THE LAW SOCIETY

Directory of
EXPERT WITNESSES

The Experts' Specialism Index

There are over 35,000 specialisms listed by expert witnesses. You may use the subject index in the main body of the Directory to access experts through key headings. However, this list enables you to find experts using the range of words the expert witnesses have used to describe their own particular expertise. Please let us know if you find this additional service helpful.

LAW SOCIETY
CHECKED
1996
EXPERT WITNESSES

FT

LAW & TAX

© Pearson Professional Limited 1995

ISBN 0752 003070

Published by
FT Law & Tax
21-27 Lamb's Conduit Street
London WClN 3NJ

A Division of Pearson Professional Limited

Associated offices
Australia, Belgium, Canada, Hong Kong, India, Japan, Luxembourg,
Singapore, Spain, USA

Printed in Great Britain by Bell & Bain, Glasgow.

Specialist areas of work

The numbers referred to are the numbers allocated to each entry in Section D *Expert Witness Profiles*.

Abnormal Psychological Reactions/Psychiatric Disorder

1094
Following personal injury in childhood and adolescence

Acceleration/Radiation/Decompression Injuries

2108
Medicine

Access/Contact Disputes

1507
Assessment of risk of further abuse/harm
Psychological/psychiatric assessment
Recommendation for treatment/rehabilitation

Access Equipment

255
Accidents
Contentious technical matters
Equipment failure
Personal injury eg doors, floors, stairs, ladders, scaffolding

Accident

80
Accidents
Cosmetics
On-site investigation
Paints and polymers
Problem solving
Trading standards

737
Emergency medicine

1179
Emergency hospital in-patient care
Medical accidents

1272
Emergency medicine

1367
Accident
Breakage
Breakdown
Dynamics
Fatigue
Fracture

1965
Equipment mis-use
Falling
Slipping
Tripping

2465
Accidents
Cosmetics
On-site investigations
Paints and polymers
Problem-solving
Trading standards

Accident Claims

593
All accident enquiries – particularly industrial and motor
Locus reports
Photographs covering all aspects of enquiries and injuries
Process service and all general enquiries
Witness proofed

Accident/Emergency

41
Personal injury
Road Traffic Accidents (RTA) investigation
Road traffic accidents

784
Initial care of injured patients
Minor fracture care
Minor injury care
Resuscitation

1121
Hand injuries
Patient care
Resuscitation
Soft tissue injuries
Whiplash injuries

1166
All aspects of Accident and Emergency (A/E) medicine
Cardiopulmonary resuscitation
Emergencies and resuscitation
Management/assessment of Accident and Emergency (A/E) patients
Multiply-injured (trauma) patients
Trauma

1169
Emergency medicine
Pre-hospital care
Trauma – all degrees of injury severity

1513
Head injury (early aspects of care)
Pre-hospital care especially first aid and ambulance
Resuscitation
Trauma
Wounding

1551
Hand injuries
Head injuries
Orthopaedics

2247
Ambulance care
Resuscitation
Spinal injury
Trauma in general

2312
General practice emergencies
Hyperbaric medicine

2568
Injuries
Negligence/standards of care
Resuscitation
Scarring
Soft tissue injuries
Trauma

Accident/Injury

2370
Accidents at work
Industrial injury
Road traffic accidents
Sporting injuries
War pensions

Accident/Injury Compensation

472
Assessing loss of earnings and pensions
Reports for insurance companies
Reports for plaintiff or defendant

Accident Investigation

110
Industrial machinery accidents
Lifting accidents
Slipping and tripping accidents

185
Bicycle accident
Claiming assessments
Component failure
Electric shock
Electrical machinery
Hazard identification
Health and safety regulations
Hydraulic machinery
Industrial accident
Load handling
Loss of earnings
Manual handling
Mechanical machinery
Motor vehicle accident
Personal injury
Playground equipment
Transport equipment

219
Analysis of expert witness reports
Identification of hazards
Recreation of accident by experiment

533
Fire and explosions at oil/gas/chemical plants
Personal injury (causes) at oil/gas/chemical plants
Personal injuries arising from fire/explosions/chemical spills (causes)
Pollution incidents

553
Bicycle accident
Claiming assessments
Component failure
Electric shock
Electrical machinery
Hazard identification
Health and safety regulations
Hydraulic machinery
Industrial accident
Load handling
Loss of earnings
Manual handling
Mechanical machinery
Motor vehicle accident
Personal injury
Playground equipment
Transport equipment

852
Effect of alcohol, medication and
 drugs
Human factors
Mechanisms and dynamics of injury
Personal injury causation

1025
Marine accidents
Personal injury
Road traffic

1500
Accident and vehicle photography
Motorcycle assessment generally
 (accident-related)
Occupational accidents
Other personal accidents
Road traffic accidents (motorcycle
 specialist)

1655
Accidents with manufacturing
 machinery
Woodworking machinery specialists

1973
Defence and plaintiff reports
Liability report
Location photographs
Location plans – detailed or scale
Video reconstruction

2065
Locus plan provision (to scale)
Photography services
Road traffic investigation
Vehicular traffic accident
 investigation including motorcycle
 accidents
Video services

2094
Detailed site plans, photographs and
 video
Mathematical modelling of accidents
Speed surveys
Tachograph analysis
Vehicle examination
Vision profiles

2220
Agriculture
Construction/building
Docks
Education
Hospitals and nursing homes
Industry/industrial premises
Offices and shops
Sport and leisure
Transport, road traffic and highways

2221
Agriculture
Construction/building
Docks
Education
Hospitals and nursing homes
Industry/industrial premises
Offices and shops
Sport and leisure
Transport, road traffic and highways

2222
Agriculture
Construction/building
Docks
Education
Hospitals and nursing homes
Industry/industrial premises
Offices shops
Sport and leisure
Transport, road traffic and highways

2223
Agriculture
Construction/building
Docks
Education
Hospital and nursing homes
Industry/industrial premises
Offices and shops
Sport and leisure
Transport, road traffic and highways

2224
Agriculture
Construction/building
Docks
Education
Hospitals and nursing homes
Industry/industrial premises
Offices and shops
Sport and leisure
Transport and road traffic

2225
Agriculture
Construction/building
Docks
Education, sport and leisure
Fires and explosions
Hospitals and nursing homes
Industry/industrial premises
Offices and shops
Offshore oil/gas
Transport, road traffic and highways

2226
Agriculture
Construction/building
Docks
Education
Hospitals and nursing homes
Industry/industrial premises
Offices and shops
Sport and leisure
Transport, road traffic and highways

2227
Agriculture
Construction/building
Dock
Education
Hospital and nursing homes
Industry/industrial premises
Offices and shops
Offshore oil/gas
Sport and leisure
Transport, road traffic and highways

2231
Accidents caused by building defects
Traffic accident scenes – measured
 surveys

2261
Accident prevention
Policies and practices of highway
 authorities
Road safety
Road traffic accident investigation
Safety audit
Surveys, plans, photographs and
 video duties

2398
Motor vehicle examination and
 damage assessment
Photography
Plan drawing
Statement taking and enquiries
Tachograph reading and analysis
Traffic accident investigation and
 reconstruction

Accident Investigation/Marine

552
Document perusal and opinion
Litigation reports and expert witness
Main and auxiliary machinery
 failures/damages
Marine claims investigation
Personal injury investigation
Refrigeration – cargo, machinery,
 equipment

Accident Investigation/Reconstruction

53
Department of Transport Examiner
 (motor cycles)
Department of Transport/Ministry of
 Transport (MOT) examiner cars and
 motor cycles
Faculty of procurators and solicitors
 seminars
Haulage industry
Road safety lectures
Traffic-related issues

242
Crash helmet examinations
Seat belt examinations
Site visits
Tachograph chart analysis
Vehicle component examinations
Wheel and tyre examinations

745
Full Road Traffic Accident (RTA)
 reconstructions
Mathematical analysis
Second opinions given on
 reconstructions
Sketch plans/photographs for use in
 court

1400
Interviewing of witnesses
Photography
Plan drawing

1698
Agricultural accident investigation
Pre-accident vehicle valuation
Road traffic accident reconstruction
Vehicle damage assessment

1779
Car, motorcycle, Heavy Goods
Vehicle (HGV) accidents
Contributory negligence of seat belts
(not used)
Injuries from seat belts
Scene examinations and plan
preparation
Seat belts (forensic examination of)
Speeds of vehicles from skidmarks,
debris, etc
Vehicle examinations

Accident Investigation/Reconstruction/ Analysis

988
Defence and plaintiff reports in civil
cases
Defence reports in criminal road
traffic offences
Investigation/analysis of accidents at
work
Investigation/reconstruction of road
traffic accidents
Scale plans/photography/accident
scene reports

Accident Investigation/Reporting

554
Accident investigation and
reconstruction reports
Health and safety at work (not
disease/chemicals)
Industry and other workplaces
Machine failure and breakdown
analysis
Machine specification compliance
(performance etc)
Road accidents [not Heavy Goods
Vehicle (HGV)]

Accident Investigator

272
Consultant engineer

Accident Neurosis

2077
Compulsive gambling
Post-traumatic stress disorder
Professional negligence/medical and
nursing
Substance misuse/alcohol and drugs
Suicide

Accident/Orthopaedic Surgery

468
'Whiplash' injuries
Fractures; joint injuries, dislocation or
disease
Musculoskeletal disease and injury
Recreational and sport injuries
Repetitive Strain Injury (RSI)
Road traffic, personal and industrial
or occupational injury

Accident/Personal Injury

875
Industrial injury

1271
Caused by construction/demolition
Caused by tripping
Reconstruction
Road/pavement condition

2530
Accident investigations and injury
claims
Occupational hazards and risks

Accident Plans

2114
Motor car
Motorcycle
Pedestrian

Accident/Trauma Personal Injury

920
Post accident pain/complications
Referral clinic for back/neck pain

Accidents Fatal

1285
All aspects

1286
All aspects

1287
All aspects

1288
All aspects

1289
All aspects

1290
All aspects

1291
All aspects

Accidents/Injuries in the Workplace

344
Health and safety procedures/practice
Workplace (including office)
disciplines: property, facilities,
productivity, personnel, information
technology, environment,
construction
risk assessment (including manual
handling, PPE, etc)

Accidents/Injuries/Trauma/Emergency Medicine

1926
Medical negligence
Soft tissue injuries

Accidents Relating to the Built Environment

2201
Buildings sites etc
Persons and property in the
workplace

Accountancy

27
Accountancy and tax matters to do
with private companies
Commercial and business matters
Personal and business taxation
Sole traders, partnership

169
Accounting records
Computations of loss of profits,
quantum of damages
Duties of accountants
Duties of directors
Generally accepted accounting
practice
Requirements of the Companies Act

257
Business interruption
Fee disputes
Matrimonial
Practice/partnership acquisition and
disputes
Professional negligence

496
Alleged fraud
Claims for loss or damage
Claims of negligence
Contractual disputes
Share valuations
Tax investigations

508
Business interruption/loss of profits
Commercial claims
Matrimonial
Personal injury

642
Fraud
Negligence claims
Personal injury claims
Quantification of loss
Valuations

771
Business valuations
Commercial disputes
Dependency claims
Fraud claims
Loss of earnings: self
employed/employed
Matrimonial disputes and related
claims

831
Department of Social Security (DSS)
and Inland Revenue categorisation
appeals
Fraud – business, mortgage, leasing
Inland Revenue and Customs and
Excise investigations
Internal business disputes
Loss of property claims, eg
insurance, defective equipment
Personal injury, fatal accident and
medical negligence loss claims

962
Fraud
Loss of profit, income or pension
quantum
Professional negligence: accountants
Valuation of businesses

1040
Accountancy fee/negligence disputes
Matrimonial asset/income
investigations
Personal injury claims re loss of
earnings
Private company minority interest
unfair prejudice
Private company share valuation
Taxation

1047
Loss of profits/business interruption
Matrimonial – financial settlements
Partnership disputes
Personal injury – loss of earnings

1496
Divorce
Fraud
Medical negligence
Personal injury
Professional negligence

1647
Accounts – misleading, fraudulent
Divorce reports
Professional negligence
Tax investigations

1745
Business acquisitions and disposals
Business valuation
Forensic accounting
Loss of profits

1818
Analysis of accounts
Assessment of financial loss
Personal financial statements
Share valuation
Taxation

1934
Business interruption: defence and
plaintiff reports
Loss of profits calculation (eg
personal injury damages)

1945
Accounting and auditing
investigations
Business valuations
Commercial disputes/loss of profits
Fraud claims
Personal injury claims/loss of
earnings
Professional negligence claims

1959
Calculation of losses
Fatal accident claims
Motor accident claims
Share valuation

2095
Audits of limited company
Business valuation
Partnerships
Professional negligence
Sole traders

Accountancy/Audit/Financial Services

36
Asset tracing
Fraud and theft
Investment appraisals
Loss of profits/earnings claims
Personal injury
Professional negligence

Accountancy/Auditing/Quantum

1455
Accountants' negligence
Accounting disputes
Breach of warranties
Disputes re purchase and sale
agreements
Fraud
Share valuation

Accountancy/Auditing/Taxation

1110
Loss of profit claims (breach of
contract etc)
Partnership agreements
Personal injury/accident claims – loss
of earnings/pension benefits
Schedule taxation

**Accountancy/Commercial
Problems/Disputes**

472
Insurance compensation for business
interruption
Loss of profits/consequential loss
claims
Partnership disputes
Shareholder disputes

**Accountancy/Finance
Arbitration/Litigation**

1014
Accounting enquiries
Completion accounts re sale of
business
Dispute resolution – companies and
partnership
Financial claims
Partnership and business valuations
Share valuations

Accountancy/Financial

2546
Divorce settlement disputes –
financial issues
Feasibility and viability reports
Forensic accountancy investigation
and report
Loss of profits/earnings qualification
Professional negligence liability
establishment and quantum of loss
Share valuation/business valuation

**Accountancy/Forensic
Accounting/Litigation Support**

1438
Matrimonial litigation support
Personal and trust taxation
Share and business valuations

Accountancy/Insolvency

1298
Corporate and individual
arrangements and fraudulent
trading defence reports
Fraud investigations
Personal injury/defence and plaintiff
reports
Share valuation and loss of earnings

Accountancy Investigations

652
Acquisition investigations
Company/business accounts analysis
Due diligence reporting
Share valuations

Accountancy Support

1637
Compensation/damages
Music business/extraction industry
Professional negligence
Purchase/sale of business
Taxation
Valuation and intellectual property
Valuation and shares

Accountancy/Taxation

651
Business valuations – unincorporated
Loss of profits claims
Personal injury calculation of losses
Share valuations for private
companies
Specialist industries – family
companies, doctors, farmers, other
professional practices
Valuations of businesses in divorce
cases

1868
Commercial litigation – loss of profits,
valuations
Fraud – investigations, Inland
Revenue and Value Added Tax
(VAT) fraud
Partnership disputes
Professional negligence – accounting
negligence

Accountancy/Taxation/Finance

660
Analysis of profitability for small
business (turnover to ?8m)
Investment return appraisal
Loss of profit calculations
Profit analysis for business
acquisition and disposal
Share valuations
Tax calculation for small businesses
(turnover to ?8m)

Accountants

138
Accountants' fees
Business and share valuations
Partnership entitlements

2253
Accountant's negligence
Insurance disputes
Loss of profits/business interruption
Professional negligence
Valuation of business (goodwill)

**Accountants/Negligence Claims
against**

138
Auditing and due diligence work
Failure to detect fraud
Failure to detect money laundering
Negligence claims against
accountants
Preparation of financial statements
Tax compliance and planning

**Accountants'/Financial Advisers'
Negligence**

1014
Back duty investigations of accounts
Negligence of accountants
Negligence of financial advisers
Other accounting investigations

Accountants' Professional Negligence

387
Inadequate auditing of unquoted
companies
Incorrect taxation advice given to
clients

459
Accounts preparation
Audit
Taxation

1428
Audit
Computers
Fraud
Investigations
Share valuations
Taxation

Accounts Analysis/Reports

736
Agricultural businesses
Agricultural estates

Acoustic/Noise/Vibration Control

1608
Auditorium and room acoustics
Control of noise from building
 services
Planning and noise
Sound insulation in buildings

Acoustics

13
Auditorium and studio acoustics
Room acoustics

1569
Tape-recording analysis and
 authentication

1716
Building

2048
Acoustics in buildings
Auditoria and conference centres
Commercial buildings
Sound insulation
Studios

Acoustics/Environmental

2053
Community noise
Construction noise and vibration
Environmental impact assessments
 PPG24 etc

Acoustics/Noise/Vibration

14
Deafness due to noise (noise
 induced hearing loss)
Environmental impact assessment of
 noise
Noise from construction and minerals
 extraction sites
Noise nuisance
Occupational noise
Sound insulation
Transport noise (road, rail and air)

199
Building acoustics
Concert/opera/theatre acoustics
Electroacoustics
Environmental noise impact
Industrial noise
Speech intelligibility

1190
Acoustic defects in buildings
Assessment of product performance
 (noise/vibration)

1522
Assessments, surveys, planning
 applications and litigation support
Building acoustics – insulation and
 property development
Environmental noise impact –
 countryside, transportation,
 quarries, airports, leisure pursuits
Industrial and power generation
 projects (eg renewable energy,
 wind energy farms)
Noise-at-work assessments –
 industry, amplified music
Residential complaints eg clubs,
 kennels, schools/nurseries, shoots,
 traffic/transport etc

1896
Environmental noise nuisance
Industrial noise exposure and
 hearing damage risk assessment

2376
Hearing damage – noise
 assessments (1989 Noise At Work
 Regulations, etc)
Licensing – entertainment noise;
 evidence to licence hearings
Nuisance – abatement notices
 (industry, construction,
 entertainment and neighbours)
Planning – environmental impact
 assessment (road, rail and airport
 schemes; retail, commercial,
 residential and industrial
 developments); planning inquiries
 and parliamentary private bills
Professional negligence – building
 design (acoustics noise and
 vibration control)
Sound insulation – testing (building
 regulations etc)
Speech intelligibility

Acquired Brain Injury/Orthopaedic Trauma (including hand injuries)

17
Assessment of environment
Assessment of functional ability
 (including physical and cognitive
 ability – memory, concentration,
 problem-solving, judgement)
Assessment of need (ie therapy,
 environmental adaptation, specialist
 equipment)
Work assessment

Acquired Neurological Disorders

2018
Augmentative communication
 systems
Dysartrina (motor speech disorder)
Dysphasia (language disorder)
Feeding and swallowing disorders
Head injury, cerebral vascular
 accident etc

Acquired Speech/Language Disorders

2115
Acute neurological accident
Chronic neurological impairments
Head injury
Swallowing disorders
Voice disorders

Acquisitions/Mergers

1079
Corporate tax
Personal tax
Shareholder disputes and warranty
 claims
Valuations of businesses/shares
Value Added Tax (VAT)

Actions Against Directors

221
Disqualification of director
Dissatisfied minority shareholders
Insolvency

Actuarial

24
Divorce (pension rights)
Industrial injury
Loss of pension rights
Road accidents

Actuarial Assessment of Damages for Loss of Income/Pension

187
Loss of earnings/pension following
 unfair dismissal or redundancy
Loss of earnings/pension in cases of
 personal injury or death

189
Division of pension on divorce
Quantification of loss of
 earnings/pension
Valuation of loss of pension following
 divorce

2023
Divorce
Loss of pension rights
Personal injury
Wrongful dismissal

Actuarial/Investment

382
Disputes between pension funds
Lloyd's of London market disputes
Professional negligence

895
Actuarial calculations
Investment and tax advice
Valuations of trusts

1564
Investment
Life assurance
Pensions
Personal injury
Trusts

Actuarial Management of Financial Institutions

2023
Corporate damages
Policy holder damages

Actuarial Valuation of Trust Interests

2023
Tax valuations
Trust partitions
Valuations for Lloyds membership

Adhesion Science/Technology

43
Adhesives and their failure in use
Surface preparation for adhesive
bonding
Testing of adhesives and of adhesive
joints
Use of adhesives as a production
technique

Adhesives

22
Independent laboratory testing
service
Labels
Self-adhesive materials
Tapes: single- and double-sided

Adhesives/Polymers

484
Adhesion of paints and surface
coatings
Chemistry of adhesives
Durability and failure of adhesive
bonds
Effect of liquids (particularly
perfumes) on plastics
Permeation and diffusion in plastics
and rubbers

Adoption

20
Adoption
Assessment and consultation in child
abuse
Child care planning and placements
Child custody disputes
Contact in both public and private law
cases

313
Twins

378
Adoption and contact issues
Assessments
Complaints against local authority
and voluntary agencies

596
Adoption and fostering
Child abuse – sexual, physical or
emotional
Custody dispute cases
Insurance claims in accidents or
crimes
Parenting capacity
Young offenders

1561
Adoption
Public law and private law
Thirty-six years' experience in
probation and social services work

1581
Adoption
Child abuse
Child care and wardship
Fostering
Matrimonial disputes and proceedings
Mental Health Act Tribunals
Psychiatric aspects of personal injury
Psychiatric assessment in criminal
cases
Residence/custody and contact for
children

1762
Adoption and fostering
All forms of abuse (emotional,
physical, sexual)
Ethnic minorities
Post-traumatic stress syndrome
Serious offenders

1859
Adoption and fostering
Behavioural and emotional disorders
occurring in childhood and
adolescence
Child abuse and neglect, including
child sexual abuse
Parenting and child care, including
contact after parental separation

2266
Adoption and fostering
Adult and adolescent sexual abuse
of children
Attachment/custody/access disputes
Emotional abuse
Failure to thrive (non organic)
Physical abuse, including children's
bullying
Risk assessment

2348
Adoption/fostering
Assessment of child abuse
Assessment of family in crisis
Assessment of parenting capacity
Assessment of rehabilitation
Severely disturbed and troubled
children

Adoption/Care Proceedings

see also Child Care

2027
Contact with birth relatives following
adoption
Frequency and type of contact in
adoption and care proceedings
Merits of adoption compared with
other alternatives
Rehabilitation of children to their birth
families

Adult Eyewitness Testimony

608
Identification from photographs,
parades or confrontations
Photofits, artist's impressions and
other computer systems
Recognition of vehicles

Adult Psychiatry

1215
All aspects

Adults/Older People

607
Cognitive behaviour therapy
Consultation on clinical environments
Dementias
Neuropsychological assessment
Post-traumatic stress disorder
Testamentary capacity

Adults with Learning Difficulties

523
Ability to parent/criminal cases

Advanced Materials

128
Analysis of failures in materials
Composite materials/fibre-reinforced
materials
Design of structures

Adverse Drug Reactions

2404
In hospital or in general practice

Advice to Lawyers

793
Assessment and safety of scientific
evidence
Co-ordination of scientific
investigations
Cross-examination briefing
Explanation of scientific evidence,
context, relevance, principles and
techniques, strengths and
weaknesses
Lectures to lawyers and others

Adviser in Children Act Matters/Public/Private Law

641
Children with special needs
Contact difficulties
Parental disputes
Residence order conflict

Advising on Financial/Business Aspects of Legal Disputes/Claims

2129
All aspects

Advisory Services

1387
Consumer safety
Due diligence
Health and safety
Product labelling
Quality systems
Trading and consumer law issues

Aerial Photography, Interpretation of

536
Boundary interpretation from aerial
photography
Land use interpretation
Measurement from survey aerial
photography

Aeronautical Engineering

619
Aircraft engines and spares litigation
Aircraft maintenance litigation
Condition of air transport aircraft
Efficiency of aircraft and engine
maintenance organisations

Agent to the Legal Profession

2056
Civil accidents
Insurance claims
Interviewing witnesses
Obtaining evidence of means (re:
Applications for legal aid)
Road accidents

Agri-environment

1920

Flood and coastal protection – cost benefit appraisals

Impact and causes of erosion of soil material from agricultural land

Impact of extreme weather conditions on agriculture

Agricultural (Estate Management)

2388

Advice on agricultural aspects of planning applications

Agricultural Claims

1106

Crop damage and losses

Farm buildings

Land drainage

Livestock losses and damage

Road traffic accident damage

Agricultural/Construction Site Machinery

255

Accidents

Contentious technical matters

Defective machinery

Personal injury

Agricultural Consultancy

1131

Agricultural appraisals for planning applications and appeals

Agricultural divorce: apportionment of farm business

Agricultural holdings legislation

Calculations of earning capacity of farms in rental disputes

Dairy cow and milk quota management

Farm budgeting and farm business appraisals

Farm management accounts and analysis

Report preparation in tenancy succession disputes

1379

Agricultural odours

Agricultural pollution

Agricultural wastes

Application of sewage sludge and trade wastes

2235

Agricultural practice

Farm management and consultancy

Feasibility studies

Valuations and insurance valuations

Agricultural Disputes

1746

Advice on sporting rights

Litigation and disputes in respect of agricultural and sporting properties, including tenancies

Valuation of farms, estates and sporting rights

Agricultural Engineering

350

Engineering and maintenance

Operator training and responsibilities

Product liability

Safety

971

All aspects

Agricultural/Environmental Engineering

2538

Choosing and using farm machines

Energy audits

Environmental assessments

Equipment for land-based industries

International strategies for farm mechanisation

Soil mechanics

Agricultural/Horticultural Businesses Management/Economics of

1920

Assessment of liability and quantum in relation to farm accidents

Assessment of liability and quantum of most types of claim in agricultural horticultural disputes

Budgets and investment appraisals

Farm and horticultural business analysis to assess viability and profitability

Agricultural/Horticultural Crop Growth/Storage

555

Chemicals – pesticides, fertilizers and weedkillers

Composts

Crop damage

Disease and pest problems

Glasshouse crops

Spray drift/pollution

Agricultural Land (Quality) Classification

841

Surveys for planning inquiries etc

Agricultural Machinery Consultancy

1542

Agricultural engineering

Agricultural tyres

Machinery design, performance and safety

Personal injury

Training course design

Agricultural Planning

82

Diversification schemes

Feasibility studies

Planning appeals

Agricultural/Residential Valuations

751

Capital and rental valuations

Compulsory purchase

Growing crops

Partnership and matrimonial division

Tenant right

Valuations of live and dead farmstock

Agricultural/Rural Aspects of Town/Country Planning

1920

Appraisals of agricultural dwelling and building requirements

Countryside resource – building and land use assessments

Environmental impact assessment of development proposals

Impact of development on agriculture and farm businesses

Soil movement planning to mitigate impacts

Soil survey for land quality and soil resources

Agricultural Valuations

1312

Boundary disputes

Live and deadstock

Rental arbitrations

Tenant rights

Valuation of growing crop

Valuation of heritable valuations

Agriculture

4

Animal and crop husbandry (including exotic species)

Health and safety/personal injury (agriculture/equine)

Loss assessment due to accidents, compulsory purchase etc

29

Ability to fund borrowing

Partition

Profitability and viability of farms

82

Compensation claims

Labour and employment

Land purchase

Machinery

Rents

Valuations

248

Arbitrations

Compensation

Landlord and tenant

Milk quotas

Valuation

350

Codes of practice

Crops

Environmental care, assessments

Practical procedures

Safety/agricultural accidents/damage

Soils and environment

406

Cattle

Chainsaw accidents

Crop spray damage

Farm machinery

Horses

Horticultural accidents

Poultry

687

Dairying

Farm economics

Forage and grass production and conservation

Livestock/cattle and sheep

Personal injury in agriculture

Quantum calculations

1106
Consequential losses
Insurance claims
Negligence in advice
Staff accidents

1171
Agency
Compulsory purchase and
    compensation
Rent review and landlord and tenant
Valuation

1385
Alternative enterprises
Farm business reviews and
    restructuring
Farm stock and machinery valuation
Marketing
Ongoing farm business management

1433
Assessments of viability and
    consequential loss
Consequential loss due to injury,
    professional negligence and error
    by supplier
Liability for personal injury
Preparation of reports and court
    appearance
Viability in relation to divorce
    settlements and planning appeals

1520
Agricultural planning
Crop production
Farm finance
Insurance claims
Organic farming
Ruminant livestock

1805
Crop production and grassland
Dairy, beef and sheep production
Farm and labour management
Machinery use
Quantum assessment

Agriculture/Horticulture

279
Accident and injury
Crop and livestock loss
Quotas

Agriculture/Horticulture/Rural Affairs

446
Expert evidence for planning appeals
Farm buildings
Farm dwellings
Reports and appraisals on
    feasibility/viability

684
Crop and livestock loss assessment
Personal and business net worth and
    income assessments for domestic
    litigation
Personal injury – liability and loss
    assessments
Product and service liability claims
Rural planning consent and appeals

Agriculture/Property

2236
Matrimonial disputes
Professional indemnity
Rent reviews
Valuation of all property

Air Conditioning/Process Cooling Systems

971
All aspects

Air Pollution

6
Indoor pollution
Industrial sources – stacks, fugitive
    emissions, etc
Modelling – pollutant formation,
    emission, deposition, dispersion
Odour nuisance and food tainting
Particulates, asbestos, Respirable
    Particles (PM10)
Planning inquiries
Smoke from fires

Air Pollution/Air Quality

2534
Air quality impact studies
Air quality studies for planning
    applications
Dust from construction and mineral
    operations
Indoor air quality
Traffic pollution

Air Sampling

971
All aspects

Air Transport

2261
Air transport demand
Airline competition
Airport industry analysis

Aircraft Operations

619
Accident and damage litigation
Efficiency of air transport operators
Insurance claim litigation
Suitablilty for purpose of air transport
    aircraft

Airphoto Interpretation: Land Resources

2564
Access disputes
Boundary litigation
Dated land use changes
Land use disputes

Airport Engineering/Runway, Taxiway/Apron Pavement Design, Construction/Maintenance

91
Drainage
LIghting installations
Operational safety
Repair and maintenance
Surface operational characteristics
Surface treatments

Alcohol

797
Analysis of blood and urine
Back calculations
Driving under the influence of alcohol
    and drugs

1222
Back tracking estimations
Effect of further doses

2498
Role in accidents

Alcohol-Related Driving Offences

1132
Breath-alcohol measurement in
    subjects with lung diseases, eg
    asthma

Allergy

827
Chest diseases – asthma
Diseases related to allergy
Side effects of steroids

2150
Medicine

Alterations

1922
Enhancement of faded writings
Ink comparisons
Recovery of erased or obliterated
    entries

Alternative/Augmentative Communication

2018
'Low tech' communication boards
Computer operated electronic
    communication systems
Digitised and synthetic speech output
    devices

Alternative Dispute

728
Expert determinations
International arbitrations
Mediation and negotiated settlements

1022
Dispute reconnaissance
Investigation, analysis and resolution
    of issues
Mediation assistance

1331
Arbitration
Expert determination: general
Expert determinations: share and
    other valuations
Mediation

1638
Mediation and conciliation

Alternative Dispute Resolution

511
All Aspects

1917
Surveyor negligence
Valuer negligence

Aluminium

454
Casting
Extrusion
Failure investigation
Forging
Molten metal treatment and safety
Rolling

Amputees/Upper/Lower Limb

1209
Civil litigation

Anaesthesia

197
Intensive care
Obstetric analgesia and anaesthesia
Pain management
Palliative care and pain/symptom
  relief
Regional analgesia
Vascular anaesthesia

231
Anaesthesia for caesarean section
Awareness during general
  anaesthesia
Epidural/spinal anaesthesia and
  analgesia
Obstetric anaesthesia and analgesia
Pain relief during labour
Tracheal intubation

1295
Awareness
Dental/obstetric anaesthesia
Drug interactions
Intensive care
Pre-post-operative care
Spinal/epidural anaesthesia

1799
Consent
Day stay anaesthesia
For general and vascular surgery
For urological surgery
Monitoring
Neuro anaesthesia
Protocols

Anaesthesia Intensive Care

71
Burns
Post-operative care
Smoke inhalation

273
Neonatal anaesthesia
Neonatal surgical intensive care
Paediatric anaesthesia and intensive
  care
Paediatric pain and airway problems

1571
Anaesthetics apparatus
Anaesthetics techniques
Cardio-thoracic anaesthesia
Paediatric anaesthesia

2378
General anaesthesia
Intensive therapy
Regional anaesthesia
Resuscitation and emergency
  medicine

Anaesthetic Care, Pre-/Per-/Post-Operative

1660
All aspects – especially intensive care
Anaesthesia for vascular surgery

Anaesthetics

336
General anaesthesia
Pain relief
Regional anaesthesia including
  epidurals

700
Day-care
Dental
General
Gynaecology and obstetrics
Neurosurgery
Orthopaedics

1458
All other non-specialised anaesthetics
Anaesthesia for children
NOT neurosurgery, cardiac surgery

Analysis

80
Chemicals
Cosmetics
Forensic
Metals
Paint, polymers and waxes
Solvents

1367
Accident
Breakage
Breakdown
Dynamics
Fatigue
Fracture

1387
Customer product safety
Food analysis
Legionella testing
Microbiology
Nutritional analysis
Product liability appraisals

2465
Chemicals
Cosmetics
Forensic
Metals
Paints, polymers and waxes
Solvents

Analysis for Explosives Traces

581
All aspects

Analysis of Corporate Performance

1145
Company performance and specific
  incidents
Evolution of company performance
Specific performance and factors –
  sales and profits
Understanding company performance

Analysis/Testing/Provider of Experts

2359
Animal nutrition
Batch processing
Chemicals
Civil engineering
Control of Substances Harmful to
  Health (COSSH) regulations
Dyes etc
Electrical faults
Environmental
Explosions
Fires
Fumes
Gas
Health and safety
Lightning protection
Materials, corrosion
Mechanical stress and fatigue
Mining
Noise

Pollution
Solvents
Spectrography
Structural mechanics
Textiles
Ventilation
Veterinary

Analytical Chemistry

108
Environmental modelling

581
Examination of environmental
  samples for explosives pollution

Analytical Chemistry to the Diagnosis/Management of Human Disease, Application of

801
Clinical chemistry
Clinical toxicology
Drug and alcohol impairment of
  drivers
Forensic toxicology
Workplace screening for drug abuse

Analytical Investigations

1616
Chemical
Environmental
Forensic science
Pharmaceuticals
Vegetable and petroleum oils

Ancillary Relief/Matrimonial

2414
Financial investigation and analysis
Share valuations

Animal Cruelty/Misuse

2342
Agriculture: miscellaneous provisions
Food poisoning in animals
Honey bees
Professional negligence by veterinary
  surgeons
Protection of Animals Act 1911- all
  aspects

Animal Nutrition

337
Animal feed formulation,
  manufacture, supply and use
Animal husbandry
Dairy cattle, beef cattle, calves,
  sheep, goats
Mineral and vitamin premixes
Pigs, poultry, rabbits

2359
Analysis, testing and provider of
  experts

Animal-Related Litigation

1795
Dog related matters
Horse accidents/civilian and military
Planning ecology
Wildlife cases

Animals/Diseases of Non-domesticated (Zoo/Pests/Free-Living)

1330
Diseases of amphibians
Diseases of birds (all species) – cage, aviary and free-living
Diseases of otters
Diseases of reptiles
Psittacosis (Chlamydia psittaci infection)
Veterinary pathology

Anti-Discriminatory Practice/Equal Opportunities

2314
Acting against racism, sexism, ageism, discrimination based on disability, sexuality and religion

Anxiety Disorders/Depression

2269
Agoraphobia and panic
Depression
Obsessive-compulsive disorder
Personality disorders
Post-traumatic stress disorder

Apparel Design/Manufacture

1987
Clothing sizes for women, men and children
Copyright
Mediator BAE qualification
Public relations client/consultant disputes
Quality assessment
Stock valuation

Aquatic Biology

1992
Conservation of native species
Crayfish
Fish farming
Fisheries
Introduction of non-native species
Pollution
Water quality issues

Arab/Islamic Law

1158
Egypt

Arab Law

2037
Contracts, labour, investment, banking, arbitration, litigation, patents and commercial

Arbitration

see also specialist area eg Building, Construction, Engineering Etc

98
Commercial disputes

171
Accounting negligence
Business interruption
Expert witness work
Professional negligence

192
Breach of contract
Breach of warranty
Business valuations/insurance claims
Commercial disputes
Loss of profits/businessinterruption
Machinery.equipment not fit for purpose
Product liability

424
Building contracts

486
Landlord and tenant

493
Construction disputes

530
Arbitration and dispute resolution
Commercial landlord and tenant
Leasehold reform
Restrictive covenants
Valuation of commercial and industrial property
Valuation of residential property

622
Building

647
Construction

657
Construction

716
Agricultural Holdings Act 1986
Arbitrations acts
Wildlife and Countryside Act 1981

790
Building and construction

880
Arbitration
Landlord and tenant
Rent review (commercial)
Valuation of commercial property for all purposes

962
All aspects

1124
Quantity surveying

1285
Determinations and arbitraions

1286
Determinations and arbitrations

1288
Determinations and arbitrations

1289
Determinations an arbitration

1291
Determinations and arbitration

1332
Arbitration
Company valuations
Loss of profits
Partnership dissolutions

1381
Construction

1512
All aspects

1595
Commercial property
Industrial
Offices
Retail

1692
Appointment as witness in such matters
Appointment to act as arbitrator or independent expert

1754
Compulsory purchase
Arbitrations
Compensation
Conveyancing negligence (quantum effects)
Doctors' and dentists' rents
Landlord and tenant disputes
Lease extensions

1784
All aspects

1840
Construction

1912
Building adjudication
Building arbitration
Building contracts
Building costs
Measurement of building works
Quantity surveying practice and procedure

1981
Alternative dispute resolution
Arbitration
Breach of warranty claims

2098
Advocaccy in smaller cases
Architectural and design negligence
Building arbitration
Building litigation
Defects investigation and reporting
NHBC arbitration

2166
Building disputes
Delapidation and repairing obligations
Rent reviews
Service charges
Valuation disputes

2325
Building

2354
Computer disputes

2477
Loss of profits

2489
Building

2528
Construction

Arbitration/Alternative Dispute Resolution (ADR)

98
Matrimonial disputes
Parnership splits

622
Forensic Engineering

642
Alternative Dispute Resolutions
Arbitrator
Expert adjudicator
Lay advocacy
Mediator

1218
Civil engineering and building
Contractual disputes
Disputes generally
Personal injury, occupational health and safety

Arbitration/Dispute Resolution

1229
Action as arbitrator, mediator or
conciliator
Pursuance or defence of arbitration
disputes

2507
Civil/structural engineering
Conciliation and mediation

Arbitration/Expert Determination

928
Allocation of capital assets following
local authority boundary changes
Aquisition and merger disputes
Share purchase agreements

Arbitration/Litigation

2408
Court attendance, giving evidence,
public enquiry evidence
Expert witness
Scotts schedules, meeting of experts
Surveys, investigations, reports

Arboriculture

202
Accidents/insurance claims involving
trees
Tree preservation orders
Tree root damage to buildings

1074
Amenity valuation of trees
Effects of tree roots on buildings, etc
Effects on the tree of damage to tree
roots
Tree management

1278
Tree accidents
Tree damage
Treeroots/buildings

1303
Contraventions of statute and
planning law
Industrial injuries
Insurance claims – building
subsidence
Third-party injuries or damage

2280
All aspects

2478
Planning appeals
Tree preservation orders
Tree safety
Trees in relation to buildings

Arboriculture Consultancy (Tree Management)

1135
Hazard analysis of trees
Tree design schemes
Tree inspection
Tree law – conservation/TPOS/
boundaries etc
Tree surveys
Tree valuation

Arboriculture/Forestry/Urban Forestry

1725
Electric utility vegetation management
Health and safety at work
Local plans and supplementary
planning guidance
Planning and development – appeals
Public inquiries
Special projects, study and
commissions
Training and continuing professional
development
Tree preservation orders
Trees and building failure
Trees and pollution control
Vegetation and environmental law

Architect

1095
Copyright
Defects liability (construction)
Professional liability

2379
Building contract administration
Fees
Professional conduct and
performance
Terms of appointment

Architect/Historic Buildings/Conservation

1892
Architectural history
Architecture: design, repair and
alterations
Condition surveys
Listed building and conservation area
legislation
Public inquiry work

Architect in Respect of Building Design/Contract/Construction

403
Analysis of client requirements
Detailed design
Efficacy of design, construction and
performance
Examination and advice on the
inception and feasability of a
proposed or completed building
Inspection of buildings and advice on
the adequacy of planning
Investigation of defects and remedial
possibilities
Operations on site and advice on the
adequacy of contraction
Production information
Programming
Project planning
Tender action
The suitability of the Scheme design

Architect's Professional Indemnity

1366
Building disputes
Negligence claims against architects

Architects/Construction Disputes

1526
Analysis of construction delays
Assessment of contractual disputes
Investigations of building defects
Professional negligence

Architects/Consultants on Design for Disability

2310
Access audits of buildings
Assessments of clients' housing
needs
Citizen's Charter
Providing realistic and pragmatic
design solutions
Providing specialist housing cost
reports for Personal Injury (PI)
claims
Training in disability awareness
Training on building regulations

Architects Designing for Special Needs/Disabilities

1615
Ancilliary expenses (selling agents,
conveyancing, removals)
Bridging loans
Building survey
Building working drawings
Completion of maintenance and
retention release certification
Contract Interim Payment Certification
Contract final accounting
Contract in progress inspection
Costed report on requirements
Costed reports on particular
conversions
Design and planning service
Estimated additional maintenance
and running costs
Grant applications
Independent research
Loss of Do It Yourself (DIY) abilities
Obtaining competitive payment
certification
Occupational certification
Property search
Relocation
Remote control installations
Special fittings and equipment
installations
Specifications
Tender documentation for
competitive building tenders
VAT zero rate certification

Architects' Appointment

2147
All aspects

Architects' Practice/Procedure

517
Architect's appointment
CDM regulations
JCT contracts

Architects' Practice/Procedure

312
Professional negligence

379
Negligent architectural design and
ccontract administration

403
Advice on architects appointment,
professional, technical and
administrative performance
Copyright infringement
Employer and contractor obligations
and responsibilities

1085
Professional negligence

1594
Building design, construction and use

1233
All aspects of design and construction
Construction defects and failures

1925
Alleged malpractice and breach of
 contract
Arbitration and court attendance
Contract delays, extras, negligence
 and disputes
Insurance and professional indemnity
 claims and counter claims
Interpretation of contract documents
 and drawings
Scott schedules and special
 drawings for court presentation

2147
Building contracts

2542
Professional Negligence

Architects' Professional Negligence

550
All aspects

Architects' Professional Services

2126
Forms of contract and contract
 administration
Negligence
Professional misconduct

Professional performance

Architects' Services

694
Construction
Contract administration
Design/team management
Practice administration
Project management

Architects'/Surveyors' Negligence

355
Architects' negligence
Negligent building surveys

Architectural/Building Acoustics

2053
Architectural acoustics
Building services noise and vibration
Recording and Television (TV)
 studios

Architectural Construction Products

723
Cladding
Curtain walling/slope glazing
 (including fire rated products)
Doors (including fire rated products)
Glass/glazing
Surface finishes
Windows (including fire rated
 products)

Architectural/Construction Technology

1847
Contractual problems and disputes
 analysis
Design and technical building
 analysis
Investigation of building defects and
 failures and related problems
Litigation and arbitration advice
Mediation

Architectural Consultancy

1426
Negligence

Architectural Design

321
Curtain walling
Defects investigations
Housing
Windows

Architectural Services

1803
Adequacy of design, specification
 and construction
Fees and service provision
Provision of contract administration

Architecture

123
Preparation of costings and reports
 on the extra cost of running special
 accommodation
Preparation of costings and reports
 upon the special housing needs of
 the severely disabled

199
Asbestos
Building defects
Cladding
Contract disputes
Fire safety
Professional practice

223
Building and construction defects
Building construction and technology
Building contracts
Building failures
Fee disputes
Professional negligence

328
Building contracts
CDM and building regulations
Negligence
Town planning

351
Conservation areas
Historic and other listed buildings
National and local design
 policy/guidance analysis
Practice matters/criticism/mediation
Sensitive townscape and landscape

669
Action for any party
Contracts for and costs of
 architectural services
Professional negligence
Relationships connected with building

815
Contract disputes
Delay and extensions of time
Design and workmanship
Personal injury
Professional negligence
Programme and drawing analysis
Technical failures

915
Building defects
Historic buildings and conservation
 areas
Planning appeals for historic
 buildings and conservation areas

1161
Building contract disputes
Building defects – commercial,
 leisure, residential and medical
 buildings
Claims for professional fees
Disputed subcontractor claims
Disputes between contractor and
 subcontractors
Improper contract administration
Infringements of copyright
Party wall infringements
Practical completion certificate
 improperly withheld
Responsibilities of an architect

1185
Administrative failures
Contractor disputes
Design failures
Professional appointment disputes
Technical failures

1529
Architects' duties under health and
 safety regulations
Architects' duties under planning and
 similar regulations
Architects' duties under various
 forms of contract
Architects' negligence claims
Professional liabilities of architects

1759
Building defects
Planning

1812
Contract law

1984
Community architecture
General design
Hospice design
Housing design
Planning field

2029
Building contracts
Building failures
Building technology
Construction defects
Fee disputes
Professional negligence

2039
Copyright

2193
Architects' responsibilities
Building construction
Building surveying
Contractual disputes
Personal injury
Procedural disputes

2281

Boundary disputes
Building contracts
Building disputes
Building technology
Design and construction
Workmanship and defect
 investigations

Architecture/Building Construction

180

Administration of the design and
 construction process
Appointment of architect
Boundary disputes
Building defects
Building regulations

265

Compliance with standards, statutory
 requirements, good practice
Construction defects
Contract/contract responsibilities
Fire, fire precautions, investigation
Materials, components, systems

349

Arbitration
Building failures
Damp problems
Performance of windows
Professional practice
Roofing problems

1457

Adjoining owner, building disputes
Alternative dispute resolution
Architectural fee disputes
Construction contract disputes
Negligence claims relating to
 construction

1956

Building technology
Ecclesiastical buildings
Giving evidence in court
Historic buildings
Metal roof coverings
Professional negligence

2107

Building maintenance/refurbishment
Historic buildings conservation

2111

Arbitration
Defective building works
Historic buildings – planning and
 construction/extension
Mediation
Professional negligence

2388

Architectural design and detail:
 fit-for-purpose, etc
Construction law
Construction quality
Contract law
Contract practice and procedures

Architecture/Construction Technology

1181

Acting as expert witness
Analysis of contractual problems and
 disputes
Design and technical building analysis
Investigation of building failure and
 related problems
Providing advice in connection with
 litigation and arbitration

Architecture/Engineering

2325

Appointments and client agreements
Buildings – conservation and historic
Defective work
Defects of design and documentation
Planning appeals

Architecture/Equine

761

Studs and stables, their construction
 and design
Wide-ranging contacts, both
 nationally and internationally

Architecture/Equine Building Design/Planning

2438

Design of equine buildings
Design of stables
Design of stud farms
Planning of stud farms

Architecture/Professional Standards

2039

Architects duties
Fees
Negligence
Terms of appointment

Architecture/Surveying

289

Building disputes
Court hearings
Plan and survey preparations for
 court hearings
Planning, listed building and
 conservation area appeals
Professional negligence

Architecture/The Building Industry

2308

Arbitration/dispute resolution
Construction problems/defects
Contract disputes
Design problems/defects
Performance related to
 contract/appointment
Professional appointments

Arms/Armour/Militaria

1015

Cataloguing arms, armour and
 militaria
Determination of age, origin and
 authenticity
Identification of arms, armour and
 militaria
Law relating to ownership and use of
 edged weapons and crossbows
Restoration and conservation of
 arms, armour and militaria
Valuation for all purposes

Army Training

263

Command direction
Man management, absence and
 desertion
Military discipline and codes of
 conduct
Physical fitness and recreation
Road transport
Staff direction

Arson

see also Fire

800

Arson Assessment of evidence
Detection of accelerants ie petrol
Re-examination of scene

Artificial Intelligence

1773

Expert systems
Intelligent systems
Neural networks

Artist/Illustrator

2211

Diagrammatical illustrations and
 plans of accident locations
Drawings/sketches/diagrams of sites
 and causes of accidents
Other drawings, diagrams, etc as
 specified

Asbestos Disease/Mesothelioma

1304

Medico-legal work

Asbestosis

1474

Medicine

Asian Languages, Interpreting in

1251

Gujarati
Hindi
Katchi
Urdu

Assault/Injury

1793

All aspects

Assessment

2209

Assessment of attainments
Cognitive assessments
Neuropsychological assessments of
 visually impaired people

Assessment/Legislation

2524

1981 and 1993 Education Act
Children Act

Assessment of Needs

395

Brain injury
Certain other catastrophic injury

Asset Recovery

514

Analysis of offshore corporate
 structures
Asset tracing
Quantifying loss

Asset Tracing

see also Forensic Accountancy,
 Fraud

124
Asset tracing
Business purchase
Customs and excise/Value Added
 Tax (VAT)
Earnings history
Inland revenue
Insurance claims

134
Drugs

1495
Asset tracing
Fraud Investigation
Litigation support

Auction/Valuation Practice: Fine Art/Chattels

2015
Auction practice and procedures
Bases of valuation
Catalogues, publicity etc
Family division
Negligence
Valuation practice and procedures

Audio Engineering

637
Compliance with BS6259, BS7449,
 BS6340, BS5839 etc
Contractor competence assessment
Fit for the purpose and deemed to
 satisfy approval
Performance audit of complete audio
 systems
Performance verification of audio
 system components

Audio Post-Production/Mastering

430
Audio restoration/forensic

Audio/Video

936
Audio systems equipment
Audiotape examination and
 transcription
Image examination (moving, stills
 from video or photographic
 cameras) using computer aids
Video and audio material
 enhancements
Video electronics equipment
 (cameras, recorders, displays)

Audiology/Deafness

1417
Evoked response audiometry
Industrial deafness assessment
Pure tone audiometry

Auditing

169
Account reports
Auditing standards
Auditors' duties
Financial assistance
Solicitors' accounts rules,
 accountants' report rules

1959
All other regulatory audits
All statutory audits

Auditory Problems

586
All aspects

Austrian Law

1422
Civil and commercial litigation
Company and commercial law
Employment and labour law
Family law
Inheritance and probate
Personal injury

Authentification of Suspect Documents/Handwriting

2424
Alleged forgery authentification –
 legal documents
Anonymous letters
Documents – scientific examination –
 source, quality, age/date
Forensic apparatus – ink changes
Forensic tests
Graffiti – identification of graphic
 creations
Handwriting – critical comparison
 with 'accepted genuine' handwriting
 and/or signatures
Identify signs of authorship
Identifying features
Microscope photograph, infra-red
 and ultraviolet evidence

Authorship Attribution using CUSUM Technique

756
Attribution of text and (transcribed)
 spoken utterance - disputed
 statements
records of interview, suicide notes
 and letters, anonymous
 communications

Automatic Engineering

745
Defective vehicles/tyres/components
Diagnosis of failures
Inspection of accidental damage and
 repairs
Quality of repair work
Unmerchantable quality of vehicles

Automobile

see also Motor Vehicle, Road
 Transport, Road Traffic, Vehicle

Aviation

268
Air accidents
Airframe, engine, radio, systems
 failures
Airline incidents following crew
 mismanagement
Flying training
Infringements of flying/operational
 regulations

619
Aircraft engines and spares litigation
Aircraft maintenance litigation
Condition of air transport aircraft
Efficiency of aircraft and engine
 maintenance orginisations

1676
Advice on contracts and to investors
Advice on safety matters
Advice to aircraft operators
Certification of prototype and used
 aircraft
Compliance with certification and
 operating requirements
General advice on maintenance and
 manufacturing

1689
Third-world helicopter operations

1730
Arbitration
Buying, selling and valuation of
 aircraft
CAA and FAA statutory requirements
Engineering/technical disputes
Professional negligence

1881
Aircraft accident investigation
Failure and defect analysis
Fire and explosion investigation and
 analysis
Professional negligence
Sabotage

Aviation Consultancy

689
Airworthiness
Aviation engineering
Civil Aviation Authority (CAA), JAA
 and EAA requirements
Engineer licensing and training

Aviculture

401
Behaviour
Bird health and welfare
Bird keeping
Cage birds
Diet
Plumage

Back Care

1729
Back education
Moving and handling training
Risk assessment

Back Injury

1434
Nursing practice
Personal injury

Back Pain, Arthritis, Work-Related Injury

1240
Arthritis
Back pain
Drug problems
Fibromyalgia
Vibration White Finger (VWF)
Whiplash injuries
Work-related injury – tenosynoritis,
 carpal tunnel

Bacterial Infection

744
Antibiotics – therapeutic and
 prophylactic

Ballistics

989
Accidents resulting from firearms and ammunition
Failures of firearms and ammunition
Interior and exterior ballistics
Trajectories, penetration and impact analysis

1937
Chemical spray devices eg CS spray canisters
Examination and testing o firearms and ammunition
Exterior ballistics calsulations
Gunshot discharge residues
Reconstruction of shooting incidents
Scene visits
Wound ballistics analysis

2317
All aspects

Bank/Building Society Lending

1891
Historic and market contextual analysis of professional negligence claims
Overdrafts, term loans, consumer and commercial
Regulatory and compliance environment of financial services sector
Relationship – solicitors, valuers and accountants with financial institutions

Banking

107
Acquisitions and mergers
Corporate finance

315
Centralised lending
Credit analysis
Lending to corporate sector
Lending to property sector
Mortgage lending

742
International banking
Investment banking
Mortgage lending
Retail banking operations
Trade finance

1164
Commercial banking
Company valuations
Corporate finance
Merchant banking
Mergers and acquisitions

2371
Correspondent bank

2471
Any kind of mediation

2479
Corporate finance
International banking
Project finance
Secured lending
Unsecured lending

2525
All aspects

Banking/Financial Services

420
Banking practice and operations
Capital markets and securities
Credit and security for lending
Payments and settlement, including card technologies
Trade finance
Treasury operations and risk management

Banking/Financial Technical Matters

2173
Assessment/consultancy for 'investors in people'

Banking Merchant

2041
Corporate finance
Project finance

Banking Merchant/Corporate Finance

293
Company advice
Corporate governance
Stock market flotation, funding, investor relations
Strategy – growth, acquisitions, disposals, defence
Unquoted and quoted companies

Banking Practice/Procedure

995
Facility documentation
Instructions to professional advisors
Structure of facilities
Underwriting of secured and unsecured facilities
Valuations of property and other forms of security

2432
Collecting banker
Constructive trust
Negligence claims
United Kingdom (UK) banking practice

Banking/Trade Finance International

2371
Documentary collections
Documentary credits
Drafts and transfers
Foreign banknotes trading, quoting and shipping
Foreign exchange trading and quoting
Gold trading (London gold) and teals (Hong Kong gold)
Guarantees, including performance guarantees, letters of comfort
Loans/advances (pre- and post-shipment finance) with or without trust receipts

Batch Processing

2359
Analysis, testing and provider of experts

Behaviourally Disturbed Adolescents/Children

2266
Absconding, risk assessment
Drug abuse
Fire setting
Secure accommodation assessment
Serious offender assessment
Violence, including self harm

Biological Forensic Science

see also Forensic Science

1060
Body fluids, grouping, DNA, hairs, plant materials
Drugs and alcohol – drink drive calculations

Biological Spoilage

671
Damage to bulk products such as cereal grains and feedstuffs
Deterioration of oils and lubricants
Microbiological contaminants in water cooling systems

Biology/Law

729
Genes and criminality

Blood

2356
Blood grouping
Body fluids
Fibres
Hairs

Bloodstock Contacts

761
Studs and stables, their construction and design
Wide-ranging contacts, both nationally and internationally

Bone/Joint (Musculo-Skeletal) Injury/Diseases

2186
Fractures – limb and spine
General orthopaedics and accident induced injury to limbs
Hand injuries – nerves and tendons
Joint replacement – hip and knee surgery

Bone Marrow Failure/Malfunction

2337
All Aspects

Bone Marrow Transplantation

439
All Aspects

Bones/Joints/Injuries to

1263
Dislocations
Fractures
Hand injuries
Subluxations

Border Dispute Resolution

1206
Boundary delimitation, demarcation
and management
Cartography
Maritime boundaries/law of the sea
Territorial conflict

Boundaries/Land Disputes

235
Building disputes

346
Clarification of undefined boundaries
Deep plan preparation
Personal injury and road traffic
accident plans and reports
Professional indemnity review and
comment
Rights of way
Title investigation

379
Boundary disputes
Building disputes
Dilapidation claims
Negligent architectural design and
contract administration
Negligent structural surveys

448
Boundary disputes
Building disputes
Dilapidations and condition surveys
and schedules
Party wall awards and disputes
Professional negligence

481
Building disputes

535
Building constuctions

647
Surveying

703
Surveying

874
Boundary disputes
Liability reports
Mobile homes (park homes)
New dwellings
Old building – conversion
Vernacular buildings – alterations
and repairs

890
Surveying

1201
Surveying

1365
Boundary disputes
Building surveys
Inferior or negligent construction
Royal Institute of Chartered
Surveyors (RICS) surveys

1393
Investigation, demarcation
Survey and resolution of disputes
relating to land, property and
concession boundaries

1404
Boundary demarcation
Boundary plans
Boundary surveys
Interpretation of maps and plans
Land surveys/areas/boundaries

1426
Boundary disputes
Building-related disputes
Construction contract disputes
Dilapidations/repairs/maintenance
Negligence/structural surveys etc
Party-wall matters

1640
Boundary demarcation disputes
Building defects
Dilapidations claims
Professional negligence

1720
Boundary disputes
Building disputes
Personal injury claims
Professional negligence

1757
Surveying

1796
Surveying

1814
Boundary disputes
Building design and construction
disputes
Insurance claims for property defects
Professional negligence
Schedules of condition, repair and
dilapidation

1849
Surveying

1863
Boundary demarcation
Boundary dispute analysis
Boundary dispute resolution
Conveyance plan preparation
Giving evidence in court
Land registry liaison

1865
Surveying

1878
Accident and other plans
Boundary disputes
Building defects

1921
Building disputes
Costings and recommendations
Local knowledge with residential
valuations – matrimonial
Preparation of plans and drawings
Valuations on disputed property

1955
Boundary and party wall matters
Defective design
Diagnosis of building defects
Dilapidations
Personal injury claims
Professional negligence
Standards of materials and
workmanship

2114
All aspects

2184
Boundaries/land
Building contracts (costs and/or
defective wokmanship)
Building defects/dilapidations
Personal injuries (arising from
buildings or land)
Windows/double glazing defects

2283
Surveying

2344
Building and land

2550
Boundary and right of way disputes
Business valuations
Partnership disputes
Personal injury
Quantum assessments

Boundary Disputes

2
Boundary disputes
Dilapidations

50
Boundary disputes
Building disputes
Commercial and residential property
Landlord and Tenant Act
Professional negligence

87
All aspects

156
Residential

206
Property litigation

772
All aspects

861
Residential

1045
Architectural design and
technological disputes
Boundary disputes and land surveys
Building regulation applications
Dilapidations and insurance claims
Professional negligence and damage
assessment
Project management and
construction supervision
Structural surveys and home buyers
reports

1077
Boundary disputes
Property alterations and
refurbishments
Property surveys
Subsidence, fire and flood damage

1085
Building industry

1151
Land and building

1171
Residential

1369
Litigation involving property

1446
Building disputes

1888
All aspects

2171
Building disputes

2197
Construction, building

2231
Residential

2261
All aspects

2402
Boundary demarcation and resolution

2406
All aspects

2439
Boundary disputes
Brickwor problems
Contractor/customer disputes
Double galzing
Woodwork problems

2542
Building industry

Brain Injury

395
Assessment of needs

442
Assessment for rehabilitation –
  equipment, case management and
  care needs
Case management
Household management
Support to client and family

Brain Injury/Assessment /Rehabilitation

2545
Assessment of traumatic brain injury
Assessment of whiplash injury
Assessment/treatment of
  psychological reaction to physical
  trauma
Medical negligence relating to brain
  injury
Rehabilitation and/or long-term care
  of brain-damaged people

Brain/Spinal Cord

614
Brain disease
Brain injury
Head injury
Nerve injury

Breach of Contract

234
CE marking
Lifting equipment
Machinery safety systems
Pressure systems

1516
Solicitors' alleged breach of contract

Breach of Contract/Warranty

1481
All aspects

Breach of Duty

517
Architect's appointment
CDM regulations
JCT contracts

Breach of Professional Practice Rules

1516
Solicitors

Breach of Warranty/Commercial

2414
Sale and purchase agreements

Breast Specialist

656
Assessment of breast problems
Management of breast problems
  (excluding implants)

Bridge Engineering

2388
All aspects

Bridges

1705
Minor bridges and footbridges
Short-span bridges

British Standards

2287
British standards
Building regulations
Codes of practice
European standards
National house building council
  standards
Working places regulations

Building

see also Construction, Arbitration,
  Architect, Surveyor, Surveying, Civil
  Engineering and the particular type
  of building

134
Design/construction

320
Cladding
Flooring
Raised access floors
Roofing
Windows

1576
All Aspects

1652
Building disputes
Expert witness work
Personal injury (building defects)

1784
Dampness and condensation
Leadwork
Roofing
Structural defects
Windows and double glazing

1875
Acceleration
Delays and disruptions
Extensions of time
Loss and expense
Quantity surveying
Valuations/final accounts

1912
Building adjudication
Building arbitration
Building contracts
Building costs
Measurement of building works
Quantity surveying practice and
  procedure

1916
Commercial
Domestic
Industrial
Public

2287
British standards
Building regulations
Codes of practice
European standards
National house building council
  standards
Working places regulations

2389
Investigating defects in buildings
Investigating structural failures

Building/Architectural Acoustics

637
Building regulation requirements
Inadequate sound insulation
Inappropriate acoustic environment
Performance and other critical
  spaces – fit for the purpose
Special requirements eg near
  airports, roads or industry

Building/Associated Professional Disputes

274
Building failures and defects
Professional contract and design
  negligence
Prolongation and loss and expense
  claims
Town planning disputes and appeals

Building/Civil Engineering

139
Loss and expense claims
Matters of quantum related to value
  of works carried out, additional
  works, delay

1056
Approximate estimating
Bills of quantities
Cost reporting and forecast of final
  costs
Elemental cost analysis
Feasibility studies
Final accounting and fluctuations

1105
Approximate estimating
Bills of quantities
Cost reporting and forecast of final
  costs
Elemental cost analysis
Feasibility studies
Final accounting and fluctuations

1155
Claims against professionally
  indemnified and insured
  practitioners
Claims for disruption and extension
  of time
Claims for loss, expense and damage

1475
Contractural obligations
Costing
Health and safety, procedures,
  regulations
Personal injury accidents
Site management procedures
Temporary works

1990
All aspects

2167
Construction accident investigation
Construction litigation support
Defects reports and workmanship
surveys
Interpretation of financial reports –
claims, counter claims
Technical reports on specifications,
methods of measurement

Building/Civil/Structural Engineering/Defects/Repairs

887
Building components and materials
Condensation risk/vapour control
Engineering materials
Glazing
Highway design, construction and
maintenance
Masonry
Rainwater goods/gutters/downpipes
Reinforced concrete
Roofing and cladding
Waterproofing and tanking
Wind damage

Building/Civil Engineering/ Engineering Contracts

1919
Docks and harbours
Heavy structural steelwork
Major concrete repair works
Major temporary works – heavy lifts
Multi-storey buildings
Roads and bridges

Building/Civil Engineering Construction

2038
Claims
Quantum

Building/Civil Engineering Failures

280
Damp/water penetration, basement
tanking
Foundations failures including
subsidence, heave, land slip,
settlement and consolidation
In situ reinforced pre-cast concrete
and post-tensioned concrete
Masonry brick, block and stonework
Structural steelwork and timber
related problems
Vibration, dynamic analysis

Building Compliance

690
Compliance with NHBC
Compliance with building guarantee
Compliance with building regulations
Compliance with contract (JCT or
others)

Building Component Failures

110
Building fabric generally
Flooring

Building Condition/Defects Analysis

299
Agricultural building problems
Design and management of remedial
works
Dilapidations claims
Disputes relating to boundary
positions
Insurance claims for building damage
Schedules of condition

Building Conservation

235
Architectural history
Conservation philosophy and
principles
Listed buildings and conservation
areas
Planning applications, appeals and
inquiries
Restoration and refurbishment
Traditional structures, building
techniques and materials

Building/Construction

69
Foundation failures
Subsidence/heave

94
Foundations/underpinning
Masonry
Reinforced concrete
Structural steelwork
Timber construction

144
Alterations
Conversions
Extensions
New housing
Old buildings

363
Defective construction
Defective design, professional
negligence
Defective structural surveys,
professional negligence

479
Assessment of quality of work
Extension of time claims
Loss and expense claims
Standard forms of building contracts
Valuation of works carried out

589
Cladding
Design
Detailing
Foundations
New and old construction,
refurbishment
Structure
Weathering envelope

690
Defects in buildings
Defects in drains
Fabric failure
Scott schedules
Subsidence claims

790
Arbitration
Measurement and evaluation of
construction works
Professional negligence actions
relating to construction professionals
Project management and project
co-ordination
Quantity surveying

811
Cracking
Damp penetration
Defects
Drainage
Subsidence
Temporary works

957
Building defects and diagnosis
Construction insolvency
Delay, disruption, loss and expense
Liquidated and ascertained
damages, set off
Measurement and valuation
Professional negligence
Project management
Rights to light, party walls

1365
Boundary disputes
Building surveys
Inferior or negligent construction
Royal Institute of Chartered
Surveyors (RICS) surveys

1529
Building contracts – delays and
disruptions
Building regulations
Cladding of buildings – roofs and
walls
Movement in structures – expansion
and other joints
Water penetration – including
basements

1609
Building surveying
Defects costing and analysis
Dilapidations
Materials and workmanship
Professional negligence
Schedule of condition

1640
Boundary demarcation disputes
Building defects
Dilapidations claims
Professional negligence

1814
Boundary disputes
Building design and construction
disputes
Insurance claims for property defects
Professional negligence
Schedules of condition, repair and
dilapidation

2098
Advocacy in smaller cases
Architectural and design negligence
Building arbitration
Building litigation
Defects investigation and reporting
NHBC arbitration

2201
Defect diagnosis
Defects and negligence/contractor,
 surveyor, architect
Dilapidations/scott schedules
Including France, Belgium, Saudi
 Arabia, Holland
Party walls and boundary disputes

2213
Building regulations
Damp proof course installation/damp
 proofing
General building and roofing work
NHBC
Replacement windows/double
 glazing/conservatories

2231
Building defects
Surveys

2287
Foundations
Rain penetration and dampness
Rendering, plastering and screeding
Roofing and cladding
Stone and masonry
Structure

2382
Commercial building
Industrial building
Professional negligence/building
Residential building

2438
Construction details
Standards of workmanship

2541
Advice in remedial/rectification work
CDM services
Evidence in building construction
 quality
Full building specification and
 architectural services
Interpretation of building contracts

Building Construction/Allied Trades

2336
Construction cost management
Evaluation of distribution costs
Evaluation of loss and expense
Expert reports on quantum
Measurement and valuation of
 variations
Prolongation claims

**Building Construction/Architectural
Practice**

312
Professional negligence

**Building/Construction
Claims/Disputes**

343
Construction insolvency
Costs of defects
Development costs
Extensions of time and loss/expense
Project co-ordination

2156
Compliance with regulations
Cost of construction work
Standards of workmanship

Building Construction/Contracts

1842
Commercial
Health/hospitals
Industrial
Leisure
Residential
Retail

1884
All aspects

Building/Construction Defects

2019
Foundation failures/subsidence
Investigation of structural failures
Material failure investigations
Professional negligence

**Building/Construction Defects for
Insurers, Investigation of**

1943
EL, PL and CAR insurance claims
Professional indemnity claims
Risk assessement for underwriters

Building Construction/Design

2147
Damp penetration
Defective construction
Delapidations and maintenance
Noise nuisance
Subsidence
Vibration damage

Building Construction Quality

1815
Approval of building works
Cost advice on building works
Design and specification of work
Supervision of building works

**Building/Construction/Quantity
Surveying**

121
All types of quantum claims relating
 to construction
Construction procurement
Contract practice and procedure

707
Children's play areas and equipment
Health and safety legislation in the
 building and construction industry
Measurement and evaluation of
 construction works
Professional negligence actions
 relating to construction professionals
Project management and project
 co-ordination
Quantity surveying

2025
Building defects
Building site accidents
Health and safety at work
Historic buildings
Personal accidents in the workplace
Structural design defects

**Building Construction/Repair/Land
Disputes**

2344
Boundary disputes
Buildings/insurance claims
Design/supervision/survey
Measurement of land and buildings
Negligence claims

Building Construction/Surveying

1567
Building contractual disputes
Building defects
Insurance related claims
Landlord and tenant disputes
Professional negligence
Structural survey

Building Construction/Valuation

535
Boundary disputes
Construction defects and disputes
Dilapidations
Insurance
Professional negligence – valuation
 and building surveying
Repair notices

Building/Construction Work

1533
Contractual disputes
Professional negligence
Progress of works
Quality of work
Repair and refurbishment of buildings

**Building/Construction-Related
Disputes**

1792
Building and land surveying
Building control (building regulations)
Dilapidations and schedules of
 condition
Drainage
Insurance claims
Personal injury where building fabric
 is contributory
Project management

Building Contract Claims/Disputes

424
Client/architect/surveyor disputes
Conciliation and mediation
Practising arbitrator
Professional negligence

1233
Building defects
Quantity surveyor practice
Valuation of building and civil
 engineering works

Building Contracts

1091
Contract administration
Extension of time assessments
Loss and expense assessments
Practical completion assessments

2014
All aspects

2147
Architects' duties

2325
Administration
Arbitration and litigation support
Claims assessment
Delay and consequential loss
Professional negligence

2494
All aspects

Building Contracts Claims

634
Advising on defective workmanship
and materials

Building Contracts/Disputes

1151
Negotiation of setlement of claims
Preparation of reports on relevant
circumstances
Provision of evidence in court and at
arbitrations

Building Defects

265
Analysis of defects/reasons for failure
Investigation of defects/analysis of
responsibilities
Investigation of fire, fire spread

355
Building contracts – defective work
Landlord and tenant repairing
obligations

550
Brickwork
Cladding
Condensation
Curtain walling
Flooring
Raised car park decks
Roofing
Timber
Windows

772
All aspects

969
Accidental water/oil spillage
Air infiltration (excessive)
Condensation
Inadequate plant room space
Internal pollution
Solar heat gains

1238
Buildings
Cladding
Concrete
Construction defects
Foundations
Housing
Masonry
Material testing
Soil mechanics
Steel
Structural engineering
Structural surveys
Timber

1815
Analysis of buildings
Cost advice
Identification of causes
Remedial works

1842
All aspects

2396
Asphalt
Brickwork
Dampness/rot/infestation
Epoxy floor finishes
Industrial Roofs and Claddings
Traditional roof coverings

Building Defects/Disputes

621
Contract disputes
Disputes between client and builder
Disputes between landlord and tenant
Repairs and closing orders
Standards of builders' work

Building Defects/Disrepair

520
Architectural, drainage and design
defects
Damp, water penetration and related
problems
Defects in precast and reinforced
concrete construction
Housing and small commercial
buildings
Structural cracking in all building
types
Subsidence of foundations

Building Design/Construction

1257
Construction defects of all kinds
Contract administration disputes and
claims
Delay and additional cost claims
Professional indemnity and other
insurance claims
Property fraud
Property valuation disputes

Building Design/Construction/Failure

517
Flat-pitched roofs
Interior and exterior finishes
Repair, renovation and alteration
Steel frame and lightweight cladding
Timber frame
Traditional construction

Building Design/Construction/Use

1594
Architect's terms of appointment –
fees and services
Building contracts
Building maintenance
Contractor's negligence – delays,
cost overruns and bad work
Conversion and refurbishment of
existing buildings
Dilapidations and building defects
Health and safety regulations
Listed and historic buildings
Planning and building regulations
Professional negligence – delays,
cost overruns and bad work
Specification of materials

Building Design/Defects

1161
Building contract disputes
Building defects – Commercial,
leisure, residential and medica
buildings
Claims for professional fees
Diputes between contractor and
subcontractors
Disputed subcontractor claims
Improper contract administration
Infringements of coopyright
Partty wall infringements
Practical completion certificate
improperly withheld
Responsibilities of an architect

Building Design/Planning

761
Studs and stables, their construction
and design
Wide-ranging contacts, both
nationally and internationally

Building Disputes

235
Boundaries
Building contracts
Dilapidations
Landlord and tenant

481
Boundary disputes
Building contract disputes
Building contract financial disputes
Building contract work quality
disputes
Party wall disputes
Professional negligence in building
contract fraud

551
Architect's appointment
Building regulations and planning
acts compliance
Construction failures
Daylight obstruction and right to light
Defective design
Professional negligence (architect)

1007
Diagnostic
Forensic
Professional negligence

1151
Boundary disputes
Disputes relating to building
ownership
Disputes relating to building works
Disputes relating to insurance claims
on real property
Rights of light disputes

1428
Consequential loss on share
purchase agreement – warrantees

1446
Boundary disputes
Building works disputes
Workmanship disputes

1816
Contract claims
Defective works
Delays and extensions of time
Health and safety
Project management
Quantity surveying

1888
Building contract law
Quality of work, compliance with
regulations etc
Value of work

1921
Building disputes
Costings and recommendations
Local knoeledge with residential
valuations – matrimonial
Preparation of plans and drawings
Valuations on disputed property

2166
Arbitration

2171
Boundary disputes
Defective building work
Professional negligence
Repairing covenants

2260
Claims for loss and expense and
   disruption
Outstanding defects or uncompleted
   work
Professional negligence
Quantum generally

2406
All aspects

2489
Arbitrations
Dilapidations
Disputes on occupation of buildings
Planning appeals

2554
Adequacy of materials and
   workmanship
Building insurance claims
Contractual matters
Defect diagnosis and advice of
   remedial work
Disputes arising out of damp-proofing
   works/roofing works
Disputes arising out of neighbouring
   construction

Building Disputes (Small Works)

2131
Contractual
Quality
Specifications

Building Engineering

1681
Cladding
Ferrocement
Foundation settlement/subsidence
Glass reinforced plastics and cement
Materials failures
Steel and reinforced concrete
   structures

**Building Engineering
(Mechanical/Electrical)**

622
Alternative dispute resolution
Arbitration
Breach of contract actions
Defective Premises Act claims
Litigation
Professional negligence claims

Building Engineering Services

see also Building Services
   Engineering

599
Measurement and valuation
Quantum
Specialist sub-contractors

655
Boiler plant and refrigeration plant
Compressed air and gas systems
Heating, ventilation, air conditioning
Hot and cold water supply systems
Plumbing and sanitation installations
Steam and condensate installations

983
Air conditioning and ventilation
Boilers and boiler plant
Engineering plant
Heating
Hot and cold water services
Steam and condensate

1749
Air conditioning
Appointments and contracts
Commissioning and handover
Controls and building management
   systems
Energy conservation
Heating and hot water

2245
Gas supply and combustion
Hot and cold water services
Oil supply and combustion

2408
Boilers, flue emissions
Heating, central heating, warm air
Investigation into electrical fires
Legionella disease investigations
Noise (acoustic) investigations of
   engineering services
Ventilation, air conditioning,
   refrigeration
Water treatment, water audits

**Building Engineering
Services/Environmental/Vertical
Tranportation**

598
Electrical engineering services
Fire protection services
Lifts
Mechanical engineering services
Public health services

Building Envelope Details

815
Basements
Construction tolerances
Damp and condensation
Flat and pitched roofs
Stairs
Walls, brick and stone
Windows, dpc's, flashings

Building Failures/Investigation

21
Condensation and mould growth
Dampness
Daylighting and sunlighting
Personal injury, slipperiness of
   finishes and design features
Thermal effects and conditions
Water penetration

2029
Dry rot investigation
Roofs
Water penetration

Building Industry/Architecture

1085
Boundary disputes
Building contract disputes
Building disputes generally
Defective construction/workmanship
Negligence claims

Building Insurance

2
Fire damage
Subsidence

1652
Fire damage claims
Negotations with insurers
Repair specifications
Subsidence claims

**Building Investigation/Reports in
Connection with Litigation**

1743
Brick structures
Cladding
Defective building/construction
   relating to landlord and tenant
   disputes
Defective buildings and construction
   causing personal injury
Defective buildings and construction
   general
Defective foundations
Foundations
Reinforced concrete
Steel structures
Subsidence
Timber construction

**Building Investigation/Testing of
Building/Civil Engineering
Materials/Components**

595
Blockwork
Cladding
Glazing
Plaster, screed and render
Reinforced and prestressed concrete
Roofing

**Building/Landscape
Contracts/Sub-contracts**

2039
Architects' instructions
Certificates
Delay and extensions of time
Obligations
Partial possession
Practical completion

Building Legislation

481
Building regulations
Town and country planning

Building Litigation

2542
Boundary disputes reports
Building disputes reports and expert
   opinion
Defective building reports and expert
   opinion
Professional negligence, architects
Subsidence of buildings including
   claims and remedial work

Building Litigation/Arbitration

2132
Contractual disputes/claims/variations
Defects/cost of repairs
Sub-contractors' disputes
Subsidence/insurance claims
Valuations/final accounts/quantum
   merit claims

Building Litigation Support

889
Assessment of quantum

Building Material Technology/Structure

306
Brickwork and blockwork as a
  material and structure
Damp penetration of walls and roofs
Subsidence of walls and floors
Thermal insulation of masonry walls
Timber roof structures
Wet and dry screeding of concrete
  floors

Building Matters/Residential Property

2231
Boundary disputes
Cracks and settlement/subsidence
Defective replacement windows
Defects in general
Surveys
Valuations

Building Negligence

690
Duty of care
Negligent advice of surveyors
Negligent construction
Standard of construction

Building Problems

1652
Diagnosis of building defects
Pre-purchase surveys and reports
Repair specifications

Building/Property

2184
Boundaries/Land
Building contracts (costs and/or
  defective workmanship)
Building defects/dilapidations
Personal injuries (arising from
  buildings or land)
Windows/double glazing defects

Building/Property Disputes

2
Boundary disputes
Contractual disputes
Defective workmanship
Dilapidations

1775
Building disputes
Construction disputes
Contract disputes/JCT Minor Works
  Agreement
Landlord and Tenant Act, 1985
Professional negligence/surveyors

Building Repair/Refurbishment

1666
Coatings
Concrete repairs
Masonry repairs
Terracotta repairs

Building/Residential Property

156
Boundary disputes
Building disputes
Residential tenancies
Valuation (capital and rental)

Building Services

47
Air conditioning
Control systems
Electrical mechanical
Ventilation

185
Commercial buildings
Domestic and industrial refrigeration
Domestic buildings
Heating systems (gas/electric/oil
  fuelled)
Public buildings
Ventilation/air conditioning systems
Water systems

553
Commercial buildings
Domestic and industrial refrigeration
Domestic buildings
Heating systems (gas/electric/oil
  fuelled)
Public buildings
Ventilation/air conditioning systems
Water systems

1410
Air and water systems
District heating
Heating and air conditioning
Industrial and agricultural
  environments
Thermal insulation

Building Services Engineering

see also Building Engineering
  Services

359
Air conditioning
Boiler plant
Heating
Steam
Ventilation
Water services

1556
Conceptual design
Feasibility studies
Installation and commissioning
Safety reviews
System performance
Technical audits

1759
Electrical services
Environmental services
Mechanical services
Public health
Transportation

1876
Air conditioning and ventilation
  systems
Control systems
Domestic hot and cold water systems
Electrical distribution systems (airing
  and equipment)
Heating systems (small and large
  scale)
Mechanical systems (including
  compressed gas networks)

2130
BS7671 – 16th Edition IEE Regs
Building services ventilation
Electricity at work act
Fire alarms, detection of fire
  protection
Lighting systems

2246
Air conditioning
Boiler plant
Consulting engineers' fees and terms
  of engagement
Heating and hot water systems
Ventilation

2366
Design faults
Personal accident
System failures

2405
Air conditioning and ventilation
Boiler plant – oil, gas and coal-fired
Energy conservation and controls
Hot and cold water distribution
  systems – domestic, commercial
  and industrial
Low-pressure hot-water heating
  systems – domestic, commercial
  and industrial
Steam and high-temperature
  hot-water heating systems

Building Services Engineering – General

983
Catering equipment
Control system
Cooling and refrigeration
Fire protection
Public health and plumbing
Sound and noise

Building Services/Lifts/Escalators

504
Cranes
Escalators
Fork lift trucks
Hoists
Lifts
Miscellaneous lifting equipment

Building Services/Mechanical/Electrical/Building Construction

547
Building fabric construction
Electrical installations
Energy usage throughout the building
Heating appliances – gas, oil and
  solid fuel
Plumbing installations
U value calculations

Building Services/Public Health Engineering

1090
Air conditioning
Electrical services
Fire protection systems
Heating and ventilation

1517
Air conditioning
Electrical services
Fire protection systems
Heating and ventilation

Building/Structural Engineering

2452
Building defects
Building site accidents
Health and safety at work
Historic buildings
Personal accidents in the workplace
Structural design defects

Building Structures

1705
Defects to low-rise buildings
(foundations, general)
Defects to low-rise buildings
(masonry, steel, concrete, timber)

Building Survey Disputes

2158
Building works
Landlord and tenant
Structural survey
Subsidence and insurance claims
Valuation – residential

Building Surveying

109
Building repairs and renovations
Construction defects
Repairing covenants
Schedules of condition
Schedules of wants of repair
Water penetration into buildings

195
Boundary disputes
Building defects
Building subsidence/settlement
problems
Dilapidations

235
Building defects (analysis and
remedy)
Home buyers reports
Professional negligence
Structural surveys

321
Building defects
Maintenance
Party walls
Property management
Repairs

329
Defects in buildings
Dilapidations
Extensions of time
Maintenance
Party wall/boundary disputes
Workmanship

379
Boundary disputes
Building disputes
Dilapidation claims
Negligent architectural design and
contract administration
Negligent structural surveys

448
Boundary disputes
Building disputes
Dilapidations and condition surveys
and schedules
Party wall awards and disputes
Professional negligence

592
Building defects
Design and refurbishment
Quality of workmanship

808
Building contracts
Building defects
Building regulations
Property valuations
Town and country planning

874
Boundary disputes
Liability reports
Mobile homes (park homes)
New dwellings
Old buildings – conversion
Vernacular buildings – alterations
and repairs

1127
Building construction
Dilapidations
Mortgage valuations
Service charge
Surveys

1128
Building defects/residential,
commercial and industrial
Building disputes/residential,
commercial and industrial
Professional negligence claims

1308
Building surveys
Dilapidations
Fire insurance valuations
Project monitoring
Repair and maintenance

1372
Listed building, repair, maintenance
and development
Management of listed residential flats

1426
Boundary disputes
Building-related disputes
Construction contract disputes
Dilapidations/repairs/maintenance
Negligence/structural surveys etc
Party-wall matters

1683
Building Construction
Building Contracts
Building Surveys
Building regulations
Dilapidations
Maintenance and repair of buildings

1720
Boundary disputes
Building disputes
Personal injury claims
Professional negligence

1796
Building disputes
Surveyors' negligence – structural
surveys

1878
Accident and other plans
Boundary disputes
Building defects

1955
Boundary and party wall matters
Defective design
Diagnosis of building defects
Dilapidations
Personal injury claims
Professional negligence
Standards of materials and
workmanship

1965
Conditions
Dampness
Deleterious materials

2402
Defects diagnosis
Dilapidations
Professional negligence

Building Surveying/Building Related Problems

2439
Boundary disputes
Brickwork problems
Contractor/customer disputes
Double glazing
Woodwork problems

Building Surveying/Construction

1077
Boundary disputes
Property alterations and
refurbishments
Property surveys
Subsidence, fire and flood damage

Building Surveying/Defect Investigation

102
Building construction/regulations and
acts
Building design/refurbishment project
management – town and country
planning
Construction disputes/claims
Defects – double glazing, fitted
kitchens etc
Public consumer complaints/faults
Structural surveys and reports

Building Surveying/Design

1045
Architectural design and
technological disputes
Boundary disputes and land surveys
Building regulation applications
Dilapidations and insurance claims
Professional negligence and damage
assessment
Project management and
construction supervision
Structural surveys and home buyers
reports

Building Surveying Practice

2396
Building condition
Competence and duties
Contract administration
Planned maintenance
Practice and procedure
Structural surveys

Building Surveying/Surveyors

362
Alteration, extension and conversion
of buildings
Building defect investigation/analysis
Negligence claims against surveyors
Residential pre-purchase (structural)
surveys (excluding valuations)
Schedules of dilapidations/condition

Building Technology

2039
Design standards
Failures of materials and components
Unforeseen events
Workmanship

Building Works

870
Cost of building works
Cost of reinstatement after fire or accident
Dilapidation reports and costs of reinstatement
House extensions and alterations
Quality of workmanship and materials

Buildings

240
Basements
Contaminated ground
Floors
Foundations
Structural elements
Subsidence and heave

359
Commercial industrial public and domestic buildings
Contractual disputes
Defence and plaintiff reports
Design disputes
Installation disputes
Professional negligence

525
Defects

755
Boundary disputes
Building contract disputes
Double glazing problems
Negligence claims
Subsidence/foundation problems

1635
Age historic development and features of interest of old buildings
Suitability of old buildings for listing or delisting

1750
Mechanical and electrical engineering
Structural engineering

1754
Building defects
Building disputes
Fire damage
Housing Act disrepair
Insurance claims
Party wall awards
Personal injury (loss of ability and home adaptations)
Schedules of dilapidations
Subsidence
Survey negligence
Tree root damage

1953
Defects

1965
Defects

2550
Defects

Buildings (New/Existing)

1998
Building services (air conditioning and heating)
Contract and project management
Health and safety in buildings
Legionnaires' disease
Personal injury
Sick building syndrome (indoor air quality)

Buildings/New/Existing/Old/Historic

1741
Asbestos contamination, sulphate attack, damp
Building movement subsidence/settlement/underpinning/shrinkage
Condition at time of sale
Masonry and timber with particular reference to old historic buildings
Professional negligence
Structural design – all materials
Temporary works – scaffolding/trenches

Buildings Structures/Foundations

981
Ancient buildings
Bridges
High rise buildings
Industrial buildings
Subsidence and foundation failure

Bulk Oil Operations

356
Charter party and demurrage claims
Contamination and pollution
Load and discharge supervision
Oil loss and cargo retention clause (ROB)
Safe port and ship to ship operations

Burn Injury

1777
Acute management of major burn
Burn scar reconstruction
Burn scarring and disfigurement
Burns in children
Non-accidental burn injury
Skin grafting and reconstructive surgery

Burns

2422
All aspects

Burns/Plastic Surgery

541
Aesthetic surgery
Burns
Hand surgery
Industrial injuries
Microsurgery
Road traffic injuries

Business

626
Corporate management

Business Advice

see also Commercial Disputes

1929
Financial analysis
Financial strategy
Growth strategy
Overhead reduction

Business Disputes

2263
Advising minority shareholders in private limited companies
Partnership disputes
Share valuations

Business/Employment Interruption

1646
Consequential loss claims
Fatal accidents
Personal injury
Wrongful dismissal

Business Equipment/Related Contracts

1682
Equipment specifications – capabilities, pricing, industry norms
Industry practices
Leasing
Purchasing procedures
Service contracts

Business Interruption/Loss of Profits

387
Losses incurred by sole traders, partners and directors of unquoted companies

Business/Share Valuation

505
Partnership disputes
Shareholder disputes

1646
Business and goodwill valuations
Share valuations
Shareholder and partnership disputes

2024
Business sale/purchase
Consequential loss
Contractual disputes
Matrimonial
Partnership dissolution

Businesses

221
Company bust-ups
Partnership disputes
Valuations

C

Cancer

563
Hodgkins disease
Lung cancer
Lymphomas
Testicular cancer

1982
Breast
Gastrointestinal and rectal
Gynaecological
Lung
Prostate
Thyroid

2150
Medicine

Cancer Diagnosis/Treatment

653
Breast cancer
Colorectal cancer
Cytotoxic chemotherapy in cancer treatment
Delay in diagnosis of cancer
Endocrine therapy in cancer treatment
Lymphoma
Radiotherapy in cancer treatment

Cancer/Malignant Disease

2233
General treatment of cancer and
  allied disease
Induction of cancer by carcinogens,
  radiation and other hazards
Industrial cancer
Problems arising out of negligence,
  particularly misdiagnosis, overdose
  and radiation damage

Cancer Medicine/Oncology

1950
Adjuvant therapy
Breast Cancer
Chemotherapy
Organisation of services
Palliative care
Quality of life

Cancer/Treatment

2259
Chemotherapy
Gynaecological cancer
Head and neck cancer
Industrially acquired cancers
Radiotherapy

Cancer Treatment/Radiotherapy/Oncology

476
Breast cancer
Gynaecological cancer (ovary, cervix,
  endometrium)
Lung cancer
Skin cancer
Urological cancer (bladder, prostate,
  testis)

Canine

1382
Animal behaviour
Dog breed identification (ie Pit Bull
  Terriers)
Ferrets and ferreting
Use of dogs in fieldsports

Canine Behaviour

390
Agillity dog training
Altering canine behaviour (therapy)
Assessing canine behaviour
Pet dog obedience
Police dog training and handling
Preparing reports on canine
  behaviour
Security dog training and handling
Working trials dog training

Canine/Feline Behaviour Consultancy

1699
Author of many pet behaviour papers
  and best-selling books
Consultant to veterinary and pet
  trade companies
Control and injury cases; acts
  relating to control of dogs, and
  injuries caused by dogs
Legal consultant animal welfare
Referral practice for veterinary
  surgeons
Treatment of pet behaviour problems
  (10 years in practice)

Capital Valuations/Rental Valuations of Residential, Commercial/Industrial Properties

1365
General practice professional
  problems

Carbon Monoxide Poisoning in the Domestic Setting

862
All aspects

Cardiac Medicine

2299
Especially ischaemic (coronary) heart
  disease

Cardiac/Respiratory Pathology

521
Interventional cardiovascular
  pathology
Occupational lung disease

Cardiology

2312
All aspects

Cardiology/Cardiovascular Disease

679
Angioplasty
Cardiac catheterisation
Coronary artery disease
Heart valve disease
Interventional cardiology
Nuclear cardiology

1021
All aspects of cardiac pacing
Invasive and non-invasive
  investigations
Post-operative cardiac surgical care

1153
Heart disease
High blood pressure
Vascular disease

1392
Coronary artery disease and
  coronary arteriography
Examination of the cardiovascular
  system

1441
Ischaemic heart disease
Traumatic heart conditions

Cardiology Fetal

1337
All Aspects

Cardiothoracic Surgery

1974
Intensive care
Paediatric Surgery

Cardiovascular Disease

188
Hypertension
Myocardial infarction

Cardiovascular Medicine

1429
Bacterial endocarditis
Coronary artery disease/angina/heart
  attacks
Heart failure
Heart rhythm disturbances
High blood pressure

Care Audits

2181
Acute units
Community units
Nursing homes
Operating theatres
Residential homes

Care/Elderly

789
Stroke

Care/Future Needs/Costings, Assessment of

1177
Care
Equipment
Structural alterations

Care Needs

9
Advocacy/care management
Care management/keyworker
Household and personal care needs
Lifting and handling
Transport/access to the community

Care Packages

100
Domestic help to 24hr nursing care –
  via 120 branches of BNA

Care Requirements

2304
Need for future care (NOT qualified
  nursing care)
Value of gratuitous care provided in
  the past

Career Structure/Earning Assessment in Case of Accident/Injury

1309
Analysis of earnings by occupational
  area and geographical region.
  Career options and levels of
  earnings in Europe, America, South
  America and Australia.
Career profiles in cases of personal
  injury – plaintiffs and defendants
Employment practice
Job market analysis and review of
  disadvantage on the labour market

Careers Counselling/Occupational/Geographical Evaluation of Employment Trends/Earnings

Career assessment generally
Career assessments after physical
  and psychological injury
Case reports for plaintiff/defendants
  – CICB/Tribunal and cases in UK
  and abroad

Cargo

see also Marine, Ship

95
Heating in products
Moisture content
Spoilage caused by funghi and
  bacteria
Spoilage caused by insects and mites
Ventilation of cargoes

356
Cargo recovery and salvage claims
  monitoring
Collision damage assessment
Liability and quantum assessment
Personal injury claims arising
Repair supervision and pollution
  monitoring

631
Breath tests
Deterioration of shipped and
  transported goods
Drink/drive cases
General forensic and chemical
  analysis
Prescribed and prohibited drugs
Ships' cargoes

1802
Analytical Chemistry
Contaminated land and water
Oil, gas and petrochemicals
Quality control and cargo
  contamination
Workplace atmosphere

Cargo/Carriage of Goods by Sea

1236
Deterioration of cargoes
Personal injury

Cargo Claims

356
Container loss and lashing
  calculations
Draft surveys and preshipment
  inspections (PSI)
Dry bulk contamination and outturn
  loss claims
Heavy lift and deck storage
  supervision
Road haulage and CMR claims

Cargo Contamination

1464
Contaminant and adulterant analysis
Witnessed analytical programmes

Cargo/Goods in Transit Litigation

1454
Carriage by sea
Containerised cargo
Road haulage

Cargo Quality Disputes

6
Chemical interactions
Contamination problems during
  storage, carriage and handling of
  chemicals and petroleum products
Interpretation of test results;
  problems in sampling and analysis
Mitigation

Cargo Security

1454
Containerised
Marine

Carpet Complaints

2088
Adherence to Office of Fair Trading
  (OFT) and British Standards
  Institute (BSI) recommendations
Arranging laboratory testing
Assessing information available from
  manufacturer and retailer
Information before point of contract
Validity of complaint

Carpet/Floorcoverings

1221
Carpet, sheet and tiles
Linoleum, sheet and tiles
Sub-floor preparation
Vinyl, sheet and tiles

Carpet Installation Procedures

2088
Cheap and shoddy workmanship
Compliance with BS 5325
Incorrect techniques
Installation safety
Responsibility
Subfloor preparation

Case Management

1737
Assessment of need with
  recommendation and costs
Care planning and implementation
Counselling
Monitoring and review

Case Management of Disabled People/Brain Injury

2051
Assessment for special equipment
Housing adaptations for disabled
  people
Identification of care needs
Lifestyle planning
Recruitment and training of carers
Rehabilitation in the home/community

Case Management/Receivership

1810
Counselling and guidance
Hiring of carers, therapists etc
Purchase and design of housing
Purchase of equipment, transport etc
Reassessments for Public Trust
  Office

Casting

454
Direct chill semi-continuous
Gravity
High pressure
Investment
Low pressure
Sand

1877
Application, removal, care and
  aftercare of patients in plaster of
  Paris or synthetic casts

Causes of Damage to Products in Ships/Store

95
Heating in products
Moisture content
Spoilage caused by fungi and
  bacteria
Spoilage caused by insects and mites
Ventilation of cargoes

Cerebral Palsy

1209
Civil litigation

2018
Augmentative communication
  systems
Feeding and swallowing disorders
Motor speech assessment
Receptive and expressive language

Chemical Analysis

118
Blood/urine alcohol
General chemical analysis

1204
All matters relating to chemicals
Drink-drive litigation

Chemical Effects on Human Health

327
Asbestosis and mesothelioma
Asthma
Dermatitis
Dust and fume
Hazardous substances
Smoking and health

Chemical Engineering

467
Commissioning of chemical plant
Construction of chemical plant
Design engineering
Process engineering
Project engineering
Project management

533
Oil and gas production
Salts, chloralkali and inorganics
  manufacture

Chemical Hazards

671
Environmental impact
Investigation and managment of
  incidents involving chemical spills
Reactive chemicals and mixtures
Release and dispersion of hazardous
  gases and vapours
Storage, transport and handling of
  dangerous materials
Toxicity and flammability
Unstable chemicals

Chemical/Microscopical Analysis

1
Asbestos
Chemicals at work
Foodstuffs
General chemistry
Pollution/contamination
Road traffic

Chemical Pathology

407
All aspects

Chemicals

80
Chemicals
Cosmetics
Forensic
Metals
Paint, polymers and waxes
Solvents

423
Fertilisers
Fine chemicals
Manufacturing, plant operation and
construction
Petrochemical
Purity and specifications
Valuation and markets

1394
Analysis
Reactions
Toxicity

1624
Analysis and identification of
chemicals
Chemicals in the environment
Effects of chemicals on humans
Effects of chemicals on plastics,
rubbers etc

2359
Analysis, testing and provider of
experts

2465
Chemicals
Cosmetics
Forensic
Metals
Paints, polymers and waxes
Solvents

Chemicals/Effect on Health

480
Safety of chemicals in the workplace
Safety of cosmetics, consumer
products
Safety of household products

Chemicals/Materials

2437
Adhesives
Industrial safety – chemicals and
materials
Paints and coatings – general and
emulsion paints (speciality)
Polymers and resins, including
applications
Textile and paper treatments
Toxicity of chemicals (non-medical
aspects)

Chemicals-Related Accidents

1741
Chemical reactions – deterioration of
materials
Container failures
Exposure – acute effects and
precautions
Plant, equipment failures
Product liability aspects
Public liability aspects

Chemistry

108
Environmental modelling

581
Examination of environmental
samples for explosives pollution

801
Clinical chemistry
Clinical toxicology
Drug and alcohol impairment of
drivers
Forensic toxicology
Workplace screening for drug abuse

1616
Chemical
Environmental
Forensic science
Pharmaceuticals
Vegetable and petroleum oils

1802
Alcohol in blood, breath and urine
Analytical chemistry
Contaminated land and water
Oil, gas and petrochemicals
Quality control and cargo
contamination
Workplace atmosphere

2073
Antioxidant mechanisms and use in
technology and medicine
Degradable polymers
Polymer chemistry and technology
Polymer recycling
Polymer stabilisation

Chemistry/Physics/Engineering of Materials

2160
Additives for polymer systems
Alternative dispute resolution
Environmental impact of polymer
materials
Fire smoke, toxic gas problems
Health and safety aspects of polymer
materials
Intellectual property (particularly
patent litigation)
Misuse of confidential information
Plastics; rubber; surface coatings;
adhesives; fibres
Polymeric materials and composites
Product liability (including failure of
building materials)

Chemotherapy

1982
Misuse
Overdose

Chest/General Surgery

1304
Medico-legal work

Chest Injury – Accidental

2017
All aspects

Chest Medicine

149
Asbestos-related problems
Asthma-occupational/non-
occupational
Chest injury following Road Traffic
Accidents (RTA)
Inhalation injury
Mesothelioma
Testing failed alcohol breath test

Chest Medicine/Allergy

1621
Adverse reactions
Occupational disorders

Child Abuse

804
Assessment of suitability for
treatment of perpetrators
Child sexual abuse
Risk assessment of admitted or
suspected perpetrators

938
All aspects

1075
All aspects

1212
All aspects

1507
Assessment of procedure
Assessment of risk of further
abuse/trauma
Child sexual abuse
Consultation services to solicitors
Opinion/recommendation for further
treatment/rehabilitation
Post-traumatic stress disorder
Psychological/psychiatric assessment

Child Abuse/Child Protection

190
Child abuse
Cot death
Infanticide
Non-accidental injury

427
Contact
Placement issues

462
Competence and credibility: children
as witnesses
Contact and residence disputes:
effects of children
Risk assessment of parents

1907
Addictions and alcohol abuse
Learning difficulties
Special needs

2266
Adoption and fostering
Adult and adolescent sexual abuse of
children
Attachment/custody/access disputes
Emotional abuse
Failure to thrive (non organic)
Physical abuse, including children's
bullying
Risk assessment

2513
Child sexual abuse

Child Abuse/Medical Evidence in Sexual Assault

1975
Child physical abuse
Child sexual abuse
Rape and other sexual assault on
adults

Child/Adolescent/Family Forensic Psychiatry

2105
Adolescents difficult to manage/place
Adolescents who commit serious
offences
Child-care legislation cases and risk
assessment
Compensation cases (children and
adolescents)
Post-sexual abuse

Child/Adolescent/Family Psychiatry

177
Access, custody and adoptions
Child sexual abuse and
non-accidental injury assessments
Family assessment, risk assessments
Personal injury (psychiatric)
Post-traumatic stress disorder

178
Care proceedings
Compensation with regard to
psychological consequences of
injury and abuse (including sexual
abuse)
Disputed residence, contact, adoption

184
Child abuse/sexual, physical,
emotional
Childhood psychological trauma
Complex child-care issues
Fostering, adoption, substitutive care
Post-traumatic stress disorder

215
Anorexia nervosa
Bereavement
Childhood trauma but NOT child
sexual abuse
Munchausen-by-proxy
Parenting assessment
Trans-racial adoption

596
Adoption and fostering
Child abuse – sexual, physical or
emotional
Custody dispute cases
Insurance claims in accidents or
crimes
Parenting capacity
Young offenders

701
Claims for damages
Custody and access disputes
Disputed care orders

1006
Accident and compensation
Child abuse of all kinds
Contact/access/custody

1548
Adoption
Child abuse
Child neglect and emotional abuse
Child sexual abuse
Custody disputes
Post-traumatic stress disorders in
children

1581
Adoption
Child abuse
Child care and wardship
Fostering
Matrimonial disputes and proceedings
Mental Health Act Tribunals
Psychiatric aspects of personal injury
Psychiatric assessment in criminal
cases
Residence/custody and contact for
children

1684
Adolescents in trouble with the law
Custody and access
Parenting capacity
Physical and sexual abuse
Sequelae of accidents, physical and
emotional trauma

1762
Adoption and fostering
All forms of abuse (emotional,
physical, sexual)
Ethnic minorities
Post-traumatic stress syndrome
Serious offenders

1859
Adoption and fostering
Behavioural and emotional disorders
occurring in childhood and
adolescence
Child abuse and neglect, including
child sexual abuse
Parenting and child care, including
contact after parental separation

2089
Child abuse
Child care and parenting assessment
Juvenile offenders – psychiatric
assessment
Psychological effects of accidents
and injuries

2458
Assessment of parenting capacity
Child abuse and neglect
Children in care
Contact and residence disputes
Parental mental illness
Psychological injury

Child/Adolescent Mental Health

2348
Adoption/fostering
Assessment of child abuse
Assessment of family in crisis
Assessment of parenting capacity
Assessment of rehabilitation
Severely disturbed and troubled
children

Child/Adolescent Psychology

259
Assessments under the Children Act
Custody and contact disputes
Developmental profiles
Intellectual and neurological
evaluations
Personal injury reports

Child/Adult Mental Impairment

259
Psychological factors in mitigation
Psychological profiles
Risk of offending
Therapeutic needs

Child/Adult Assessment

427
All aspects

Child Care

see also Adoption

378
Adoption and contact issues
Assessments
Complaints against local authority
and voluntary agencies

427
All aspects

494
Failed sterilisation/vasectomy –
costing of child-rearing
Loss of dependency – loss of
mother's services, loss of financial
dependency
Other claims related to child care

1442
Care proceedings

2358
Assessment of attachment and
bonding
Contact and custody disputes
Risk assessment for child abuse

Child Care Proceedings

20
Adoption
Assessment and consultation in child
abuse
Child care planning and placements
Child custody disputes
Contact in both public and private law
cases

1561
Adoption
Public law and private law
Thirty-six years' experience in
probation and social services work

Child Development

2229
Assessment of problematic behaviour
Effect of trauma on children
(non-divorce)
General assessment/cognitive,
emotional

Child Development/Behaviour

2352
All aspects

Child/Educational Psychology

1466
Emotional and behavioural difficulties
Specific learning difficulties/dyslexia

1492
Dyslexia and specific learning
difficulties
Education Act
Individual assessment (psychometric
and educational)

2524
Accident damage, negligence
Behaviour difficulties/parent handling
Behaviour difficutlies and accident
damage
Brain injury (educational and
functional seuelae)
Dyslexia (including adult assessment)

Child Health/Illness

228
Allergy
Asthma
Child abuse
Child sexual abuse
Immunisation practice
Professional negligence

539
All childhood illnesses
Joint diseases – rheumatology,
    arthritis

Child Neurology

1144
All Aspects

Child Protection/Child Care

670
Psychological and behavioural
    sequelae of abuse
Psychological issues in fostering,
    adoption and contact arrangements

1138
Comprehensive assessment
Initial assessment
Risk assessment
Therapeutic intervention

Child Protection/Sexual Abuse/Children Act

2155
Effects of all forms of abuse
Group work with victims of abuse
Interviewing children – validation work
Post-traumatic stress disorder
Separation/loss work
Sexual development of children
Work with perpetrators of abuse

Child Psychological Assessment (Learning Difficulties)

1466
Emotional and behavioural dificulties
Specific learning difficulties/dyslexia

Child Psychological Assessment/Behaviour Difficulties

2524
Behaviour difficulties and accident
    damage
Behaviour difficulties/parent handling

Child Psychological Assessment/Learning Difficulties

1492
Dyslexia and specific learning
    difficulties
Education Act
Individual assessment (psychometric
    and educational)

2524
Accident damage, negligence
Brain injury (educational and
    functional sequelae)
Dyslexia (including adult assessment)
Pre-school, mental handicap and
    autism
Sensory/physical disability including
    visual impairment
Special educational needs

Child Psychology

105
All aspects

670
All aspects

2266
Behaviourally disturbed
    adolescents/children

2463
Child abuse – physical, emotional
    and sexual effects on development
Emotional and behavioural problems
Emotional development
Emotional effects of family separation
    and loss

Children

see also Relevant Discipline eg
    Psychology, Psychological,
    Speech/Language Therapy

73
All aspects

1431
All aspects

2352
All aspects

2524
Assessment and legislation

Children Act/Child Abuse

462
Competence and credibility: children
    as witnesses
Contact and residence disputes:
    effects of children
Risk assessment of parents

Children/Adults with Moderate/Severe Learning Difficulties

512
General purpose educational
    assessment to establish level of
    competence for legal defence
    purposes

Children/Families

2314
Extended families role for children
Foster care issues
Identify needs of children, especially
    of black and ethnic minority children

Children/Families, Assessment of

1442
Care proceedings

Children/Injuries to

220
Child protection
Personal injury to children

Children with Emotional/Behavioural Difficulties

2517
All aspects

Children with Special Needs

1907
Developmental problems
Educational problems
Special educational provision
Work within 1981 Education Act

Children's Evidence

608
Analysis of videotaped interviews
Assessment of credibility of
    statements
Impact of court appearance on
    children

Children's Learning Difficulties

1466
Emotional and behavioural difficulties
Specific learning difficulties/dyslexia

1492
Dyslexia and specific learning
    difficulties
Education Act
Individual assessment (psychometric
    and educational)

2524
Accident damage, negligence
Behaviour difficulties and accident
    damage
Behaviour difficulties/parent handling
Brain injury (educational and
    functional sequelae)
Dyslexia (including adult assessment)

Children's Pathology

190
Child abuse
Cot death
Infanticide
Non-accidental injury

427
Contact
Placement issues

462
Competence and credibility: children
    as witnesses
Contact and residence sidputes:
    effects of children
Risk assessment of parents

1907
Addictions and alcohol abuse
Learning difficulties
Special needs

2266
Adoption and fostering
Adult and adolescent sexual abuse of
    children
Attachment/custody/access disputes
Emotional abuse
Failure to thrive (non-organic)
Physical abuse, including children's
    bullying
Risk assessment

2513
Child sexual abuse

Chiropractic Malpractice

253
All Aspects

Chronic Fatigue

2464
Chronic fatigue syndrome
ME/post viral fatigue
Stress-related conditions

Chronic Pain

614
Head pain
Spinal pain

693
Post-operative pain
Road traffic accidents (RTA)
Spinal injury

City of London, Money/Capital Markets

1824
Employment contracts
Regulation
Remuneration and career expectancy

Civil Aviation

268
Air accidents
Airframe, engine, radio, systems failure
Airline incidents following crew mismanagement
Flying training
Infringements of flying/operational regulations

689
Airworthiness
Aviation engineering
Civil Aviation Authority (CAA), JAA and EAA requirements
Engineer licensing and training

1676
Advice on contracts and to investors
Advice on safety matters
Advice to aircraft operators
Certification of prototype and used aircraft
Compliance with certification and operating requirements
General advice on maintenance and manufacturing

1689
Third-world helicopter operations

1730
Arbitration
Buying, selling and valuation of aircraft
CAA and FAA statutory requirements
Engineering/technical disputes
Professional negligence

1881
Aircraft accident investigation
Failure and defect analysis
Fire and explosion investigation and analysis
Professional negligence
Sabotage

Civil/Criminal Litigation

1924
Collation and preparation of evidence
Defence and plaintiff enquiries re preparation
General assistance in case preparation
Personal interviews and detailed proofing of witnesses

Civil Engineering

see also Quantity Surveying, Building and the Particular Structure eg Swimming Pool, Road

47
Blast/Impact
Bridges
Chimneys
Foundations
Power Stations
Tunnelling

69
Drilling and boring techniques
Ground anchorages
Piling
Testing techniques

201
Building defects

240
Contaminated ground
Earthworks
Ground movements
Harbours and dry docks
Highways and bridges

335
General

391
Contract entitlements and evaluations
Contract interpretation/administration
Measurement and valuation of work/claims
Quantity surveying

493
Drainage
Earth and rock dam construction
Earthworks design and construction
Pavement engineering
Road construction

582
Development control, highways issues
Road planning, design and construction
Road traffic/accidents investigations

659
Grouting
Slope Stabilisation
Tunnelling

792
Drainage
Estate roads
Foundations
Groundworks
Harbours and jetties
Maintenance
Piling
Quality assurance
Quay headings
Reinforced concrete
Retaining walls
Sewerage

811
Earth retaining works
Foul and surface drainage
Roads
Swimming pools

814
Construction
Contractual disputes
Design
Operation and maintenance
Related personal injury claims
Water treatment

943
Asphalt and coated macadam pavement disputes
Remedial advice
Technical assessments

1218
Alternative Dispute Resolution
Arbitration
Disputes generally

1482
Environmental engineering, contaminated land, remediation scheme
Foul drainage, sewerage, pumping stations
Highway/traffic engineering, road traffic accidents, road safety
Marine civil engineering, quay walls, jetties, ports and harbours
Road/heavy duty industrial paving, infrastructure design
Surface water drainage, land drainage

1681
Artificial sports surfaces
Land reclamation
Piling
Pipelines
Reservoirs
Retaining walls
Slope stability

1741
Construction site accidents
Construction work (general)
Excavations
Falls
Ladder accidents
Road building
Roofing accidents
Scaffolding accidents

1750
Bridges
Highways
Infrastructure

1759
Geotechnical engineering
Ground contamination
Land drainage
Structural engineering

1909
Coastal erosion control
Computer programs and software
Planning applications
Subsidence and settlement

2013
Bridges
Deep excavations
Design defects
Reinforced and prestressed concrete
Structural steelwork

2113
Hydraulic engineering
Waste water disposal

2261
Bridges
Construction
Contractual disputes
Earthworks
Highway engineering
Retaining walls
Road design

2305
Drainage
Earthworks
Forensic investigations
Retaining structures
Roads

2336
Evaluation of disruption costs
Evaluation of extra costs
Expert report on quantum
Measurement and valuation of
  variations
Prolongation claims

2359
Analysis, testing and provider of
  experts

2366
Drainage and sewerage
Highways
Traffic and transportation

2388
Alkali silica reaction in structures
Basement construction and leakage
Buildings
Concrete defects
Contract supervision, management
  and administration
Foundations and heavy structures
Highways, railways, bridges
Marine works
Overseas projects
Sheet piling defects
Structural damage due to ground
  movement

2389
Bridge scouring
Coastal protection
Contract disputes
Harbours, jetties, quays
Marine works
Underwater engineering work
  (qualified diver)

2500
Civil engineering aspects of personal
  injury accidents
Earthworks – earth retaining structure
Flood investigation and alleviation
Foul and surface water
  sewerage/pumping
  stations/pressure mains
Highway engineering
Industrial pavements
Waste water treatment (domestic,
  livestock, industrial)

2501
Cofferdams and diaphram walls
Defence installations
Harbours and drydocks
Major structures (steel and concrete)
Offshore platforms (steel and
  concrete)
Roads and pavements
Sewerage and stormwater drainage

2507
Contract administration
Forms of contract
Measurement, value and contract
  claims
Planning and output
Professional negligence
Sub-contract disputes

Civil Engineering/Building/ Construction

540
Accidents (construction sites,
  personal and traffic)
All ICE and JCT forms of contracts
Building and civil engineering design
  and construction
Building defects including subsidence
Health and safety at work
Safety at sports grounds legislation

1650
Construction disputes
Professional negligence

Civil Engineering/Building Contracts

1233
Claims for disruption and prolongation
Loss and expense quantum
Programmes – critical path analysis

Civil Engineering/Building Investigations

1616
Aggregates
Bituminous materials
Building products
Concrete and cement
Earthworks

Civil Engineering/Construction

2178
Building
Structural engineering
Tunnel and underground work

Civil Engineering/Construction Failure Investigation

2046
Chemical analyses
Cladding
Concrete
Resource evaluations (quarries)
Soil and rock site investigations
Stone/marble/granite etc

Civil Engineering/Design/Construction

1665
Engineering geology
Geotechnical engineering
Hydraulics, fluid flow in pipes and
  channels
Radioactive waste management
Rock stabilisation
Site investigation/ground investigation
Solid waste management
Underground construction, including
  foundations, tunnelling and
  underground caverns for pumped
  storage power stations

Civil Engineering/Geotechnical

301
All matters relating to the building
  and construction industry
General disputes and negligence
Geotechnical and related matters
Health and safety
Personal injury

698
Earthworks
Engineering geology
Foundations and settlement
Ground investigation
Land drainage
Landslides and slope stability

1199
Earthworks
Foundations
Geosynthetics (geotextiles and
  geomembranes)
Geotechnical engineering (soil
  mechanics)
Reinforced soil
Retaining walls

Civil Engineering/Mechanical/ Electrical Engineering

1875
Acceleration
Delays and disruption
Extensions of time
Loss and expense
Quantity surveying
Valuations/final accounts

Civil Engineering/Mechanical/ Hydraulics

1318
Air entrainment and flow control
Anchoring of ships
Cavitation and cavitation erosion
Hydro-electric spillways and river
  control
Large-scale flow systems
Water supply and pumping

Civil Engineering/Public Health

1558
Drainage and sewerage
Infrastructure
Professional fees
Sewage treatment including small
  sewage treatment works
Topographical surveys

Civil Engineering/Structural

28
Building construction
Working practices

94
Foundations/underpinning
Reinforced concrete
Roads and drainage
Structural masonry
Structural steelwork
Structural timber

125
Bed and breakfast houses
Building construction
Building design
Commercial buildings and
  underpinning works
Community centres
Industrial buildings
Office buildings
Residential care homes
Restaurants

529
Building construction, structural
  design and failure
Cladding of buildings, masonry and
  brickwork
Cold storage and industrial buildings
Foundation design and construction,
  piling
Precast, reinforced and prestressed
  concrete
Structural steelwork design and
  construction

734
Building defects – investigation
Insurance claims
Professional negligence

826
Building and construction defects
General building construction and
  construction practice
Masonry design and construction
Reinforced concrete design and
  construction
Structural steelwork design and
  construction
Temporary works and construction
  methods

879
Foundation engineering
General building construction and
  good practice
Retaining walls
Road pavements
Structural refurbishment and
  restorations
Structures in concrete, steel,
  masonry and timber
Subsidence/settlement investigations

1044
Building technology
Foundations
Masonny, brickwork and blockwork
Reinforced concrete
Steelwork
Water penetration

1077
Foundation underpinning
Infrastructure and site development
Structural investigations

1090
Concrete repairs
Docks and harbours
Multi-storey buildings
Piling
Roads and bridges
Structural steelwork

1129
Building contract control
Building foundations and
  superstructures
Civil engineering contracts
Civil engineering projects
Insurance claims: subsidence, fire etc

1517
Concrete repairs
Docks and harbours
Multi-storey buildings
Piling
Roads and bridges
Structural steelwork

1533
Building defects and failures
Foundations, subsidence and
  settlement
Heavy civil engineering – power
  stations
Industrial and commercial buildings
Multi-disciplinary projects
Stuctures – steel, concrete, masonry

1666
Masonry
Reinforced concrete structures
Steelwork structures
Structural timber

1897
Building structures
Cladding – natural stone, brick,
  aluminium, precast concrete
Foundations
Glazing structures
Paving – including block paving
Piling

2316
Construction defects – all kinds –
  structure and weather shield (NOT
  weather seals)
Design defects – structure, civil
  engineering, infra-structure (roads,
  drainage, retaining walls)
Disputes on professional brief/fees
Disputes relating to good practice
  (civil/structural engineering) and
  allocation of professional
  responsibilities
Materials defects in construction
  materials – concrete, steel,
  masonry, timber (NOT rot)

2536
Collapsed or unstable scaffolding or
  temporary works
Estimating costs of building or repairs
Flooding of premises
Scotts schedule
Structural integrity of buildings

Civil Engineering/Structural/ Highway/Public Health/ Environmental

1261
Environmental impact
Pipe-line failures
Public utility works
Social and indirect project cost
  assessment
Structural movement and failure
Trenchless technology

Civil Engineering/Structural/Building Disputes

475
Construction defects
Cost of works disputes
Design failure
Professional negligence

Civil Engineering/Structural/ Environmental Management

1554
Assessment of structural
  damage/structural condition
Condition reports on buildings
Contract disputes/arbitration
Foul/storm drainage, urban/arterial
  drainage
Reports/assessment of
  environmental problems

Civil Engineering/Surveying

661
Sewerage, sewage treatment,
  industrial effluents
accident investigation, fall, trip, slip
drainage, land drainage, flooding,
  rivers, pollution
infrastructure, highways
personal injuries, safety, health and
  safety
professional negligence, fees

Civil Engineering/Transportation/ Roads

1338
Road design/improvement
Sewers and drains
Traffic impact studies

Civil Engineering/Works Evaluation

319
Mechanical and electrical engineering
Water and waste treatment works

Civil/High Technology

2153
Electrical appliances
Electronic equipment
Telecommunications ROPT

Civil Litigation

1041
Business interruption and loss of
  profit claims
Financial services
General contractual disputes
Intellectual property
Personal injury and medical
  negligence
Shareholders and joint venture
  disputes

1209
Amputees (upper and lower limb)
Cerebral palsy
Head injury leading to
  physical/intellectual incapacity
  (hemiplegia)
Other injuries leading to
  disability(brachial plexus, knee/hip
  injuries, hand injuries etc)
Paraplegia/quadriplegia (tetraplegia)
Whiplash

Civil/Structural Engineering

2387
All aspects

Civil/Structural Engineers

426
Advice on ill-considered structural
  alterations
Assessment on
  stability/incompatibility of
  post-remedial works
Buildings – investigations into default
Concrete – defects, reinforcement
  corrosion
Drainage – investigation into flooding
  of houses
Subsidence, heave and land slip –
  foundations etc

Cladding

436
Composites
Gaskets
Glass
Leakage
Sealants
Stone

Cladding Technologies

1067
Curtain walling
Windows and glazing (including UPVC glazing)

Claims Discovery Work

531
Coverage disputes (asbestos and pollution)
Lloyds' members and agents, disputes
Professional liability
US general liability

Claims Management

1938
Audits of binders and cover holders records
Claims handling procedure analysis
Claims systems appraisals

Clinical Biochemistry/Chemical Pathology

407
Alcohol
Drugs

Clinical Child Psychology

105
Adoption and fostering
Child protection
Child sexual abuse

670
Cognitive-behavioural psychological therapy
Disorders of behaviour, emotions and development
Family and social influences on psychological disorders

Clinical Endocrinology

191
Disorders of growth
Disorders of sexual development
Disorders of the adrenal cortex
Pituitary disorders
Thyroid disorders

Clinical Forensic Medicine

393
Clinical forensic medicine
Forensic pathology

735
Drink and drug related offences
Fitness for interview
Fitness to detain
Physical assault
Sexual assault/both children and adults

765
All aspects

852
Fitness to detain in custody
Fitness to interview
Medical forensic evidence
Medical negligence in primary and custodial health care
Road Traffic Act alcohol backtrack estimations

938
Assault (physical)
Child abuse (non-accidental injury)
Child sexual assault
Domestic violence
Drug misuse in crime
Drunken driving
Sexual assault

1212
Assault/interpretation of wounds and injuries
Child physical and sexual abuse
Drugs and alcohol misuse (Road Traffic Act)
Medical negligence in general medical practice
Rape
Sexual offences

1301
Assaults, interpretation of injuries
Child abuse, physical and sexual
Fitness for custody and interview
Safety of toys
Sex offences

1348
Child abuse
Interpretation of injuries
Medical care of detained persons
Sexual offences

1718
Fitness to interview of police detainees
Interpretation of injuries
Police surgeon and the Road Traffic Act

1793
Actual/grievous bodily harm
Drink and drug offences under Road Traffic Act
Drugs
Sexual crime
Woundings

1893
All aspects of clinical forensic medicine except sexual offences

1979
Drink/drug driving and behaviour
Fitness to be detained/interviewed
Injury interpretation (assault)
Sexual assault

2410
Sexual assault in adults
Sexual assault in children

Clinical Forensic Medicine/Medical Negligence

1075
Child abuse
Drink driving and alcohol related offences
Medical negligence involving General Practitioner (GP) or police surgeon
Medical negligence, multiple specialities – overall appraisal when personal injury
Physical abuse, injuries and bruising
Sexual assault

Clinical Forensic Medicine/ Odontology

1093
Aircraft and other transport accidents
Disasters

Clinical Neurology

2241
All aspects

Clinical Physiology

2150
Medicine

Clinical Practice in Chest Medicine

1797
All aspects

Clinical Science

341
Osteopathy
Psychosocial and biomechanical aspects of lower back trouble

Clothing

1987
Clothing sizes for women, men and children
Copyright
Mediator BAE qualification
Public relations client/consultant disputes
Quality assessment
Stock valuation

Collision/Salvage

356
Cargo recovery and salvage claims monitoring
Collision damage assessment
Liability and quantum assessment
Personal injury claims arising
Repair supervision and pollution monitoring
Speed and angle of blow reports

Colorectal Surgery

774
Anal sphincter injury
Colorectal cancer
Diverticular disease
Incontinence
Inflammatory bowel disease
Post-obstetric injury

Colorectal Surgery/General Surgery

2385
Colonoscopy
Colorectal cancer
Functional bowel disease
Incontinence
Inflammatory bowel disease

Commercial

624
Business valuation
Contractual disputes
Insurance claim assessment
Loss of profits/earnings
Partnership disputes

1171
Agency-industrial, retail and office
Compulsory purchase and
  compensation
Development land consultancy
Landlord and tenant-rent review etc
Valuation

2253
Accountants' negligence
Insurance disputes
Loss of profits/business interruption
Valuation of business (goodwill)

Commercial Disputes

see also Relevant Dispute eg
  Directors, Corporate, Insolvency

29
Breach of contract and warranty
Business viability
Nuisance
Partnership and shareholder disputes
Product liability and loss of profits
Share and business valuations

72
Business valuations
Loss of earnings/profits
Partnership disputes
Share valuations

76
Competition disputes
Construction claims
Document management
Expert determinations
Lost profit claims
Post-acquisition disputes
Professional negligence

133
Breach of contract
Business valuations
Loss of profits/business interruption
Product liability

138
Accountants' fees
Business and share valutaions
Partnership entitlements

214
Business/company valuations
Loss of profits claims
Partnership disputes

221
Company bust-ups
Partnership disputes
Valuations

316
Business and assets valuation
Loss of profit claims
Warranty claims

360
Breach of contract
Business valuations
Loss of profits/business interruption
Share valuations

387
Losses incurred by sole traders,
  partners and directors of unquoted
  companies

397
Breach of contract
Breach of warranty
Construction disputes
Product liability
Section 459 disputes and share
  valuations

425
Breach of contract
Business disruption claims
Valuation of business

441
Business valuations
Damage claims
Loss of profits/business interruption

449
Business interruption
Contested take-overs
Warranty and contract disputes

456
Finance
Fraud/asset tracing
Loss of profits/earnings

457
Breach of contract
Breach of warranty
Business valuations
Loss of profits

505
Partnership disputes
Shareholder disputes

533
Chemical specifications and
  performance
Construction and operation of
  oil/gas/chemical plants
Performance of computer systems

601
Loss of profits/business interruption

624
All aspects

635
Breach of contract
Business valuations
Loss of profits/business interruption

728
Breach of contract
Breach of warranty
International business valuations
Loss of profits/business interruption

767
Business valuations

791
Directors disqualification

821
Consequential loss

833
Breach of contract
Breach of warranty
Business interruption
Business valuations
Insurance claims
Loss of profits
Product liability

839
Inspections and reports
Machinery and equipment failures
Performance audits
Technical review of contracts

921
Contractual disputes
Fraud
Loss of profits

924
Plaintiff and defence reports
Taxation advice re settlement of
  proceedings
Valuation of Business
Valuation of shares in family
  companies

927
Breach of contract
Business valuation
Loss of profits/business interruption

928
Breach of contract
Breach of warranty
Business and share valuations
Director's disqualifications
Intellectual Property claims
Loss of profits/business interrruption
Partnership disputes
Share valuation

929
Breach of contract
Breach of warranty
Business and share valuations
Computer disputes
Loss of profits: business interruption
Partnership disputes

977
Breach of contract
Business valuations
Loss profits/business interruption
Product liability
Shareholder disputes

979
Breach of contract and warranties
Business and share valuations
Loss of profits/business interruption
Pensions fund management

1004
Building construction
Project management
Structural engineering

1029
Business valuations
Loss of profits
Share valuations

1041
Business interruption and loss of
  profit claims
Financial services
General contractual disputes
Intellectual property
Personal injury and medical
  negligence
Share holders and joint venture
  disputes

1054
Business and share valuations
Loss of profits/business interruption

1058
Breach of contract
Breach of warranties
Business valuation
Partnership disputes
Property and construction disputes
Shareholder disputes

1062
Business valuations
Construction contract disputes
Fraud and false accounting
Loss of profits/business interruption
Partnership disputes

1111
Business valuations
Loss of profits/business interruption

1115
Business/valuation
Environmental
Loss of profits/business interruption

1160
Sale and purchase of shares
Security for costs
Taxation

1173
Breach of contract
Business interruption
Business valuation
Loss of profits

1284
Breach of contract/warranty
Earnout/completion of account
  disputes
Loss of profits/business interruption

1285
Breach of contract and warranty
  claims
Business and share valuations
Insurance claims
Intellectual property disputes
Libel and slander
Loss of profits claims
Purchase and sale disputes
Security for costs applications
Shareholder and partnership disputes

1286
Breach of contract and warranty
  claims
Business and share valuations
Insurance claims
Intellectual property disputes
Libel and slander
Loss of profits claims
Purchase and sale disputes
Security for costs applications
Shareholder and partnership disputes

1287
Breach of contract and warranty
  claims
Business and share valuations
Insurance claims
Intellectual property disputes
Libel and slander
Loss of profit claims
Purchase and sale disputes
Security for costs applications
Shareholder and partnership disputes

1288
Breach of contract and warranty
  claims
Business and share valuations
Insurance claims
Intellectual property disputes
Libel and slander
Loss of profit claims
Purchase and sale disputes
Security for costs applications
Shareholder and partnership disputes

1289
Breach of contract and warranty
  claims
Business and share valuations
Insurance claims
Intellectual property disputes
Libel and slander
Loss of profit claims
Purchase and sale disputes
Security for costs applications
Shareholder and partnership disputes

1290
Breach of contract and warranty
  claims
Business and share valuations
Insurance claims
Intellectual property disputes
Libel and slander
Loss of profit claims
Purchase and sale disputes
Security for costs applications
Shareholder and partnership disputes

1291
Breach of contract and warranty
  claims
Business and share valuations
Insurance claims
Intellectual property disputes
Libel and slander
Loss of profit claims
Purchase and sale disputes
Security for costs applications
Shareholder and partnership disputes

1299
Breach of contract
Business valuations
Insurance claims
Loss of profits
Professional negligence –
  accountancy
Professional negligence – others

1317
Loss of profits
Matrimonial
Sole trader and partnership valuations
Unquoted company valuations

1332
Arbitration
Company valuations
Loss of profits
Partnership dissolutions

1335
Business valuation
Evaluation of claim
Loss of profits/business interruption

1390
Business valuations
Loss of profits/business interruption
Patent breach
Warranty

1428
Consequential loss on share
  purchase agreement – warrantees

1450
Loss of office claims
Loss of profits/business interruption
Partnership disputes
Share/business valuation

1502
Business valuation
Loss of profits
Product liability

1562
Breach of contract
Contractual warranty and claims
Loss of profits and loss of earnings
  claims
Valuation of business and other
  commercial assets

1646
Business and goodwill valuations
Share valuations
Shareholder and partnership disputes

1673
Accounting negligence claims
Business valuations
Loss of profits
Theft

1732
Contractual disputes
Fraud

1740
Business valuations
Loss of profits/business interruption

1758
Breach of contract
Breach of warranty
Business valuations
Loss of profits/business interruption

1766
Breach of contract
Loss of profits
Share valuations

1768
Breach of contract
Loss of profits/business interruption

1839
Breach of contract or warranty
Loss of profits/business interruption

1928
Board disputes
Loss of profits
Partnership disputes
Tax
Valuations including those for S459
  claims

1940
Breach of contract of warranties
Business interruption/consequential
  loss of profits
Business valuations
Director, shareholder and partnership
  disputes
Product liability
Security for costs applications

1966
Business valuations
Loss of profits/business interruption
Matrimonial and divorce
Medical practice disputes
Partnership disputes

1981
Alternative dispute resolution
Arbitration
Breach of warranty claims
Business interruption
Expert determination
Fraud investigations and asset tracing
Loss of profits claims
Share and business valuations
Tax investigations

2007
Business valuations (including
  goodwill)
Loss of profits/business interruption
Share valuations

2024
Breach of contract
Breach of warranty
Business disposal/acquisition
Business sale/purchase
Consequential loss
Contractual disputes
Losses on contractual disagreement
Matrimonial
Partnership dissolution

2129
Breach of contract
Business valuations
Loss of profits

2162
Accounting/taxation negligence
Business valuations
Inland revenue and customs and
   excise investigations
Share valuations

2163
Breach of contract
Breach of warranty
Business valuation
Divorce settlements
Fraud/asset tracing
Loss of profits/business interruption
Taxation aspects

2174
Claims for breach of warranties and
   business failures
Insurance claims
Loss of profit calculations
Partnership disputes
Professional negligence, for both
   plaintiff and defendant
Share valuations

2175
Business valuations
Loss of profits

2188
Breach of contract
Loss of profits/business interruptions
Partnership disputes
Product liability

2216
Breach of contract
Defence and plaintiff reports
Product liability

2263
Advising minority shareholders in
   private limited companies
Arbitration
Attending meetings of experts
   pursuant to RSC Order 38.38
Breach of contract
Business interruption
Partnership disputes
Share valuations

2330
Breach of contract
Breach of warranty
Business valuations
Loss of profits/business interruption
Product liability

2331
Breach of contract
Breach of warranty
Business valuations
Loss of profits/business interruption
Product liability

2332
Breach of contract
Breach of warranty
Business valuations
Environmental
Loss of profits/business interruption
Product liability

2333
Breach of contract
Breach of warranty
Business valuations
Loss of profits/business interruption
Product liability

2397
Contract breach and termination
Expert testimony
Financial modelling
Insurance claims
Intellectual property
Loss of profits and damages

2477
Business valuations
Shareholder and partnership disputes

2495
All aspects

Commercial Disputes/Arbitration

192
Breach of contract
Breach of warranty
Business valuations/insurance claims
Loss of profits/business interruption
Machinery/equipment not fit for
   purpose
Product liability

Commercial Disputes/Engineering

74
Breach of contract
Consequential loss
Fitness for purpose
Product liability
Professional negligence
Project management

Commercial Disputes/Forensic Accounting Support

1915
Business/share valuations
Fraud
Loss of profit/business interruption
Minority shareholder action
Partnership disputes

Commercial Disputes/Fraud

2459
Business interruption/loss of profits
Fraud
Matrimonial dispute
Partnership disputes
Professional negligence
Share valuations

Commercial Disputes/Insurance

1022
Adjustment of insurance claim
   involving loss of profits and litigation
   support
Breach of contract
Critical analysis of claim, causal link,
   consequences and quantum
Loss of profits/business interruption
Loss of use
Other liabilities including product
   liability

Commercial Disputes/Insurance Claims

2134
Breach of warranty
Consequential loss claims
Partnership disputes

Commercial/Domestic Accidents

40
Inadequate lighting
Lifting injuries and lifting equipment
Machinery or equipment (inc kitchen
   equip) or inadequate (inc guarding)
Product liability or
   quality/sub-standard product

Commercial Engineering Consultant

1352
Expert assessment of merchandise,
   commercial and industrial
   equipment and buildings

Commercial Vehicle/Construction Plant/Compressed Gases Installations

939
Commercial vehicle and trailer
   chassis, suspension, axles, wheel
   security
Commercial vehicle bodywork
   construction and mounting
Compressed gases systems and
   cylinder storage
Metal fabrication, welded or bolted
Off-road vehicles and light
   construction plant, hydraulics
Road tankers for liquids, powders,
   cryogenic and compressed gases

Commercial Vehicle Engineering

2062
Design, development and testing –
   all classes
Heavy haulage and abnormal loads
Military and off-road vehicles
Scammell and Leyland vehicles
Special-purpose wheeled vehicles
Vehicle recovery – all kinds

Commercial, Industrial/Domestic

2408
All aspects

Communication Disorders/Adult/Paediatric

997
Acquired speech and language
   disorders
Developmental speech and language
   disorders
Hearing impairment
Voice disorders

Communications

2291
Intensive training of lawyers in
   dealing with the press and conduct
   of radio and television interviews
Production, writing, filming, editing of
   medical accidents and personal
   injury videos, used in court as
   evidence based on medical
   background supplied in advance by
   other experts acting on instructions
   of solicitors and their clients

Communications (Digital/Voice)

2262
Data loss
International standards and
  conformance
Malicious call disputes
Misuse of radio/cellular telephones
Tampering, misuse, interruption with
  systems/data

Community Occupational Therapy

1889
Advice on adaptations to property
Advice on equipment in the home
Medico-legal work
Physical disability assessment

Company

1145
Company performance and specific
  incidents
Evolution of company performance
Specific performance and factors –
  sales and profits
Understanding company performance

Company Law

791
Directors disqualification matters

Company Valuations

1061
Estate valuations
Inland Revenue negotiations
Share valuations
Shareholder disputes

Company Valuations/Profit/Cost Structure Analysis

1145
Accounting analyses (FCMA)
Company valuations (discounted
  cash flow and P/E methods)
Forces driving costs and profits

Compensation

124
Accident
Consequential loss
Divorce
Earnings loss
Professional negligence
Profits loss

Compensation/Loss of Earnings

2324
Directors' loss of office claims United
  Kingdom (UK) and international
Insurance claims for loss of earnings
  or prospects
Loss of earnings through accident or
  dismissal
Loss of future earnings due to death
Mediation on dismissal

Competence to Make Wills/Give Evidence/Plead

1103
All Aspects

Competition/Monopolies

712
Analysis of markets
Analysis of productivity and
  profitability
Company policy and strategy
Corporate finance and acquisitions
Corporate financial performance

Component Failure Investigation

1616
Materials testing
Metallurgical analysis
Non-destructive testing

Composite Materials

802
Composites manufacture and
  processing (all matrix resins)
Finished product quality/suitability
Phenolic resin matrix composites
Raw material supply
SMC/DMC

1182
Carbon fibre/resin composites
Design, service behaviour
Glass fibre/resin composites
Raw materials, manufacture

Compressed-Air Work (Tunnelling)

717
Bone necrosis (osteonecrosis)
Brain damage (scans; psychometrics)
Decompression illness (bends;
  barotrauma)
Fitness (to work; to resume work)

Compulsory Purchase/Compensation

716
Motorway and new road
  compensation
Pipelines

772
Blight Notices
Compulsory purchase
Part 1 Land Compensation Act 1973

Computer Aided Design/Administration

694
Computer Aided Design (CAD)
  management
Computer Aided Design (CAD)
  systems
Computer Aided Design (CAD)
  techniques

Computer/Communication Equipment

2003
Environmental controls
Use by disabled people

Computer Consultancy

1081
Computer systems/failure to perform
Computer systems/fraud involving,
  and other crime
Computer systems/hardware and
  software value
Computer systems/misuse of, abuse
  of
Computer systems/problems with
  bespoke software or software
  development
Computer systems/viruses, hacking,
  security

1113
Hardware
Power supplies

Computer Dispute Resolution

2354
Advice
Arbitration
Expert determination
Mediation
Neutral fact finding
Pre-trial Alternative Dispute
  Resolutions (ADR) reviews

Computer Disputes

664
Communications
Copyright
Criminality (eg hacking)
Management of projects
Systems analysis

1532
Computer dispute mediation
Contract disputes
End-user v supplier disputes
Hardware disputes
Project management disputes
Software disputes

2354
Software copyright
Software licensing, consultancy,
  software development
Systems procurement, systems
  integration, system performance

Computer Evidence

399
Computer misuse, fraud and hacking
Computer security
EDI
Legal reliability of computer systems
The Internet and other networks
Trusted third party services

Computer Reconstruction 3D

2474
Animation sequences
Lines of sight
Scenes of crime

Computer Software

1544
Bespoke software
Computer consultancy
Financial software
Transport systems

2566
Fourth generation computer
languages
Software copyright
Software quality procedures and
negligence

Computer Software Consultancy Disputes

1428
All aspects

Computer Strategy/Selection

307
Defining system requirements,
software, hardware
Developing computer strategy
Ensuring timely and effective
implementation
Evaluation of results
Selecting systems to meet
requirements

Computer Systems

796
Computer Misuse Act
Computer failures
Computer networks
Computer security and fraud
Data Protection Act
Software copyright

1025
Mathematical modelling
Real time data acquisition and
process control
SCADA
Simulation
Small company systems

Computer Systems/Disputes/Accidents

1741
Computer networks
Implementation of computing systems
Software design and development

Computer Systems/Information Technology

567
Computer performance disputes
Fraud involving falsification of
computer records
Fraud involving transfer of money via
bankers automated clearing service
Software copyright infringement
Testing of software and hardware
systems
Theft of computer hardware and/or
software
Valuation of computer hardware and
software

1773
Feasibility studies
Hardware and software design and
programming
System implementation
System requirements definition
System sizing and loading
Testing and acceptance

Computer Systems/Installation

1481
All aspects

Computer Systems/Software

399
ADR and mediation
Computer contracts and litigation
IT training and professional
development
Project management and
review/troubleshooting
Software quality, reliability and
provability
Software specification, design,
construction, testing and
implementation

Computer Systems/Tactical Review

307
Establish business objectives for
systems
New project feasibility studies
Recommend future actions,
personnel, systems
Review effectiveness of current
system/solution

Computer-Related/Disputes

5
Breach of contract
Computer facilities organisation and
methods
Fitness for purpose
Product liability
Professional negligence
Project management
Systems performance

Computers

15
Computer crime
Hardware contracts
Intellectual property
Software contracts

340
Automation – process and
manufacturing
Copyright and patent infringement
Piracy and theft
Project management
Quality
Software

580
Acceptance tests
Expert reports
Failed computer systems
Hardware
Software
Support
System tests

642
Contract terms and failures
Copyright
Crime
Fraud
Hardware and software
Misuse

1872
Industry commercial practices
including pricing
Procurement involving issues of
merchantable quality, fitness for
purpose
Project management involving issues
of best/reasonable practice, duty of
care
Reliability of computer-generated
information, PACE 84 requirements
Safety critical systems (computers
that can kill or harm)

2018
'Low tech' communication boards
Computer operated electronic
communication systems
Digitised and synthetic speech output
devices

2256
Computer applications
Networks
Personal computers (PCs)
Software engineering

Computers/Holmes

325
Access for unused material, data and
evidence
Investigation of serious and complex
crime

Computers/Information Technology

1175
Breach of contract
Copyright and intellectual property
Patents
Performance and sizing

Computers/Information Technology (IT)/Information Systems

743
Breach of contract
Computer crime
Fitness for purpose/satisfactory
quality
Intellectual property
Personnel/employment issues
Professional negligence

1420
Health service computing
Hotel/leisure
Manufacturing/logistics/distribution/reta
iling

2262
Computer misuse disputes
Contractual disputes
Copyright, and software title, patents
and reverse engineering
Data protection/all aspects
Databases, database management
systems, data title
Employment contracts
Health and safety/all Video Display
Units (VDUs) and all Information
Technology (IT) equipment and
workplaces
Performance/sizing/operability/user
interfaces
Software protection
System security

Computers/Management Consulting

1378
Broad knowledge of computer
  applications
Computer acquisition and
  requirement definitions
Computer contract negotiation
Project management
Software development
Standard industry procedures

Concrete Technology

2141
Assessment of structures
Concreting processes
Repair of structures
Specification and supervision of
  repairs

Condition of Buildings

2325
Geotechnical conditions
Service life
Water, egress and ingress
Wind assessments

Condition Surveys

2405
Air conditioning and ventilation
Boiler plant – oil, gas and coal-fired
Cold-water storage and distribution
Heating systems – steam and water
Hot-water storage and distribution
Plumbing and drainage

Consequential Loss

652
Loss of earnings

1428
Building disputes
Fatal accidents
Fire claims
Matrimonial
Personal injury
Share purchase agreement warranty
  claims

Conservation

1984
Conservation areas
Housing
Listed buildings
Repairs and maintenance

Construction

see also Building, Arbitration,
  Surveying, Civil Engineering and
  the particular type of construction
  eg Curtain Walling

11
Building pathology
Professional negligence

128
Analysis of failures in materials
Composite materials/fibre-reinforced
  materials
Design of structures

240
Building
Civil engineering
Foundation engineering
Soil mechanics
Structural engineering

338
Estimating
Insolvencies
Planning
Procurement
Project management
Quality/defective work

391
Breach of
  contract/entitlements/evaluation
Cause and liability for defects
Contract
  interpretation/administration/managem
  ent
Measurement and valuation of
  works/claims
Quantity/building surveying
Tendering/estimating

599
Contractual claims
Measurement and valuation
Mechanical and electrical
  engineering services
Professional negligence
Quantum

647
Arbitration
Building disputes
Cost
Materials
Standards of workmanship

948
Architect/employer disputes and fee
  recovery
Architectural practice
Building defect investigation and
  analysis
Building surveys
Building works related to injury or
  disability
Employer/architect disputes and fee
  mitigation
Planning appeals
Rights of light and boundary disputes

1032
Advising on arbitral procedure
Estimating building costs
Post-contract valuation of building
  works

1125
Defective construction
Foundations, drainages
Reinforced concrete
Steelwork
Structural design
Timber structures

1238
Bridges
Buildings
Construction contracts
Construction defects
Dams
Docks
Drainage
Dredging
Engineering contracts
Fraud
Harbours
Highways
Lock gates
Marine engineering
Mediation
Project management
Railways
Road surfacing
Sea outfalls
Sewerage

Tunnels
Waste disposal
Water structures
Water supply
Water systems

1261
Construction design and
  management
Construction methods
ICE and JCT conditions of contract
  and contract procedures
Safe working in construction

1381
Arbitration/alternative dispute
  resolution
Design/construction – building works
Diagnosis of defects and remedial
  action
Maintenance and repairs
Professional negligence – building
  works
Scott schedules

1447
Quantum/liability – claims
  (loss/expense)
Quantum/liability – extension of time
Quantum/liability – final accounts

1453
Contracts with particular emphasis
  on interpretation, claims, quantum,
  delay analysis, breach of contract
  etc
Technical aspects of construction

1501
Civil engineering and building
Concrete materials and structure
Ground conditions and piling
Quality management
Reinforced and prestressed concrete
Standards of design and construction

1512
Fabrication and erection
Pre-commisioning
Subcontracts
Testing

1639
Geotechnical engineering
Piling and foundations
Site operations

1709
Building defects resulting in personal
  injury
Design defects
Professional negligence by
  architects, surveyors and designers
Structural defects (excluding civil
  engineering)

2014
Building defects
Component failures
Design liability
Health and safety
Materials assessment
Professional negligence

2040
Building/construction disputes
Expert witness reports
Insolvency matters – values of work
  carried out/to be carried out on
  incomplete contracts
Preparation and settlement of
  construction claims
Valuation of construction work and
  repair work

2326
Construction accidents
Construction disputes
Professional negligence
Structural failures
Subsidence

2408
Court attendance, giving evidence,
  public enquiry evidence
Expert witness
Scotts schedules, meeting of experts
Surveys, investigations, reports

2494
Building defects
Component failures
Design liability
Health and safety
Materials assessment
Professional negligence

**Construction (Including Professional
Negligence)**

55
All aspects

Construction Accidents

159
Machinery hazards
Manual handling
Personal protective equipment
Scaffolding

971
Cranes
Demolition
Excavations
Scaffolding

Construction Arbitration/Litigation

2528
Domestic extension and alteration
  mediation
Extension of time claims evaluation
Insolvency practice
Loss and expense claims
  ascertainment
Quality of work assessment
Valuation of work quantification

Construction/Architecture

2197
Boundary disputes
Building quality disputes
Construction defects
Contractual claims
Design negligence
Party wall disputes
Rights to light

Construction/Building

80
Construction materials
Corrosion
Material testing and failures
On-site investigation
Paint
Polymers

632
All aspects

675
Building contracts and claims
Building work relating to historic
  buildings
Defects in buildings
The practice of architecture
The work of building contractors and
  sub-contractors

682
Expert witness
Programming, planning
Project management
Property management
Quantity surveying
Valuation audit

2465
Construction materials
Corrosion
Materials testing and failures
On-site investigations
Paint
Polymers

**Construction/Building/Civil
Engineering**

1623
Adjudication
Arbitration
Financial and contractual
Mediation
Quantity surveying
Subcontracts

**Construction/Building/Civil
Engineering Disputes**

2123
Disruption on site; site supervision
Estimating
Extensions of time
Liability for costs incurred in
  construction
Quality of workmanship and materials
Values of work executed

**Construction/Building/Civil
Engineering International**

2329
Arbitration and Alternative Dispute
  Resolutions (ADR) procedures
Civil and structural engineering
Conditions of contract [United
  Kingdom (UK) and international]
Construction in the Middle East
Delay and disruption
Duties of engineer and consultant

Construction/Building Sector

1375
Elements of construction eg cladding
Foundations
Structures

Construction/Civil Engineering

260
Defects inability
Extensions of time
Loss and expense
Measurement and quantum

873
Contract administration
Contract documentation
Contract management
Geotechnics and foundations
Law and dispute resolution
Natural disasters, blast and dynamics

Construction Claims

1321
Commercial developments
Main contract claims
Sub-contractors' claims

Construction Claims/Contract Advice

511
All Aspects

**Construction Claims/Disputes/
Arbitration**

2157
Extension of time
Loss and expense
Measurement of construction works
Set off
Validity of liquidated and ascertained
  damages
Valuation of construction works

Construction Claims Litigation

2495
All Aspects

**Construction Commercial
Management**

2320
Cost engineering

Construction Consultants

2228
Analysis of defects
Drafting and writing of health and
  safety plans
Party wall surveyor
Reports and surveys of property –
  domestic and commercial

Construction Contract Disputes

657
Arbitrator – acted in connection with
  Construction Contarcts Disputes,
  appointed by president of the Royal
  Institution of Chartered Surveyors
  (RICS)
Construction cost consultancy
Quantity surveying
Value management

1856
Delay/direct loss/expense

Construction Contracts

1233
Claims for disruption and prolongation
Valuation of construction work

1875
Acceleration
Delays and disruption
Extensions of time
Loss and expense
Quantity surveying
Valuations/final accounts

1914
Management of contract conditions
Measurement of construction work
  as per rules
Quantification of loss and
  expense/disturbance issues
Valuations of construction work and
  variations thereto

Construction Contracts/Building/Civil Engineering

2500
Contract procedures
Duties and responsibilities of engineering consultants (and other professionals)
Duties and responsibilities of parties to the contract

Construction Cost Consultancy

857
All aspects

Construction Costs

2285
Building costs
Civil engineering costs
Loss and expense claims
Prolongation claims
Small building works
Water engineering costs

Construction Defects

1091
Forensic investigation
Technical assessment

2382
Component failure
Condensation/mould growth
Dampness and water penetration

Construction Disputes

330
Ascertainment of disruption expense
Ascertainment of prolongation expense
Assessment of delay to progress
Disruption to progress
Value of variations
Value of work done

810
Building quantum and contract
Civil engineering quantum and contract

944
Negligence disputes against architects

1526
Analysis of construction delays
Investigations of building defects
Professional negligence
assessment of contractual disputes

1813
Boundary disputes
Building disputes

2379
Contract performance
Defence and plaintiff reports
Investigation of design and construction failures
Standards of workmanship

2382
Contract administration
JCT forms of contract
Preparation of Scott schedules

2561
Contract advice
Contract claims
Defects
Estimates of building adaptations for personal injury victims
Estimates of construction costs for insurance
Evaluation of completed works
Preparation of Scott schedules
Procedural advice

Construction Disputes/Building Surveying/Architecture

1812
Boundary disputes
Contract law and administration
Cost consultancy
Defects in construction and design
Facilities management
Professional negligence in property and construction matters
Project management
Quantity surveying
Schedules of conditions and dilapidation
Structural engineering

Construction Disputes/Litigation

493
Accident investigation
Arbitration
Contractual claims
Failure investigations
Forensic engineering
Public inquiries

812
Defective workmanship claims
Forensic investigations (buildings and sites)
Forensic reports (expert witness)
Latent damage defects claims
Negligence claims

1346
Litigation and arbitration support – expert reports
Main and subcontract review
Management of projects including critical path analysis
Preparation/defence and/or management of claims
Professional negligence
Quantity surveying from bills of quantities to final account

1923
Contract claims/professional negligence
Environmental impacts
Latent defects
Licensing applications
Personal injury
Town planning appeals

Construction/Electrical Safety

413
Builders' hoists
Contact with overhead lines and underground cables
Portable/transportable plant/equipment
Site distribution systems

Construction/Engineering

2338
Construction accident investigation
Defects investigation
Loss adjusting support
Programming – cause and effect analysis, extension of time claims
Project and construction management
Quantum – loss and expense claims and analysis

Construction/Engineering Contract Disputes

583
Extension of time awards
Planning – analysis of factors of delay/disruption on planned work sequence
Quantification of loss and expense arising out of delays/disruption

Construction Engineering/Management

1919
Analysis of programmes
Extensions of time
Interpretation of technical provisions of contract
Methods and sequences of construction

Construction Engineering Safety

1811
Accident/injury investigation
Expert evidence
Reports/statements for legal proceedings
Safety of systems of work

Construction Failures

1803
Adequacy of design, specification and construction
Compliance with planning and building regulations
Component design and failure
Safety and building design

Construction Failures/Claims Analysis in Building/Civil Engineering

1819
Construction costs
Contract administration
Defective workmanship and materials
Design defects
Professional negligence
Project management

Construction Industry

411
All aspects

Construction Industry Contractual Disputes

1776
Architects'/engineers' instructions
Direct loss and expense
Extensions of time
Measurement
Quantum
Variations and final accounts

Construction Industry Professional Evidence in

251

Disputes between architects and clients on professional negligence/competence

Disputes between contractors/employers in contracts on defects, constructional errors and quality compliance

Informal mediations between building owners/architects and contractors in dispute

Construction Industry/Property Disputes

238

Construction matters related to poor/incorrect workmanship

Contract costs and claims

Contract valuation disputes

Interpretation of contractual matters

Party wall disputes

Construction Methodology

2013

Erection of structures

Heavy lifting and sliding

Moving structures

Scaffolding

Temporary works

Construction/Oil Sector

546

Critical path network analysis

Delay and disruption quantification

Loss and expense arising from delay and disruption

Management and control of projects

Construction/Personal Injury

331

Building technology

Contractor's all risks, 21.2.1, party wall, professional indemnity

Hydrology

Product liability, hazards, buildng materials

Construction Planning/Programming

1090

Critical path analysis

Extension of time

1517

Critical path analysis

Extension of time

Network analysis

Construction/Project Management

1840

Arbitration

Building contract law

Contract administration

Defective works

Inter-professional relationships

Construction/Property-Related Disputes

2446

Building defects

Dilapidations

Landlord and tenant

Professional negligence

2549

Main contractor/end user client

Process engineering

Subcontractor/main contractors

Traditional procurement/design and building

Construction/Quantity Surveying

1838

Final accounts

Loss and expense claims

Quantum

1977

Damages arising from poor construction

Evaluation of construction costs

Loss/expense arising from construction contract

Measurement of buildings

Opinion on employer's agent

Opinion on fees

Construction Quantum Disputes

2547

Programme disputes

Simple planning issues

Construction Services

76

Cost analysis

Critical path method analysis

Expert planning and programming analysis

Lost profit and expense claims

Project management

Construction Technique/Management

2126

Building standards and practice

Contract administration

Materials and methods

Supervision of work

Technical standards

Construction Vehicles/Plant

723

Access equipment (design/manufacture/use/performance evaluation)

Cranes (design/manufacture/use/performance evaluation)

Pavers (design/manufacture/use/performance evaluation)

Product liability assessment

Constructional Steelwork

1735

Construction failures

Manufacturing processes/production engineering

Quality management systems

Welding/bolted connnections

Consultant/Valuer of Gemstones/Jewellery

451

Damage and identification

Jewellery manufacture

Particular expertise in diamonds and jade

Trade description

Values

Consumer Disputes

2507

Landscaping

Pavings

Consumer Safety

1189

Child safety

General product safety regulations

Product design

Product liability

Warnings and instructions

Contraception/Women's Health Care

1341

Cervical smear tests (cytology)

Contraceptive methods

Family planning services

Menopause care

Reproductive health, eg sexually transmitted disease within general practice and family planning clinic services

Contract

2014

Building contracts

Building procurement

Collateral warranty

Partnership

Professional appointments

Project management

2104

Defective electrical installations

Disputes relating to defective equipment

Failure of electrical apparatus and cables

2494

Building contracts

Building procurement

Collateral warranty

Partnership

Professional appointments

Project management

Contractual Claims

632

Claims by members of public versus suppliers of equipment

Construction and building claims

Performance of equipment versus contract specification

1056

Consequential loss

Delay

Disruption

Loss and Expense

Loss of profit

Overheads

1105

Consequential loss

Delay

Disruption

Loss and expense

Loss of profit

Overheads

Contractual Dispute

205
Breach of contract
Breach of warranty aspects
Evaluation of losses through failure
  of contracted item
Product liability

550
All aspects

Contractual Matters

2141
Claims evaluation
Conditions of contract
Contractual disputes

Control of Substances Harmful to Health (COSHH) Regulations

2359
Analysis, testing and provider of
  experts

Conveyancing

1068
General competence
Mortgage fraud

2394
Commercial conveyancing
Landlord and tenant
Mortgages
Residential conveyancing

Conveyancing Negligence

1764
Domestic conveyancing
Fraud
Mortgages
Negligence
Professional conduct
Residential estate conveyancing

Cooking/Sterilisation/Pasteurisation

787
Food production
Frying
Grilling
Microwave
Radio frequency

Copyright

1091
All aspects

Copyright in Architecture

2039
Evaluation of similarities and
  relationships
Implied licences to reproduce
Moral rights
Originality and distinction
Sole and joint authorship

Corporate Finance

1929
Acquisitions/due diligence
  investigations
Business planning and financial
  forecasting
Debt financing
Stock market flotations
Valuations of shares and businesses
Venture capital

Corporate Fraud

1673
Accounts-evaluation and
  interpretation
Income tracking
Incomplete records investigation
Report writing and expert witness
Systems analysis
Tax investigations

Corporate Governance/Controls

845
Corporate strategy
High-level controls
Role of board of directors

Corporate Management

626
Business strategy
Marketing (strategy and audit)
Personnel policy and systems
Reward and renumeration systems

Correspondent Banking

2371
Account relationships
Agency arrangements
Confidential test key arrangements
Joint venture between banks –
  arrangements
Syndicated loan arrangements
Training facilities

Corrosion

357
Cathodic protection
Corrosion in concrete
Metals, coatings and linings
Monitoring
Sour service

891
Cathodic protection
Chemical cleaning
Chemical treatments
Coatings
Corrosion engineering design
Corrosion testing
Failure investigation
Inhibitors
Marine corrosion
Materials selection
Metallurgy
Microbiological corrosion
Monitoring (corrosion)
Paints
Process industry corrosion

1425
Alloy and corrosion mechanisms
Anodic protection
Boiler failure investigation
Catalysis
Cathodic protection
Coating failure analysis and
  specifications
Electro chemistry
Fracture/fatigue/investigation
Glass reinforced plastics
Machinery life-assessment
Marine coatings
Marine engine failure investigation
Metallurgy
Microbial analysis and corrosion
NDT project management
Paint/coating sciences

Resins and polymers
Ship tank surveys
Surface replication
Welding sciences

1465
Chemical and petrochemical plant
  corrosion
Marine
Testing

1577
Atmosphere
Chemical plant
Industrial corrosion
Marine corrosion
Process equipment
Water systems

1995
Atmospheric corrosion
Corrosion in fresh water wells
Corrosion of stainless steels
Marine corrosion
Stress – corrosion

Cosmetic Surgery

1534
Abdominoplasty
Breast reduction and augmentation
Facial aesthetic surgery (including
  nose, eyelids and ears)
Liposuction
Scar revision
Thigh lifting

Cosmetics

80
Accidents
Cosmetics
On-site investigation
Paints and polymers
Problem solving
Trading standards

2465
Accidents
Cosmetic
On-site invesigations
Paints and polymers
Porblem solving
Trading standards

Cost of Disability

1460
Additional cost of leisure activities
  and holidays
Additional cost of mobility
Additional household expenditure
Aids and equipment requirements
All aspects of spinal cord injury
Cost of help and assistance

Counselling/Therapy

691
Counselling for relationship
  difficulties, divorce, etc
Post Traumatic Stress Disorder
  (PTSD) – intervention
Psychological therapy for anxiety,
  stress, depression, etc

1599
Counselling for PTS
Debriefing/counselling following
  critical incidents
Psychological therapy for anxiety
  states, phobias, depression,
  relationship difficulties etc

Covert Surveillance Operations

2065
All aspects

Cranes

413
Electrical safety

504
Cranes
Escalators
Fork lift trucks
Hoists
Lifts
Miscellaneous lifting equipment

723
Cranes design, manufacture, use,
  performance evaluation

971
Construction accidents

1270
Material damage losses

Cranes/Hoists/Lifts/Slinging

971
All aspects

Cranial/Spinal Surgery

994
All aspects

Credit Card Fraud, Investigation of

1890
All Aspects

Credit Insurance

1971
Credit insurance/reinsurance
Financial guarantee
  insurance/reinsurance – resolution
  of disputes; advice on
  development/company acquisition

Credit Policy

1891
Lending assessment
Lending process flows
Organisational structures
Preparation of technical manuals
Risk management
Strategic and risk planning

Criminal

see also the Relevant Crime eg
  Drugs, Fraud

221
Fraud
Tax prosecutions
Theft

928
Banking frauds
Fraud defence
Fraud investigations
IT fraud work
Money laundering

1111
Drugs trafficking – asset tracing and
  proceeds assessment

1940
Drug trafficking
Insolvency and Companies Act
  offences
International fraud investigations

2263
Fraud
Reporting for the Defence of the
  Crown
Theft

2333
Defence witness

Criminal Defence Preparations

644
Accident plans and photographs
Alibi preparation
Crime scene investigations
Witness proofing and statement
  taking

Criminal Fraud

1476
Accountancy/bookkeeping
Audit investigation work
Corporate tax
Inland Revenue investigations
  (special office)
Value Added Tax (VAT) fraud

Criminal/High Technology

2153
Abstraction of electricity
Cellular/mobile radio
Computer misuse/personal
  organisers
Fire
Payphone fraud/theft

Criminal Matters Involving General Practitioners

542
Allegations of indecent assault
  involving general practitioners

Criminal Proceedings

1706
Credibility of testimony
Disputed confessions
Evaluating difficulties/mental health
  problems
Fitness to plead
Mental vulnerability and suggestibility
Psycho-linguistic analyses of
  video-taped evidence

Criminal Work

463
Assessment of intellectual ability
Personality assessment

Criminal Work/Legal Aid

2433
Patterns of wounding and injury

Criminalistics

797
Blood and body fluid detection and
  analysis
Contact trace transfer
Crime scene examination
Doexribonucleic Acid (DNA) profiling
Interpretation of blood splashing
Marks and impressions

Crop Production/(All Crops)

667
Crops for freezing, canning,
  dehydration
Crops for medicinal purposes
Plant breeding
Seed production and technology
Variety evaluation and introduction

Curtain Walling

see also Construction

436
Air penetration
Failures
Glass breakage
Sealants
Structural detachment
Water leakage

Daily Living Assessment

2304
Cost of special equipment
Difficulties with domestic/household
  tasks
Difficulties with personal care
Need for extra services
Problems with mobility/transport
Suitability of housing

Daily Living Problems of Disabled People

752
Accommodation needs
Aids and equipment
Care
Mobility
Recreation

Damage to Goods in Transport/Storage

912
Protection against compression
Protection against corrosion
Protection against impact
Protection against shock and
  vibration

Damaged Vehicle Assessment

834
Assessment of damaged vehicle
  salvage value
Detailed cost assessment of damage
Reports on quality of repairs
Reports on vehicle condition
Vehicle pre-accident valuation

Damages Quantum, Assessment of

1752
Loss of pension rights on divorce
Loss of pension rights on
  wrongful/unfair dismissal
Personal injury/fatal accident

1871
Loss of pension rights on divorce
Loss of pension rights on
  wrongful/unfair dismissal
Personal injury/fatal accident

Dangerous Substances

971
Classification
Labelling

Data Communication Systems

5
Contracts management
Fitness for purpose
Forensic engineering
Installations
Quality assessments
Safety compliance
Systems performance

Deafness

1305
Noise induced hearing loss
Ototoxicity
Traumatic deafness

1417
Evoked response audiometry
Industrial deafness assessment
Pure tone audiometry

Decoration

144
Interior and exterior painting
Specialist paint finishes eg graining,
   marbling, dragging, stencilling, etc
Wallcoverings and hanging

Defect Investigations

1852
Engineers' reports (domestic surveys)
Site investigations/inspections
Subsidence investigations

Defective Building Work

2550
All Aspects

Defective Equipment in Buildings

525
All Aspects

Defective Equipment in Ports/Harbours

525
All Aspects

Defects/Deterioration in Structures/Materials

1953
Accidents (involving defects or
   deterioration in materials)
Biocides (fungicides, insecticides,
   pesticides)
Building chemicals (preservatives,
   fire retardants, coatings)
Building environment (dampness,
   humidity, sick building syndrome)
Cot death (toxic gases from mattress
   deterioration as primary cause)
Health problems (from deterioration
   or use of chemicals)

Defects/Failures (Building/Construction)

1965
Dampness and water ingress
Design and 'as-built' detailing
   assessment
Fire damage
Problems with construction materials
   and products
Specification and workmanship
   assessment

Defence Expert in Forensic Cases

1770
Evaluation of Deoxribonucleic Acid
   (DNA) carried out in forensic cases

Defence/Plaintiff Reports

1881
Presentation of detailed technical
   analysis for the lay reader
Use of colour diagrams and graphics
   to explain technical issues

Delay/Disruption/Loss/Expense on Construction Projects

1819
Analysis of loss and expense
Causation of delay and disruption
Consequential loss
Critical path analysis
Forms of construction contract

Dental

137
Damage to jaws
Damage to teeth
Facial trauma
Management of oral medicine cases
Management of oral surgery cases

Dental Injury

916
Accidental
Criminal

Dental Negligence

916
Clinical dentistry: professional
   negligence
Condition and prognosis reports:
   clinical examinations

Dental/Oral/Maxillofacial Problems

2136
All Aspects

Dental Practice

911
Consent
Crown and bridgework
Dental record cards
Dental treatment planning and X-rays
Gum diseases
Root filling work

2000
Cosmetic work
Dentures, bridges, crowns, veneers
Facial pain
Full mouth reconstructions
Gum treatment
Root canal treatment
Second opinions

2144
Implants
Minor oral surgery

Dental Surgery

1661
Dental negligence
Oral surgery
Restorative dentistry

2339
Assessment of dental injuries
Negligence

Dentistry

see also Forensic Dentistry

236
Crown, bridge, denture and implant
   reconstruction
Expert witness reports
Facial reconstruction by prosthesis
Full case management of personal
   injury problems
Head and neck pain and muscular
   dysfunction
NB Medical malpractice on behalf of
   plaintiff not considered

699
Facial trauma

2319
Car accidents
Dento-legal
Implantology
Litigation
Negligence
Restorative dentistry

Dentistry/Forensic Odontology

126
All Aspects

Dentistry, Restorative

1780
All aspects

Deoxribonucleic Acid (DNA)

1418
Genetic markers in problems of
   identification

1770
Evaluation of Deoxribonucleic Acid
   (DNA) carried out in forensic cases

Deoxribonucleic Acid (DNA) Evidence

2363
Deoxribonucclleic Acid (DNA)
   paternity determinations
Expert advice
Independent Deoxribonuccleic Acid
   (DNA) testing laboratory for forensic
   casework
Medical genetics advice
Veterinary and environmental
   genetics advice

Derivatives

207
Clearing and settlement
Documentation
Exchanges and SFA regulations
Investment advice
Negligence
Risk management and control

Dermatology

79
Especially occupational dermatoses
such as eczema

90
Cryosurgery of skin
Laser surgery of skin
Medico-legal matters in dermatology
Occupational dermatology

518
Industrial dermatitis
Laser therapy of the skin
Medical negligence involving
dermatology and laser therapy
Psychiatric aspects of dermatology

527
Clinical dermatology
Industrial dermatology

544
All Aspects

1011
Occupational skin disease, including
dermatitis
Skin diseases due to accidents

1130
Occupational skin diseases

1336
Chloracne
Coal mining hazards
Embalming hazards
Industrial dermatitis
Keloids and scars
Neoplasms

1477
All Aspects

1605
Allergy
Skin and psychiatric disease and
disfigurement
Skin disease
Skin surgery including laser surgery

1626
Contact dermatitis
Hair disorders
Occupational skin disease

1648
Industrial dermatitis
Paediatric dermatology
Topical corticosteroids psoriasis

2012
Connective tissue diseases of the
skin
Industrial and contact dermatitis
Medico-legal aspects of skin diseases
Occupational diseases of the skin
Radiation and the skin

2070
All Aspects

2282
All Aspects

2306
Trichology

2522
All Aspects

Design/Construction of Building Structures

134
Diagnosis/repair of defects in building
structures
Management of engineering design
Overcladding/modernisation of
postwar estates
Scandinavian house-building
construction

Design Consultancy

123
Preparation of reports where poor
design or inappropriate
specification have resulted in
severe injury

2013
Civil engineering
Professional negligence
Structural engineering

Design Defects

1091
Forensic investigation
Technical assessment

Design/Faulty/Negligent/Defective

2537
Capital equipment
Consumer products
Household goods
Industrial equipment
Manufactured goods
Personal injury

Design/Manufacture Disputes/ Arbitration

2137
Copyright
Fitness for purpose
Patent infringement

Design/Planning/Conservation

2126
Design briefs and architects'
instructions
Design competition juror/assessor
Design critiques and assessments
Listed and historical buildings
Planning enquiries

Design/Planning Enquiries

1792
All aspects

Determinations/Arbitrations

1285
Arbitrations
Expert determinations
Mediation
Valuations

1286
Arbitration
Expert determinations
Mediation
Valuations

1287
Arbitration
Expert determinations
Mediation
Valuations

1288
Arbitration
Expert determinations
Mediation
Valuations

1289
Arbitration
Expert determinations
Mediation
Valuations

1291
Arbitration
Expert determinations
Mediation
Valuations

Development

869
Disputes relating to development
agreements

Development/Access Planning

2261
Access planning for developments,
business parks and shopping
centres
Car parks
Cycle routes
Impact assessment of roads and
road traffic
PPG13 and sustainable development
Traffic forecasting, modelling and
economics
Traffic generation

Development Consultancy

957
Infrastructure
Mainstream development
Urban regeneration

1275
Building contracts
Building surveying
Construction defects
Project management
Supervision and management of
major development projects

1980
All mainstream development
Infrastructure projects
Urban regeneration

Development of Land/Commercial/Residential

1763
Landlord and tenant
Problems of development (eg
access, easements, viability)
Valuation of development sites
Valuation of land

Development Planning Engineering Support

826
Accident analysis and highway safety
All major developments, particularly
new settlements
Car park design and analysis
Conceptual layout and junction
design
Negotiation of legal agreements
Traffic impact analysis

Diabetes

1066
Diabetes – diagnosis, childhood diabetes, diabetes in pregnancy, hypoglycaemia, diabetic neuropathy, food complications of diabetes

2108
Medicine

Diabetes/Endocrinology

2276
Medical aspects of insulin treatment including hypoglycaemia

Diabetes/Hypoglycaemia

1686
Diabetic hypoglycaemia
Diabetic ketoacidosis
Driving and diabetes
Non-diabetic hypoglycaemia

Diabetes Mellitus

1179
Hypoglycaemia
Insulin therapy

Dilapidations

2166
Arbitrations
Preparation of schedules
Settlement of claims and compensation

Directors

see also Commercial Disputes, Corporate Governance, Corporate Insolvency

Disability

752
Daily living assessment

2304
Daily living assessment

Disability (Physical)

1177
All age groups and most disabilities

2512
Health Services
Social Services

2514
Assessment of functional abilities
Assessment of life skills
Recommendations for equipment/aids/appliances
Recommendations for home adaptations
Transport recommendations eg adaptations, alternative vehicle

2517
Neurological conditions – cerebral palsy
Orthopaedic conditions
Other medical conditions

Disability/Cerebral Palsy/Adult

2030
Assessment of behavioural problems
Assessment of cognitive functioning
Assessment of employment potential
Assessment of specific learning disabilities
Counselling

Disability for Personal Injury Claims, Assessment of

2218
Aids and equipment
Amputations
Back injuries
Brachial plexus lesions
Care needs
Head injury
Housing needs
Neurological disorders
Orthopaedic injuries
Paediatrics
Spinal cord injury
Transport

Disability Medicine

145
Accidents resulting in disability
Medical care of people with disabilities
Memory loss following head injury
Pressure sores
Rehabilitation of neurological patients
Stroke

Disability Resulting from Personal Injury/Accidents/Negligence, Costs of

317
Aids and equipment
Daily living
Holidays and leisure
Personal care and domestic help
Transport

Disability/Special Needs of People with Injuries/Physical Disabilities

437
Analysis and quantification of care needs
Costs of specialist adaptations eg stairlifts
Costs of specialist equipment eg wheelchairs
Housing difficulties caused by disability

Disabled

2408
Facilities for the Disabled

Discrimination

2314
Acting against racism, sexism, ageism, discrimination based on disability, sexuality and religion

Dispute Resolution

98
Commercial disputes
Matrimonial disputes
Partnership splits

642
Alternative Dispute Resolutions (ADR)
Arbitrator
Expert adjudicator
Lay advocacy
Mediator

Disputes

138
Accountants' fees
Business and share valuations
Partnership entitlements

Disputes/Computing/Information Technology

1175
Breach of contract
Copyright and intellectual property
Patents
Performance and sizing

Disputes/Ownership of Land/Buildings

1151
Boundary disputes
Disputes relating to building ownership
Disputes relating to building works
Disputes relating to insurance claims on real property
Rights of light disputes

Diving (Recreational/Professional)

717
Bone necrosis (osteonecrosis)
Brain damage (scans; psychometrics)
Breathing apparatus (air; mixed gas)
Decompression illness (bends; barotrauma)
Diving accidents (in water)
Fitness to resume diving (after accidents or illness)

Diving Accidents/Injuries

2238
Commercial (professional) divers
Equipment failure
Loss of earnings
Military divers
Sport (recreational) divers
Underwater physiology

Divorce

see also Matrimonial, Family and Particular Expertise eg Valuation

142
Pension rights on divorce

360
Business valuations
Evaluation of assets and liabilities
Share valuations

449
Income streams and taxation advice
Valuation of businesses and unquoted shares

456
Asset tracing
Business valuations
Taxation

457
All aspects

895
Investment advice
Loss of pension rights
Valuation of 'reasonable'
  requirements

1029
Commercial valuation

1111
Business valuations
Income evaluation

1299
All aspects

1637
Pension matters
Pre-nuptual agreements
Professional negligence

1932
All Aspects

2129
Financial settlements
Investigations

2253
All Aspects

Divorce/Partnerships Disputes

2125
Business and share valuations
Forensic accounting

Divorce/Separation

924
Petitioner and respondent reports
Taxation advice re settlements of
  proceedings
Valuation of business
Valuation of shares in family
  companies

Divorce Settlements

2488
Business and share valuations
Income evaluations
Taxation advice

Doctors' Surgery Valuations

1692
For national health service rent and
  rates scheme
For partnership change

Document Analysis

800
Forged documents
Identification of suspect typefaces
Ink identification

Document Examination

see also Forensic Document
  Examination

793
Alterations, erasures, additions
Counterfeit document identification
Indented writing
Ink examination, analysis,
  comparison
Watermarks, post marks

797
Altered documents
Counterfeit documents
Handwriting and signatures
Indented impressions
Ink analysis
Sequencing of documents and entries
Typewriting, photocopying and
  modern office technology

1262
Comparison of inks
Detection of forgery
ESDA testing of documents
Identification of handwriting
Identification of photocopy documents
Identification of typescript

2356
Altered documents
ESDA
Handwriting comparisons
Ink comparisons
Signatures and forgery
Typing and printing

Documents

1060
Altered documents
Handwriting comparison
Indented writing (ESDA)
Typewriter/printer comparison

Dog Training

390
Agility dog training
Pet dog obedience
Police dog training and handling
Security dog training and handling
Working trials dog training

1382
Animal behaviour
Dog breed identification (ie Pit Bull
  Terriers)
Ferrets and ferreting
Use of dogs in fieldsports

Domestic Animals

2192
Behaviour, environment, nutrition
  and welfare
Environmental pathology
Products of animal origin
Professional negligence
Zoonoses

Domestic Violence

1142
Battered woman syndrome
Counselling of battered women
Post-traumatic stress disorder

1907
Marital/partner violence

Double-Glazing

421
Investigation of failures

Drainage

335
Foul water drainage systems and
  disposal
Foul water treatment works
Surface water drainage and drainage
  systems

980
Flooding
Storm water
Surface water

Drainage Consultancy

132
Flooding of land and property
Hydraulic analysis
Pollution surveys
Sewer construction
Sewer design

Drainage Installations

1869
Closed Circuit Television (CCTV)
  inspections
Condition surveys
Design defect diagnosis
Ex-flitration damage investigations
Quantum and reports
Trenches repair recommendations

Dredging

153
Capital dredging
Dredging contracts
Hydrographic survey
Maintenance dredging
Measurement

913
Beach replenishment
Excavation of marine foundations
Reclamation of land with hydraulic fill
Sea outfall trenches

Drink Driving

118
Blood/urine alcohol
General chemical analysis

631
Breath tests
Deterioration of shipped and
  transported goods
Drink/drive cases
General forensic and chemical
  analysis
Prescribed and prohibited drugs
Ships cargoes

674
Alcohol calculations (breath and
  blood)
Medico-scientific aspects

863
Back calculations
Blood alcohol
Breath alcohol

938
All aspects

1075
All aspects

1204
All matters relating to chemicals
Drink-drive litigation

1511
All aspects

1802
Alcohol in blood, breath and urine
Analytical chemistry

Drink Driving 'Back-Calculations'

421
Effects of other chemicals on test
   results

Drink Driving/Alcohol Related Cases

800
'Hip flask' defence calculations
Blood/breath alcohol concentration
   calculations
Consideration of interfering
   substances
Investigation of 'unusual' metabolism
Investigation of irregularities in
   machine results
Investigation of irregularities in
   procedure

2154
Analysis and interpretation
Criminal and defence investigations
Employment and discipline disputes

2490
Back calculation or back tracking
Blood alcohol analysis
Drug interaction
Expert opinion and review of
   documentation

Drug Trafficking Quantum

472
All Aspects

Drug-Induced Injury

1585
All Aspects

Drug-Induced Injury/Malpractice in Relation to Drugs

1727
All aspects

2409
General practice (medical)
Pharmaceutical medicine

Drugs

134
Drug trafficking

797
Analysis and identification
Body fluid analysis

1036
Adverse reactions
Drugs and driving
Hazardous substances
Interactions
Pharmacology and therapeutics
Side effects

1940
Drug trafficking

2356
Drugs of abuse (possession, supply
   and production)
Prescribed drugs

2370
Adverse effects
Civil service
Drug reactions
Stress-related diseases

Drugs/their Effects in Humans

1632
Drugs of abuse testing
Interpretation of forensic toxicology
Opiate drugs – morphine, heroin,
   buprenophene
Pharmacodynamics – drug action
Pharmacokinetics – drug levels
Use of drugs in medicine

Drugs/Medical Malpractice in Relation to

1585
All Aspects

Dyes etc

2359
Anaslysis, testing and provider of
   experts

Dysfunctional Families/Individuals

1907
Learning difficulties of parents
Marital/partner violence
Parenting skills
Workplace stress

Ear/Nose/Throat

906
Deafness, especially industrial
   deafness
Ear Nose and Throat (ENT)

1253
Deafness, tinnitus and vertigo due to
   trauma, particularly industrial and
   road traffic accidents
Medical litigation for Ear, Nose and
   Throat (ENT) problems
Occupational deafness and tinnitus
Upper respiratory and airway
   problems with toxins in industry

1578
Ear Nose and Throat (ENT)
Industrial deafness
Laryngeal and pharyngeal injury and
   disease
Nasal and sinus disease and nasal
   polyposis

2552
Ear Nose and Throat (ENT)
Hearing and deafness

Ear/Nose/Throat Conditions

1671
Noise-induced deafness
Trauma to the ear, nose or throat

2383
Head and neck surgery
Laser surgery in Ear, Nose and
   Throat
Medico-legal work for plaintiff and
   defendant
Noise-induced hearing loss

Ear/Nose/Throat Disease

2099
Deafness – ear surgery
Ear Nose and Throat (ENT)
Noise-induced deafness and tinnitus
Occupational rhinnitis (nasal mucosa)

Ear/Nose/Throat Surgeon (Consultant)

136
Ear Nose and Throat (ENT)
Medical negligence
Noise induced hearing loss
Occupational rhinitis
Trauma to ear, nose and throat

Ear/Nose/Throat Surgery

1102
Ear Nose and Throat (ENT)
Ear, nose and throat diseases and
   injuries
Occupational noise-induced
   deafness and tinnitus
Occupational rhinitis

1493
Ear Nose and Throat (ENT)
Otology/noise-induced deafness

1537
General Ear, Nose and Throat (ENT)
   surgery
Oto-neurology
Otology
Paediatric Ear, Nose and Throat
   (ENT) surgery

1726
Facial nerve injury
General Ear, Nose and Throat
   surgery
Hearing and balance disorders
Industrial hearing loss

2468
All other Ear, Nose and Throat (ENT)
   surgery but NOT otology
Cancer of the head and neck
Neck surgery
Skull base surgery

Ecological Studies

2384
Habitat assessment
Implications of environmental
   legislation

Ecology

1074
Botanical surveys
Habitat creation
Habitat management
Habitat transference
Impact assessment

Economics

2009
Competition and monopoly
Economic effects
Environmental impact

Education

1277
Management
Special education
State and private
Statementing

1706
Assessments of special educational
   needs
Disputed 'statements' of educational
   provision
Dyslexia
School phobia, truancy and
   attendance problems

Education/Higher

1113
Course provision
National Vocational Qualifications
(NVQs)
Standards
Student placement

Education Reports for People with Disabilities

575
Coping with disability in education
Guidance on study options

Education/Training

1115
Assessment of courses
Examination moderation
Practical experience reviews
Review of education programmes

Educational/Child Psychology

603
Child care placements and
management
Emotional and behavioural difficulties
Family proceedings ('Section 8
orders')
Learning difficulties
Special educational needs

Educational Psychology

1316
Disability and handicap
Dyslexia and specific learning
difficulties
Education acts and special needs
Individual assessment
Pre-school work

2209
Children, young people and adults
with multiple disabilities
Emotional and social needs
Learning difficulties, specific and
non-specific
Visually impaired children, young
people and adults

Educational Safety/Premises/ Workshops

971
All aspects

Effluent Discharge Regulation

438
Calculation and evaluation of
discharge limits
Discharge authorisation appeals
Discharge consent applications
Environmental discharge charges
Planning inquiries, expert witness
experience
Water audit of industrial premises

Electrical

see also under Engineering

2104
All aspects

Electrical Accidents

971
All aspects

Electrical Building Services

727
Ancillary systems eg lightning
protection
Fire detection and alarm systems
Lighting installations
Power systems and distribution
Standby generation and systems
Sub-stations and switchgear

860
Design procedure
Fire
Health and safety
IEE Regulations and Electricity at
Work Regulations
Lighting

Electrical/Electro-Mechanical Engineering

1601
All Aspects

Electrical/Electronic Engineering

185
Answering machines
Communication systems
Contractual claims
Control systems
Cost and value assessment
Data capture
Earthing systems
Electric shock
Electrical appliances
Electricity cost assessment
Electricity generation, including
nuclear plants
Electro-magnetic fields
Electronic components
Forensic analysis of magnetic tapes
Illegal abstraction of electricity
Information Technology (IT) systems,
digital communications
Power distribution systems
Telecommunication fraud
Wiring regulations

553
Answering machines
Communication systems
Contractual claims
Control systems
Cost and value assessment
Data capture
Earthing systems
Electric shock
Electrical appliances
Electricity cost assessment
Electricity generation, including
nuclear plants
Electro magnetic fields
Electronic components
Forensic analysis of magnetic tape
Illegal abstraction of electricity
Information Technology (IT) systems,
digital communications
Power distribution systems
Telecommunication fraud
Wiring regulations

Electrical/Electronic Systems

74
Contracts and projects management
Fitness for purpose
Forensic engineering
Installation engineering
Quality assessments
Systems and product design
Systems performance

Electrical Engineering

99
All electrical/lighting systems in
industrial/commercial/domestic
installations
Audio/visual systems, presentation
systems
Data and voice communications
Lift installations
Security systems/fire alarms/intruder
alarms/Closed Circuit television
(CCTV)

465
EMC (electromagnetic compatability)
Electricity at work regulations
Health and safety
Meter fraud
Product engineering

796
Arson and fires with an electrical
source
Electrical accidents, electric shock
injuries
Electrical equipment design and
installation
Electrical patent actions
Electrical wiring defects and
professional negligence
Electricity meters

1357
Induction motors
Linear electric motors
Rotating electrical machines

1383
Abstraction of electricity
Allocation of electricity costs
Compliance with Electricity at Work
Regulations
Compliance with IEE Wiring
Regulations
Electrical accidents
Electrical installation design

2130
Earthing systems
Electricity supply regulations
LV distribution
Lightning protection
MV distribution
Protection and discrimination

2222
Electrical accidents (shocks/burns)
Electrical equipment malfunctions
Electricity transmission/distribution
(HV)
Industrial/domestic electricity
supplies (MV, LV)

2224
Electrical accidents (shocks/burns)
Electrical equipment malfunctions
Electricity tranmission/distributions
(HV)
Fire investigation (electrical faults)
Industrial/domestic electricity
supplies (MV, LV)
Passenger and goods lifts (electric)

2421
Control systems
Electrical installations
Electrical safety
Electricla generators, motors and
transformers
Power utilisation and control
Power generation and distribution

Electrical Engineering Consultancy

93
All matters regarding electromagnetic
interference (EMI)
Environmental health and electricity
Inspections related to standards of
electrical installations
Investigative analysis of
cause/reason for all types of
electrical faults

Electrical Engineering/Industrial Safety

1391
Building services installations –
power, lighting and alarms
Electrical accidents – shock and
burns to persons and animals
Electrical equipment – safe operation
and maintenance
Industrial high and low voltage power
systems
Machinery safety
Safe systems of work

Electrical Engineering Services

969
Communications
Controls
Electric power
Fire detection/protection
Lighting and emergency lighting

Electrical Engineering Systems for Buildings

1107
Electricity Generation and
Emergency Supplies
High and Low Voltage Electrical
Supply and Distribution
Lighting, Communications,
Information Technology
Protection Security and Alarm
Systems; Lightning Protection
Specialist Engineering Plant and
Equipment
Uninterrupted Power Supplies for
Computers

Electrical Faults

2359
Analysis, testing and provider of
experts

Electrical Installations/Equipment

297
Design, erection and verification of
electrical systems
Electricity at work regulations
IEE – BS7671 wiring requirements
Portable appliance testing

Electrical/Mechanical Engineering

661
Electrical distribution, fault and
protection
building engineering services
drives, control, process control,
instrumentation
personal injuries, safety, health and
safety, accident investigation
plant, industrial services, mechanical
handling
professional negligence, fees

1001
Building services – investigations
Electricity meters – alleged fraud
Electrocution investigations
Laboratory testing of engineering
equipment
Manufacture/development of special
equipment
Photocopiers – alleged unfit for
purpose

2334
Contract management
Design verification
System design

Electrical Safety

2031
Audio-video products
Domestic appliances
Luminaires

Electrical Safety/Electric Shock/Burns

413
Electrical testing/repair of
products/systems
High and low voltage distribution
switchgear and control gear
including building services
Radio frequency/microwave heating
Rotating machinery –
generators/motors
Static
Welding

Electrical Safety/Electrical/Electronic Control Systems

413
Guard interlocking and
electrosensitive safety systems
Lifts, cranes, hoists
Manufacturing dangerous machinery
Process plants
Programmable electronic systems
Robots and mechanical handing

Electricity

2191
Electricity at Work Regulations 1989
Electricity meter accuracy and
electricity charges disputes
Electricity supply companies'
distribution systems
Expert witness in coroners' courts
General electrical safety matters
Industrial, commercial and domestic
electrical installations

Electronic Engineering

282
Contractual disputes
Electricity at work regulations
Fire investigations
Personal injury
Technical investigations and reports

796
Copyright actions
Electronic equipment design and
defects
Electronic patent actions
Gaming machines
Product design liability
Security systems, fire and intruder
alarms

Electronics

740
Computer hardware
(microprocessor) design
Digital signal processing (DSP)
High speed digital systems
Image processing of generation
Television and video broadcast
systems

1113
General

2256
Communications
Industrial electronic machine control
Patent/copyright/IPR
Process control

2262
Control and instrumentation
Litigation over accident or 'Act of
God' natural peril damage
Microprocessor-based equipment
Process control systems including
plcs

Electronics/Computers

465
Hardware, software
Photocopies
Systems, real-time
Vascar and radar (police speed traps)

Emergency Care

1272
Ambulance aid
First aid

Emergency Medicine

737
All Aspects

Employability/Rehabilitation Services

543
Accident and injury
Long-term care costing
Loss of earnings
Medical records analysis
Provision of expert opinion
Vocational evaluation and
assessment

Employment

see also Quantum, Income Loss,
Loss of Earnings

494
Breach of contract – assessment
regarding quantum
Loss of earnings

1299
All aspects

1530
Assessment of aptitude
Assessment of future
employment/earnings prospects
Conduct of employment agency or
business
Salary and job market surveys

1589
Career mapping and audit
Career transition management
Continuity planning
Employee appraisal systems
Job search strategies
Personal written and verbal
communications

1689
Effects of pre-accident employment
history
Efforts to mitigate loss
Future employment prospects
Loss of earnings

Employment Advisers

186
Occupational therapists' reports
(plaintiff and defence cases)
Personal injury claims

Employment Consultancy

408
Career planning and development
consultancy
Occupational and employment
assessment
Vocational training consultancy

525
All Aspects

1326
Advice on Smith v Manchester
implications
Assessment of future employment
prospects
Assessment of loss of earnings
Assessment of vocational
rehabilitation and resettlement

1374
Assessment and advice on training
Careers and earnings analysis
Employment case management
Furnishing of labour market
information
Labour market research
Vocational assessment of people
with disabilities

1941
Employment legislation
Pay and benefits
Recruitment/career counselling

2377
Employment tribunals
Fatal accidents
Job information
Labour market surveys
Matrimonial settlements
Medical negligence
Personal injury
Quantum calculations/forensic
accountant's report
Rehabilitation of people with
disabilities

Employment Consultant

525
All Aspects

Employment/Disability

926
Availability of work
Employment skills and prospects
Sheltered employment
Training and rehabilitation

Employment/Equal Pay

813
Assessment of claims – relative
value of applicant and comparator
work
Reward structures
Witness at industrial tribunals
Written reports for industrial tribunals

Employment Law

1706
Bullying/harassment
Disciplinary disputes
Fairness in selection for recruitment,
promotion and redundancy
Job evaluations on equal value
disputes
Psychological problems at work
Work-induced stress in duty of care
disputes

Employment/Pensions Disputes

1285
All aspects

1286
All aspects

1287
All aspects

1288
All aspects

1289
All aspects

1290
All aspects

1291
All aspects

Employment Rehabilitation

485
Fitness for work
Training
Vocational guidance
Work design

Employment Reports for People with Disabilities

575
Disability assessments
Educational and training guidance
Psychometric testing – aptitudes
Psychometric testing – personality
Vocational guidance

Employment Research

485
Earnings
Employment trends
Labour force characteristics
Occupational and career structures
Skill shortages

Endocrinology

885
Clinical pharmacology
Diabetes
Growth disturbance
Menopause and infertility
Reproductive endocrinology
Vascular disturbance

2108
Medicine

2169
Diabetes
Information science and technology

Endocrinology/General Physician

161
Pituitary diseases
Thyroid diseases

Energy

969
Conservation
Control
Cost
Excessive consumption

Energy Conservation

1410
System non-performance

1749
Air conditioning
Appointments and contracts
Commissioning and handover
Controls and building management
systems
Energy conservation
Heating and hot water

Energy Policy

2302
Dealing with local and central
government
Government responses
Industry structure
Institutional
Regulation

Energy/Power

1601
Communications
Diesel power plant
Electric railways
Power plant performance testing

Energy/Process Engineering

1681
Chimneys
Cooling towers
Industrial structures
Storage tanks
Vessels

Engineer/Accident Investigator

272
Automobile assessors and valuers
Consulting mechanical and
automobile engineers
Road traffic accident investigation
and reconstruction
Third party employers' liability and
factory accident investigation

Engineering

see also under the relevant type of
engineering eg Electrical, Chemical,
Mechanical

74
Breach of contract
Consequential loss
Fitness for purpose
Product liability
Professional negligence
Project management

562
Accidents
  construction/machinery/general
Building services and district heating
Civil/structural concrete, steel, plant
Construction materials
Contract and fee disputes
Explosions, blast damage and
  demolition
Foundations/geotechnical piling,
  underpinning
Machinery disputes
Planning applications and
  environment
Silos and retorts
Valuations
Water, sewerage, drainage

671
Intrinsic safety
Effects of fires on structures
Explosion and flameproof equipment
Failures and incidents involving
  electrical, mechanical and chemical
  engineering
Investigation of losses
Product liability
Water damage

677
Chemical analysis
Component failure investigations
Material testing
Non-destructive testing
Quality assurance
Specification disputes

742
Chemical
Electrical
Mechanical

1352
Expert assessment of merchandise,
  commercial and industrial
  equipment and buildings

1376
Building structural collapse
Consulting engineer
Machinery malfunction
Personal injury

1497
Accidents and personal injury
Agriculture
Automotive power
Civil
Construction
Liability and negligence claims

1583
Technical assessments in criminal
  and civil matters

1681
Foundation

1852
Defect investigations

1895
Chemical engineering
Civil engineering and construction
Electrical engineering
Fairground and leisure parks
Mechanical engineering
Mining engineering and tunnelling

2327
Air-conditioning and all mechanical
  ventilation
Construction contracts and
  sub-contracts
Consulting engineer
Dispute resolution board/arbitration
Fuels (oil, gas, etc) and boiler plant
Professional appointments (eg
  engineers, architects, quantity
  surveyors)
Space-heating and hot/cold water
  installations

2338
Building, civil and structural
  engineering
Heavy and process engineering
Marine engineering and shipbuilding
Mechanical and electrical engineering
Petrochemical and offshore
  installations
Production engineering

2425
Building and structural engineering
Design and costing of repairs to
  buildings
Engineering geology
Geotechnical engineering

2427
Civil and structural engineering
Geotechnical engineering
Ground engineering
Occupational health and safety
Piling
Slope stability/failures
Vibration whitefinger

2506
Accident reconstruction
Damage evaluation
Environmental
Fire damage evaluation/investigation
Forensic investigations
Industrial training

Engineering Advice on Highway Law

985
Excavation and reinstatement by
  statutory undertakers
Housing estate road development
  and private street works
Personal injury and vehicle accident
  claims
Public rights of way

Engineering Consultancy

692
Lifts and escalators

2216
Engineering contracts
Finite element analysis/modelling
Industrial computer systems
Mechanical engineering design
Project management
Safety assessment/audit

Engineering Consultancy/Noise/Vibration

963
Building acoustics
Environmental acoustics – noise and
  vibration
Industrial acoustics – hearing
  damage risk assessment
Noise/vibration nuisance
  investigations
On-site acoustic testing eg building
  elements
Transportation noise monitoring and
  assessment

Engineering Design

1512
Detailed engineering and design
Plant layout
Process engineering
Systems engineering

Engineering Geology

788
Civil engineering construction
  problems
Concrete technology
Engineering geomorphology
Geomaterials

1281
Ground and groundwater behaviour
Slope stability
Subsidence

2119
Engineering geology in glaciated
  areas (slopes stabilities etc)
Floodding and drainage disputes
  (Lands Tribunal claims etc)
Public inquiries into floodpain
  developments etc
Water aspects of planning
  applications
Water resources problems,
  boreholes, low flows etc

2305
Earthwork claims
Mining
Soils investigation

2388
Derelict and contaminated land
Engineering geological mapping and
  field assessments
Quarries and resource surveys
Site investigations
Slopes, landslides, embankments
  and cuttings

Engineering Geology/Geotechnical Engineering

659
Dams and reservoirs
Ground water engineering
Site investigation
Slopes and quarries
Tunnels and caverns
Waste management and disposal

1143
Construction materials
Contractual claims
Earthworks
Foundations
Slope stability
Supervision of site investigations

Engineering Infrastructure

826
Highway and drainage strategies
(including phasing) and design
Housing, industrial, retail, commercial
and leisure developments
Strategic and cashflow planning
Strategic services provision including
negotiations with statutory
authorities
Urban regeneration

2388
Drainage
Highways
Mains services supplies
Traffic

Engineering/Personal Injury

372
Consulting engineer
Forensic
Industrial injuries
Mining and tunnelling accidents

Engineering/Quantum

682
Civils; tunnelling : dams : heavy
structures
Expert witness
Industrial
Mechanical and electrical
Power stations, roads, rail,water
Sewerage

Engineering/Scientific Services

281
Engineering failure analysis/accident
reconstruction
Mechanical engineering
Personal injury investigation
Railway engineering
Road traffic accident reconstruction
Transportation accident investigations

Engineering Services

552
Damage reports
Failure analysis
Inspections
Investigations
Personal injury investigation
Safety systems

Engineering Services/Domestic/
Commercial/Industrial

570
Air conditioning and refrigeration
Combustion problems with fuels
Heat losses/gains
Industrial ventilation
Safety aspects of heating and
ventilating

Engineering Structural/Civil
Engineering

574
Building construction
Building structures/building failures
Construction site
Design negligence
Foundations
Reinforced concrete
Structural steelwork
Structural timber

English/Welsh Domestic Buildings

1635
Age.historic development and
features of interest of old buildings
Suitability of old buildings for listing
or delisting

Entertainment Safety

2034
Management
Night clubs
Outdoor events
Planning
Risk assessment
Training

Environment

4
Climatology
Ecology and ecotoxicology
Land restoration
Odour and dust dispersion
Water storage and disposal
Water/air/soil contamination

396
Air emission monitoring and
abatement
Contaminated land investigations
Environmental impact assessments
Noise monitoring and abatement
Odour complaints

522
Agriculture
Archaeology
Ecology
Landscape assessment
Soil science

923
Clinical waste management
Environmental monitoring
Food hygiene
Health and safety
Housing

974
Asbestos-related claims
Contaminated land
Entomology
Environmental auditing
Environmental due diligence –
property transactions
Environmental impact assessment
Shipping pollution claims

1376
Exposure in the workplace
Health and safety
Land/acquatic contamination
Noise and vibration

1616
Analytical investigations

1887
Environmental health
Environmental impact assessment
Environmental protection
Food hygiene, safety and composition
Occupational health and safety
Sanitation

2287
Building waste
Condensation
Contaminated land and radon gas
Energy conservation
Noise nuisance and abatement

2425
Environmental sciences

2426
Landscape design and
aftercare/assessment
Soils and agriculture

2427
Air quality
Contaminated land
Environmental assessments
Landfill engineering
Landscape/visual
appraisal/assessment
Noise
Subterranean gas
Waste management

Environment/Air

492
Acoustic insulation
Air quality (transport and industrial
emissions)
Occupational hygiene
Transport noise (traffic, airport, rail)
Vibration

Environment/Conservation

729
Criminal damage
Environmental impact assessment
reports – quality
Wildlife

Environment/Contaminated Land

582
Investigation of soil and groundwater
contamination
Landfill gas
Methane gas
Petrol contamination
Reclamation of contaminated sites

1275
Environmental assessments
Implications of contamination
Rectifying contamination

Environment/Contaminated Land
Assessment/Remediation

2025
Design or reclamation schemes
Environmental liabilities
Site investigation

1499
Design or reclamation schemes
Environmental liabilities
Site investigation

Environment/Contaminated Land,
Wastes/Land Reclamation

2388
Chemical contamination/hazardous
waste
Conceptual design of remedial
measures
Ground investigation
Groundwater pollution
Landfill gas hazard assessment and
control
Liability assessment
Mine gas hazard assessment and
control

Environment/Contamination of Land

2387
Effects on water and wider
  environmental qualities
Reclamation quality assurance
Remediation solutions
Revegetation of reclaimed land
Risk assessment
Site investigations
Subterranean fire risk assessments

Environment/General

188
Carbon monoxide poisoning
Illness related to poor housing
  conditions
Inability to produce intoximeter
  sample

Environment/Land

492
Contaminated land studies
Landfill gas/methane
Review of analytical practice

Environment/Planning

1463
Effect of development on viability
Justification for agricultural dwellings,
  appraisals
Land use, classification and quality
Occupancy conditions, agricultural
  dwellings

Environment/Water

492
Drinking water quality (chemical and
  bacteriological)
Effluent treatment
Groundwater quality
Surface water quality (rivers,
  streams, drainage)

Environmental

2359
Analysis, testing and provider of
  experts

Environmental/Acoustics

2053
Community noise
Construction noise and vibration
Environmental impact assessment
Planning assessments PPG24 etc

Environmental Analysis

1464
Atmospheric emissions
Contaminated soil and groundwater
  analysis
Fire debris analysis
Nuisance odour characterisation

Environmental Assessments

350
Environmental care
Land-based processes
Life cycle analysis

Environmental Auditing/Environmental Impact Assessment

2369
All aspects

Environmental Consultancy

957
All aspects

1787
Air pollution
Environmental impact assessment
Noise

1980
Environmental assessment

Environmental Damage

1932
Breach of contract
Business interruption
Commercial disputes
Loss of profits

Environmental Engineering

493
Asbestos contamination
Contaminated land investigation and
  remediation
Environmental assessment
Groundwater contamination
Landfill gas migration and control
Landfill planning and engineering

1649
Environmental engineering audit
Noise/sound measurement and
  vibration analysis

2025
Clinical waste treatment and disposal
Contaminated land
Incineration
Landfill design and engineering
Mineral resource development
Rust consultanting
Waste disposal

2113
Contaminated land assessments
Marine pollution of shellfish waters
Planning and licence matters – waste
  disposal sites
Waste management and pollution
  control

2230
Clinical waste treatment and disposal
Contaminated land
Incineration
Landfill design and engineering
Mineral resource development
Waste disposal

2305
Environmental assessment
Asbestos Contamination
Audits
Contaminated land
Contaminated land investigation and
  remediation
Environmental impact assessment
Groundwear contamination
Landfill
Landfill design and engineering
Landfill gas migration and control
Landfill planning and engineering
Mineral resources development
Waste disposal
Waste regulation and strategic
  planning for waste disposal sites
Waste regulation and strategic
  plannning for waste disposal sites

Environmental Engineering/Building Services

1991
Distribution pipework and associated
  equipment
Gas and liquid petroleum gases
Hot and cold water
Storage vessels, tanks

Environmental Engineering/Heating Systems

1991
Boilers, pumps, chimneys, pipework
Carbon monoxide poisoning
Heat emitters/associated controls
  and equipment
Steam, high pressure hot water
  (medium and low)

Environmental Engineering/Pollution Control

2388
Contaminated land assessment and
  remediation
Environmental assessment
Landfill
Wastes management

Environmental Geology

2388
Geological aspects of contaminated
  land
Geological aspects of landfilling
  wastes
Groundwater protection
Landfill gas migration assessment
  and control
Mine gas hazard assessment and
  control

Environmental Health

154
Assessment of environmental
  statements and reports
Environmental contamination by
  chemicals
Environmental impact assessment
Health risk assessment
Housing – nuisances, occupancy etc
Impact of industrial chemicals
Land contamination
Noise and air pollution and its
  environment
Pest control and its enforcement
Timber treatment, damp proofing

1196
Assessment of environmental
  statements and reports
Environmental contamination by
  chemicals
Environmental impact assessment
Health risk assessment
Impact of industrial chemicals
Land contamination

1946
House inspection and report
Landlord and tenant
Statutory nuisance
Unfit housing

Environmental Health/Safety

2435
Air quality
Environmental protection compliance
Health and safety compliance
  including Control of Substance
  Harmful to Health (COSHH)
Nuisance including dust, odour and
  noise

Environmental Issues

1282
Environmental audit and assessment
Odour assessment and control
Planning matters
Safety in the agriculture and food
  industries
Wastewater disposal and pollution
Water quality and contamination

Environmental Law

2423
BS7750
Contaminated land
Environmental-audit
Haz-chem

Environmental Management

81
Air pollution
Contaminated land
Corporate environmental strategy
Environmental auditing
Environmental hazard and impact
  assessment
Environmental management systems
Landfill design and gas management
Landscape design
Mineral working
Noise and vibration
Waste management
Wastewater treatment
Water pollution

Environmental Pollution/Contamination

see also Pollution and the particular
  type eg Oil

77
Groundwater pollution,
  contamination, quality
Soil pollution, contamination, quality
Water pollution

867
Chemical analysis
Civil Engineering
Remedial estimates
Risk assessment
Site investigation

868
Chemical analysis
Civil engineering
Remedial estimates
Risk assessment
Site investigation

953
Advice on environmental pollution
  ACT-IPC
Environmental assessments/auditing
Expert witness in cases with
  contaminated land, air, water
Implementation of environmental
  management systems
Monitoring services provided

1522
Air pollution – industrial and
  petrochemical plants
Investigation of dust and noxious
  emissions
Investigation of land contamination –
  building/housing development
Land and water contamination –
  industrial/petrochemical plants
Renewable energy eg methane gas
  plants

Environmental Protection

1084
Emission monitoring
Environmental assessments
  (BS7750)
Flammability
Waste treatment/management
Water analysis

2313
Contingency/emergency plans
Environment management/systems
Industrial effluent treatment
Operating procedures
Pollution prevention and control
Sewage treatment

Environmental Protection/Pollution

450
Incineration
Waste gas treatment
Waste handling and treatment
Wastewater treatment and impact

Environmental Risk Assessment

108
Risk modelling

Environmental Science

1281
Landfill
Methane problems
Reclamation

2265
Acoustics: noise, noise control
Environmental impact assessments
Environmental radioactivity
Hazardous materials
Pollution: water, air, ground, ecology
Waste management

Environmental Water Quality

438
Environmental impact assessment
European Union (EU) environmental
  directives
UK water and environmental
  legislation
Water quality objectives and
  standards

Epidemiology

2204
Adverse reactions to drugs

2395
'Cluster' investigations
Causal inference
Childhood leukaemia and cancer
Ionising radiation
Non-ionising radiation
Occupational exposures

Epidemiology of Anaesthesia

1458
Deaths associated with operations

Epilepsy

586
All aspects

Equestrian

see also Stablelads

502
Accidents and injuries to riders,
  drivers and third parties
Carriage driving and horse-drawn
  vehicles
Disputes concerning riding schools
  and tuition of pupils
Racing
Show jumping, horse trials and all
  competitive activities
Traffic accidents involving motor
  vehicles

1480
Accidents
Competition
Riding
Safety
Training
Valuations

1584
Buying and selling horses
Care of horses
Riding of horses
Training of horses (show jumping,
  dressage, cross-country,
  point-to-pointing)

1972
Purchase/sale of horses
Riding accidents
Valuations

Equestrian/Horse Racing

761
Artificial galloping surface and
  menages
Gallops/training grounds – their
  construction, design and
  maintenance
The racehorse, its racing, training
  and stabling

Equestrian/Horse Riding Instructions/Techniques/Procedures

2341
Giving evidence in court
Handling and schooling horses
Liability claims
Schooling horse and rider for
  dressage and jumping
The care of the horse/safe handling
Training students for examinations
  and teaching

Equestrian/Horse-Drawn Vehicles

1230
Carriage driving activities
Coaching and four-in-hand driving
Harness horse training
Horse driving trials
Private driving and showing
Trade and commercial horse-drawn
  vehicles

Equestrian/Horse-Related Accidents/ Problems

1256
Buying and selling
Horse management
Horse training – flat and jumping
Riding in company –
  roads/hunting/countryside
School management
Training riders in schools
Training riders on own horses

Equestrian/Horse-Related Cases

211
Accidents to horses, people, vehicles
  and property
Assessing and arbitrating
Registered as expert witness with
  British Horse Society

Equestrian Safety

370
Equestrian accidents generally
Equine/human injury
Health and safety (equine and
  human)
Horse related traffic accidents
The highway code

Equestrian Training

83
Horse behaviour
Teaching skills

Equine Buildings

761
Studs and stables, their construction
  and design
Wide-ranging contacts, both
  nationally and internationally

2438
Design of equine buildings
Design of stables
Design of stud farms
Planning of stud farms

Equine Veterinary Consultancy (Horses Only)

2442
Behavioural abnormalities of horses
Defects of the horse's spine
Obscure lamenesses
Opinions on suitability of horses for
  purchase
Structure and movement problems in
  competition horses

Equipment Performance in Industrial/Commercial/Domestic Fields

876
Design, manufacture, installation and
  maintenance of equipment
Diagnosis of equipment malfunction
  and failure in heavy and light
  industry, machine tools, automotive,
  food, packaging, hoists and
  passenger lifts

Ergonomics

243
Human performance
Manual handling
Product design
Safety
Task analysis
Workplace design

341
Low back disorders
Upper limb disorders
Work-related injury

358
Manual handling injuries
Product design and evaluation
  (safety)
Repetitive strain injuries (RSI)
Work environment design and
  evaluation
Work-related upper limb disorders
  (WRULD)
Work-station design and evaluation

1388
Display screen/office assessment
Job analysis and design
Man/machine interface design
Manual handling
Workplace design and assessment

2368
Industrial health and safety
Manual handling
Product safety
Work-related upper limb disorders

Ergonomics/Health/Safety at Work

1159
Display screen equipment use
Manual handling
Repetitive Strain Injury (RSI)/upper
  limb disorders
Stress
Work equipment use
Workplace design

Escalators

504
Cranes
Escalators
Fork lift trucks
Hoists
Lifts
Miscellaneous lifting equipment

Estate Agency

1808
Commission dispute arbitration
Estate Agents Orders and
  Regulations 1991
Law of agency – practice and
  procedures
The Estate Agents Act 1979
The Property Misdescriptons Act
  1991

Estate Agency/Valuations

2234
Country houses, cottages
Farms and estates

Ethics in Psychiatry

23
Competence to consent
Confidentiality
Professional misconduct by
  doctor/therapists

Evaluation of Damages

800
Costs of losing valuable asset for
  business/domestic purposes
Costs of nuisance caused by noise,
  smells or other pollution
Direct costs of death or disability
Distress and inconvenience

Evaluation of Loss of Income

800
Costs incurred because of
  death/disability of the homemaker
Damage to earnings prospects
  through unfair dismissal
Loss of earnings through death or
  disability
Spouse's pensions entitlement in
  divorce cases

Evidential Photography

2211
Accidents: industrial, commercial and
  public
Causes of accidents
Interiors and exteriors of accident
  sites
Personal injury

Expert Determination or Arbitration

928
Acquisition and merger disputes
Allocation of capital assets following
  local authority boundary changes
Share purchase agreements

Expert Opinion/Expert Witness

972
Assessment of pleadings and
  statements
Case merit advice to counsel
Comment on other expert opinion
Documentation for discovery
Experienced expert witness
Taking statements/substantiation
  facts

Expert Witness

74
Affidavits
Counsel conferences
Court attendance
Legal aid
Pleadings
Quantum
Reports
Scott schedules
Technical inspections

Expert Witness Services

1311
Animated graphical evidence
Critical path analysis
Electronic storage and retrieval of
  data
Forensic engineering
Planning and programming

Expert Witness Works

866
Evidence in court
Paraplegic claims
Specialist reports

Experts

471
Expert practices
Expert standards

Experts Location/Identification of Suitable Additional

2467
All aspects

Explanation of Expert Reports

1292
All Aspects

Explosion Investigation/Civil/Criminal

794
Debris analysis/flammable liquids, chemical analysis
Isolation of evidential material/appliances, debris
Mathematical calculations and evaluation of potential
Scene examination/gas and flammable liquids

Explosions

2359
Analysis, testing and provider of experts

Explosives

671
Blast effects
Handling
High explosives
Investigation of incidents
Pyrotechnic mixtures
Safe distances

800
Examination of residual levels of explosives
Home-made explosives

Explosives Act 1875

1070
Investigation of firework accidents

Explosives Investigation

581
Examination and assessment of explosive devices
Examination of post-explosion debris
Examination of suspected bomb-making materials
Investigation of aircraft crashes for possible explosives involvement

Eyes/Medico-legal

495
Eye injuries
Negligence
Ophthalmology

Facial Comparison/Analysis

1421
Facial anatomy
Image processing
Mensuration
Photographic and video analysis
Shape description and computer vision
Statistics

Facial Deformity

2026
Surgical correction of jaw deformity
Surgical correction of soft-tissue deformity

Facial Injury/Dental

137
Damage to jaws
Damage to teeth
Facial trauma
Management of oral medicine cases
Management of oral surgery cases

Facial Trauma

2026
Corrections of post-traumatic deformity
Facial fractures
Soft tissue injuries to head and neck region

Facilities for the Disabled

2408
Heating, sanitation, access

Factory Accident Investigation

566
All Aspects

Factory Accidents/Work-Related Diseases

159
Dermatitis
Machinery hazards
Manual handling
Personal protective equipment
Slipping

Failure by Fatigue/Fracture of Metallic Structures/Components

1031
All Aspects

Failure for Medical Reasons to Provide Breath Sample

665
High blood pressure, diabetes
Respiratory impairment (asthma etc)

Failure Investigation

357
Evaluation of documentation
Expert witness work
Laboratory testing
Site investigations

Failures/Collapses/Disasters in Construction, Investigation of

1943
Defective roofs, Failed floors
Defective sewerage and water pipelines
Defective structural steelwork
Defective tanking and waterproofing
Masonry failures
Piling and foundation failures
Pre-stressed and in-situ concrete failures
Timber frame damage

Fairground Equipment

130
Accident investigation
Safety reports

Families/Lesbian

904
All aspects

Family

see also Divorce, Matrimonial and the type of work eg Psychology, Social Work

29
Assistance in planning cross-examinations
Budgets
Rule 2.63 questionnaires
Taxation considerations
Valuations of businesses and partnerships (including farms)

221
Disputed probate
Structure of marital settlements
Tax aspects of marital settlements
Tracing and consolidating marital assets
Valuing businesses on marital break-ups

927
Business valuations
Duxbury calculations
Pension rights
Whole man/woman valuation in divorce

1481
All aspects

Family Assessments

523
Individual needs/group interaction

Family/Child Care Legal Proceedings

232
Assessment of adults' ability to parent children
Assessment of the risk of adult abuse of children
Legal aid

Family Functioning

259
Attachments
Parenting abilities
Rehabilitation potential
Risk assessments

2229
Effects of separation and abuse
(including reports for Guardian ad
Litems)
General assessment

Family Planning/Women's Health

258
All aspects

Family Proceedings/Children's Act

1706
Assessing adults' intellectual abilities
Assessing children's emotional and
developmental needs
Assessing childrens' intellectual,
social and emotional development
Assessing childrens' vulnerability to
future harm
Assessing parenting abilities
Attachment, bonding and separation
anxiety
Child abuse (sexual, physical,
emotional)
Disputed care, supervision,
residence, contact orders
Domestic violence
Family assessments
Risk assessment of parents re:
abuse and neglect

Family Psychology

2463
Family breakdown
Family interactions – effects on
children
Parenting competence
Rehabilitation of children to parents

Farm Building Construction

1920
Design and supervision of
construction of most types of farm
building
Suitability of irrigation systems (fixed
and portable) for
design/specification
Suitability of pollution control
equipment for application

Farm Business Management

1167
Assessing losses to total business
Divorce
Partnership dissolution

1463
Feasibility studies
Financial planning and monitoring
Preparation and assessment of
insurance claims
Viability and profitability appraisals

Farm Management

82
Arable crops
Budgets and costings
Contract farming
Finance
Livestock
Management performance

1106
Bank referrals
Budgeting and account analysis
Business profitability
Divorce
Quantum calculations

Fatal Accidents

1428
Consequential loss on share
purchase agreement – warrantees

Fee Disputes

2095
All Aspects

Fenestration/Domestic

1911
Conservatories
Original windows and doors
Patio doors
Replacement doors
Replacement windows

Fenestration/Framing

1911
Curtain walling and similar cladding
Doors
Entrances, shop fronts
Glazed structures
Glazing – patent, overhead
Windows

Fenestration/Glass, Glazing/Infill

1911
Accidents
Double glazing and multiple glazing
Panelling
Structural glazing

Fetal Cardiology

1337
All Aspects

Fidelity Policies

1481
All aspects

Finance

1929
Corporate finance

**Finance/Investment Business
Problems**

221
Appropriate advice
Financial Services Act compliance

Finance/Investment Disputes

204
Insurance disputes
Litigation between stockbrokers and
clients
Matrimonial financial disputes

Finance/Investment/Insurance

1885
Compensation for
misleading/incorrent illustrations
Reserving techniques of general
insurance (eg Lloyds)

Financial Consultancy

1413
Extortionate credit bargains
Finance and mortgage broking
(private and commercial)
Fraudulent selling of investment
bonds often linked to insurance
policies
Professional negligence and
malpractice

Financial Due Diligence

514
Corporate backgrounds
Mergers and acquisitions
Venture capital and other financing

Financial Economics

382
Damages calculations
Financial investigation and analysis
Lease financing
Project viability appraisal
Valuation of intellectual property
rights

Financial Markets/Advice

1213
Endowment policies
Equity/gilt markets
Foreign exchange
Futures and options
Investment and financial planning
advice
Investment management
Mortgages
Pensions

Financial Services

284
Building society practice
Imprudent lending
Lending policies
Mortgage fraud
Mortgage lending practices

1886
Commercial and domestic loans
Investment advice
Life assurance sales
Mortgages
Pensions provision
Pre-retirement counselling

Financial Services/Investment Advice

1788
Negligent investment advice: life
assurance, packaged investment
products
Structured settlement
Valuation of losses following
negligent financial planning advice

Financial Services/Regulation

1788
Compensation schemes
Ombudsmen
Regulatory authorities

**Financial
Services/Regulation/Litigation**

928
All Aspects

Financial Settlements

1173
Commercial
Matrimonial
Medical negligence
Professional negligence

Fine Art/Antiques

967
Furniture
Old master and modern paintings
Restoration of works of art
Valuation of works of art

1072
Furniture, silver, decorative arts,
chattels
Gallery/dealer/auction house practice

Fine Art/Antiques/General Chattels

2015
Assessment of damage
Identification, appraisal, valuation

Fine Claims

1428
Consequential loss on share
purchase agreement – warrantees

Finger/Palm Print Identification/Crime Scene Examination

497
Crime scene examination techniques
Fingerprint development techniques
Fingerprint treatments of suspect
documents
Forensic aspect of crime scene
examination
Suspect documents

Finger/Palm/Sole Print Identification

1334
Checking prosecution expert
evidence
Crime scene investigation for prints
Criminal appeals
Giving evidence in court at all levels
Internal fraud investigation for large
concerns
Lecturing
Murder

Fingerprint Analysis

2516
Comparison to establish
identity/non-identity
Examination of documents for finger
marks by chemical methods
Preparation of reports with, where
possible, significance of marks

Fingerprint Comparison/Recovery (including palm)

172
Glove mark comparison
Instrument mark comparison
Scene of crime examination
Shoe impression comparison
Tyre mark comparison

Fingerprint Consultancy

2296
Advice on all aspects of the finger
and palm prints
Fingerprint investigation in criminal
and civic matters
Forensic photography
Second opinion on prosecution
evidence

Fingerprint/Crime Scene Work

2249
Assessment/validity of evidence
Briefing
Developments of marks
Examination/marks/crime scene
Expert witness
Reports

Fingerprint Examination

1449
All Aspects

Fingerprint Identification

300
Forensic advice
Scene examination

805
Chemical treatment of paper for
fingerprinting
Court atttendance/consultation
Evidence assessed
Finger, palm and footprint
identification
Scenes of crime examination

Fingerprints

797
Detection on difficult surfaces
Enhancement of fingerprint detail
Enhancement of fingerprints in blood

1060
Comparison of finger and palm prints
Detection of latent prints
Interpretation/orientation of marks
Taking prints from individuals

1570
Checking scenes of crimes
Identification of finger marks
Scrutinising fingerprint evidence

Finishes

1965
Coatings
Flooring
Plaster
Render
Tiling (walls, floors, swimming pools)

Fire

see also Arson

797
Accelerant analysis
Accident investigation
Carbon monoxide poisoning
Electrical fires
Examination of fires and fire
damaged items
Explosion investigation
Fatalities in fires
Incendiary and explosive devices
Vehicle fires

800
Arson assessment of evidence
Detection of accelerants ie petrol
Re-examination of scene

969
Building services
Electrical
Fuel oil
Smoke control

2359
Analysis, testing and provider of
experts

Fire Damage Claims/Disputes

1155
Analysis, measurement and
assessment of damaged building
works

Fire/Explosion

323
Advice on fire and explosion
problems
Investigation of incidents
Litigation support in civil and criminal
cases

671
Behaviour of materials
Condensed phase explosions
Dust testing and hazard evaluation
Dust, mist and vapour phase
explosions
Effects of fire on structures
Electrostatic hazards
Extinguishing agents
Fire and explosion dynamics
Fire detection and protection
Heat transfer
Investigations of cause
Self-heating and spontaneous
combustion
Sources of ignition

971
All aspects

1051
Electrical and engineering-related
incidents
Personal injury claims
Product liability claims
Railway accidents

1449
Bomb scene search
Fire investigation
Scene of crime work

1616
Building fires, commercial and
domestic
Industrial and plant fires and
explosions
Marine fires and explosions
Vehicle fires

1741
All types of explosions
Failures of pressure systems and
ancillaries
Process/materials-related fires

Fire/Explosion Investigation

2350
Appliances involved in fires
Arson and fire-related fraud
Consideration of documents
Expert reports
Factors relating to fire spread
Origin and cause – on-site

Fire Investigation

794
Appliance examination/misuse, malfunction
Debris analysis/flammable liquid residues, chemical analysis
Fire scene examination and interpretation
Isolation of evidential material/appliances, debris
Mathematical calculations

1485
Criminal work involving arson and related charges
Fire – cause and origin
Fire – product liability
Fire – vehicles and mechanical plant
Legal consideration of fire brigade operations

2104
Arson
Fires of electrical origin
Ignitions of flammable gases and vapours
Murder by petrol
Suspect insurance claims

2436
Cause of fire
Fire behaviour/characteristics
Fire service operations/procedures
Human behaviour

Fire Safety Engineering

2436
Computer modelling
Contractual matters
Failure of fire protection systems
Performance of materials in fire
Performance of systems in fire
Professional negligence

Firearms

291
Determination of firearms status under Firearms Acts
Identification of firearms and ammunition
Internal and external ballistics
Proof acts and suitability for use
Safe handling and use of sporting firearms

626
Ammunition design and performance
External ballistics
Internal ballistics
Pistols, rifles and shotguns
Tank and artillery guns and ammunition
Wound ballistics

797
Analysis of missile composition, discharge residues and noxious sprays
Association of firearms with used bullets/cartridge cases
Examination of stun guns
Identification, testing and classification of firearms
Prohibited weapons and ammunition
Scene of incident investgation, range of firing and wound interpretation

1386
Classification, dating, identification, evaluation of firearms
Performance of weapons, ballistics etc
Shotguns and other weapons, both licensed and others

1795
Firearms crime scene analysis
Sporting shotguns and rifles

Firearms/Ammunition

1015
Determination of firearms status under Firearms Acts
Determination of firearms' age and origins
Firearms proof matters and suitability for use
Identification of firearms and ammunition
Internal and external ballistics
Valuation for all purposes

Firearms/Ballistics

989
Accidents resulting from firearms and ammunition
Failures of firearms and ammunition
Interior and exterior ballistics
Trajectories, penetration and impact analysis

1937
Chemical spray devices eg CS spray canisters
Examination and testing of firearms and ammunition
Exterior ballistics calculations
Gunshot discharge residues
Reconstruction of shooting incidents
Scene visits
Wound ballistics analysis

Firearms Evaluation/Testing

726
Evaluation of causes and effects
Firearms identification
Testing and examination of mechanisms

Firearms Examination/Classification

946
Classification of firearms
Firearms examination
Firearms licensing matters
Incident investigation

Firearms Legislation

291
Antique firearms and their exemption from control
Criminal offences – Firearms Acts 1968-94
Firearms act exemptions for non-certificate holders
Firearms licensing and police policy
Safe storage measures for firearms

1015
Antique firearms and their exemption from controls
Criminal offences under Firearms Acts 1968-1994
Firearms licensing and police policy relating to it
Firearms safety and good practice
Interpretation of Firearms Act exemptions for non-certificate holders
Safe storage measures for firearms

Fisheries

817
All aspects

1992
Conservation of native species
Crayfish
Fish farming
Fisheries
Introduction of non-native species
Pollution
Water quality issues

2555
All Aspects

Fitness for Purpose

1583
Assessment of deficiences and failures in supplied plant and equipment
Quality assurance in manufacture and provision of goods and services – general
Safety and hygiene in drink processing and manufacture
Safety and hygiene in food processing and manufacture

Fitted Interiors

2152
Bathrooms/planning and installation
Bedrooms/planning and installation
Kitchens/planning and installation

Fitted Kitchens/Bedrooms

140
All Aspects

Floods

969
Pipes freezing
Sprinklers
Tanks

Floor Covering Technology

1664
'Slipping, tripping and falling' accidents
Installation of all floor coverings
Moisture, humidity and rising moisture
Osmosis
Safety on floors
Substrates in building

Floor Coverings

1936
Carpet fitting
Carpets
Vinyls

Floor Safety

768
Accident investigations/slip
resistance of floor surfaces
Damaged paving and kerbstones
Stairs
Tripping accidents

Flooring

2539
Ceramic tiles
Floor finishes
Linoleum
Vinyl flooring
Wood flooring

Food

4
Food hygiene
Microbiology

154
Food safety and enforcement of food
law

239
Food contamination
Food engineering
Food packaging
Food poisoning
Food science and technology
Forensic investigation of food

787
Chill and cold chain
Cooking
Cooking/sterilisation/pasteurisation
Processing
Refrigeration
Regulations
Temperature control

1387
Customer product safety
Food analysis
Legionella testing
Microbiology
Nutritional analysis
Product liability appraisals

Food Biology

1194
Damage to marine and air food
cargoes
Expert on potatoes and sugar
Post-harvest storage and transport of
foods
Spoilage of refrigerated food

Food Claims

239
Food losses
Food poisoning and contamination
Food spoilage
Insurance claim assessment
Loss adjustment
Passing off

Food/Drink

953
Advice on quality management (BS
5750) and due diligence
Expertise in microbiology, unfit
food/food hygiene
Industrial experience in sugar
confectionary, soft drinks industries
Public analyst expertise in
examination and witness work

1583
Assessment of deficiences and
failures in supplied plant and
equipment
Quality assurance in manufacture
and provision of goods and services
– general
Safety and hygiene in drink
processing and manufacture
Safety and hygiene in food
processing and manufacture

Food/Drinks Packaging/Ergonomics/ Scientific Investigations

725
Alcohol backtracking
Exploding bottles
Foreign body adulteration in foods
and drinks
Forensic investigations [Crown
Prosecution Service (CPS)
challenges]
Health and safety and personal injury
Repetitive Strain Injury (RSI)
(ergonomics of work practices)
Stress and fracture analysis of glass

Food/Health/Safety/Consumer Goods/Analysis Testing/Advice

606
Consumer safety (especially
chemicals) advice and analysis
Food Safety Act advice and analysis
Health and safety advice and analysis
Road Traffic Act, alcohol
determinations, back calculations
etc

Food Hygiene

2544
Audit inspections
Hazard analysis
Reports in mitigation
Training

Food Hygiene Training

786
Adequacy of training
Design of training programmes

Food Industry/Packaging Industry/Process Machinery

1216
Food and allied processing machinery
Food manufacturing processes
Food packaging

Food Manufacture

2486
Environment
Equipment
Industrial injuries
Services
Storage
Technology

Food Microbiology

2071
Food contamination
Food illness
Food production

Food Poisoning

1474
Medicine

Food Products

2486
Canned vegetables
Confectionery
Dairy products
Dried foods
Edible oils

Food Quality

2486
Contamination
Control of quality
Due diligence
Foreign bodies
Hygiene
Instrumentation and control

Food Quality/Safety

1282
Animal feeds/production and spoilage
Food adulteration
Malicious tamper
Microbiological and chemical
contamination

Food Safety/Hygiene

786
Complaint investigation
Enforcement action – 'due diligence'
Food Safety Act
Food hygiene regulations
Food poisoning allegations
Risk assessment

1860
Due diligence defence (Food Safety
Act 1990)
Food poisoning investigations
Inspection of unfit/unsound food
(including meat)

1946
Due diligence
Food contamination
Food hygiene regulations
Food poisoning
Premises audits

2530
Food hygiene inspections and
standards
Food poisoning claims
Food prosecutions – investigations
and reports

Food Safety/Quality

643
'Due diligence' defence systems
Construction and layout of premises
Contamination: microbial, foreign
body, chemical
Enforcement notices
Hazard analysis critical control point
systems
Hygiene management and control
Litigation
Procurement, analysis and
examination of samples
Temperature control

Food Science/Technology

78
Food additives (flavouring and
colourings)
Food and beverage packaging
Fruit processing and fruit juices
Natural products
Soft drinks

1133
Food analysis
Food hygiene
Food quality
Foreign bodies in food (customer
  complaints)
Meat and meat products
  (composition, quality and
  presentation)
Microbiology of food

1387
Food processing controls
HACCP
Hygiene
Product development
Systems auditing

2100
Food preservation
Food production
Food safety and quality
Meat and meat products

Foot/Ankle Surgery

7
Fractures of the foot, hindfoot and
  ankle
Surgery of the forefoot
The foot and ankle in rheumatoid
  arthritis

Footwear Made to Measure

2069
Adaptations to own footwear
Calipers
Foot supports
Footwear repairs
Orthopaedic/surgical footwear

Footwear Quality of

371
Faulty footwear and reports
Foot health and faults in manufacture
Footwear injury claims
Methods and procedures of
  manufacture
Quality of components

Foreign/Commonwealth/International

1489
Conflict of laws
Diplomatic privileges and immunity
Hindu personal laws
Islamic personal and sharia law
  (marriage, divorce and succession)
Medical malpractice

Foreign Exchange/Money Markets

840
Advice on market technicalities
Consideration of dealing authorities
Investigation of suspect transactions

Forensic

see also under the specialism eg
  Document Examination

Forensic Accountancy

see also Asset Tracing, Fraud

97
Commercial litigation (contract
  disputes)
Fraud (investigation, funds tracing)
Libel
Partnership disputes
Professional negligence (auditing,
  tax, accounting)
Quantum claims (loss of profits, fatal
  injury, personal injury, medical
  negligence)

98
Loss of profit claims
Professional negligence

116
Breach of contract (including
  computer installations, construction
  and warranty claims)
Civil and criminal fraud including
  false accounting and asset tracing
Insolvency including preference and
  fraudulent trading
Other damages claims including loss
  of future profits
Personal injury and fatal accident
  claims (including medical
  negligence)
Professional negligence
Share valuations including
  S459CA1985

124
Accounts reconstruction
Business transfers
Courts martial
False accounting
Fraud
Personal injury compensation

147
Business valuation disputes
Consequential loss and business
  interrruption claims
Expert advice and independent
  arbitration
Fraud and financial irregularities
Income tax investigations
Personal injury and fatal accident
  claims
Value added tax investigations

171
Business valuations
Commercial actions
Fraud investigations
Inland Revenue investigations
Loss of profits

208
Accountants' role in matrimonial
  breakdown
Pension splitting in divorce

262
Commercial litigation
Fraud
Insurance litigation
Personal injury, fatal accidents and
  medical negligence
Professional negligence

278
Contractual disputes
Fraud and theft
Litigation support
Matrimonial disputes
Partnership disputes
Professional negligence

333
Consequential loss
Fraud and negligence
Marital breakdown
Partnership and shareholder disputes
Personal injury (plaintiff and
  defendent)

505
General forensic accounting
Loss of earnings
Professional negligence claims

576
Breach of contract – settling quantum
Fraud investigations
Matrimonial – valuations of assets
Personal injury – settling quantum
Professional negligence – settling
  quantum

610
Loss of profits
Matrimonial
Personal injury
Small commercial claims and
  disputes

623
Divorce
Drugs investigation
Fraud investigation
Insurance claims
Legal aid work (criminal and civil)
Partnership and company valuations
Tax investigations and prosecutions
Theft and money tracing

720
Accounting investigations
Damages (calculation of)
Fraud
Funds tracing
Mareva and Anton Piller injunctions
Share valuations

747
Commercial litigation
Fraud
Insurance
Matrimonial disputes
Personal injury
Professional negligence

799
Business and share valuations
Divorce, financial
  investigation/valuation
Fraud/theft, investigation/defence
Partnership disputes
Personal injury, profit/pension loss
Professional negligence

966
Disputes resolution – partnership and
  shareholder disputes, particularly
  family businesses
Fraud: investigation and prevention
Personal injury and medical
  negligence: plaintiff reports, general
  and special damages excluding
  PSLA

970
Commercial litigation
Department of Trade and Industry
  (DTI) disqualification
Fraud investigation
Matrimonial
Personal injury and medical
  negligence
Professional negligence
Share and business valuations

978
Business interruption claims
Contractual disputes
Matrimonial
Personal injury, medical negligence
 and fatal accidents
Share/business valuations
Shareholder disputes

1079
Business loss of profits
Contractual disputes
Insurance claims
Interpretation of accounts
Matrimonial disputes
Personal injury and dependency
 claims
Professional negligence

1217
Business interruption
Business/share valuations
Employment
Fraud
Personal injury
Professional negligence

1313
Breach of warranty claims
Commercial fraud
Divorce settlements
Intellectual property disputes
Loss of earnings/profits
Professional negligence
 (accountants)
Share valuations

1335
Financial modelling
Fraud
Money laundering

1360
Commercial litigation
Loss of profits and earnings
Matrimonial disputes
Personal injury
Professional negligence
Share valuations

1389
Business and share valuations
Consequential loss of profit claims
Contractual or commercial disputes
Fraud
Matrimonial disputes
Professional negligence

1408
Arbitration and dispute resolution
Breach of contract/warranty claims
Business interruption
Due diligence
Fraud, insolvency
Matrimonial
Negligence: professional and medical
Personal injury

1427
Business losses
Dependency claims
Insurance claims
Other losses of earnings
Personal injury claims

1491
Breach of warranty
Business interruptions
Business valuations
Criminal work
Debt recovery
Fatal accident
Fraud and fidelity
Loss of pension
Matrimonial disputes
Medical negligence
Personal injury
Product liability
Professional negligence
Security for costs
Structured settlements

1504
All aspects

1646
Fraud and misfeasance (civil and
 criminal)
Intellectual property infringement
Means assessment
Professional negligence claims
Revenue back duty
Shareholder and partnership disputes
Trade and contractual disputes

1657
Commercial disputes
Fraud
Matrimonial
Partnership disputes/share valuations
Professional negligence
Quantum of personal injury claims

1742
Commercial litigation
Fraud investigations
Loss of earnings claims
Professional negligence

1819
Business/share/asset valuation
General damages assessment
Intellectual property
Loss of profit and business
 interruption
Personal injury and fatal accident
Professional negligence

1829
Company valuations
Divorce settlement valuations
Personal injury claims

1915
Business/share valuations
Fraud
Loss of profit/business interruption
Minority shareholder action
Partnership disputes

1929
Fraud investigations
Personal injury – loss of earnings
Professional negligence
Profit forecasts
Valuations

1933
Business valuations
Loss claims generally
Losses under warranty
Professional negligence
 (tax/audit/accountancy)

1969
Fraud
Personal injury
Professional negligence
Share valuations (matrimonial)

2004
Breach of contract as product liability
Business valuations
Commercial and partnership disputes
Fraud and criminal work
Inland revenue investigations
Insurance litigation
Loss of profits
Matrimonial
Personal injury, fatal accident as
 medical negligence
Professional negligence

2035
Business valuations
Commercial disagreements
Commercial disputes
Consequential loss
Fraud and criminal cases
Loss of profits
Matrimonial disputes
Personal injury and fatal accident
 claims
Share valuations

2139
Commercial litigation
Fraud
Matrimonial

Forensic Accountancy/Civil Litigation

1331
Employment and pensions
Matrimonial
Personal injury and medical accident
 quantum
Professional negligence
Quantification of commercial losses
Shareholder and partnership disputes

Forensic Accountancy/Finance

66
Breach of contract and warranty
Expert financial/accounting
 determinations
Fraud and white collar crime
Professional negligence
Quantum
Share and business valuations

Forensic Accountancy/Fraud

1398
Accounts manipulation
Bank, dealing and public company
 fraud
Investigations
Money laundering and asset tracing
Regulatory enquiries and reports

Forensic Accountancy/Investigative

648
Assessment of claims for loss of
 profit/earnings in – personal injury,
 medical negligence, business
 interruption and commercial dispute
Experienced in both plantiff and
 defendant work
Regularly undertake cases funded by
 legal aid

2557
Accident and injury claims
Business and company valuation
Fraud and negligence
Insolvency related assignments
Investigations and viability reports

Forensic Accountancy/Litigation Support

1027
Business interruption and loss of profits
Insurance
Personal injury, fatal accident and medical negligence
Professional negligence

1119
Accountants negligence
Business valuations
Commercial litigation
Fatal accidents
Matrimonial disputes
Other professional negligence
Personal injury

1767
Commercial litigation
Fraud
Insurance claims
Matrimonial
Personal injury, fatal accident and medical negligence
Professional negligence

2078
Agent auditing
Business interruption claims
Expert witness
Fidelity guarantee and professional indemnity
Personal injury/special damage calculations with continuing losses

Forensic Acoustics

637
Critical analysis of noise/aural event/occurrence
Effects of masking by ambient noise
Modelling/simulation of aural event/occurrence
Quantification of sound transmission paths
Verification of audibility/intelligibility

Forensic Archaeology

1178
Establishing interval since death
Maximising evidence of death during recovery
Recovery of buried remains
Search for buried remains

Forensic Art

2491
2-D facial reconstruction
Artist impressions
E-Fits (electronic facial identification technique)
Facial mapping
Image comparison

Forensic Biochemistry/Medico-Legal

1508
Alcohol related crime and disease
Diabetes and other metabolic diseases
Drugs of abuse
Hypoglycaemia and automatism
Nutritional and environmental health
Pathology of disease

Forensic Biology/Microscopy

793
Blood stains/interpretation of nature and distribution
Blood, semen, saliva and other body fluids/identification characterization
Damage to clothing by weapons, struggle, to weapons themselves
Scenes of crime/examination, collection of evidence, interpretation, general overviews
Textile fibres, hairs/identification, significance as trace evidence, continuity and contamination issues

1307
Alcohol calculations
Body fluids/stains
Deoxribonucleic Acid (DNA)/STR
Footwear marks
Glass fragments
Hairs
Textile fibres

Forensic Chemistry

793
Chemicals/cosmetics, greases, waxes, lachrymators, general
Contact traces/glass, paint, building materials, plastics, adhesives
Drugs/analysis methods, production, legislation
Fires and explosions/scene examination, debris analysis
Marks/manufacturing, cutting, tool, footwear, tyres

1307
Explosives
Firearms
Paint and building material failures

Forensic Computer Examination

649
Examination of computer printers
Text retrieval from computer floppy disks
Text retrieval from computer hard disks

Forensic Dentistry

see also Dentistry

916
Bite mark analysis
Dental identification of human remains
Identification by bite mark

2219
Bite marks in child abuse
Bite marks in foodstuffs
Bite marks in murder, assault, rape, etc
Body identification by dental means
Negligence claims relating to general dental practice

2487
Ageing of the dead or the living
Assessment of fragments at scene of crime
Bite mark analysis (on flesh and objects)
Identification of the dead
Non-accidental child injuries involving the teeth

Forensic Diagnostic Radiology

1205
Injuries to bones and joints, especially the spine

Forensic Document Examination/Handwriting Analysis

see also Document Examination

160
Alterations of recorded detail
Handwriting (signature) examination/comparison
Inks/paper
Physical examination of documental materials
Typewriting/printing – identification

198
Altered records
Disguised handwriting
Disputed wills
Figure fraud embezzlement
Malicious and anonymous letters
Suspect signatures

514
Forensic handwriting analysis
Forgery
Questioned documents

638
Alterations/additions to documents
Anonymous letters
Comparisons of inks and papers
ESDA testing
Handwriting/typewriting comparisons
Signature comparisons

649
All other aspects of document examinations
Decipherment of indented impressions of handwriting
Examination of altered documents
Examination of counterfeit and printed documents
Paper and photocopy comparisons
Typescript comparisons

795
Examination and comparison of inks
Examination and comparison of typescript
Examination of paper and print
Examine alterations/erasures on documents/navigation charts
Signature and handwriting comparisons
Visualise indented impressions of writings by ESDA

881
Authentication of signatures
Counterfeit documents
Identification and study of photocopies
Identification of handwriting
Identification of typewritings, printing
Study of altered documents including latent impressions

1550
Anonymous letters
Detection of forgery
Handwriting identification
Obliterations/erasures/ink comparisons
Photocopies
Recovery of indentations
Typescripts/print/paper comparison

1902
Alterations and erasures
ESDA (writing impressions)
Handwriting identification
Ink analysis (non-destructive and chemical)
Signature authentication
Typewriting identification

Forensic Document Examination/Handwriting Analysis/Examination of Questioned Documents for Forgery/Fraud

1024
Examination for indented impressions (ESDA technique)
Examination for mistreatment (alterations, obliterations)
Examination of materials – paper, inks etc
Handwriting comparisons and identification
Infra red and ultra violet radiations
Stereoscopic microscopy
Typewriting comparisons and identification

Forensic Document Examination/Indented Impressions

1922
Anonymous letters
ESDA
MIssing diary pages
Rewritten statements

Forensic Ecological Studies

1795
Environment studies
River pollution
Shoot management

Forensic Engineering

622
Alternative dispute resolution
Arbitration
Health and Safety Act – breaches
Litigation
Negligence actions
Personal injury investigation

710
Engineering metallurgy
Failure analysis of components and structures
Metal fatigue
Patent litigation
Product liability
Stress analysis

1229
Analysis of building and structural defects
Building collapses
Industrial accidents on construction sites

1411
Analyis of polymers
Fracture and failure of polymers
Polymer processing
Product ergonomics
Product liability (plastic and rubber products)
Product quality

1577
Accident reconstruction/investigation
Failure analysis
Insurance claims
Mechanical engineering
Plant inspection
Product liability

1586
Blunt impact injuries
Dynamics of stab wounds
General engineering principles applied to forensic medicine
Time of death

1881
Failure and defect analysis of structures, components, machinery
Fire and explosion investigation and analysis

2311
Domestic and industrial accident investigation
Machinery and manual aspects of Repetitive Strain Injury (RSI)
Product and production machinery performance
Product liability

Forensic Engineering/Engineering Reports

261
Engineering contractual litigation
Industrial/occupational accident investigations
Lifting/slipping accidents
Occupational health investigations
Personal injury claims (litigation)
Upper-limb disorders – ergonomic studies

Forensic Engineering/Mechanical

52
Personal injury in construction accidents
Personal injury in industrial accidents
Personal injury or loss due to mechanical failure
Road traffic accident reconstruction

Forensic Entomology

729
Insect analysis in determining time and place of death
Insect biology in criminal investigations

Forensic Examinations

1084
Blood/breath alcohol
Chemical analysis
Dyestuffs – fires, chemical analysis
Fingerprints, footwear impressions
Instrument marks – glass, paint
Textiles including fibres, yarns, fabrics, clothing

Forensic Handwriting Analysis

649
Comparison of handwriting of foreign nationals
Handwriting comparisons to identify authorship
Signature comparisons to identify authorship

Forensic Learning Disability/Sex Offenders/Violence/Arsonists

462
Assessment of perpetrators of child abuse
Assessment of post-traumatic stress disorder
Competency, treatability issues

Forensic Medical Examiner/Police Surgeon

381
All Aspects

Forensic Meteorology

2307
Air pollution and atmospheric pollution
Climate and hazards
The impact of weather and climate in any aspect
Weather and insurance claims
Weather and road accidents
Weather forecasting

Forensic Odontology

435
Age assessment
Analysis of bite marks
Dental identification of individuals
Human-animal toothmark analysis

1409
Age estimation from dental evidence
Analysis of bite marks in food and other materials
Analysis of bite marks on skin for exclusion of suspects
Analysis of bite marks on skin for identification of suspect
Comparison of weapon mark patterns with weapons
Identification of living/dead persons from dental evidence
Recognition of bite marks on victim of assault

2339
Bite analysis
Post mortem identification and reports

Forensic Pathology

61
Clinical laboratory medicine
Death from natural disease
Homicide investigation
Non-fatal injuries

276
Pathology of violence; homicide and accidental injury

931
Child abuse
Death investigation – second post mortems
Fatal accidents
Homicide
Hospital mishap or negligence
Industrial disease

1035
Defence autopsies
Medical accidents, negligence cases
Medico-legal opinion, offences against the person
Medico-legal opinion, road traffic offences

1174
Autopsies
Malicious wounding/causes, mechanism

1347
Deaths in custody
Defence autopsies in homicide
Fatal industrial accidents and diseases
Identification of the dead (especially skeletal)
Pathology of trauma and death
Transporation (traffic) deaths

2413
Forensic autopsies
Interpretation of wounds and injuries

Forensic Pathology/Medicine

1588
Interpretation of injuries in the living
Post-mortem examinations
Study of physical child abuse

Forensic Phonetics

1269
Transcriptions of tape-recorded speech

Forensic Psychiatry

23
Female offenders
Personality disorders
Post-traumatic stress disorder and crime
Psychological treatment/therapy
Sexual offenders and their victims

1232
Dangerousness
Homicide
Mentally disordered offenders
Mild/borderline learning disability
Sex offenders

1310
Forced confessions

1322
Civil – post-traumatic stress disorder
Criminal – reliability of confessions
Fitness to plead/insanity
Head injury
Malingering
Mental Health Act
Mental illness and intent/automatism
Sex offenders

2128
Accident neurosis
Crime and mental disorder
Differential diagnosis functional psychoses and organic brain disease
Marriage and marital problems
Post-traumatic stress disorder
Psychiatric component of ill-health generally
Testamentary capacity – wills, Court of Protection

2543
Adult mental health in care of children
Alcohol and alcoholism
Drug abuse and dependency
Medical negligence (both sides)
Mental Health Review Tribunal (restricted cases)
Offender psychiatry – all aspects
Personal injury (plaintiff and defendant)

Forensic Psychiatry/Adolescent

2008
Forensic Psychiatry in relation to adolescents
Personal injury

Forensic Psychiatry/Civil Litigation Relating to Mental Disorder

688
Mental capacity in relation to any legal capacity
Nervous shock
Psychiatric injury – post-traumatic stress disorder
Psychiatric negligence

Forensic Psychiatry/Criminal /Civil Cases

1279
Civil work in personal injury/medical negligence
Criminal work in homicide and violent crimes
Mental health review tribunals
Other criminal cases
Sex offences

Forensic Psychiatry/Criminal Litigation Involving Mental Disorder or Brain Injury

688
Mental capacity of defendants and witnesses
Mental health review tribunal options
Mentally disordered offenders and psychiatric defences

Forensic Psychiatry/Medico-Legal Work

227
All areas of criminal psychiatric assessment
Compensation following injury
Expert witness reports and giving evidence
Medical negligence
Other professional negligence and litigation

Forensic Psychology

384
Accident investigation
Children
Educational issues
Personal injury (psychological aspects, social, domestic and employment sequelae)
Post-traumatic stress
Trauma – psychological aspects

711
Brain injury – MUA claims, personal injury
Child custody
Dementia
Diminished responsibility
Dyslexia and learning disability
Impaired intellectual functioning

964
Diminished responsibility
Disputed confessions
Fitness to plead
Post-traumatic stress disorder
Sexual offending assessment

1120
Assessment and treatment of criminal behaviour
Clinical and criminal liability
Evaluation of witness statements
Post-traumatic stress disorder
Problems of abnormal behaviour

1873
Capacity
Criminal
Defence
Disability
Risk

Forensic Science

118
Alcohol – blood/urine/breath determinations and calculations
Comprehensive forensic examination
Criminalistics (erased numbers recovery, tyreprint examination)
Criminalistics (footwear impressions, instrument marks, paint, glass)
Dangerous drugs and toxicology
Explosions and explosives – fires
Fibres
Fingerprints
Handwriting

490
Alcohol technical defences (back calculations)
Footwear marks
Glass
Paint
Tool marks

654
Advice on and interpretation of scientific reports
Alcohol-related offences
Footwear impressions
Glass comparisons
Paint comparisons
Tool and instrument impressions

671
Contact traces such as glass and paint
Evaluation of analysis of arson debris
Examining of physical evidence – tool marks, shoe prints and tyre marks

722
Alcohol – including hip flask, laced drinks, back calculations
Documents, alterations and erasures
Drugs
Fibres
Firearms
Footwear marks, impressions
Glass
Instrument marks
Intoximeter testing and breath test interpretation
Paint
Vehicle accidents and reconstruction

867
Blood alcohol
Burglary
Explosion investigation
Fire investigation
Road traffic accident

868
Blood alcohol
Burglary
Explosion investigation
Fire investigation
Road traffic accident

1060
Body fluids, grouping, Deoxriboncleic
Acid (DNA), hairs, plant materials
Drugs and alcohol – drink drive
calculations

1436
Arson and incendiary agents
Explosives traces
Firearms residues
Foot marks
Glass
Paint
Tool marks
Trace contact evidence generally

1616
Analytical investigations

1697
Audio enhancement – analysis –
authentication
Fingerprint examination
Questioned documents and forgery
examinations
Video enhancement

2400
Associates available to cover
handwriting and voice identification
and fingerprints
Contact traces
Controlled drugs
Fire investigations, explosions and
explosives
Footwear impressions and
toolmarks, ballistics
Serious crime cases from murder
downwards

2454
Body fluid analysis (blood etc)
Damage to clothing
Deoxribonucleic Acid (DNA) profiling
General biological evidence
Hair comparison
Textile fibres

**Forensic Studies on
Alcohol/Drugs/Dangerous
Chemicals**

631
Breath tests
Deterioration of shipped and
transported goods
Drink/drive cases
General forensic and chemical
analyses
Prescribed and prohibited drugs
Ships' cargoes

Forensic Systems Analysis

399
All aspects

Forensic Toxicology

843
Alcohol and drug advice
Drug analysis in body fluids
Drug analysis of suspect substances
Employee drug screening
Mass-spectrometric analysis
Road Traffic Acts alcohols (analysis
and opinion)

1618
Alcohol, drugs and poisons: analysis
and interpretation
Clinical toxicology
Employment drug testing

2328
Effects of alcohol and drugs on
humans

2518
Analysis of body fluids for
alcohol/drugs
Control of substances hazardous to
health (COSHH)
Drink driving, back calculations,
intoximeter
Effects of drugs on individuals
Long and short term effects of
chemicals
Work for HM Coroner

**Forensic Trace Evidence/
Examination/Identification**

538
Fingerprints
Footmarks
Handwriting
Toolmarks

Forestry

1074
Amenity valuation of woodlands
Continuous cover forestry
Forest ecology

1303
Contraventions of statute and
planning law
Industrial injuries
Insurance claims – building
subsidence
Third-party injuries or damage

Fork Lift Trucks

504
Cranes
Fork llift trucks
Hoists
Lifts
Miscellaneous lifting equipment
escalators

971
All aspects

Foul Drainage

2214
Reporting on problems with foul
drainage systems

Foundation Engineering

1681
Consolidation
Failures
Ground improvement
Piling
Subsidence

Fracture/Failure of Metal/Alloys

1944
Accidents with ladders and steps
Accidents with tools and gas torches
Identification of eye splinters and
surgically removed metallic bodies
Industrial accidents in metal
manufacturing industries
Product liability claims
Road traffic accidents involving
component failure

Fracture Management

7
Conservative management
Femoral neck fracture
Operative treatments

Fraud

see also Asset Tracing, Forensic
Accountancy

124
Asset tracing
Business purchase
Customs and excise/Value Added
Tax (VAT)
Earnings history
Inland revenue
Insurance claims

133
Fraud investigations

221
All aspects

285
Asset tracing and recovery
Criminal defence
Fraud investigations
Fraud prevention
Money laundering

316
Asset tracing and recovery

360
Forensic accounting
Fraud investigations
Information Technology (IT) fraud

367
Fidelity loss calculations
Fraud investigation

397
Computer fraud
Conspiracy to defraud
Fraud by employees and directors
Fraudulent trading under the
Companies Act
Misappropriation of clients' funds

449
Companies Act breaches
False prospectus
Fraudulent concealment

514
Computer related fraud
Corruption
Financial dishonesty
Securities fraud

624
Fraud investigation

728
Asset tracing
Fraud investigations
Fraud prevention
Money laundering

762
Analysis of accounts and accounting
records
Damage identification

927
Theft/false accounting loss
assessment

928
All aspects

977
Asset tracing
Fraud investigation
Fraud prevention
Money laundering

979
Asset tracing
Companies Act offences
Criminal proceedings
Fraud investigations
Money laundering

1058
Conduct of officers
Investigation of fraud
Prevention of fraud

1079
Fraud investigations

1111
Application of Companies Act
Breach of regulatory codes of conduct
Fraudulent and wrongful trading
Investigations

1202
Investigation
Money laundering
Prevention
Tracing of assets
Tracing of individuals

1284
Fraud investigations (criminal and
    civil)
Fraud prevention

1285
Asset tracing and recovery
Fraud awareness workshops and
    seminars
Fraud investigations
Fraud risk reviews

1286
Asset tracing and recovery
Fraud awareness workshops and
    seminars
Fraud investigations
Fraud risk reviews

1287
Asset tracing and recovery
Fraud awareness workshops and
    seminars
Fraud investigations
Fraud risk review

1288
Asset training and recovery
Fraud awareness workshops and
    seminars
Fraud investigations
Fraud risk reviews

1289
Asset tracing and recovery
Fraud awareness workshops and
    seminars
Fraud investigations
Fraud risk reviews

1290
Asset tracing and recovery
Fraud awareness workshops and
    seminars
Fraud investigations
Fraud risk reviews

1291
Asset tracing and recovery
Fraud awareness workshops and
    seminars
Fraud investigations
Fraud risk reviews

1299
Asset tracing
Fraud defence
Fraud investigations

1317
Detection and quantification
Police liaison

1450
Asset tracing
Fraud investigation
Fraud prevention

1476
All aspects

1495
Asset tracing
Fraud investigation
Litigation support

1636
Commodity fraud
Computer fraud
Defalcation
False accounting
Insider trading
Investment fraud

1673
Corporate fraud

1740
Asset tracing
Fraud investigations
Fraud prevention
Money laundering

1758
Fraud investigation and prevention

1928
Investigations
Tax

2087
Asset tracing
Investigation of fraud in the corporate
    sector
Money laundering

2253
Reporting on small fraud

2263
All aspects

2330
Asset tracing
Fraud investigation
Fraud prevention

2331
Asset tracing
Criminal investigations
Fraud investigations
Fraud prevention
Information Technology (IT) Fraud
    work

2332
Asset tracing
Fraud investigations
Fraud prevention
Information Technology (IT) fraud
    work
Money laundering

2333
Investigations

2477
Asset tracing
Fraud investigations
Information Technology (IT) fraud
    work

Fraud Actions

    2495
    All aspects

Fraud/Corporate Investigations

    1839
    Employee fraud or theft/defalcation
        by directors
    Establish fraudulent preference
    Evidence and quantification of losses
        arising

**Fraud Deterrence Including Computer
Fraud**

    138
    Awareness training
    Development of security policies
    Vulnerability analysis

**Fraud/False Accountancy/
Theft/Financial Irregularities**

    1932
    All Aspects

Fraud/Financial Irregularity

    205
    Establishing of method
    Examination of circumstances
    Fraud prevention
    Information Technology (IT) fraud
        and integrity issues
    Money laundering
    Tracing of assets

Fraud Investigations

    138
    Investment and assembly of evidence
    Liaison with authorities and
        insurance intermediaries
    Money laundering transactions
    Quantification of loss
    Tracing and securing assets

    506
    Asset tracing
    Investigation of the nature of a fraud
    Money laundering
    Recovery of funds
    Statutory/regulatory investigations

    507
    Asset tracing
    Investigation of the nature of a fraud
    Money laundering
    Recovery of funds
    Statutory/regulatory investigations

    2129
    All aspects

Fraud/Loss Investigation

    472
    All Aspects

Fraud/Other Criminal Activities

    1041
    Corruption
    Defalcations, burglary and theft
    Financial services and bank frauds
    General fraudulent activities
    Money laundering
    Trading whilst insolvent

Fraud/Other Financial Irregularities

    1481
    All aspects

Fraud/Regulatory Investigations

1331
Asset protections, tracing and
  recovery
Criminal fraud: prosecution and
  defence
Department of Trade and Industry
  (DTI) investigations
Insolvency investigations
Money laundering and drug trafficking
Pensions
Public sector
Revenue fraud: defence

Fraud Services

76
Asset tracing
Fraud investigation
Fraud prevention

Full Personal Functional Needs Assessment

2084
Care needs
Home adaptations
Physical and psychological
  therapeutic requirements
Preventative intervention
Specialist equipment needs

Fumes

2359
Analysis, testing and provider of
  experts

Functional/Life Quality Assessment

2461
Care needs and costings
Case management
For head and orthopaedic injuries
Home adaptation
Special equipment needs and
  costings

Funfairs/Amusement Park Accidents

971
All aspects

Furniture

1936
Beds
Cabinets
Dining furniture
Fitted furniture
Kitchens
Upholstery

Furniture/Allied Industries

746
Ergonomics
Fitted furniture
Prams and pushchairs
Structures and Standards
Upholstery

Gambling

304
Assessment of gamblers who have
  offended
Pathological gambling and criminal
  offending

Garment Manufacture

850
Failure analysis and fault definition
Pattern assessment
Statistically based inspections
  (including fabric)

Gas

1349
Accident investigation
Appliances
Boiler plant
Carbon monoxide poisoning
Central heating
Distribution
Explosion
Industry
Leakage
Metering
Natural
Pipelines
Pipes
Services
Streetworks
Supply
Utilisation
Warm air heating

2359
Analysis, testing and provider of
  experts

Gas Engineering

2225
Carbon monoxide poisoning
Gas meter fraud
Gas transmission and distribution
  systems/practice (NG/LPG)
Gas utilisation and appliance
  servicing (NG/LPG)
Heating appliance malfunctions
  (including solid fuel)

Gas Utilisation

673
Appliance design and product liability
Compliance with regulations and
  standards
Investigations of fires, explosions,
  fatalities
Quality control and industrial process
  plant
Safety of gas installations
Ventilation and flues

Gastroenterologist/General Physician

1494
Inflammatory bowel disease
Pancreatic disease (especially
  cancer)
Psychological complications of
  organic disease

Gastroenterology

179
Achalasia
Bowel disorders
Endoscopy, perforation accidents
Gastrointestinal endoscopy
Oesophageal disease and strictures

907
All aspects

1444
Diseases of oesophagus, stomach,
  intestine, and pancreas
Gastrointestinal endoscopy
Nutritional disorders

1793
Endoscopy (diagnostic)

Gastroenterology/Liver Disease

1675
Alcohol
Colitis
Gastrointestinal cancer
Hepatitis
Liver biopsy
Peptic ulcer

Gastroenterology Medical

2248
Endoscopy
Inflammatory bowel disease
Malabsorption

Gastrointestinal Disease

2067
Abdominal surgery
Colonic, rectal and anal disease
General surgery
Hernias
Non-orthopaedic injury

Genealogy

829
Probate research

General Criminal Work

1280
All aspects

General Medical Practice

137
All aspects

158
Occupational health
Personal injury

336
Complaints
Steroid litigation
Terms of service

381
Medical negligence

473
Medical negligence
Personal injury
Professional negligence

559
Family planning
General practice education
General practice obstetrics

597
Cardiology
Erectile dysfunction
Preparation of medical reports from
  General Practitioner's expert point
  of view

1089
All aspects

1154
Medical accidents
National Health Service organisation
Occupational health
Personal injury
Pharmacology
Professional negligence

1259
All Aspects

1718
Complaints and negligence

2121
All aspects

General Medical Practice/Negligence

1989
Personal injury

General Medicine

34
Diabetes
Endocrinology
Impotence (male erectile dysfunction)

141
Diabetes
Endocrinology
Metabolism

846
Diabetes
Drug interactions
Geriatric medicine
Heart and lung diseases
Immunological medicine and Aids
Intensive care medicine

933
Cardiology
Gastroenterology
Liver disease
Respiratory diseases

1048
Diabetes mellitus
Endocrinology

1066
All aspects

1117
Anticoagulation
Drug reactions
Hypertension
Sarcoidosis
Stroke
Systemic lupus erythematosus

1163
Clinical allergy
Thoracic medicine (non-invasive)

2012
Connective tissue diseases, including
  systemic lupus erythematosus and
  sytemic sclerosis
Raynauds disease
Vibration White Finger

2108
Medicine

2451
Acute and medical emergencies

2515
Acute medicine
Hypertension

General Medicine/Elderly Care

254
Aspects of long term care
Care in nursing homes
Dementia
Negligence of elderly people

General Medicine/Haematology /Transfusion

993
Bone marrow transplantation
HIV and AIDS, and infection in
  general
Haemophilia and bleeding disorders
Leukaemia
Problems with transfusion of blood
  products
Thrombosis

General Practice

542
Criminal
Medical negligence

765
All aspects

1195
General practice

1214
All aspects

General Practice/Hospital

1835
Medical litigation/Medico-legal reports

General Practice Litigation

258
Women's health and family planning

Genetics

1770
Evaluation of Deoxribonucleic Acid
  (DNA) carried out in forensic cases

1791
Embryology
Malformation syndromes
Medical management of inherited
  disease
Mental handicap
Pre-natal diagnosis

2363
Deoxribonucleic Acid (DNA) evidence

Genetics Markers in Problems of Identification

1418
Blood grouping
Deoxribonucleic Acid (DNA) profiling
Incompatible blood transfusions
PCR-based testing (eg STR systems)
Paternity testing
Stain identification

Genital Surgery

1634
Genital surgery
Penile surgery
Scrotal surgery
Testicular surgery
Vasectomy
Vasectomy reversal

Genito-Urinary Medicine

1731
AIDS/HIV
Erectile dysfunction (impotence)
Sexually transmitted diseases

Genito-Urinary Surgery/Injury/Disease

816
Impotence
Injury, cancer, surgery and disease
  of kidneys, bladder, prostate, penis
  and testes
Male fertility
Urinary incontinence (male)
Vasectomy/vasectomy reversal

Genito-Urinary Surgery/injury/Disease

2521
Infertility
Prostates – testes – kidneys
Stones
Tumours
Urine infection

Geotechnical

1338
Environmental
Foundations
Ground contamination
Landfill

1750
Foundation design
Site appraisals
Soil mechanics

2501
Contaminated ground
Foundations
Piling
Retaining walls ground anchors
Slope stability

2531
Landform interpretation
Maps and aerial photographs

Geotechnical Engineering

69
Interpretation of ground conditions
Slope stability
Soil and rock engineering

372
Foundations
Methane gas and soil contamination
Old mineshafts and workings
Structural property surveys
Subsidence

493
Chalk in foundations and earthworks
Foundation engineering and piling
Ground treatment
Landslips, slope stability and
  stabilisation
Site investigation
Subsidence and heave investigation

582
Slope stability
Soil mechanics

1281
Forensic engineering
Foundation design
Site investigation

1499
Earthworks
Foundations
Geosynthetics
Site investigations

1517
Erosion and flooding
Excavations, earthworks and
  retaining structures
Foundations, settlement, subsidence
  and land instability
Piling engineering and testing
River and coastal engineering
Slopes, landsliding

1672
Building foundation problems
Environmental engineering
Site investigation
Slope stability
Subsidence

1909
Computer software
Geology
Geosynthetics
Geotextiles
Minerals planning applications

2025
Earthworks
Foundations
Geosynthetics
Site investigations

2141
Earthwork design
Foundation design and performance
Site investigations
Slope stability and landslides

2388
Earthquake engineering
Foundations and substructures
Geoenvironmental engineering
Geological engineering
Landslips
Piling
Subsidence

Geotechnical/Foundation Engineering

2301
Earthworks and ground improvement
Engineering geology
Landslips and slope stability
Pile design and construction
Retaining wall performance
Subsidence prediction and analysis

Geriatric/General Medicine

1323
Cardiovascular disease in ageing
Dizziness
Driving and cardiovascular disease
Driving and the elderly
Falls
Syncope

Geriatric Medicine

470
Dementia
Disability
Nursing homes
Rehabilitation
Stroke

487
Acute/long-term medical/nursing care
  of elderly patients

1017
Acute medical case of the elderly
Continuing care of the frail elderly
  person
Rehabilitation after medical and
  surgical illness in the elderly

1114
Consent to treatment
Fitness to plead
Medical problems of old age
Mental problems in old age
Personal injury in the elderly
Physical disability in old age
Testamentary capacity

1830
Acute medical care of elderly
Assessment of disability
Domiciliary assessment
General rehabilitation of elderly

1904
Dementia

2563
Disability and rehabilitation in old age
Muscle and exercise physiology in
  old age

Geriatric/Medicine/Old Age

145
Abuse (physical or financial)
Alzheimers disease
Falls
Investigation and treatment
Mobility problems

Glass/Glazing

70
Curtain walling and building facades
Design and use
Domestic and commercial double
  glazing
Glass accidents
Glass products and performance
Windows and installations

Glass/Glazing Accidents

971
All aspects

Glass/Glazing/Mastics/Sealants

252
Defective windows and doors
Failures of double glazing units
Glass fractures, defects and injuries

Glass Manufacture

1396
Annealing – continuous, batch,
  toughening
Forming processes
Melting furnaces
Processing – cutting, coating,
  polishing, decorating
Raw materials – suitability

Glass Product Failure

1396
British Standards, codes of practice,
  legislation
Failure and fracture analysis

Glass Product Performance

1396
Domestic tableware
Ovenware
Products from common glass types
Release of toxic materials
Suitability for use
Technical ware including laboratory
  ware

Golf Project Development

903
Consultancy (including appraisal)
Golf architecture
Golf construction project
  management

Goods Vehicles/Technical/Operation

556
Certificate of professional
  competence
Goods vehicle accident investigation
Goods vehicle technical reports
Operator licensing and public
  inquiries
Operator licensing appeals to
  transport tribunal
Tachograph and drivers' hours

Grassland Management

1167
All aspects of grassland production
  and output
Damage assessment to grass ley
Losses from livestock damage –
  defective equipment

Ground Engineering

826
Foundation engineering and
  subsidence
Geotechnical engineering
Ground investigations
Piling
Retaining structure
Slope stability

2261
Foundations
Geology
Geotechnical engineering
Ground conditions
Landslides
Slope stability

Ground/Foundation Engineering

2305
Basements, including water
  penetration
Earth retaining structures
Forensic investigations
Foundation engineering
Ground floor slabs, including screeds
Ground treatment (grouting,
  vibroflotation, dynamic compaction)
Piling
Slopes
Soils

Ground/Ground Water Problems

646
Disputes relating to ground and
  ground water conditions
Flooding
Foundation failures
Safety/personal injury/negligence
Site investigation problems
Subsidence and heave
Unstable ground and landslips

Gynaecological Surgery

96
General and advanced diagnostic
  and therapeutic laproscopy
  including sterilisation and keyhole
  surgery (endoscopic surgery)
General gynaecological surgical
  complications

464
Minimally invasive surgery
Sterilization

Gynaecology

249
Contraception
General (NOT minimal access)
Subfertility

269
All medical and surgical areas (NOT
  endocrinology and advanced
  endoscopic surgery)

311
General gynaecological surgery
Gynae oncology
Minimal access gynaecological
  surgery

458
General gynaecological laparoscopy
  (inclucing sterilisation) but NOT
  advanced endoscopic surgery

587
Ectopic pregnancy
General gynaecology
Gynaecological surgery
Hysterectomy
Ovarian tumours
Sterilisation

856
Advanced prolapse repair and pelvic
  surgery

954
General gynaecology
Laparoscopy (but NOT advanced
  minimal access surgery)

976
Endoscopic (endometrial) surgery
Fertility – contraception
Fibroids
Hysteroscopy
Infertility
Menstrual disorders

1009
Gynaecological infection
NOT cancer surgery and NOT
  advanced endocrinology)
Premalignant disease and
  colposcopy (but NOT advanced
  laparoscopic surgery

1371
Abnormal cervical cytology
Colposcopy
Gynaecological cancer
Laparoscopic surgery

1373
General gynaecological
  laparoscopy/NOT advanced
  endoscopic surgery
General gynaecological surgery

1479
Hysteroscopic
Infertility
Recurrent miscarriages
Surgical procedures – laparoscopic

1625
Colposcopy/cytology
General surgery
Laparoscopic (minimal access)
  surgery
Oncology

1691
Special interest in
  urogynaecology/urinary tract injury

1711
Colposcopy
General gynaecology
Hysteroscopic techniques
Laproscopy (general)

1828
General gynaecological operations,
  including laparoscopy but NOT
  endoscopic surgery
Infertility, especially acquired sterility
Sexual abuse

2102
Advanced laparoscopic surgery
Endoscopic surgery including
  hysteroscopy and endometriac
  resection
General gynaecological surgery

2172
Cervical screening
Gynaecological oncology (cancer)
Gynaecological surgery

2203
Family planning (including
  sterilisation)
Therapautic termination of pregnancy

Gynaecology including gynaecological oncology

2318
All aspects

Gynaecology/Obstetrics

225
Abortion
Fertility and sterility
Genito-urinary medicine/surgery
Hysterectomy
Intra-uterine contraceptive devices
Rape

676
All aspects

1559
Abortion and sterilisation operations
Family planning
General gynaecology
NOT minimal invasive surgery
NOT specialised gynaecological
  oncology
Obstetrics

Haematology

439
Leukaemia
Lymphoma
Myeloma

993
Bone marrow transplantation
HIV and AIDS, and infection in
  general
Haemophilia and bleeding disorders
Leukemia
Problems with transfusion of blood
  products
Thrombosis

1116
Anaemias
Leukaemias, lymphomas
Thrombosis and haemorrhage

Haematology/Blood Transfusion

2505
All aspects

Haematology (Clinical/Laboratory)

2145
Blood transfusion and
  immunohaematology, including
  transfusion reaction, haemolytic
  disease of newborn
Laboratory haematology, including
  accreditation of haematology
  laboratories
Treatment and management of blood
  disorders

Hair Damage/Scalp Injury

1739
Damage from bleaching, highlighting,
  perming, straightening
Discoloration from tinting and dyeing

Hair/Scalp

569
Chemical treatments to the hair/scalp
Hair transplanting

Hair/Scalp Conditions

1999
Bleaching
Chemical relaxed processes
Hair extension processes
Micro-surgical hair transplantation
Permanent colouring using para-dyes
Permanent waving

2480
Diagnosis and recommended
  treatments where applicable
Hair and scalp damage
Monitoring treatments
Professional negligence in
  hairdressing undertakings

Hair/Scalp Damage Reports

1239
Allergic reactions
Alopecia caused through trauma
Colour damage
Perm damage
Relaxer (straightening) damage
Scalp burns (including chemical)

Hair/Scalp Problems/Litigation

111
Expert witness reports and court
appearances
Hair and scalp damage/trauma
Hair loss problems
Hairdressing negligence/litigation
Medical negligence
Transplants

Hair/Scalp-Trichology

591
All cases of hair and skin damage
Photography
Plaintiff and defence reports
Problems arising from transplants,
wigs, extensions, hairpieces

Hairdressing/Industrial/Commercial Accidents

2401
Expert Witness in the field of litigation
Fitting and removal of hairpieces and
wigs
Manufacture of hairpieces and wigs

Hand Injuries

1613
Mainly for plaintiff
Repetitive Strain Injury (RSI) [or
work-related upper limb disorders
(WRULD)]
Trauma

2568
All aspects

Hand Surgery

617
Scarring of the hand
Soft tissue injuries including nerve,
tendon and nail injuries

1534
Acute soft tissue trauma of upper
limb (not brachial plexus)
Burns of upper limb, acute and
chronic management
Dupuytren's contracture

2422
Finger and hand injuries
Microvascular surgery
Soft-tissue injuries (including nerves)

Hand/Upper Limb/Plastic Surgery

112
Hand and upper limb injuries
Plastic surgery and burns
Work-related upper limb disorders

Handwriting

213
Document compilation for court
evidence
Document examination
Malicious messages
Script
Signatures

1922
Authentication of disputed writings
and signatures
Cheques and credit agreements
Claim forms
Custody records
Police notes and statements
Wills

Handwriting Analysis

800
Altered entries
ESDA testing
Handwriting identification
Questioned signatures

930
Behavioural profiling
Comparison and examination of
handwriting and signatures
Court and tribunal witness
Forensic handwriting expert
Questioned document examiner
Scientific analysis of disputed
documents

1927
Compatibility assessment
Personnel recruitment and
management selection
Positive vetting for security
Verification of documents
Vocational aptitude

2045
Disputed handwriting
Document examination

Handwriting Disputes

650
Comparison of handwriting on
cheques and credit card fraud
Historical handwriting examination
Identification of authorship of
threatening letters
Identification of fraud in handwriting
on legal documents
Identification of fraud in handwriting
on personnel/company records and
legal documents
Signature authentication on wills,
mortgage and legal documents

Handwriting Expert

1384
Extensively equipped laboratory
including ESDA
Questioned and anonymous
handwriting to establish authorship

Handwriting Expert/Forensic Document Examiner

2492
Faxes, photocopies and
computer-generated documents
Handwriting and signature
identification and comparison
Investigation of alterations and
erasures
Paper and printing problems
Typewriting

Handwriting/Signature Identification/Comparison

1890
All Aspects

Head Injury

894
Epilepsy
Headache
Memory impairment
Post-traumatic syndromes
Psychological states

Head injury/brain injury

1094
All aspects

Head Injury leading to Physical/ Intellectual Incapacity/Hemiplegia

1209
Civil litigation

Head/Neck Surgery

2026
Facial skin cancer
Microvascular surgery
Oral cancer

Health/Safety

see also Industrial Accidents,
Machinery

1
Asbestos
Chemicals at work
Foodstuffs
General chemistry
Pollution/contamination
Road traffic

5
Incident investigation
Repetitive Strain Injury (RSI)
questions and investigations
Safety regulatory compliance
Staff relaxation plans and projects

40
Inadequate lighting
Lifting injuries and lifting equipment
Machinery or equipment (inc kitchen
equip) or inadequate (inc guarding)
Product liability or
quality/sub-standard product

74
Assessment of compliance with
safety requirements
Evaluation of events leading to injury
or death

99
Construction (design and
management) regulations
Control of Substances Harzardous to
Health (COSHH) regulations
Electricity at work regulations
Environmental Protection Act
Sick building syndrome

149
Asbestos-related problems
Asthma-occupational/
non-occupational
Chest injury following Road Traffic
Accidents (RTA)
Inhalation injury
Mesothelioma
Testing failed alcohol breath test

154
Health and safety at work and its
enforcement/claims

159
Construction accidents

234
CE marking
Lifting equipment
Machinery safety systems
Pressure systems

245
All aspects except radiation

310
All aspects

327
Asbestosis and mesothelioma
Asthma
Dermatitis
Dust and fume
Hazardous substances
Smoking and health

358
Industrial injury and accident
  investigation
Risk assessment

396
Asbestos
Construction industry accidents
Exposure to hazardous
  substances/exposure controls
Machinery safety
Manual handling/work related upper
  limb disorders
Noise exposure and occupational
  deafness
Road traffic accidents/vehicle
  inspections
Slips, trips, falls

480
Safety of chemicals in the workplace
Safety of cosmetics, consumer
  products
Safety of household products

671
All aspects

707
Health and safety legislation in the
  building and construction industry
Measurement and evaluation of
  construction works
Professional negligence actions
  relating to construction professionals
Project management and project
  co-ordination
Quantity surveying
children's play areas and equipment

786
Accident investigations
Enforement action
Manual handling investigations
Policy documentation
Risk assessment

809
Accident investigation
Application of statutory legislation at
  work
Brewing industry – working in
  confined spaces
Personal injury claims arising from
  ill-health or accidents at work
Personal injury claims from
  industrial/manufacturing/construction
  situations
Safety of manufacturing machines
  and processes
Welding, soldering, paint-spraying,
  solvents etc

882
Control of thermal environment at
  work
Control of workplace pollution
Health effects of workplace
  environments
Ventilation of workplaces
Worker exposure to substances
  hazardous to health

971
All aspects

1084
Chemical analysis
Control of Substances Hazardous to
  Health (COSHH) risk assessments
Dust
Noise
Personal protective equipment
Toxic fumes/gases

1092
All aspects

1189
Consumer safety

1388
Accident investigation
Risk assessment
Safe systems of work
Safety management
Safety procedures design
Workplace inspections

1461
Dermatitis
Dust and fume control
Hazardous substances
Safety of access and work
  environment
Safety of machines
Stairs, ladders and walkways

1475
Contractural obligations
Costing
Health and safety, procedures,
  regulations
Personal injury accidents
Site management procedures
Temporary works

1693
All aspects

1741
Chemical reactions – deterioration of
  materials
Container failures
Exposure – acute effects and
  precautions
Plant, equipment failures
Product liability aspects
Public liability aspects

1792
All aspects

1811
Construction Engineering

1895
Contaminated land
Explosives application and use
Industrial pollution
Manual handling
Materials handling
Noise and vibration
Occupational health and
  environmental hygiene
Personal protective equipment
Repetitive Strain Injury (RSI) and
  upper limb disorders
Road traffic accident reconstructions
Slips, trips and falls

1946
Accident investigation
Policy and management
Prosecution defence
Risk assessment
Safety audits

1985
Education
Leisure
Local government
Steel industry

2265
Industrial accident/injury
Occupational health
Personal accident/injury
Protective equipment failure
Public health
Risk management

2359
Analysis, testing and provider of
  experts

2368
All aspects

2388
All aspects

2396
1992 Health and Safety Regulations
Construction (Design and
  Management) Regulations

2437
Adhesives
Industrial safety – chemicals and
  materials
Paints and coatings – general and
  emulsion paints (speciality)
Polymers and resins, including
  applications
Textile and paper treatments
Toxicity of chemicals (non-medical
  aspects)

2506
Industrial accidents
Legal aid cases
Negligence
Personal injuries
Repetitive strain injuries
Safe practices of work

2530
Audits and reviews
Management of health and safety
Research and advice
Risk assessments
Safety policies, systems and
  procedures

2544
Audit inspections
Hazard analysis
Reports in mitigation
Training

Health/Safety/Accident Investigation

594
Construction industry
Machinery accidents
Manufacturing industries
Occupational ill health – asthma, skin
  disease, Repetitive Strain Injury
  (RSI), deafness
Service industries including transport
Slipping, access, manual handling

Health/Safety/Accidents

1522
Accident investigations – road traffic,
  transport
Control of Substances Hazardous to
  Health (COSHH) assessments
Engineering analyses – equipment
  faults
Industrial diseases
Industrial injuries and accidents

Health/Safety at Work Act

1461
British Standards
Guidance and approved codes of
practice
Industry recommendations
Labelling requirements
Legislative requirements
Training and instruction

Health/Safety Litigation/Transport

2335
Accidents at work
Chemical handling and transportation
Expert witness
Fork-lift truck/warehouse litigation
reports
Safety of loads (reports for counsel)
Transport of dangerous goods

Health/Safety Management

1864
Accident investigations, reports and
opinion
Appeals against notices issued by
Health and Safety Executive and
Environmental Health Officers
Manual handling injuries
Personal injury

Health/Safety/Marine/Mechanical/ Industrial

552
Access equipment – ladders,
scaffolding etc
General machinery damages or
defect investigation
Litigation reports and expert witness
Metal and woodworking machinery-
personal injury
Noise exposure – tests and advice
Personal injury – plant, tools and
equipment

Health Care Generally

1063
Care in the community
Costs of care generally
Health/nursing care in Europe
Health/nursing care in North America
Personal injury and insurance reports
Professional nursing negligence

Health Service Management

2116
Regional health authority
Trust management

Hearing/Tinnitus/Balance Disorders in Children/Adults

1903
Birth related hearing disorders, noise
induced hearing loss
Head injuries
Whiplash injuries

Heating

983
Air conditioning and ventilaation
Boilers and boiler plant
Engineering plant
Heating
Hot and cold water services
Steam and condensate

1749
Air conditioning
Appointments and contracts
Commissioning and handover
Controls and building management
systems
Energy conservation
Heating and hot water

1831
Boilers
Central heating
Gas systems
Pumps
Radiant heating
Warm air heating

1876
Air conditioning and ventilation
systems
Control systems
Domestic hot and cold water systems
Electrical distribution systems (airing
and equipment)
Heating systems (small and large
scale)
Mechanical systems (including
compressed gas networks)

Heating Appliances

547
Building fabric construction
Energy usage throughoout the
building
Heating appliances – gas, oil and
solid fuel
Plumbing installations
U valve calculations

Heating/Domestic/Commercial

2245
Boiler examinations
Carbon monoxide poisoning
investigations
Investigations into reported defects

Heating/Flues/Chimneys/Plumbing/ Environmental Matters

2092
Chimney and flues and all fuels
Damp and dampness problems
Environmental matters
Heating systems and heating
appliances – all fuels
Plumbing – hot and cold water etc
Ventilation

Heating Installations

1869
Combustion gases, fluing and venting
Condensation problem
Design fault diagnosis
Quantum and reports
System failure investigations
Workmanship appraisals

Heating/Plumbing Engineering

622
Alternative dispute resolution
Arbitration
Environmental Protection Act actions
Housing Act – breaches
Landlord and tenant claims
Litigation

Heating/Ventilation

1931
Air conditioning
Building services engineering
Claims
Commercial, industrial and domestic
heating and ventilation
Compressed air
Control of noise
Gases
Heating
Inspections
Procurement routes
Steam and condensate
Ventilation
Water services

Heavy Civil/Structural Engineering; Building; Petrochemicals

1049
All aspects

Heavy Goods Vehicle Operation

640
Giving evidence in court
Health and safety
Operational and statutory
requirements
Personal injury
Planned maintenance
Professional negligence

Height Evaluation

2474
Determine heights of suspects from
security camera film/Closed Circuit
Television (CCTV)

Helmets

1612
Biomechanics of head injuries
Horse riders' helmets
Industrial helmet performance
Motorcycle helmet performance

Hepatobiliary Surgery

2292
Damage to bile ducts
Other complications of
cholecystectomy
Portal vein damage

High-Rise Building Accidents

1968
Operators using rope techniques,
abseiling/jumars

Highway Authorities

798
Duties, policies and practices of
authorities
Highway and road maintenance
systems
In-house advice on climatology and
meteorology
Road conditions due to weather

Highway Engineering

335
Earthworks design
Highway design
Pavement design
Planning matters relating to above
Road construction
Traffic engineering

826
All aspects of urban highway
　engineering
Contracts, detailed design and
　contract preparation
Feasability studies including route
　location, environmental and
　economic appraisal and public
　consultation
Safety audits

2387
All aspects

2388
Bridge design and maintenance
Envrionmental appraisal
Highway design and maintenance
Transport planning

Highway Improvements

942
Assessing traffic implications
Compliance with BS 5489
Compliance with the Department of
　Transport's design criteria for public
　highways
Determining minimum land take
　requirements

Highway Maintenance

826
Block paving
Claims against the highway authority
Construction and maintenance
　materials
Obstructions within the highway
Signs and bus shelters
Winter maintenance

2462
Accidents related to highway defects
Defects causing accidents to
　pedestrians
Defects causing accidents to vehicle
　users
Management of highway
　maintenance
Obligations and practices of highway
　authorities
Standards of highway maintenance

Highway Maintenance/Management

985
Highway surfacing, reconstruction
　and associated contracts
Load construction materials and
　processes
Winter maintenance management

Highway/Traffic Engineering

115
Highway engineering
Infrastructure planning
Traffic engineering
Transportation planning

582
Highway design and capacity
Highway safety
Planning inquiries and appeals
Traffic data collection and analysis
Traffic generation studies
Traffic impact assessments
Traffic modelling

1203
Advising private and public sector
　clients on development proposals
Design of on- and off-site highway
　and drainage infrastructure
Preparation of environmental
　assessments
Preparation of specifications and
　contract documents
Preparation of traffic impact
　assessments
Site supervision

Highways

503
Highway design
Responsibilities of highway authorities
Road safety
Traffic engineering
Traffic impact

985
Engineering advice on Highway Law

Highways/Buildings/Structures

1271
Dampness/cracking/decay
Failures
Fire damage/repair
Floor slabs/pavements
Retaining walls
Settlement/subsidence/underpinning

Highways, Assessment of

2387
All aspects

Histopathology

393
Cardiac (heart) pathology
Lung pathology

2118
General diagnostic histopathology
　and cytopathology
Post-mortem examination

Histopathology/Cytopathology

237
Breast cytology
Cervical cytology
Malignant melanomas
Testicular tumours
Urological pathology

Hoists

504
Cranes
Escalators
Fork lift trucks
Hoists
Lifts
Miscellaneous lifting equipment

971
All aspects

Home Care

494
Costing and care during recovery
Home nursing-care – on-going care
Housekeepg services costing of
　commercial help

Horse

see also Equestrian

Horticulture/Arboriculture/Crops

2470
Assessment of quantum for crop
　failure or loss
Contamination of soils and composts
Herbicide and pesticide damage
Personal injury and health and safety
Pollution affecting crops and the
　environment
Tree surveys and inspection, tree
　root damage

Horticulture/Landscape

1098
Commercial landscape litigation
Envrionmental/product liability
Insurance claims assessments
Landscape environment impact
Private garden litigation
Professional negligence of
　landscape/garden contracts
Public inquiries
Valuations of contractual works

Horticulture/Plant Pathology

2028
Brassicaceae
Environmental stresses especially
　cold and damage
Plasmodisphorc brasical
Powdery mildews
Rhododendron

Hotel Development

1207
Hotel planning disputes
Hotel valuation
Market and feasibility appraisals
Proof of need assessment
Site appraisals
Technical services disputes

Hotel Investment/Finance

1207
Business planning
Financial due diligence
Financial viability appraisal
Project financing

Hotel Operations

1207
Food and beverage operations
Hotel operational audits
Leisure centre/club operations
Management contract disputes
Sales and marketing
Staffing requirements

Household Consumption/Living Standards

1738
Financial costs of child rearing

Household Goods

2031
Bicycles
Ceramicware
Cool bags/vacuum flasks
Furniture
Gym equipment
Leisure products

Housing

866
Housing alterations and extensions
Sheltered homes, special needs
  groups

1984
Housing association
New build and rehabilitation
Private
Self help

2430
Boundary disputes
Building defects
Professional negligence re surveys
  and valuations

2544
Agency services
Compulsory purchase orders,
  clearance and demolition orders
Disrepair (landlord and tenant,
  Housing Acts and Defective
  Premises Act)
Renewal area declaration
  reports/area house condition
  surveys
Renovation grant procedures
Statutory nuisance

Housing Accommodation for Disabled People

669
Acting for plaintiff or defendant
Adequacy of existing housing for the
  injury
Assessment of housing needed in
  'the ordinary course of events'
French language cases
Housing needed for the injury
Various cost solutions in a 'shopping
  list'

Housing Adaptation/Design

1177
Agent for disabled facilities grant
  applications
Proposals in conjunction with
  architects

Housing Disrepair

1327
Disrepair under section 11 of the
  Landlord and Tenant Act 1985
Personal injury
Statutory nuisance
Unfit housing

Housing Disrepair/Condensation/ Mould Growth

524
Fitness for human habitation
Inspections and reports on condition,
  schedules of work
Statutory nuisance

Housing Disrepair/Dampness

549
Breach of repairing obligations
Dampness diagnosis
Energy audits
Overcrowing/HMDs/fire safety
Statutory nuisance
Unfitness assessments

2473
Breach of repairing obligations
Houses in multiple occupation
Overcrowding
Property inspections
Statutory nuisance
Unfitness assessments

Housing Disrepair/Landlord/Tenant

1064
Breach of repairing obligation
Dampness diagnosis
Fire safety
Housing in multiple occupation
Overcrowding
Unfitness assessments

Housing/Environmental Assessments

9
Adaptations to existing property
Advice on the design of
  domestic/residential accommodation
Housing assessment
Liaison with architects/builder
Processing of grant applications
Workplace assessments

Housing/Environmental Health

524
Hazardous building (design and
  materials)
Multi-occupied housing
Overcrowding
Pest control

1658
Accident investigation

Housing for Immigration Purposes

549
Adequacy of accommodation
Overcrowding assessment
Unfitness assessment

1064
Adequacy of accommodation
Overcrowding assessment
Unfitness assessment

Housing Needs of Disabled People

1220
Assessing and quantifying alterations
  and adaptions
Design and management of plaintiffs'
  housing projects
Designing specialised new-build
  housing
Inspecting properties to assess
  suitability
Quantifying additional
  maintenance/Do It Yourself (DIY)
  work

2149
All aspects

Human Food/Agriculture

2490
Chemical and microbiological
  analysis
Environmental
Expert opinion and review of
  documentation
Food poisoning
Quality assurance aspects of
  production and analysis (HACCP)

Human Genetics

1970
Identification of individuals by genetic
  tests (serological, Deoxribonucleic
  Acid [DNA])

Hydraulic Engineering

2141
Flood alleviation and flooding
  compensation
NRA permission and procedures
Pipelines
Pumping stations
River erosion and control
Weirs and river structures

Hydrogeology

271
Contamination investigation
Export review
Groundwater resources assessment
Impact assessment for
  mining/quarrying

Hydrography

713
Dredging
Environmental status
Port operations
Quality of charts and depth surveys
Tides and tidal streams
Writing contracts for hydrographical
  surveys, monitoring and reporting

Hypnotherapy

1466
Appropriate clinical applications

Ice Rink Design/Planning Consultancy

1276
Ski slopes

Ill Health/Environment

991
Ill health arising from substandard
  housing
Ill health resulting from working
  environment

Imagery Analysis

1293
Photogrammetry
Photographic interpretation
Video analysis

Immigration

2473
Adequacy of accommodation reports
Assessment for overcrowding
Fitness for human habitation

Income Loss

see also Employment, Quantum,
  Loss of Earnings

2024
Compensation claims
Dependency claims
Medical negligence
Personal accident

Incontinence

145
Constipation
Faecal incontinence
Incontinence in people with
  disabilities
Urinary incontinence
Use of urinary catheters

Industrial Accidents

see also Relevant Industry,
  Machinery, Health/Safety, Safety

537
Chemical hazards
Dangerous goods transport
Land-use planning for hazardous
  industries
Nuclear safety
Offshore oil and gas
Petroleum refineries

1519
Adherence to regulations/safety
  procedures
Injury in a factory/site environment

Industrial Accidents (Including Building Sites)

40
Component and material failure
  (NOT structural failure)
Falls from ladders, scaffolding and
  access equipment
Inadequate lighting
Lifting equipment and lifting injuries
Machinery or processes defective or
  inadequate (inc guarding)
Tripping and slipping
Unsafe procedures

Industrial Accidents (NOT Road or Chemical), Investigation of

1943
Accidents associated with loading
  and unloading
Accidents associated with moving
  plant
Accidents on building sites

Industrial Disease

49
Beat conditions knee, hand and
  elbow
Industrial asthma
Industrial deafness
Upper limb disorders

Industrial Disputes

49
All Aspects

Industrial Engineering

839
Design
Manufacturing engineering
Oil and gas, on-shore and off-shore
  topsides and production facilities
Painting, lining and coating
Quality assurance and quality control
Water treatment, filtration and
  specialist process equipment

2506
Contractual
Extraction
Manufacturing
Mechanical/electrical
  systems/machinery
Process
Production/machinery loss evaluation

Industrial/Environmental Toxicology

327
All Aspects

Industrial Hazards

6
Chemical spills, including transport
  accidents and corrosive or toxic
  risks
Control of Substances Hazardous to
  Health (COSHH)
Explosion, including blast, missiles,
  flammable atmospheres, runaway
  reactions
Fire, including flammable materials,
  ignition, propagation and toxicity of
  smoke
Hazardous waste – transport,
  storage, handling, treatment
Planning inquiries, Control of
  Industrial Major Accident Hazards
  (CIMAH)
Risk assessment and environmental
  impact assessment

Industrial Injuries

2032
All Aspects

2293
Accidents
Over-use

Industrial Injuries by Gases/Vapours/Dusts

2369
Assessment of pollution abatement
  systems
Assessment of ventilation systems
  for gas removal adequacy
Risk studies for potentially polluting
  or dangerous operations
Toxicity studies of gases, vapours
  and dusts

Industrial Injuries/Noise at Work

637
Compliance with 1989 Noise at Work
  Regulations
Machinery noise and workplace
  environment
Noise at work assessments

Industrial/Mechanical Engineering

683
Accidents at the workplace,
  mechanical
Accidents when using machines
Health and safety
Kitchens: inspections of quality and
  accidents, both commercial and
  private
Lifting and carrying accidents
Slipping, tripping and falling accidents

Industrial Noise Hearing Damage Claims

84
Expert witness – defence and plaintiff
  reports

Industrial/Personal Injury

192
Breach of safety regulations (EC or
  British)
Machinery/equipment malfunction
Machinery/equipment misuse
Product/packaging failure

Industrial Roofing

466
Condensation analysis
Failure investigation
Good practice
Profiled metal
Structural performance
Thermal performance

Industrial Safety

255
Accidents
Contentious technical matters
Doors and physical security of
  buildings
Machine and equipment failures
Manual handling, lifting equipment
Personal injury
Woodworking machine accidents

1583
General industrial safety
Lifting equipment – safe use and
  operation
Pressure systems – safe use and
  operation
Test, inspection and certification
  requirements relating to above

2313
Accident prevention
Emergency plans
Maintenance procedures
Operating procedures
Safety management/systems

2403
Accident investigation
Occupational health
Occupational safety
Safety legislation
Safety management

Industrial Storage Structures

1690
Concrete industrial floors
Industrial storage systems

Industrial Tribunals

282
All Aspects

Infection

1930
Antibiotic therapy
Diagnosis and treatment of infection
Gentamicin (aminoglycoside) toxicity
Hospital infection
Post-operative infection
Prevention of infection

Infectious Diseases

1565
Gastroenteritis and food poisoning
Hepatitis
Meningitis
Septicaemia
Viral infections

2204
AIDS
Chemotherapy
Vaccinations and immunisations

Information System Implementation

1773
Project management
Quality standards and quality systems
Supplier evaluation and selection
System performance and technical
review
Tenders

Information Technology

116
Contract negotiation
Dispute resolution
Project management
System performance
System selection
System specification

1532
Business software
Computers
End-user/supplier disputes
Project management
Software applications

1593
Assistance in settlement of computer
disputes
Computer industry commercial
practice
Project management and
implementation

Information Technology/Computer Software/Computer Systems

352
Computer contracts
Software QA
Software design and production
Software project management

Information Technology in Banking

420
Accounting and management
information systems
Computer security
Payments and clearing systems

Inhalation/Traumatic Respiratory Disorders

2483
Chest injuries
Dust diseases of the lung
Occupational asthma

Injuries/Disability Reports

1209
All aspects

Injuries/Transport Accidents

1913
Injury mechanisms
Lorry under run guards
Restraint of load/people in vans and
minibuses

Injury/Disability in Old People

1141
All aspects

Insolvency

147
Company voluntary arrangements

449
Business rescue and viability studies
Directors' conduct
Fraudulent and wrongful trading
Quantification of relevant losses

511
All Aspects

1284
Directors' disqualification/DTI
investigations
Expert witness
Wrongful/fraudulent trading

1957
Corporate reconstructions
Corporate recovery
Corporate viability investigations

1981
Asset recovery and realisations
Asset tracing
Fraud investigations
Insolvency proceedings
Regulatory authority matters

2459
Directors' negligence
Offences under the Insolvency Act

2546
Corporate insolvency – liquidation
and other routes
Forensic accountancy investigation
and report
Personal insolvency – bankruptcy
and voluntary arrangements
Professional negligence – liability
and quantum

Insolvency/Construction Dispute Resolution

1470
All Aspects

Insolvency/Corporate

505
Directors' disqualification
Forensic accounting
Formulating claims against
directors/creditors
Investigation of wrongful trading
claims

Insolvency/Corporate Recovery

316
Directors' disqualification
Professional negligence

Insolvency Investigations

138
Management irregularities
Misappropriation of assets
Tracing hidden or misappropriated
assets

Inspection/Investigation of Wood in Buildings

2288
Assessment of deterioration by
fire/water/decay etc
Assessment of quality of new build,
materials and/or workmanship
Comparison of works with
British/European standards and
requirements
Identification of wood species
In-situ grading for quality and/or
structural strength

Inspection/Preparation of Critical Reports Mainly in Respect of Residential Property

1850
Boundary disputes
Defective buildings/works
Defects in buildings etc as the cause
of personal injury
Professional negligence
Survey inspections and reports on
buildings
Tenants' Sect II claims

Inspection/Testing

1465
Condition monitoring
Inspection of plant and equipment
Non-destructive testing

Instrumental/Control Systems

534
Agricultural machinery
Animal weighing and feed control
Crop drying and storage equipment
Crop weighing and grading
Dairy parlour monitoring and control
Greenhouse environment

Instrumentation/Control/Automation Engineering

1148
Distributed control systems (DCS)
Instrumentation standards
Potentially explosive atmospheres
Process control
Programmable logic controllers (PLC)
Supervision control and data
aquisition (SCADA)

Insurance

5
Claim assessment
Determination of accedence
Loss adjustment
Professional negligence
Quantum
Technical inspections

74
Claim assessment
Professional negligence
Technical inspections

360
Claims for loss of profit including
business interruption

367
Calculation of quantum of claims
Insurance litigation
Property and liabilty claims
Subrogation

457
Claim assessment
Claim audit
Insurance litigation

471
Disclosure
Policy interpretation
Professional standards of brokers
 and intermediaries

511
All Aspects

677
Claim assessment
Investigations – engineering
Plant and component assessment
Refrigeration

742
Life insurance
Mortgage protection

780
Materiality and misrepresentation
Non-marine insurance generally
Professional indemnity
Working of Lloyds of London
 insurance market

977
Claim assessment and audit
Negotiation advice

978
Claim assessment
Claims audit
Insurance litigation

1111
Claims assessment
Claims audit

1202
Accident investigation
Financial status reports
Investigation of suspect claims
Surveillance
Tracing and intervening of witnesses

1284
Claim assessment

1335
Claim compilation and assessment
Insurance litigation
Loss of profits/business interruption

1450
Claims assessment
Fire and loss of profits
Small claims advice

1681
C A R policies
Claim validity
Design/construction defects
Technical issues

1758
Claim assessment
Insurance litigation

1817
UK retail general insurance –
 insurance agency law and practice

1940
Claims assessment reports: plaintiff
 and the defendant insurance
 companies
Insurance litigation

2129
Claim assessment
Insurance litigation

2331
Claim assessment
Claims audit
Insurance litigation

2332
Claim assessment
Claims audit
Insurance litigation

2333
Claim assessment
Insurance litigation

Insurance (Non-Life)/Insurance Broking

1419
Business interruption
Contractors all risks
Fire and perils
Household and other personal
 insurances
Insurance broking
Liability (employer's, public and
 products)
Motor (including motor trade)
Theft
Transit

Insurance Adjuster

1352
Business interruption
Fire losses
Liability claims
Theft/burglary
Transportation damages
Water damages

Insurance Archaeology

769
American law
Insurance history
Insurance policy reconstruction
Lloyd's of London
Policy analysis
Solvency analysis

Insurance/Banking/Other Financial Services

1481
All aspects

Insurance Claims

359
Flood damage – cause and effect
Personal injury caused by hot
 pipes/hot water

397
Allegedly fraudulent claims
Consequential loss
Material loss
Recovery actions

762
Claim assessment
Insurance litigation

Insurance Claims/Quantum

1455
Fraudulent claims
Loss of profits

Insurance Disputes

474
Broker negligence cases
Non-marine broker negligence cases
Non-marine commercial and
 personal lines (UK only)

Insurance Disputes/Commercial

1886
Employers liability
Fire and consequential loss
Indemnities (professional and
 directors)
Motor
Products liability
Public liability

Insurance Disputes/Domestic

1886
Household
Medical
Mortgage indemnity
Motor
Subsidence
Travel

Insurance Investigation

118
Fires
Industrial accidents
Personal injury
Vehicle accident reconstruction

2087
Accident investigation
Investigation of public and
 employers' liability claims

Insurance/Life Assurance

1168
Disputes between brokers and
 insureds ie agency
Disputes between insured and insurer
Insurance brokers professional
 negligence claims
Legal liability claims
Property and life insurance

Insurance Loss Adjusting

1938
Bankers
Business interruption
Civil and structural engineering
Fire investigations
Jewellers block
Liability
Oil and gas
Personal accident
Subsidence
Theft and fraud

2509
Claims assessment for buildings,
 plant and machinery

Insurance/Management of Chattels

2015
Insurance claims, disputes – for
 insurers or insured
Management practice (chattels)
 including insuring
Negligence
Retrospective valuation reports
Storage and handling procedures

Insurance/Personal Injury

1115
Claims assessment
Loss of earnings claims

Insurance/Property/Business Interruption Claims

1028
Professional negligence of loss adjusters

Integrated Overview of Complex Cases

1292
Advising on how to improve quality of medical evidence
Advising on schedule of special damages relating to disabilities
Discussing medical evidence with counsel
Reviewing quality of medical evidence
Selecting an appropriate expert for difficult cases

Intellectual Property

76
Copyright tribunal
Licence of right
Patent infringement claims

514
Conflict of interest
Corruption or misuse of corporate information
Insider trading

712
Authorship of software
Authorship of technical (engineering) papers/reports
Design

721
Licence conditions
Licence negotiations
Licences of right
Patent infringement damages
Patent royalties
Royalties

928
All Aspects

1202
Breach of copyright
Protection of confidential information
Seizure
Use of trade marks

1411
Confidential information on materials (analysis)
Patents: infringement/validity
Patents: obviousness/design development

1481
All aspects

Intellectual Property Disputes

921
Licensing disputes

Intellectual Property/Libel, Enfringement of

205
Damages
Quantification of commercial effect

Intellectual Property/Patent/ Copyright/Registered Design Disputes

2537
All aspects

Intellectual Property/Patents

1451
Mechanisms
Patent searches
Products – consumer
Products – domestic
Products – motor accessory
Products – nursery/juvenile

2526
Non-mechanical equipment

Intellectual Property, Patents

1367
All aspects

Intensive Care

1774
All aspects

Intensive Care Medicine

2451
Complications of intensive care
High dependency care
Intensive care outcomes
Medical and surgical intensive care

Interior Finishes

1321
Suspended ceilings

Internal Medicine

127
Hypertension (blood pressure)
Renal disease

907
All aspects

1112
Accident and industrial illness compensation
Health care negligence
Hospital acute medical illness including intensive care
Occupational illness
Thoracic medicine

1444
All aspects

2150
Medicine

Interview/Statement/Locus Service

2161
Interviewing participants, evaluation of events relating to accidents
Obtaining of witness statements for automobile incidents
Provision of detailed locus diagrams and photographs

Interviewing of Witnesses/Victims/ Suspects

322
Interviewing children
Interviewing people with learning disability
Investigative interviewing
Police interviewing
Training and evaluation of interviewers

Interviews/(Audio/Video Recorded/ Written)/Analysis Assessment of

1211
Interviewee (adult;child) behaviour – verbal/non-verbal
Interviewer behaviour – verbal/non-verbal (form; effects)
Interviewer conduct (observation of legal and official guidance) and information management

Investigation

see also Litigation Support

124
Asset tracing
Business purchase
Customs and excise/Value Added Tax (VAT)
Earnings history
Inland revenue
Insurance claims

958
Criminal defence work
Insurance fraud investigations
Interviews of witnesses (civil and criminal)
Investigation of fraud
Road accident reports (locus and photograhs)
Tracing missing persons

1495
Asset tracing
Fraud investigation
Litigation support

Investigation/Private Investigation Work

2380
Evidence gathering
Statement taking
Surveillance

Investigative Processes/Collated Evidence, Assessment of

1211
Critical episode reconstruction
Multiple-source testimony analysis

Investigators

1100
Accident reconstruction
General investigation
Locus reports
Photography
Witness interviews

Investigatory Services

1924
All aspects of investigatory work
International probate matters

Investment

935
Actuarial practice involving finance
and investment: pension funds
Assessing damages and financial loss

Islamic Law

2037
Family law and succession,
commercial, civil and criminal

Italian Law

823
Civil proceedings
Commercial law
Company law
Insolvency law
Private International law
Property law

Jewellery

451
Damage and identification
Jewellery manufacture
Particular expertise in diamond and
jade
Trade description
Values

2277
Diamond grading
Gem testing
Valuation of jewellery, watches,
silver, antiques, coins
Valuations for probate, insurance,
sale, security

Jewellery/Gems/Valuations

2208
Hallmarking
Identifying gems including testing
Jewellery manufacture
Trade practices
Valuations, theory and practice

Jewellery/Gemstone

1162
Coloured gemstone testing, natural,
synthetic origin
Determination whether damage has
accidental origin or is inherent fault
Diamond certification, grading, testing
Precious metals
Valuation for all purposes

Jewellery Manufacturing

2277
Stock control systems
Stock valuation
Trading standards

Jewellery Retailing

2277
Stock control systems
Stock valuation
Trading standards

Kenya Law of

1489
African customary law
Civil and criminal law and procedure
Land law
Probate and administration

Kidney Medicine/Renal Medicine/ Nephrology

2096
Continuous ambulatory peritoneal
dialysis
General nephrology
Haemodialysis
Hypertension
Kidney transplantation (but not
surgical aspects)
Renal failure

Knitwear Design

170
Copyright
Design for hand-framed production
Design for industrial machine
production
Garment construction methods
Production troubleshooting
Sample cutting
Stitch pattern graphs (including
intarsia and jacquard)

Laboratory Facilities

2135
Chromatography
Light microscopy
Spectroscopy and spectrometry
Thermogravimetry

Laboratory Management

1282
Biotechnology
Microbiology

Laboratory Safety

971
All aspects

Land

1754
Easements
Restrictive covenants
Rights of way
Town planning
Valuations

Land Drainage

1665
Flooding
Water rights disputes

2214
Preparing remedial work proposals
for flooding problems
Reporting on flooding problems

Land Management/Consultancy

2234
Agricultural tenancy issues
Development
Estate/farm management
Milk quota
Rent reviews

Land Restoration Advice

841
For reinstatement of open cast
mining etc
For reinstatement of pipelines etc

Land Surveying

87
Boundary dispute resolution
Calculation of areas and volumes
Engineering surveys
Measured building surveys
Topographical surveys

2261
Boundary disputes
Measured building surveys

Land Transfer/Professional Negligence

1123
Commercial conveyancing
Domestic conveyancing
Office management by solicitors
Office procedures by solicitors

Land Use Planning

2388
Development plan policy
Social and economic analysis

Landfill

271
Design of landfill sites
Hydrogeology of landfill sites

2531
Landfill gas emission
Settlement

Landlord/Tenant

448
Commercial and residential property
dilapidations for tenants and
landlords
Residential property dilapidations
against local authorities

481
All Aspects

486
Arbitration
Independent expert
Lease renewals
Rent reviews

647
Dilapidations
Housing Act claims
Lease renewals
Rent review

772
Commercial – rent reviews, lease
renewals, and schedules of
dilapidations
Residential – valuations, dilapidations

844
Commercial properties
Industrial properties
Leisure properties
Office properties
Retail properties

1308
Lease renewals
New leases
Rent reviews

1439
Car parks
Casinos
Lease disputes
Lease renewal
Motor trade property
Rent review

2131
Compensation
Dilapidations
Eviction

2431
Dispute over diminution in the value
of reversions
Renewals under Landlord and
Tenant Act 1954 Part 2
Schedules of dilapidations

Landlord/Tenant (Commercial)

754
Lease disputes, claims and actions
Rent review disputes and arbitrations
Section 18 dilapidations – diminution
in value actions

Landlord/Tenant/Compensation

1446
Compulsory purchase matters
Dilapidations
Lease renewals
Rent reviews
Service charges
Water Act claims

Landlord/Tenant Disputes

1923
Counterclaims for possession
Disrepair
Statutory nuisance

Landlord/Tenant Disputes (Residential/Commercial)

2554
Damp problems
Defect diagnosis and advice on
remedial work
Interpretation of landlord and tenant
obligations under leases
Interpretation of repairing covenants
in leases
Leasehold dilapidations
Procedural matters under statute

Landscape

1095
Design

Landscape Architecture

469
Heritage landscape
Landscape assessment and
landscape planning
Master planning and development
Open space and recreation
Power industry
Waste management and minerals

1358
All aspects

1952
Derelict land reclamation
Environmental impact assessment
Forestry/forest design
Landscape design
Visual and landscape impact of
development

2387
Environmental assessment
Landscape design
Visual impact assessment

Landscaping

2507
Consumer disputes paving

Laryngology

1305
General laryngology
Voice disorders

Lasers

1183
Laser applications
Laser technology

Law Costs Consultancy Work

1002
Commercial/mercantile
Intellectual property
Medical negligence
Personal injury

Learning Difficulties/Assessment/ Advice

1844
Assessment of psychological
sequelae of neurological damage
(RTA)
Children Act 1989 assessments
Dyslexia and dyspraxia in children
and adults
Special educational needs
Special educational needs tribunals

Learning Difficulties/Impact on Parenting Competence

2463
Assessment of ability to learn
acceptable standards of parenting
skills
Assessment of concepts of parenting
Impact of parental learning difficulties
on children's development
Learning difficulties assessment

Learning Disability

1156
Asperger's syndrome
Assessment of abuse
Assessment of parenting ability
Autism
Communication disorders

Learning Disability/Mental Handicap

462
Disposal/treatability
Disputed confessions
Intelligence
Witness competency

992
Parents with learning disabilities
Sexual abuse of children and adults
with disabilities

Lease Disputes

2202
Dilapidations
Lease renewals
Rent reviews
Schedules of condition
Service charges

Legal Aid Instructions

280
Domestic property failures
Neighbour trespass, nuisance and
damage
Personal injury – defective
pavements/structures
Personal injury – defective roads
Personal injury – site accidents
including scaffolding
Personal injury at place of work

Legal Costs

636
Advising on solicitors' costs and
obtaining reductions
Recoverable costs with specific
regard to commercial litigation and
personal injury
Solicitor and client costs

Leisure Properties/Businesses including Hotels/Licensed Trade

1746
Litigation and disputes in respect of
all leisure properties
Management consultancy, including
feasibility studies and appraisals
Sales and purchases of all types of
leisure properties
Valuation of all types of leisure
property, including hotels and public
houses

Leisure Property

2303
Caravan sites
Caravans – touring and static
Shooting rights

Lending

2432
Clearing bank lending
Contributory negligence claims
Mortgage lending – commercial
Mortgage lending – residential
Recovery and realisation procedures
Securities

Lending/Credit Approval Procedures

845
Corporate loans
Credit analysis and documentation
Foreign bank branch operations
Project financing
Property loans
Relationships with professional firms

Lending Negligence

1891
Best practice
Compliance environments – internal and external
Fraud investigation reporting
Residential and commercial lending

Lending/Retail (including Mortgage)/ Commercial

247
Bank lending
Bank procedures
Mortgage lending (residential, commercial)
Retail banking customer service
Retail banking strategic management

Leukaemia Treatment/Diagnosis

2337
Anaemia
Blood disorders in general
Blood transfusion
Bone marrow transplantation

Licence Applications

2114
Betting offices
Off/on licence premises

Licensed Leisure/Entertainment Property

600
Capital and mortgage values
Chattels and inventory valuation
Damages and negligence claim assessment
Justices licence applications
Rating
Rent review and associated case law

Life Assurance

187
Actuarial aspects of life company management
Quantification of loss as a consequence of bad advice or maladministration

1188
Bad advice under Financial Services Ace (FSA)
Company sales
Demutualisation
Transfers

Life Assurance/Pensions Financial Services

471
Disclosure
Policy interpretation
Professional standards

Lifts

413
Electrical safety

504
Cranes
Escalators
Fork lift trucks
Hoists
Lifts
Miscellaneous lifting equipment

525
All Aspects

971
All aspects

Light Level Determinations

800
All aspects

Lighting/Environment

1853
Light pollution
Obtrusive light from road/sports lighting, floodlighting etc

Lighting Standards/Design

1853
Commercial and industrial lighting
Fundamental and technical aspects of visual perception
National and international standards
Sports lighting
Street and motorway lighting

Lightning Protection

2359
Analysis, testing and provider of experts

Litigation

80
Accidents
Cosmetics
On-site investigation
Paints and polymers
Problem solving
Trading standards

303
Court attendance

359
Commercial industrial public and domestic buildings
Contractual disputes
Defence and plaintiff reports
Design disputes
Installation disputes
Professional negligence

791
Negligence claims
Partnership dissolution claims

914
Business valuation
Loss of profits/business interruption
Other assessments of quantum

1652
Building disputes
Expert witness work
Personal injury (building defects)

2465
Accidents
Cosmetics
On-site investigations
Paints and polymers
Problem-solving
Trading standards

Litigation Support

see also under relevant cause of action eg Construction, Personal Injury and type of support eg Investigation, Forensic Accountancy

74
Affidavits
Counsel cconferences
Legal aid
Pleadings
Quantum
Reports
Scott schedules
Technical inspections

124
Asset tracing
Business purchase
Customs and excise/Value Added Tax (VAT)
Earnings history
Inland revenue
Insurance claims

171
Matrimonial
Personal injury

322
Interviewing children
Interviewing people with learning disability
Investigative interviewing
Police nterviewing
Training and evaluation of interviewers

506
Breach of contract and warranty claims
Business valuation disputes
Insurance claims
Personal injury
Regulatory enquiries
Sale of business disputes

507
Breach of contract and warranty claims
Business valuation disputes
Insurance claims
Personal injury
Regulatory enquiries
Sale of business disputes

972
Assessments of pleadings and statements
Case merit advice to counsel
Comment on other expert opinion
Documentation for discovery
Experienced expert witness
Taking statements/substantiation facts

1292
Advising on how to improve quality of medical evidence
Advising on schedule of special damagesrelating to disabilities
Discussing medical evidence with counsel
Reviewing quality of medical evidence
Selecting an appropriate expert for difficult cases

1311
Animated graphical evidence
Critical path anallysis
Electronic storage and retrieval of data
Forensic engineering
Planning and programming

1331
Database and document
 management
Recovery of data
Secure communications
Visual presentations

1495
Asset tracing
Fraud investigation
Litigation support

1881
Presentation of detailed technical
 analysis for the lay reader
Use of colour diagrams and graphics
 to explain technical issues

2161
Interviewing participants, evaluation
 of events relating to accidents
Obtaining of witness statements for
 automobile incidents
Provision of detailed locus diagrams
 and photographs

2291
Intensive training of lawyers in
 dealing with the press and conduct
 of radio and television interviews
Production, writing, filming, editing of
 medical accidents and personal
 injury videos, used in court as
 evidence based on medical
 background supplied in advance by
 other experts acting on instructions
 of solicitors and their clients

Litigation Support/Forensic Accountancy

277
Fraud
Loss of profits
Negligence

296
Business and share valuations
Loss of profits/business interruption
Matrimonial disputes
Personal injury (loss of earnings)
Professional negligence
Taxation disputes

1988
Compensation of loss of
 trade/earnings
Examination of accounting records
 and accounts
Health care industry
Insurance claims/quantum
Partnership disputes

2551
Business valuations
Loss of profits reports
Matrimonial disputes
Partnership disputes
Personal injury
Share valuations

Litigation Support in Reinsurance Related Disputes

428
Document discovery/treaty
 reinsurance related matters
Expert testimony on market practice
Quantifications of issues in dispute

Liver Diseases

1444
Diseases of liver and bile ducts

Liver Transplantation

2292
All aspects

Lloyd's/Insurance/Reinsurance

1846
Broker/underwriter relationships at
 Lloyd's
Negotiation of American casualty
 business in London market
Run-off reinsurance and reinsurance
 to close

Local Plans

844
Appearance at local plan inquires
Appearance at structure
 examinations in public

Locksmithing

461
Auto security
Forensic locksmithing
Key systems
Product testing
Safes
Technical consultancy

Locomotor System Disorders

1833
Bone and joint trauma
Medical negligence
Soft tissue disorders

Logistics

777
Distribution systems
Inter-modal transport
Loss of use insurance claims
Materials and inventory management
Road transport costs
Road transport operations
Supply chain management
Warehousing

Loss of Career Prospects

926
Education, training and qualifications
Promotion and reputation

Loss of Earnings

see also Employment, Income Loss,
 Quantum

142
Breach of contract
Loss of pension rights
Personal accident

926
Dependency claims
Pay As You Earn (PAYE) earnings
Self employed profits

Loss of Earnings Claims

459
Farmers
Schools/education
Self employed

Loss of Earnings from Personal Injury Quantification of

200
Fraud
Matrimonial disputes
Professional negligence
Tax investigations/back duty

Loss of Earnings Quantification of

2162
Loss of pension entitlement
Loss of profits/business interruption
Loss of salaries/wages

Loss of Earnings Reports/Personal Injury

2340
Deceased
Medical negligence
Road traffic
Workplace

Loss of Income or Value/Examination/ Evaluation of Claims

205
Consequential loss of profits
 following fire or disruption
Extra costs of operation

Loss of Profit

see also Quantum

1636
Breach of contract
Breach of warranty
Business interruption (fire/flood/etc)
Personal injury and fatal accidents
Product failure

Loss of Profit Claims

138
Breach of contract
Business interruption
Fraud, defalcation or misappropriation
Intellectual property, patent and
 copyright infringement
Misrepresentation and warranties

221
Breach of contract/warranties
Fraud or misappropriation
Interruption of business due to fire,
 flood, illness etc
Product failure

1061
Industrial disputes
Personal injury

Loss of Profits/Business Interruption

367
Construction
Environmental
Financial loss
Product liability

Loss of Profits/Earnings

1481
All aspects

Loss of Profits through Business Interruption/Personal Injury

668
All aspects

Loss Prevention/Risk Analysis

671
Design studies
Environmental protection
Fire and explosion protection
Hazard identification and assessment
Process safety
Project and contract management
Risk management
Total safety management

Lung disease

1982
Industrial lung disease
Mesothelioma

Lung Disorders

1132
Asthma related to poor housing
conditions
Chest conditions due to inhalation of
toxins
General asthma management
(hospital or community)

Machine Components

1693
Bearings
Chains
Couplings
Gears
Pistons and rings
Seals

Machine Condition Monitoring

310
Bearing monitoring
Condition monitoring for machinery
maintenance
Rolling element bearing assessment
Rotating machinery condition
monitoring
Vibration and shock measurement

Machine Failure

2388
Design
Maintenance
Manufacture
Operation

Machinery

see also Industrial Accidents,
Health/Safety

1693
Engines
Gearboxes
Mechanical handling equipment
Process plant
Turbines and compressors

Machinery Accidents/Manufacturing Systems

971
All aspects

Machinery for Docks, Harbours/Waterways

1092
Access ramps
Bridges
Flood control
Lock gates
Slipways
Sluices

Magnetic Resonance Imaging

758
Computed Tomography (CT)
Ear, Nose and Throat (ENT) radiology
Musculo-skeletal including trauma
Ultrasound

Management Consultancy

293
Cost/profit improvement
Crisis management
Information systems
Marketing
Mergers and acquisitions
Strategy

Management Systems

1087
ISO9000 type specifications
Quality systems

Manual Handling Accidents

971
All aspects

Manual Handling Operations

1057
Assessment – safe systems of work
Health and social care services
Industry
Stress calculations
Training, trainers, employees

Manufacturing/Commercial Sectors

1041
Chemical and allied industries
Clothing industry
Man-made fibres industry
Textile industries

Manufacturing Engineering

2224
Consumer product defects
Linotype and printing
machinery/process
Machinery defects/disputes
Manufacturing
processes/practices/materials

Manufacturing Machinery

1655
Accidents involving personal injury,
especially on woodworking
machinery
Mechanical and electro-mechanical
failures
Patent infringements

Mapping/Cartography

1393
Contractual disputes and
professional negligence
Evaluation of current and historical
maps as evidence
Geographic information systems
(GIS)

Marine

see also Naval, Ship

671
Cargo containment
Chemical and fire incident
management and investigation
Fire and explosion losses involving
ships and their cargoes
Hazardous and bulk cargoes
Offshore structures and facilities
Salvage arbitration
Transportation of hazardous materials

1616
Cargo damage and personal injury
investigations
Cargo loss and contamination
investigations
Claims assessments and
investigation
Custody transfer
Navigation and charter party disputes
Petroleum oils, petrochemicals and
vegetable oils
Salvage and distressed cargo

2207
Collisions
Founderings
Groundings
Personal injuries
Safe port disputes
Shiphandling

Marine Accidents

1350
Interpretation of facts
Navigational data assessment
Vessels up to 24 metres
(pleasure/fishing/work/sport)

Marine Casualty Investigations

2264
Collisions
Fires on board ships
Groundings
Machinery failures of ships
Ships refrigeration failures
Structural failures

Marine/Coastal/Inland Waters

628
Collisions – casualty – sinkings and
groundings – investigations
Dredging and hydrographic surveys
– pilotage
Jetty construction – moorings and
anchorages
Personal injury claims – health and
safety at work
Ports – docks and harbours –
operation and management
Tugs and towage of ships and crafts

Marine Consultants/Surveyors

1656
Bunker quality disputes
Cargo damage/condition surveys
Charter party and bill of lading
  disputes
Collision and grounding investigations
Hydrographic related work
Investigations into personal injuries
  and fatalities
Liquid cargo loss and contamination
  investigations
On and off hire surveys
Pre-hire condition and suitability
  surveys
Ship damage/condition surveys
Ship description and performance
  disputes
Speed, consumption and
  performance analysis
Stevedore damage assessments
Tank coating condition and suitability
  surveys
Unsafe port disputes
Yacht surveys

Marine Engineering

8
Damage to ship's hull and machinery
Naval architecture

185
Corrosion protection
Damage control (fire fighting, salvage
  pumping etc)
Dock gates
Loading/unloading equipment
Lock gates
Marina, dock, port and harbour
  installations
Maritime electrical installations
Moving bridges
Power generation and distribution
Propulsion equipment
Roll on/Roll off (RORO) facilities
Shore services (water, power, fuel,
  waste)

261
All aspects

332
Casualty investigations (collisions,
  grounding, fire)
Hull and machinery damage
Reefer cargo and plant damage
Ship sale and purchase inspections
  and disputes
Speed, consumption and bunker
  quality disputes

356
Auxiliary and reefer operations
Fuel oil quality claims
Main engine operations
Maintenance and operational
  standards
Speed and consumption calculations

553
Corrosion protection
Damage control (fire fighting, salvage
  pumping etc)
Dock gates
Loading/unloading equipment
Lock gates
Marina, dock, port and harbour
  installations
Marine electrical installations
Moving bridges
Power generation and distribution
Propulsion equipment
Roll on/Roll off (RORO) facilities
Shore services (water, power, fuel,
  waste)

766
Cargo gear failures
Ship performance analysis

1894
Propulsion machinery for medium-
  and high-speed diesel
Small ship auxiliary machinery and
  systems
Small ship power transmission
  machinery

2309
Marine engineering systems and
  equipment
Performance of marine fuels in
  engines
Ship and engine performance

Marine Insurance/Reinsurance

2217
Cargo
Facultative reinsurance
Hull
Treaty reinsurance

Marine/Maritime

1665
Oceanology/oceanography
Offshore safety
Ship hulls (eg VLCCs, bulk carriers,
  dredgers)
Structural engineering

Marine Metallurgy

88
Engineering and structural failures in
  ships
Engineering component and
  structural failures in industry
  (petrochemical and engineering
  plant)

Marine Mutual/P/I Insurance

2469
Cargo damage – port of refuge
  reports
Collision – sinking – grounding
Condition/valuation – damage claims
  and assessment
Coroner's office report
Safe operation of passenger RoRo
  ferries – pilotage
Shipboard personnel injury – loss of
  life

Marine/Nautical

2164
Bulk carrier operations
Casualty investigation – ship and
  cargo (wet and dry)
Charter party disputes
Liquid cargo movements – claims,
  causation, performance
Oil pollution and removal
Tanker operations

Marine Navigations (Master Mariner)

332
Cargo disputes (timber, bulk,
  containers, steel)
Casualty investigations (collisions,
  grounding, fire)
Navigation and meteorology; voyage
  planning
Personal injuries aboard all types of
  ships
Unsafe ports and charter party
  disputes

Marine Operations

1250
Collision investigation
Marine high-speed transportation
Surveys

Marine Safety Including Docks

971
All aspects

Maritime Civil Engineering

2274
Berths for grounding vessels
Marine structures
Piling and foundations
Retaining walls
Steel and concrete structures,
  including bridges

Maritime/Offshore Engineering

280
Abandonment of offshore structures
Construction of sea defences
Dredging
Long sea outfalls
Offshore pipelines
Underwater construction

Market Analysis/Market Dynamics

1145
Evolution of markets
Market behaviour
Market events and specific incidents
The forces driving markets

Marketing

899
Advertising
Agency practice
Client/agency relations
Consumer products
Market research
Survey research

Marketing Consultant

2291
All aspects

Marketing/Social Research

2009
Advertising claims
Consumer information
Employee research
Licensing and planning applications
Passing off (copyright and
trademarks)
Public opinion polls
Surveys (consumer and industrial) or
polls

Martial Arts/Civil Law

775
Fatal accident
Insurance
Personal injury
Professional negligence

Martial Arts/Criminal Law

775
Assaults
Murder and manslaughter
Offensive weapons

Martial Arts/Forensic

775
Techniques used in crime
Weapons used in crime

Masonry Construction

1662
Brickwork cracking/spalling
Masonry accidents on site
Masonry design calculations
Masonry site defects
Masonry staining
Workmanship

Material Damage Claims

632
Analysis of failure of installed plant
and machinery
Cost of repairs and replacements
Failure of and damage to
construction plant and machinery
Fire damage to plant and machinery

Material Damage Losses

1270
Contractors' plant
Fire and flood damage
Mobile cranes
Monitoring of repair costs
On-site investigations

Materials

1465
Chemical, petrochemical and
engineering plant corrosion
Design and fabrication
Failure investigations
Metals
Non-metallic materials
Transport and shipping

Materials Consultancy

2046
Corrosion/inland and marine
Failure investigation
Glass, plastics, ceramics
Metallurgy/ferrous and non-ferrous
Non-destructive testing
Welding

Materials/Corrosion

2359
Analysis, testing and provider of
experts

Materials Examinations

2042
Accident investigations involving
materials
Chemical and surface analysis
Environmental issues
Failure analysis
Physical and mechanical testing

Materials Failure Analysis

152
Composites failures
Materials related personal injury
Metallurgical failures
Paint/linings failures
Plastics failures
Welding failures

Materials Failure Investigations

2046
Bolting problems, failures
Castings
Materials testing
Petrography and metallography
Roads and bridges

Materials Joining/Testing

781
Brazing: metals, testing quality
Engineering: fitness for purpose,
merchantable quality
Failure: analysis, investigation, metal,
structural
Inspection: non-destructive, quality
Materials: failure analysis, selection,
testing
Metals: corrosion, defects, fatigue,
fracture, testing
Non-destructive testing: quality,
equipment, inspection
Testing: materials, products, quality
Welding: metals, equipment, testing,
quality
X-ray: hazards, legislation,
protection, safety

Materials Science/Polymer Chemistry

2058
Adhesives, chemical and surface
analysis
Coatings, paints, rubbers, plastics,
composites
Corrosion and metallurgy
Oil/petrol properties and cargo
contamination
Valve lining and lubrication
Water analysis

Materials Testing

1182
Chemical and analytical testing
Glass and ceramics
Metals and alloys
Physical and mechanical testing
Plastics and rubbers

Maternal (Pregnancy) Medicine

1033
Hypertension and renal disease
Medical disorders of pregnancy
especially

Mathematics (Applied)/General

2566
Formulae and algorithms
Mathematical modelling
Probability and risk analysis
Technical and commercial
applications of mathematical
methods

Matrimonial

see also Divorce

833
All aspects

977
Income and asset investigation
Share valuations

978
Investigations into income and assets
Share valuations

1377
Assessment of individuals' estates
Lloyd's underwriter losses
Pension rights
Share valuations/business valuations
Trust valuation

1390
Accountants' reports/analysis of
business, earnings capacity,
valuations

1428
Consequential loss on share
purchase agreement – warrantees

1450
Asset tracing
Share/business valuation

1502
Defence and plaintiff reports
Quantification of income
Valuation of business

1562
In private companies and other
commercial assets
Valuation of business shares

1845
Calculation of assets/liabilities of
parties
Calculation of gross and net income
of parties
Forensic accountancy re affidavits
and questionnaires
Investigation of incorrect
accounts/returns

1915
Business valuations
Net asset statements
Potential earnings/pension
entitlements
Unquoted share valuations

1940
Assessment of earning capacity
Business valuations
Investigation work
Pension valuations

1966
Business Valuations
Loss of profits/business interruption
Matrimonial and divorce
Medical practice disputes
Partnership disputes

2007
Asset valuation
Evaluation of penson rights
Plaintiff/respondent reports

2163
Divorce settlements

2174
Asset tracing
Business valuations

2263
Business evaluations
Clean break settlements
Effects of taxation
Reports on behalf of either husband
  or wife

2333
Company valuation
Expert witness work
Schedule of needs

2459
Business interruption/loss of profits
Divorce settlements
Fraud
Matrimonial dispute
Partnership disputes
Professional negligence
Share Valuations

Matrimonial Actions

2495
All aspects

Matrimonial/Ancillary Relief Proceedings

652
Company/business accounts analysis
Financial investigation and analysis
Share valuation

Matrimonial And Familly Disputes

1286
All aspects
1288
All aspects

Matrimonial And Family Disputes

1285
All aspects
1287
All aspects
1289
All aspects
1290
All aspects
1291
All aspects

Matrimonial Disputes

397
Duxbury calculations
Family business issues
Pensions
Share valuations
Tracing of assets

472
All Aspects

757
Assessment of income
Dependency claims
Forensic investigation of undisclosed
  income or assets
Valuation of assets (including
  business and shareholdings)
Valuation of pension rights

979
All aspects

1284
All aspects

2477
All aspects

Matrimonial/Family Law

1839
Advice on structured settlements
Calculation of capitalized
  maintenance
Pension aspects and splitting of
  pension rights
Valuation of shares and businesses

Matrimonial Proceedings

767
Business valuations
Funding of settlements
Identification of assets
Taxation

Matrimonial Settlements

133
Business valuations
Valuation of assets and liabilities

Measurement Surveying

2402
Archive research
Area and volume circulation
Boundary demarcation and resolution
Monitoring of structures
Preparation of reports
Re-establishing boundaries – setting
  out

Meat Industry

2357
Abattoirs
Business systems – methods of work
Catering
Custom and practice – techniques
Food Safety Act – due diligence
Goodwill transference/profitability
  disputes
Health and safety – industrial injuries
Hygiene inspections
Manufacturing
Quality and specification disputes
Retailing
Trades descriptions
Wholesaling

Meat/Poultry Industry

385
All aspects of legislation relevant to
  the food industry
Expert witness for identification,
  quality/misrepresentation for
  consumer services
Fraudulent insurance claims where
  quality/microbiological spoilage is in
  question
Health and safety/accident reports for
  personal injury claims
Litigation with regard to installation of
  plant in meat packing plants and
  abattoirs
Specialist anatomical identification –
  retail cuts to carcase

Mechanical

975
Agricultural Road Traffic Act offences
Agricultural construction and use
  regulations
Agricultural health and safety
Agricultural machinery
Workshop machinery and equipment
  condition reports

Mechanical/Building Services Engineering

210
Air conditioning systems
Drainage systems
Gas systems
Heating systems
Hot and cold water systems
Housing disrepair
Ventilation systems

1391
Commercial litigation – breach of
  contract, warranty etc
Heating, ventilation and air
  conditioning
Industrial plant, boiler plant and
  steam services
Insurance claim investigation
Personal injury
Safety

Mechanical/Electrical Building Services

1756
Air conditioning
Compressed gas systems
Energy control systems and
  management
Fuel technology
Heating and ventilation
Plumbing systems (domestic and
  commercial)

2033
Adequacy for purpose and
  effectiveness
Application to all building types
Contribution to the comfort and
  wellbeing of users
Contribution to the deterioration of
  building materials
Effect on lease agreements
Effects of plant and equipment
  failures

Mechanical/Electrical Design

1424
Expert witness work
Hydraulic systems design
Industrial and aviation off-highway
 vehicle design
Project leadership
Transport system design
Waste-to-energy system design

Mechanical/Electrical Engineering

32
Acoustics
Building services
Environmental
Machinery
Refrigeration
Thermodynamics

2509
Construction
Energy utilisation
Industry

Mechanical/Electrical Engineering Services

342
Commercial disputes – expert
 opinion/witness
Equipment condition review –
 insurance claims
Equipment design, manufacture,
 installation and operation failure
Mechanical, electrical and HVAC
 design service
Personal injury claims – expert
 opinion/witness

Mechanical/Electrical Engineering Services for Construction

1897
Design performance and
 management of air conditioning
 systems
heating
lighting and power
plumbing and drainage
ventilation, natural and forced

Mechanical/Electrical Installations

1233
Claims for disruption and prolongation
Subcontract tendering and
 management
Valuation of services installations

Mechanical/Electrical/Marine Engineering

1649
Accident investigations
Agricultural/farming machinery
All types of machinery and
 mechanical equipment
Fabrication/welding
Fork lift trucks/lifting equipment
Product liability/testing
Sound/noise measurements

Mechanical Engineering

99
All heating, ventilation, air
 conditioning, water supply to all
 types of building
Compliance with standards and
 regulations
Control systems
Energy efficiency/environmental
 performance
Machines/mechanical handling
Noise control/acoustics

128
Analysis of problems associated with
 structural failure
Design of structures
Structural integrity

185
Accident investigation
Accidents
Bulk handling machinery
Consultant engineers' performance
 and fees
Dock gates
Electro-mechanical appliances
Engineering plant and equipment
Factory machinery
Health and safety
Hydraulic equipment
Lifting machinery
Lock gates
Moving bridges
Prime movers (engines for
 generators)
Printing machinery
Rotating machines
Workshop machinery

525
All Aspects

553
Accident investigation
Accidents
Bulk handling machinery
Consultant engineers' performance
 and fees
Dock gates
Electro-mechanical appliances
Engineering plant and equipment
Factory machinery
Health and safety
Hydraulic equipment
Lifting machinery
Lock gates
Moving bridges
Prime movers (engines for
 generators)
Printing machinery
Rotating machines
Workshop machinery

626
Aerodynamics
Computing systems (applications)
Fluid dynamics
Materials science and testing
Thermodynamics

796
Automotive and other engines
Defects in mechanical structures and
 machinery
Ergonomics and personal injury
Gas meters
Heating, fuels and air conditioning
 systems
Machinery accidents
Manufacturing systems
Mechanical patent actions

989
Failure analysis of components and
 machines
Fracture and fatigue of engineering
 materials

1357
Gyroscopes

1693
Accident investigations
Design advice
Failure investigations
Patent disputes
Tribological problem solving

2221
Consumer product defects
Cranes and lifting equipment
Fairground equipment
Machinery defects/disputes
Mechanical handling equipment,
 including forklifts

2223
Construction equipment/site accidents
Consumer product defects
Cranes and lifting equipment
Machine tools; machine shop practice
Machinery defects/disputes
Mechanical handling equipment
 (including forklifts)
Power station equipment

2225
Agricultural machinery/practice
Chain drives, Conveyors,
 Earthmoving plant/construction
 equipment
Consumer product defects (including
 gas containers)
Cranes and lifting equipment
Fire sprinkler systems
Flour and feed milling
Machinery defects/disputes
Mechanical handling equipment
 (including forklifts)
Military bridging/engineering
Pleasure park/fairground
 rides/practice
Plumbing/water supply
Road accident analysis
Vehicle handling/braking and tyres

2226
Asbestos felt manufacture
Bitumen handling plant
Boiler plant and steam ancillaries
Carpet making and finishing
 machinery
Consumer product defects
Cranes and lifting equipment
Machinery defects/disputes
Mechanical handling equipment
 (including forklifts)
Papermaking machinery

2227
Consumer product defects
Cranes and lifting equipment
Fairground equipment
Machinery defects/disputes
Mechanical handling equipment
 (including fork lift trucks)

2412
Computer system analysis and
  services
Control systems
  (industrial/aero/marine)
Fluid power systems and components
Research and development
Technical journalism (including
  German)
Theatre control systems

2421
Diesel engines, steam and gas
  turbines
Industrial plant, machinery and
  installations
Manufacturing machinery
Mechanical handling machinery
Mining machinery
Safety of machinery

Mechanical Engineering Accidents

1741
Domestic accidents (slips, trips and
  scalds)
Agricultural and construction
  machinery and equipment
Fork lift trucks
Heavy GoodsVehicle (HGV)
Hydraulics
Industrial deafness claims
Machinery guarding
Marine accidents
Maual handling
Mechanical handling and storage
  (ladders)
Playground accidents
Road traffic accidents
Slipping falls
Wodworking machinery

Mechanical Engineering/Control of Machinery

310
Automatic control
Computer control
Computer numerical control
Control of high speed machinery
Numerical control
Programmable logic control

Mechanical Engineering Design

1700
Chemical process plant – design and
  operation
Dynamics and stress analysis –
  mechanical and electrical equipment
Engineering design including
  machinery design
Patent analysis
Road and rail vehicle stability and
  safety
Vibrations and noise control –
  mechanical and electrical equipment

Mechanical Engineering/Machine Tools/Robotics

310
CNC (Computer Numerical Control)
  of machine tools
Machine tool control systems
Numerical control
Programmable controllers
Robotics

Mechanical Engineering/Personal Injury

323
Investigation of engineering incidents
Litigation support in civil and criminal
  cases

Mechanical Engineering/Products

723
Design
Fitness for purpose
Manufacturing
Performance evaluation
Product liability assessment
Use of engineering products

Mechanical Engineering Services

969
Air conditioning/treatment
Boiler plant
Chimneys
Heating
Refrigeration
Ventilation

Mechanical/Environmental Engineering Systems for Buildings

1107
Air Conditioning
Automatic Control Systems
Heating and Ventilation
Piped Water and Gas Systems
  including fire systems
Plumbing and Drainage Systems
Specialist Mechanical Engineering
  Plant and Equipment

Mechanical Failures

2137
Failure of machinery
Failure of mechanical engineering
  components
Failure of mechanisms

Mechanical Handling

1092
Conveyors and elevators
Cranes
Fork lift trucks and straddle carriers
Industrial tractors and trailers
Pumps
Winches

Mechanical/Hydraulic/Pneumatic Engineering

1826
Guarding of machinery
Health and safety in the workplace
Hydraulic engineering
Maintenance of machinery
Supervision and management of
  staff, craft, operators
Total quality management

Mechanical Industrial Engineering

1069
Accident and floor slip investigations
COSHH regulations
Civil works and plant
Environmental protection
Finishing processes
Handling and conveying equipment
Health and safety
Loss adjustment investigations
Machinery and machine tools
Machinery metal and woodworking
Patent infringement investigations
Project management
Quality assurance investigations
Storage warehousing mechanical

Mechanical/Manufacturing Engineering

2222
Consumer product defects
Cranes and lifting equipment
Machinery defects/disuptes
Manufacturing
  processes/practices/materials
Mechanical handling equipment

Mechanical Process/Environmental Engineering

1090
Accidents, fires, explosions, personal
  injury
Incineration and other combustion
  plant
Mechanical failures including welding
Plant malperformance and failures
Pollution and environmental impact
Public inquiries

1517
Accidents, fires, explosions, personal
  injury
Incineration and other combustion
  plant
Mechanical failures including welding
Plant malperformance and failures
Pollution and environmental impact
Public inquiries

1553
Accidents, fires, explosions, personal
  injury
Incineration and other combustion
  plant
Mechanical failures including welding
Plant malperformance and failures
Pollution and environmental impact
Public inquiries

Mechanical Services in Building

727
Air conditioning, heating and
  ventilation
Central plant including boilerhouses
Piped gas installations
Piped systems for water services
Soil and waste pipework installations
Underground services

Mechanical Stress/Fatigue

2359
Analysis, testing and provider of
  experts

Mechanical/Structural Engineering

1200
Accident investigations
Design, manufacture, application and
  operation of: mobile cranes, lorry
  loaders, access equipment
Mechanisms and structures of
  machinery

Medical

1546
Disability insurance
General practitioner negligence
Personal injury

Medical Accidents

106
Assessment of damages resulting
  from misplaced vesicant (cytotoxic
  chemotherapy) injections

1222
Drug adverse effects
Factors altering drug disposition
Time course of drug action

Medical Accidents/Personal Injury/Professional Negligence/Court Evidence

1478
General joint and bone injury
Hand injury
Spinal injury
Trauma involving the
  musculo-skeletal system

Medical Appeal Tribunals

1033
Industrial injury
Severe disabilities allowance

Medical Conditions

1179
Emergency hospital in-patient care
Medical accidents

Medical Education

473
General practice – primary health
  care
Training, career development and
  education for general
  practice/primary health care

Medical Ethics

1511
All aspects

Medical Literature Searches/All Subjects

1467
Curriculum vitae checking (medical
  practitioners)
Drug therapy/adverse reactions
Medical treatment/complications
  arising
Surgical treatment/complications
  arising

Medical Litigation

1836
All aspects

Medical Manpower

86
Appropriate responsibilities for
  medical staff at all levels
Medical staffing levels

Medical Negligence

41
Accident and emergency medicine

230
Psychological effects

241
All aspects

309
General practice negligence

339
Child health surveillance
Family planning
General practice standard of care
Minor surgery

432
Legal aid
Professional negligence

579
All aspects

674
Medical accidents

715
Loss of amenities and personal
  injuries
Psychiatric medical and professional
  negligence, due to negligent
  medical and psychiatric treatment

828
General medical council/professional
  disciplinary matters
General medical practice negligence
Medical service committee hearing
  matters

855
All areas in general
Neurology in particular

920
Accident and emergency
General surgery

991
Professional negligence involving
  general practitioners

1036
Defence and plaintiff reports
Expert witness work
Negligence and breach of statutory
  duty of medical practitioners,
  pharmacists and corporate bodies

1075
All aspects

1103
PTSO
Professional practice and standards

1324
Ethics hearings attendance
Medical reports, defence and plaintiff

1348
General practice

1406
Claims against general practitioners

1448
Adverse effects of drugs
Opinion or diagnosis and treatment
  by psychiatrists
The effects of prescribed medication

1511
All aspects

1804
All aspects

1981
Defence
Plaintiff
Structured settlements

2074
General practice
Legally (as well as medically)
  qualified
Personal injury

2076
All aspects

2298
Orthopaedics
Trauma

2373
Claims

Medical Negligence Claims for Plaintiff/Defendant

2433
Accident and emergency department
  claims

Medical Negligence/for Doctor or Patient

1613
All aspects

Medical Negligence/from 1997

1136
All aspects

Medical Negligence/General Practice

542
All aspects

1026
All aspects

Medical Negligence/Orthopaedics

2372
All aspects

Medical Negligence/Personal Injury

1285
All aspects

1286
All aspects

1287
All aspects

1288
All aspects

1289
All aspects

1290
All aspects

1291
All aspects

2467
Anaesthetics
Forensic medicine
General practice
Geriatrics

Medical Photography

2103
Medico-legal photography
Scientific and technical photography

Medical Practice

1195
General practice

1280
General criminal work
Postgraduate medical education

Medical/Professional Negligence

96
All aspects

2066
Diabetes
Endocrinology
General medical matters

Medical Psychology/Psychological Aspects of Medical Disorders

1592
Post-traumatic stress (in adults)
Psychological aspects of chronic pain (in adults)

Medical Records Collection

2467
Conversion to usable form
Identification of discrepancies
Travel to storage site for copying

Medical Reports

101
For solicitors
for CICB

Medical Specialities

336
Choice of appropriate experts
Complaints
Overview/interpretation of medical records

Medical Staffing/Terms/Conditions

700
All aspects

Medical Statistics

1249
Multiple sclerosis
Severe head injuries
Statistical analysis and interpretation (generally)

Medical Training

1822
Medical competence
Medical negligence

Medicine

1272
Medicine

1474
Asbestosis
Food poisoning
Occupational and industrial medicine and injury
Personal injury
Professional negligence/medical negligence
Work-related upper limb disorders Repetitive Strain Injury (RSI)

2108
Acceleration, radiation, decompression injuries
Diabetes
Endocrinology
General medicine
Personal injury
Physics in medicine

2150
Allergy
Cancer
Clinical physiology
Internal medicine
Occupational lung disease
Thoracic and respiratory disease

Medicine Legal Aspects of

1347
Alcohol and driving
Asbestosis and other industrial diseases
Child abuse issues
Industrial trauma
Medical negligence (especially fatal)
Non-fatal trauma (criminal and accidental)

Medicine/Preliminary Reports/All Medical Specialisms

1753
General medicine
General practice
General surgery
Obstetrics and gynaecology (particularly cerebral palsy)
Orthopaedics
Paediatrics

Medico-Legal Case Preparation

2121
Helping solicitors to commision appropriate reports
Identifying relevant medico-legal issues

Medico-Legal Compensation Injury Claims

1431
Post-traumatic stress
Psychological effects of accidents

Medico-Legal Reporting

905
Personal injury
Soft-tissue injuries of all types

2351
Road traffic accidents/industrial accidents, tripping accidents, etc

Medico-Legal Work

715
Chronic pain syndrome
Fitness to plead
Post-traumatic stress disorder

Menstrual Hormonal Imbalances

588
Postnatal depression
Premenstrual syndrome

Mental Capacity/Capability

2358
Psychometric testing of intelligence, memory and personality

Mental Health

100
All aspects

230
Admissibility of evidence
Diminished responsibility
Fitness to plead
Insanity
Intent (capacity for forming intent)/automatism
Reports for sentencing
Reports of detained patients

Mental Health Nursing

1063
In hospital, nursing home, residential care home

1402
Community care
Elderly care
Hospital care
Nursing competence
Schizophrenia
Supervision of patients at risk

Mental Health/Psychiatric Rehabilitation

548
Competence to care for self, others, property
Functional performance reports to determine capacity

Metal Failure Analysis

1995
Diesel engine failures
Fatigue
Forensic investigations
Manufacturing defects
Marine failures
Structural failures

Metallurgical Failures/Problem Investigations

224
Advisory/consultancy/metals related
Metal corrosion
Metal fracture/cracking
Metal heat treatment
Metal wear

Metallurgy

454
Aluminium
Non-ferrous metals

1577
Material corrosion
Material failures
Material specification
Materials examination
Materials testing/analysis
Patent infringement

1722
Alloy developments, particularly
  steels
Criminal cases involving knives etc
Failure analysis
Metal resource availability
Patent applications – alloy
  composition
Road traffic accidents

Metallurgy/Corrosion

455
Corrosion
Corrosion consequent to fires
Fatigue
Fractures
Marine corrosion
Metallurgical failures

Metallurgy/Materials Science

671
Collapse of structures
Component and system failures
Corrosion
Design and fabrication appraisal
Failure of metals, polymers and
  composite materials
Pressurised reactor and
  non-pressurised container failures

797
Accident investigation
Failure of systems and components
Forensic examination of metals and
  materials

Metals/Refractories

1147
Accidents: vehicles, domestic
  appliances, mechanical handling
Failures: automotive, central heating,
  industrial fixings, marine
Injuries: building collapse, furniture,
  cycles, foundries
Materials/process: wrong selection,
  poor performance/maintenance low
  product quality
Patent litigation: steelmaking, metal
  processing, refractories

Metals/Testing/Analysis

224
Chemical analysis
Corrosion testing
Mechanical (physical) testing
Microscopical examination
Non-destructive testing
Weld testing

Meteorology

950
All criminal activities (weather)
Construction (weather)
Personal injury (weather)
Road traffic accidents (weather)

1715
Assessment of the accuracy of
  weather forecast
Climate worldwide
Investigation of weather events
  worldwide
Storm analysis

Microbiology

671
Damage to bulk products such as
  cereal grains and feedstuffs
Deterioration of oils and lubricants
Microbiological contaminants in water
  cooling systems

1645
Hepatitis
Human immunodeficiency virus
Rubella
Virology

Microbiology/Bacteriology

2243
Disinfection
Food hygiene
Food safety
Medical microbiology
Sterility, especially medical devices
Sterilization

Microbiology Medical

1101
Antibiotic chemotherapy; prophylactic
  antibiotics
Clinical examination of patients not
  undertaken
Hospital-acquired infection; viral
  infection
Infections; post-operative infection
Medical bacteriology; medical virology

Microwave/Radio Frequency Technology Research/Design/Manufacture

1126
Antenna design and measurements
EMC
Electronics safety aspects
Manufacture
Microwave communications
Patents
Radar
Radio frequency communications
Surveillance security

Midwifery

1254
Antenatal care
Community midwifery
Intrapartum care

Military

263
Allegations of negligence by Ministry
  of Defence
Driver training
Land, sea and air movement
Road safety services
Traffic accidents and procedures
Transport operations

Minerals

2428
Land quality
Mineral site restoration and afteruse

Mining

753
Open pit mining
Opencast coal
Surface mining and quarrying

2359
Analysis, testing and provider of
  experts

2428
Mining remediation
Mining research
Mining stability

Mining Engineering

1909
Mining subsidence
Planning applications
Treatment of abandoned mine
  workings
Treatment of mine shafts

Mining/Geological Consultant

753
Alluvial mining
Cassiterite and columbite mining
Evaluation
Expert witness in geological and
  mining matters
Exploration
Mine evaluation
Mine operation
Mine planning
Opencast coal
Restoration

Mining/Minerals

2425
Abandoned mine entries
Environmental impact of blasting
Evaluation of mineral ventures
Mineral planning
Minerals valuation and management
Mining and minerals surveying

2426
Air pollution

2427
Compulsory acquisitions
Mine operators' agreements
Mining contracts
Personal injury claims
Problems from abandoned mines
Subsidence damage

Mining/Surveying/Building

760
Building construction
Subsidence engineering
Surveying

Mobile Home Parks

2283
Condition of units
Valuation

Mortgage/Credit Broking

886
Compliance with Consumer Credit Act
Duties and obligations of broker to
  customer
Duties and obligations of broker to
  lender

Mortgage/Finance Lending

886
Arrears policy and procedures
Compliance with Consumer Credit Act
Establishment of solicitor and valuer panels
Lending policy
Repossession policy and procedures
Underwriting policy and procedures

Mortgage Lending/Residential/Commercial

256
General mortgage market conditions
Marketing and sales of mortgage products
Repossessions and sales
Self-certification/non-status schemes
Underwriting policy and procedures

Mortgages

731
Contributory negligence: valuers versus lenders
Lending criteria
Mortgage indemnity claims
Mortgage products
Negligence: lenders versus valuers

Mother/Baby Assessment

523
Parenting ability/relationship

Motor Accident/Industrial/Personal Injury

1587
'Whiplash' injury
Head injury
Orthopaedic injury
Soft tissue injuries
Spinal injury

Motor Accident Reconstruction

303
All aspects

Motor Trade/Property/Business/Valuation

2303
Business losses
Landlord and tenant
Petrol filling stations
Professional negligence – valuation aspects
Retrospective valuations

Motor Vehicle Consultant Engineer

998
Accident and crime scene photographs
Court process serving
Examination of vehicles used in the importation of drugs etc
Investigation of criminal and civil offences
Statement, affidavit and evidence recording
Tracing and interviewing witnesses

Motor Vehicle Examination/Assessment

303
Accident damage assessment
Claims investigation
Condition report
Negotiation and arbitration
Valuation report

1005
Accident investigation relative to mechanical failure
Cause/s of mechanical failure
Condition of vehicle/components (roadworthiness)

2185
Collision damage repair methods and costs
Diminution in value following collision and repair
Fire and theft
Investigating vehicles damaged by industrial contamination
Investigation of mechanical/electrical breakdown
Valuations

Motor Vehicles

130
Accident damage assessment
Valuation

797
Accident investigation and reconstruction
Component failure
Examination of crash helmets
Forensic examination of vehicle components

975
Construction and use regulations
Department Of Transport (DOT) and Ministry Of Transport (MOT) testing regulations
Health and safety
Road Traffic Act offences
Sales of Goods and Services Acts
Vehicle condition reports

2472
Accident reconstruction and investigation
Diminution in value
Driving offences (death by dangerous driving; without due care and attention)
Locus report on accident scenes
Quality of work completed by the motor trade etc
Quantum of claim value (repair costs, total loss value)

Motor Vehicles/Construction/Use

2220
Cars
Earth moving plant.
Heavy goods vehicles (HGVs)
Light commercial vehicles
Mechanical handling equipment (MHE)
Passenger carrying vehicles (PCVs) (buses/coaches)

Mountain Medicine

445
Cold injury – frostbite, hypothermia
Expedition medicine
Medical problems associated with altitude

Mountaineering

460
Alpinism
Avalanches
Rock climbing
Scottish winter climbing
Ski mountaineering
Snow and ice climbing

Mountaineering/Skiing Accidents

1968
Hill walking/scrambling
Rock climbing
Ski mountaineering
Skiing/avalanches

Mouth/Face/Neck Surgery

388
Dento-alveolar disease and surgery
Maxillo-facial injury
Mouth, face and neck plastic surgery
Oro-facial cancer
Orthognathic surgery
Salivary gland disease and surgery

Musculo-Skeletal Disorders

1469
Arthritis
Back and neck pain
Connective tissue diseases
Musculoskeletal trauma
Osteoporosis
Regional pain syndromes

Musculo-Skeletal Problems

666
Alleged negligence following treatment by manipulation
Spinal problems, in particular whiplash

Musculo-Skeletal Trauma

910
Acetabular and pelvic fractures
Lower limb trauma
Multiple injuries
Pathological fractures of lower limb

Musculoskeletal System Disorders

25
All Aspects

Music

1880
Breach of contract
Claims of co-authorship
Copyright in music and lyrics
Electronic adaptation (sampling)
Libel
Piracy of recordings
Plagiarism
Unlicensed reproduction and adaptation

Music/Entertainment

2148
Contracts
Films
General exploitation
Overseas entertainers in United Kingdom (UK)
Royalties
Video

Nasal Fractures

617
All aspects

National Network of Personal Injury Experts

1848
All aspects

2361
All aspects

National Reports Service on Personal Injury

2360
All aspects

Nationwide Reports Service on Personal Injury

2255
All aspects

Natural/Built Environmental Control

630
Air pollution
Building ventilation and condensation
Flood and water resource analysis
Inshore hydrography and river
  pollution
Landfill design and contamination
Subsidence and landslip analysis

Nautical/Marine Engineering

2222
Cargo handling
Quayside practice
Seamanship (motor and sail)
Ship engine room practice

Naval

see Marine, Ship

Naval Architects/Marine Engineering

203
Accident and injury on board ships
New building and ship refits
Ship safety and management
Ship security
Ship structural strength and stability
Surveying of ships, equipment and
  cargo

Naval Architecture

766
Collision analysis
Flooding and stability analysis
Performance analysis
Strandings and salvage
Tonnage calculations
Total loss analysis

1894
Fishing vessel design and
  construction
Fishing vessel stability
Pontoons and barges
Small ship design and construction
Small ship stability

2264
Conducting of inclining experiments
Investigations into capsizings,
  sinkings etc
Investigations into causes of
  structural failures
Stability analysis
Structural design (ships)

2309
Disputes regarding condition surveys
Investigations into casualties
Roll on/Roll off (RORO) safety
Ship design
Stability

2388
Fatigue cracking
Hydrostatic and dynamics
Ship strength/structural design

2540
Composite materials and structures
Failure analysis of composites
Seakeeping
Yacht and power craft performance

Naval Architecture/Shipbuilding/ Marine Engineering

394
Marine propellers and propulsion
  nozzles
Ship and boat construction
Ship and boat surveying
Ship design

Negligence

1377
Detailed knowledge of ethical
  guidelines
Practical experience of the
  application of the ethical code to all
  sizes of accountancy practice
Understanding the preparation and
  audit of business accounts

1451
Instructions for use
Office procedures
Product design
Safety at work training
Workshop procedures

1845
Medical negligence
Personal injury
Professional negligence

2561
Construction professionals'
  negligence
Contractors' negligence
Employers' negligence in
  construction contracts

Negligence Claims

1229
Fees disputes
Pursuance of, or defence of,
  negligence claims

Negligence Claims against Surveyors

1151
All aspects

Neonatal Circumcisions

2568
All aspects

Neonatal Medicine

1354
Handicap
Obstetric – neonatal mishaps

1935
Brain injury
Neonatal cases of later handicap
Preterm infants

2457
Causation of brain damage,
  especially cerebral palsy
NOT standards of obstetric care
Neonatal intensive care
Postnatal care
Resuscitation

Neonatal/Respiratory Paediatrics/ General

37
Care of the newborn
Child abuse
Medical audit
Paediatric respiratory medicine
Perinatal medicine

Nephrology (Kidney Disease)

1117
All aspects

Nephrology/General Medicine

113
Bone disease
Dialysis
General renal medicine
Metabolic medicine
Transplantation
Urinary tract stone disease

759
Diabetes
General medicine
Nephrology
Renal transplantation

Nephrology/Kidney Medicine

1503
Acute kidney failure
Complex urological problems
Dialysis and tranplantation
Intensive care

Neurological Conditions Affecting the Central/Peripheral Nervous System

2355
Epilepsy and unconscious attacks
Head injury
Headache
Multiple sclerosis
Spinal injury

Neurological/Developmental Disorders in Childhood/Adolescence

447
Acute neurological disorders eg
  meningitis
Cerebral birth injury/cerebral palsy
Epilepsy
Head injury sequelae
Neurological rehabilitation

Neurological Disorders

151
Brain injury, particularly head injury
Epilepsy
Memory loss
Parkinson's Disease and movement
  disorders
Whiplash injury

Neurological Disorders in Children

1144
Epilepsy

2002
Acquired neurological disorders in
  childhood
Cerebral palsy
Medical aspects of quantum
  determination
Perinatal brain damage

Neurological/Orthopaedic
Assessment

2364
Amputee and prosthetic rehabilitation
Back pain
Chronic pain
Head injury
Multiple trauma
Rheumatological conditions

Neurological Problems

2044
Dizziness
Epilepsy
Head injury
Headache and migraine
Peripheral nerve injuries
Spinal injuries

Neurological Surgery

398
Head injury/trauma (adult and
  paediatric)
Neurological consequences of
  industrial and other injuries, eg road
  traffic accidents
Post traumatic syndrome
Spinal injury/trauma (neck and
  lumbar)

Neurology

404
Epilepsy
General neurology
Head injury
Medical negligence

564
All Aspects

611
Cerebrovascular disease
Neurological trauma/head injury,
  whiplash injury, peripheral nerve
  diseases
Neuromuscular/peripheral nerve
  disease
Spinal cord disease

627
Epilepsy
Episodes with loss of consciousness
Head injuries
Post-traumatic syndromes

855
All other areas of neurology
Epilepsy and blackouts
Head and spinal injury
Peripheral nerve injury

945
Neurology in relation to general
  medicine

960
Epilepsy
Head injury
Headache
Neck and back injury
Pain syndromes
Peripheral nerve diseases

961
Legal aspects of epilepsy, stroke,
  dementia
Neurological aspects of injuries to
  brain, spine and nerves

1043
Epilepsy
Head injury
Headaches/dizzy spells
Peripheral nerve injury
Post-traumatic amnesia
Spine injury

1050
Blackouts
Disorder of smell sense
Head injury and sequelae
Nerve entrapment syndromes
Spinal injury

1136
Epilepsy
Head injury
Nerve injury
Spinal injury (NOT whiplash)

1144
Child neurology

1187
All Aspects

1193
Pain
Rehabilitation
Spinal problems

1205
Cerebrovascular disease
Neurobehaviour disorders
Neurological complications of trauma

1315
All aspects

1319
Head injury
Headache
Neuro-ophthalmology

1320
Neuro-ophthalmology

1399
Epilepsy
General care of neurological patients
Headache
Parkinson's disease
Sequelae of head injury, whiplash,
  spinal and peripheral nerve injury

1515
Dystomia and other involuntary
  movements
Movement disorders
Parkinson's disease

1602
Effects of disease
Effects of medical negligence
Effects of trauma

1707
Epilepsy
Head injury
Headache
Periheral nerve injury

2018
Augementative communication
  systems
Dysartrina (motor speech disorder)
Dysphasia (language disorder)
Feeding and swallowing disorders
Head injury, cerebral vascular
  accident etc

2110
Epilepsy
Multiple sclerosis

2115
Acute neurological accident
Chronic neurological impairments
Head injury
Swallowing disorders
Voice disorders

2196
General neurology
Movement disorders
Trauma

2252
General neurology
Incontinence, pelvic floor disorders
Neuromuscular disorders

2485
Brain damage
Dementia
Epilepsy
Head injury
Nerve injury
Spine injury

2567
Head injuries/brain damage
Hysteria/malingering
Medical negligence
Peripheral nerve injury
Post-traumatic epilepsy
Spinal injuries

Neurology/Adult

1380
All Aspects

Neurology/Clinical Neurophysiology

965
Brain damage
Brain death
Epilepsy
Exposure to toxic chemicals
Multiple sclerosis
Nerve damage
Parkinson's disease

Neurology/General Clinical
Neurosurgery

445
Head injuries
Medico-legal work for defendants
  and plaintiff
Multiple sclerotis
Myasthenia gravis
Negligence
Spinal injuries

Neurology/Medical

44
Clinical neurophysiology

Neurology/Neuro-Ophthalmology

1205
Epilepsy
Magnetic resonance image
Multiple sclerosis/optic neuritis
Orthopaedic neurology
Peripheral neuropathy
Stroke

Neurology/Neurological Rehabilitation

2054
Chronic pain syndromes
Epilepsy
Head injury and rehabilitation
Multiple sclerosis
Muscular dystrophy
Spinal disorders
Stroke and rehabilitation

Neurology/Neurophysiology

2068
Epilepsy
Head injuries
Nerve injuries

Neurology/Occupational Therapy

1034
Chronic progressive conditions
Trauma: stroke, brain injury, spinal
    injuries

Neurology/Psychiatry

2346
Epilepsy
Head injury – behavioural and
    cognitive problems
Non-epileptic seizures
    (pseudoseizures)
Somatoform disorders (conversion
    disorders)

Neuropathology

639
Diagnosis of diseases of the nervous
    system
Expert neuropathological opinion on
    autopsies performed by general
    pathologists
Independent opinion for other
    neuropathologists
Post-mortem examination of
    neurology and neurosurgery
    hospital deaths
Post-mortem examination of peri-
    and post-operative deaths
Road traffic accidents, especially
    head injuries

Neurophysiology

1205
Brain injuries
Nerve injuries
Spinal injuries

Neuropsychiatry

209
Brain and head injury
Electro-encephalography (EEG)
Epilepsy and automatism
Mental illness
Post-traumatic stress
    disorder/nervous shock
Sleep disorders

763
Automatism
Epilepsy
Head injury
Neurophysiology
Sleep

1225
Back pain
Brain damage
Chronic pain
Head injury

1227
Dementia
Epilepsy
Head injury
Sleep disorders

Neuropsychiatry/Organic Aspects of Psychiatry

2323
Alcohol-related organic brain disease
Automatic states, epileptic
    automatisms, amnesia, memory loss
Psychoses associated with organic
    brain disease
The psychiatry of epilepsy,
    particularly psychosis associated
    with epilepsy

Neuropsychology

31
Neuropsychological assessment
Rehabilitation of brain injury/damage

167
Environmental toxins
Neuro-disability
Neurodegenerative disease
Personal and medical accident
Rehabilitation and management
Traumatic head injury

395
Other brain damage, including
    medical negligence
Traumatic brain injury

560
Assessment of brain damage as a
    result of professional negligence
Assessment of traumatic brain injury
Correlation of neuroimaging and
    functional brain damage
Impact of perinatal injury
Rehabilitation needs assessment

1247
Cognitive assessment following brain
    injury
Emotional correlates of brain injury:
    Post Traumatic Stress Disorder
    (PTSD), depression, etc.
Management advice in cases of brain
    injury
Neuropsychological rehabilitation

1663
Assessment of IQ, memory,
    personality change, etc
Brain damage
Defence and plaintiff reports prepared
Post-traumatic stress disorder
Rehabilitation

1680
Head injury
Neurotoxicology
Post-concussional disorders

2080
Assessment

2199
Learning disability
Post-traumatic stress disorder
Traumatic brain injury

2209
Assessment of attainments
Cognitive assessments
Neuropsychological assessments of
    visually impaired people

2434
Assessment of brain damage
Rehabilitation

Neuropsychology/Assessment/ Rehabilitation

1748
Brain damage/fitness to plead
Brain damage/progressive
    neurological disease
Brain injury/accidents (RTAs and
    other)
Brain injury/assaults
Brain injury/damage/reduced
    responsibility
Intellectual function and personality
    change

Neuropsychology/Physical Disability

334
Burns and disfiguring injuries
Chronic pain
Head injuries
Post-traumatic stress disorder
Spinal injuries

Neuroradiology

63
Computerised tomography (CT)
Ear, Nose and Throat (ENT) radiology
Magnetic resonance imaging (MRI)
Orbit radiology
Paediatric radiology

2353
Brain, spine and nervous system
    imaging and interpretation
Head injury and sequelae
Inrracranial bleeding
NAI children
Spinal injury
Strokes, brain tumours and multiple
    sclerosis

Neurosurgery

287
Cranio-facial surgery
Head injuries

565
Head injury
Spine/cervical and lumbar

968
Head injury – epilepsy, headache, post-concussional syndrome, brain damage
Spinal injury – whiplash, disc injury, backache

1192
Brain and spinal tumours
Intracranial haemorrhage
Spinal disorders including disc surgery
Trigeminal neuralgia, hemifacial spasm

1205
Head injuries
Spinal diseases

1235
Spinal neurosurgery

1242
Head injuries
Intracranial tumours
Spinal injuries

1267
Cerebral vascular disease/aneurysmal rupture etc
Head injury and effects of
Paediatric neurosurgery/spina bifida, hydrocephalus etc
Spinal injury/disc herniation, cervical and lumbar

1535
Cerebral haemorrhage
Head injuries
Intracranial vascular abnormalities
Spinal degenerative disease
Spinal disc disease
Spinal injuries

1685
Acoustic neuroma
Head injury
Lumbar and cervical degenerative disease
Spinal injury
Spinal surgery

2502
Head injuries
Hydrocephalus
Neurosurgical sepsis
Spina bifida
Spinal injuries
Syringomyelia, all varieties

2529
Head injury
Spinal disease and injury
Subarachnoid haemorrhage

Neurosurgery/Neurology

877
Head injury, effects of spinal injury
Medical negligence – neurological topics
Trauma

2109
Head injuries
Neurological disorders
Neurosurgical disorders
Peripheral nerve injuries
Spinal injuries

Niche Textile Products

850
Carpets
Fabric procurement
Uniform and workwear
Upholstery

Noise

13
Building services noise and vibration
Environmental noise (industry, aircraft, gunfire, entertainment, quarries etc)
Noise nuisance/pollution – planning and litigation
Sound insulation within buildings

1329
Expert technical surveys and reports
Expert witness representation
Measurement and analysis of noise
Noise and planning
Noise at work regulation surveys
Noise control design and specification

1569
Aircraft
Industrial
Nuisance
Occupational
Planning

1716
Building
Construction
Environmental
Industrial
Occupational
Transportation

2359
Analysis, testing and provider of experts

2498
Accidents due to noise
Aircraft noise and sleep
Traffic and domestic noise

Noise Control

266
Assessment of noise control methods and installations
Industrial and environmental noise control advice

Noise Environmental

84
Noise nuisance, defence and plaintiff reports
Planning applications and appeals

1190
Assessment of noise/vibration from proposed developments
Measurement and assessment of noise, vibration from industry, roads, airfields

1827
Noise abatement notices under EPA
Prosecutions under the EPA and appeals

2388
Construction noise
Environmental impact assessment
Leisure noise
Noise in buildings
Noise planning
Transportation noise

Noise/Industrial Deafness

3
Noise-induced hearing loss investigations

Noise Measurement/Assessment

266
Assessment of noise exposure for occupational hearing loss claims
Environmental impact assessments (noise aspects)
Leisure noise assessment
Noise abatement notices
Planning applications and appeals involving industrial or environmental noise
Road traffic noise assessment

Noise/Nuisance

1622
Advice on mitigating nuisance
Environmental Protection Act
Expert witness

Noise Nuisance Litigation

637
1990 Environmental Protection Act Sections 80 and 82
1993 Statutory Nuisance Act

Noise/Personal Injury

1622
Hearing damage
Voice damage

Noise/Planning

1622
Commercial, industrial and residential development
Entertainment noise, arenas, discotheques
Environmental assessments
Expert witness at planning inquiries
Road, rail and aircraft noise
Superstores, warehouses, car parks

Noise Related to Licensing

637
Conference facilities
Leisure and entertainment facilities
Nightclubs and public houses
Outdoor stadia and 'one off' events
Public entertainment licences
Special hours certificate applications

Noise Related to Planning

637
Application of PPG24 and BS4142
Application of building regulations approved document 'E'
Commercial development
Industrial development
Leisure and entertainment development
Residential development

Noise/Vibration

1107
Engineering, architectural, industrial,
    Wind Farm and Environmental
    Acoustics
Fire alarm acoustic design
Noise and Planning Law
Noise and vibration control (passive
    and active)
Noise impact assessment
Sound conditioning systems

1631
Environmental planning
Environmental protection/nuisance
Hearing damage/noise at work
Machinery noise and vibration

2048
Building services noise and vibration
    control
Environmental and transportation
    noise
Licence applications
Noise and vibration control
Noise and vibration effects
Noise at work
Planning

2534
Environmental noise from
    construction and mineral operations
Highway noise predictions
Industrial noise control
Noise assessments for planning
    applications
Noise impact studies
Noise nuisance investigations
Vibration and building damage

Noise/Vibration/Acoustics

1704
Acoustic design
Building acoustics, environmental
    noise, traffic noise
Noise and vibration control
Noise and vibration measurement
    and prediction
Radio and television studio design
    and building

2261
Construction noise
Noise measurement
Noise nuisance
Noise prediction
Railway noise
Road traffic noise
Stadium noise

Noise/Vibration Consultancy

2093
Assessment of negligence in noise
    and vibration
Assessment of nuisance
Assessment of structural damage by
    vibration

Noise-Induced Hearing Loss

1566
Injuries to facial skeleton

Non-Mechanical Plant for Construction/Maintenance

2526
Design
Use

Non-traumatic Spinal Cord Tissues Causing Spinal Cord Damage

853
All aspects

NOT Gynaecology

872
NOT surgical complications in
    gynaecology, sterilization etc
Womens problems excluding
    pregnancy and birth

Nuclear Engineering

1376
Ionising radiations dose exposure
Nuclear safety
Radioactive contamination

Nursery Products

2031
Design evaluation
Mechanical testing
Performance Trials
Toxicological analysis

Nursing

1063
In hospital, nursing home, residential
    care home

1272
Accident and emergency
General

1402
Community care
Elderly care
Hospital care
Nursing competence
Schizophrenia
Supervision of patients at risk

1877
Expected patient outcomes
Expected standards of patient care
Manager's viewpoint
Nursing care
Orthopaedic nursing
Policies and procedures

1901
Back injuries
Community care
Independent health care sector

2420
Care of the elderly
General nursing
Health and safety at work
Health care capital planning
Nursing management
Registration and inspection of
    nursing homes

Nursing/Aids/Equipment

2290
Case management
Health care liability cases
Quantum aids and equipment
Quantum nursing care

Nursing Care

836
Evaluation of need and costs

1063
Accidents to staff in hospital, nursing
    home and residential care home
Nursing care/special care of
    patients/residents in hospital,
    nursing home and residential care
    home

Nursing/Care Assessments

100
Costing of care – past, present, future
Fee rates – available for past 10
    years
Fees for nurses, carers, nannies,
    home helps
Home care assessments
Loss of maternal value – costings

Nursing Care Reports/Assessment of Need/Past/Present/Future/Costings

2455
Community: generic, (birth to the
    elderly); also school nursing and
    special needs
Hospital settings/mainly acute
    medicine, some surgical and
    accident and emergency experience
Manual handling

Nursing/Hospital/Community

2181
Clinical negligence
Education and training
Industrial injuries
Organisation and management of
    services
Practice
Staffing levels/skill mix

Nursing in the Acute Hospital Sector

2315
Back injuries
Negligence
Standards of care

Nursing Management/Practice

783
General nursing care (at home, in
    hospital, in nursing homes)
Lifting and handling
Nursing practice (adults)

Nursing/Personal Care

2497
Back and related injuries
Matters relating to the Registered
    Homes Act 1984
Past, present and future care costs
Professional nursing matters

Nursing Policy/Practice

663
Community care
General and vascular surgery
Lifting and handling
Management of community and
    primary care services
Needs assessment
Residential and nursing home care

Nursing Reports

1208
Costs
Future requirements
Past and future care
Present circumstances

Obstetrics

86
Fetal/maternal medicine
Intrapartum care
Pre-natal diagnosis
Ultrasound

96
Diagnostic techniques
General pre-natal screening (but
NOT ultrasound or invasive)
Intra-partum care
Surgical complications

249
General (NOT intrapartum)

269
All areas of ante-partum, intrapartum
and post-partum care

311
Antenatal and intrapartum care
Community antenatal care
Information technology in obstetric
care
Prenatal screening

458
General pre-natal screening but NOT
specialist ultrasound or invasive
techniques
Intra-partum care

856
Intra partum care
Pre-natal screening (NOT advanced
invasive techniques)

872
Antenatal care
Complications for mother and baby
Labour and delivery
Miscarriage

954
Acute obstetrics/intrapartum care
General obstetrics
High risk care
Pre-natal diagnosis (but NOT
advanced ultrasound)

976
Elderly women having babies
Genetic factors

1009
Antenatal care
Intrapartum care
Post-partum care (but NOT
advanced foetal medicine and NOT
advanced ultrasound)

1373
Intrapartum care
Invasive techniques
Prenatal screening
Specialist ultrasound diagnosis

1479
Chorionic villus sampling
Fetal invasive procedure
Medical disorders in pregnancy,
especially diabetes mellitus
Prenatal diagnosis

1691
All areas except specialist ultrasound
and invasive diagnostic techniques

1711
Intrapartum care
Pre-natal screening (general)

2102
General antenatal and intrapartum
care (NOT specialist ultrasound
techniques)

2203
Antenatal diagnosis
High risk obstetrics

2318
NOT specialist ultrasound or invasive
techniques

Obstetrics/Gynaecology

51
All Aspects

59
Colposcopy and treatment of
premalignant lesions of cervix/vulva
Contraception including sterilisation
Day surgery
Emergency gynaecology
Intrapartum care and operative
deliveries
Prenatal counselling and antenatal
care (NOT specialist ultrasound on
foetal therapy)

464
Assessment of alleged clinical
negligence

696
Antenatal care, including screening
tests
Diagnosis of foetal abnormality using
ultrasound techniques
Gynaecological surgery
Intrapartum care, birth asphyxia
Ultrasound in obstetrics and
gynaecology

884
Diabetes in pregnancy
Hysteroscopic surgery
Laparoscopic surgery
Oral contraception

902
Colposcopy
Pre-conception counselling
Trans-cervical resection of
endometrium and hysteroscopy

1053
Drugs in pregnancy
High-risk pregnancy

1237
Antenatal care
Contraception
Female urinary incontinence
Gynaecological surgery
Management of labour
Sterilisation

1255
Cerebral palsy (obstetric care)
Intrapartum care (labour ward
management)
Laparoscopic and endoscopic surgery

1259
All Aspects

1368
Antenatal diagnosis of congenital
malformations
Early pregnancy loss
High-risk pregnancy
Infections in obstetrics and
gynaecology
Miscarriage
Preterm labour and birth

1412
Minimally invasive surgery using
laparoscope and hysteroscope

1432
Antenatal care/intrapartum care
Colposcopy cervical problems
Endometriosis/infertility
General gynaecology
Prenatal diagnosis

1437
Obstetrics (NOT advanced
monitoring)
Operative gynaecology (NOT
advanced laparoscopic work)

1440
All Aspects

1572
Laparoscopic and hysteroscopic
surgery
Menopause

1597
(NOT criminal cases)
Antenatal and intrapartum care
General gynaecological surgery
(NOT endoscopic)
Management of twinning
Perinatology (NOT paediatrics)
Radical pelvic surgery
(gynaecological)

2182
Antenatal dignosis of foetal
abnormality
Early pregnancy ultrasound diagnosis
Gynaecology scans/imaging
Imaging
Ultrasound scans

2297
Endometriosis
Gynaecological surgery
Infertility
Menstrual disorder

2345
Foetal damage
Gynaecological surgery
High-risk obstetrics

Obstetrics/Gynaecology; Family Planning

1654
Assisted conception
Gynaecological surgery and
complaints
Management of labour and
puerperium
Management of menopause
Management of pregnancy
Prevention and causes of cerebral
palsy

Obstetrics/Gynaecology/Medical Negligence

1630
Instrumental and non-instrumental
deliveries
Urogynaecology

Obstetrics/Gynaecology Medical/Surgical

1395
Drugs in pregnancy
Hormone replacement therapy
Infertility

Obstetrics/Maternity Care

587
Antenatal care
Birth asphyxia/cerebral palsy/birth
trauma
Diabetes and other medical disorders
in pregnancy
Fetal monitoring/fetal heartrate/CTG
Labour/delivery/episiotomy
Materno-fetal medicine/high-risk
obstetrics

Obstetrics/Medical Aspects

2016
Medical disorders of pregnancy
NOT general obstetrics and
gynaecology
Pre-eclampsia/hypertensive diseases
Prescribing in pregnancy

Occupationial Assessment Reports

2365
All aspects

Occupational Assessment Reports for Personal Injury Claims

1251
Accommodation and housing
adaptation
Assessment and recommendation of
equipment for disabled and elderly
persons
Employment assessment
Functional assessment
Personal and nursing care
assessment
Welfare benefits
Wheelchair – pressure care
assessment

Occupational Disease/Injury

674
Asthma at work
Gassing accidents
Harmful products
Industrial cancer
Repetitive Strain Injury (RSI)
Toxic substances

Occupational Diseases

933
Lead poisoning
Styrene inhalation
Vibration white fingers

Occupational Diseases/Chemical/Substances Related

1741
Chronic systemic effects of
chemicals: carcinogens
Dermatitis and other skin disorders
Pneumoconioses

Occupational Diseases/Process Related

1741
Ergonomics
Manual handling
Strain injury
Work related upper limb disorders

Occupational Environment

2534
Asbestos
Fumes and contamination
Health and safety risk assessments
Noise
Ventilation and thermal comfort
Water quality/legionella

Occupational/Environmental Health

665
Bronchitis, emphysema, cryptocenic
fibrosing alveolitis
Musculo-skeletal and other
occupational diseases
Occupational lung disease,
asbestosis, mesothelioma, asthma
Public health
Stress at work – ECG-based
research for Home Office

Occupational/Environmental Health/ Safety

1082
Environmental pollution, odours
Expert reports for legal purposes
Exposure to chemicals, dusts, fumes
Health physics
Noise
Occupational hygiene
Radiation protection
Toxic substances
Welding hazards

Occupational/Environmental Medicine

1300
Metal toxicology
Respiratory disorders

2399
Occupational diseases
Toxicology

Occupational Health

671
Advice and training
Assessment and control of the
working environment
Work-related diseases and injuries –
statutory requirements

971
Asbestosis
Carbon monoxide poisoning
Dermatitis
Noise
Occupational asthma
Upper limb disorders
Vibration White Finger (VWF)

1258
Health and safety in healthcare
environments
Loss of potential earnings as a nurse
Nursing injuries in the workplace

1587
Diving accidents
Human factors in accidents
Industrial and chemical exposures
Road Traffic Act alcohol backtrack
estimation

Occupational Health/Safety

282
Accident investigation
Personal injury
Safe systems of work

1218
Dangerous occurrences
Display screen equipment
Hearing loss
Reportable diseases
Substances hazardous to health
Work-related upper limb disorders
(WRULDs)

2032
All Aspects

2220
Ergonomics and manual handling
Ladders/scaffolding
Slipping and tripping accidents
Woodworking machines

2221
Asbestos related illness
Dermatitis
Ergonomics and manual handling
Fumes, Control of Substances
Harmful to Health (COSHH)
Industrial diseases
Ladders/scaffolding
Respiratory illness, including asthma
Slipping and tripping accidents
Woodworking machines
Work related upper limb disorder,
Repetitive Strain Injury (RSI)

2222
Asbestos related illness
Ergonomics and manual handling
Industrial diseases
Ladders/scaffolding
Noise-induced hearing loss
Respiratory illness including asthma
Slipping and tripping accidents
Wood-working machines
Work related upper limb disorders
(RSI)

2223
Asbestos related illness
Ergonomics and manual handling
Industrial diseases
Respiratory illness, including asthma
Scaffolding/ladders
Slipping and tripping accidents
Woodworking machines
Work related upper limb disorder
[Repetitive Strain Injury (RSI)]

2224
Asbestosis related illness
Ergonomics and manual handling
Industrial diseases, including
dermatitis
Noise-induced hearing loss
(deafness)
Slipping and tripping accidents
Woodworking machines
Work related upper limb disorder
[Repetitive Strain Injury (RSI)]

2225
Asbestos-related illness
Ergonomics and manual handling
Industrial diseases
Ladders/scaffolding
Respiratory illness, including asthma
Slipping and tripping accidents
Woodworking machines
Work related upper limb disorder
(repetitive strain injury)

2226
Ergonomics and manual handling
Industrial diseases, including
  dermatitis
Ladders/scaffolding
Noise induced hearing loss
  (deafness)
Respiratory illness, including asthma
Slipping and tripping accidents
Vibration white finger (VWF)
Woodworking machines
Work related upper limb disorder
  [Repetitive Strain Injury (RSI)]

2227
Ergonomics and manual handling
Industrial diseases, including
  dermatitis
Ladders/scaffolding
Noise induced hearing loss
  (deafness)
Respiratory illness, including asthma
Slipping and tripping accidents
Work related upper limb disorders
  [Repetitive Strain Injury (RSI)]

2388
Accident investigation and reporting
Confined space entry
Construction health and safety
Control of substances hazardous to
  health (COSHH)
Legal requirements on health and
  safety
Machinery and plant health and
  safety

Occupational Health/Safety/Food Safety

162
Civil claims for negligence
Documentation of policies and
  procedures
Food safety law and practice,
  including food hygiene requirements
Health and safety law and practice

Occupational Hygiene

1787
Control of substances hazardous to
  health (COSHH)
Exposure of workers to hazardous
  substances
Noise at work

Occupational/Industrial Medicine/Injury

1474
Medicine

Occupational Lung Disease

1165
Asbestos disease and other
  pneumoconioses
Aspects of lung function
Effects of lasers
Occupational asthma
Thoracic injury
Toxicology

1797
Accidental fume exposure
Asbestos/related disease
Occupational asthma
Tuberculosis

1883
Asbestos-related disease
Chest and lung injury
Effects of inhalation of fume, smoke
  and dust
Medical negligence – lung disease
Occupational asthma

2150
Medicine

Occupational Lung Disease/Thoracic Disease

2390
All aspects

Occupational Medicine

65
Accidental and non-accidental injury
Fitness to work
Management systems to prevent
  illness and accident
Occupational illness and accidents
Rehabilitation
Systems of work

498
Fitness for work
Health and safety in the National
  Health Service (NHS)
Noise-induced deafness
Repetitive Strain Injury (RSI)
Vibration-related disease [Vibration
  White Finger (VWF)]

579
Accidents
Chemical hazards
Musculo-skeletal disease
National Health Service (NHS)
  Occupational health and safety
Occupational health services
Physical hazards eg: noise, radiation
Safe working systems

852
Diving accidents
Ergonomics
Human factors in accident causation
Investigation of industrial illness
Occupational asthma
Repetitive Strain Injuries (RSI)

862
Back injuries
Gassing – especially carbon
  monoxide
Occupational health problems of
  health care workers
Solvents
Stress

1579
Medical effects of exposure to
  ionizing radiation
Medical toxicology
Occupational diseases/hazards
  within the National Health Service
  (NHS)
Work related upper limbs disorders,
  including Repetitive Strain Injury
  (RSI)

2522
All Aspects

Occupational Noise

1827
Factory improvement notices and
  appeals
Personal injury – noise-induced
  hearing loss

Occupational Pension Schemes

2367
Duties of professional
  advisers/trustees to schemes
Loss/withdrawal of Inland Revenue
  approval
Reporting and accounting
  requirements for schemes
Tax implications of approval/loss of
  approval

Occupational Psychology

1466
Occupational personality and
  aptitude assessment
Work-related stress and stress audits

Occupational Stress

375
Expatriate stress
Stress in overseas employees
Work-related stress

691
All aspects

1351
Stress audit
Stress management programmes:
  individual and group

1599
Assessment of occupational stress
  and its effects
Psychological effects of harassment
  etc
Psychological effects of industrial
  accidents

Occupational Therapy

166
Accidental injury, including head
  injury
Daily living activities costed
Equipment and building adaptations
Home and workplace assessments

324
Assessment and costings of the
  effects of disability

1226
Evaluation of extra care needs of
  permanently injured plaintiffs
Housing needs of disabled people
Specialist equipment needs

1582
Case management
Head injury assessment
Personal injury assessment

1737
Acute intervention to identify daily
  living needs and facilitate hospital
  discharge
Advice on aids/equipment and
  housing – individual clients
Assessment of need of people with
  disabilities under Local Authority
  Statutory provision
Designing and delivery of
  assertiveness/stress management
  groups

1889
Advice on adaptations to property
Advice on equipment in the home
Medico-legal work
Physical disability assessment

2133
Assessment of care needs
Case management
Provision of home adaptations
Provision of specialist equipment
Work evaluation

Occupational Therapy Assessment Reports

1088
All Aspects

Occupational Therapy Reports

1208
Specialist paediatric reports and reports regarding all disabilities

1786
Cost of past, present and future care needs
Home assessment on the functional aspects of disability including costs of specialised equipment needed
Plaintiff and defence work
Recommendations for home adaptations and rehousing needs

Occupational Therapy Reports for Personal Injury Litigation

1737
Assessment of function based on physical, emotional psychosocial daily living skills
Childcare/homemaking provision with costs
Ergonomic assessment within home/school/work (NOT vocational assessment)
Evaluation of appropriate care needs/provision with costings
Housing needs – recommendations for aids/equipment and costs
Mobility/transport needs (but NOT driving assessments)

Offences Against The Person

2356
Blood grouping
Body fluids
Fibres
Hairs

Offices

1747
Investment
Landlord and tenant work
Planning
Rating
Rent review/lease renewals
Sales and lettings
Valuation

Offshore Engineering

1765
Arctic subsea engineering
Explosions
Ice
Pipelines
Trenching
Underwater excavation

2388
Fatigue cracking
Hydrostatics and dynamics
Platform strength/structural designs

Offshore Oil/Gas

1715
Environmental loading
Floating strength and stability
Marine operations
Mooring systems
Operations of drilling platforms
Risk assessment
Soils strength
Towage and emplacement of structures and pipelines
Warranty surveying

2403
Accident investigation
Occupational health
Occupational safety
Offshore safety legislation
Safety management

Oil

356
Charter party and demurrage claims
Contamination and pollution
Load and discharge supervision
Oil loss and cargo retension clause (ROB)
Safe port and ship to ship operations

671
Damage to bulk products such as cereal grains and feedstuffs
Deterioration of oils and lubricants
Microbiological contaminants in water cooling systems

Oil/Gas

2302
Dispute resolution
Engineering project management
Gas – all aspects, technical and commercial
Investigative work, eg for adjudications
Oil and gas transportation, sales and purchase
Strategy and policy, deregulation

Oil Refining/Natural Gas

423
Gas transmission
Manufacturing, plant operation and construction
Purity and specifications
Refined oil products
Valuation and markets

Oil Spill Analysis

1464
Dispersant analysis
Estimation of biodegradation and age
Oil fingerprinting and correlation
Oil speciation
Post-spill environmental surveys

Oncology

1149
Breast cancer
Chemotherapy
Lung cancer
Prostate cancer
Radiotherapy

1243
Cancer diagnosis and treatment
Epidemiology
Predisposing causes

2300
Breast cancer
Gynaecological malignancy

Ophthalmic Conditions/Injuries

1714
Complicated intraocular lens surgery
External eye disease
Ocular infection
Trauma to cornea, lens, iris

Ophthalmic Medicine/Surgery

2001
Medical and surgical malpractice
Personal injury

Ophthalmic Surgeon

1712
Lacrimal pathology
Orbital pathology and trauma
Paediatric ophthalmology
UD pathology

Ophthalmic Surgery

1949
Diseases of children's eyes/developmental glaucoma and cataract
Diseases of the anterior segment of the eye/corneal grafting

Ophthalmology

347
Ocular trauma
Paedriatric ophthalmology

432
Cataract and intraocular lenses
Corneal pathology and injuries
Industrial injuries
Refractive surgery
Road traffic accidents

453
Cataract surgery
General ophthalmology
Glaucoma
Medical ophthalmology/retinal vascular disease
Ocular trauma
Uveitis

604
Diabetic eye conditions
General eye conditions
Injuries of the eye
Retinal conditions

858
Medical negligence
Personal injuries

987
Cataract surgery
Corneal surgery
Refractive surgery (including laser surgery)

1340
All Aspects

1356
Cataracts
Diabetic retinopathy
Drug toxicity
Genetic eye disease
Laser eye surgery
Retinal disorders and injuries

1555
Cataract surgery
Corneal surgery including laser
 surgery
Ocular trauma

1677
Ocular injuries
Paediatric and neonatal eye problems
Retinopathy of prematurity

2187
Cataract
Correction of myopia and astigmatism
Eye lasers
Glaucoma
Ophthalmic trauma

2559
Cataract surgery
Orbital disease

Ophthalmology/Medical/Surgical

848
Eye surgery
Retinal diseases

2441
Cataract and general anterior
 segment surgery
Including Glaucoma and corneal
 conditions
Including detachment and diabetes
Medical and surgical retinal
 conditions

Oral/Maxillofacial Surgery

101
Dento alveolar surgery (wisdom
 teeth, jaw cysts, jaw surgery)
Facial treatment (Road Traffic
 Accidents (RTAs) and assaults)
Orofacial malignancy

2146
Dentoalveolar surgery
Disorders of the temporomandibular
 joint
Facial trauma
Oral pathology
Reconstructive dentistry
Skin cancer

Oral Rehabilitation

1443
Endodontics

Ornithology

401
Ageing and plumage
Bird behaviour and welfare
Breeding under controlled conditions
 in captivity
Illegal possession of wild birds and
 traps
Ringing

Orthopaedic (Skeletal) Radiology

2212
Bone infection
Bone tumours
Spinal disorders
Trauma to bones or joints

Orthopaedic/Accident Surgery

1627
Adult trauma
Disability assessment
Medical negligence
Paediatric trauma

2393
All Aspects

Orthopaedic/Conditions Trauma

1563
Spinal injuries and conditions
 including discs

Orthopaedic Disorders

871
Arthritic problems – knee and hip
 replacement
Lumbar spine
Rheumatoid arthritis

Orthopaedic/Plastic Surgery

2064
Failed orthopaedic implants
Pressure sores (bed sores)

Orthopaedic/Sports Medicine

1825
Accidents at work
Disability
Psychosomatic disorders
Road traffic accidents
Soft tissue injuries
Whiplash injuries

Orthopaedic Surgeon, Consultant

2392
The hand, wrist and elbow

Orthopaedic Surgery

7
Hip and knee replacement
Ligamentous and other
 derangements of the knee
Peripheral nerve entrapments
Work-related upper limb syndromes

468
'Whiplash' injuries
Fractures; joint injuries, dislocation or
 disease
Musculoskeletal disease and injury
Repetitive Strain Injury (RSI)
Road traffic, personal and industrial
 or occupational injury

488
Paediatric orthopaedics: birth
 trauma/cerebral palsy
Spinal deformity in children
Trauma: adults and children,
 including non-accidental injury

605
General orthopaedics and trauma
Paediatric orthopaedics

733
Hand surgery
Joint replacement surgery
Osteoporosis
Rheumatoid arthritis surgery
Trauma surgery

897
Peripheral nerve injury
Trauma
Upper limb surgery

910
Lower limb surgery (adult)

1073
Foot and ankle
Hand and upper limb
Rheumatic disease surgery
Sports-related injuries

1134
Accident and emergency surgery
Trauma surgery

1157
Injuries in dancers and performing
 artists

1224
Trauma
Upper limb (including the hand)
 surgery

1713
Knee
Upper limbs and hand

1782
Conditions of the back
Conditions of the foot and ankle
Conditions of the hip
Conditions of the knee

1861
All Aspects

1910
Arthroscopic surgery
Hand surgery
Hip and knee surgery
Shoulder surgery
Spine surgery

1947
Sports injuries
Trauma – particularly complex trauma

2456
Arthroscopic surgery of the knee
Hand and shoulder surgery
Paediatric orthopaedic surgery –
 especially of hip and foot
Spinal surgery, excluding scoliosis
Total joint replacement surgery –
 hips and knees
Trauma – adults and children

Orthopaedic Surgery/Fracture Treatment

1325
Joint replacement
Orthopaedic aspects of accidents
Shoulder surgery
Trauma of locomotor system

Orthopaedic Surgery/Injuries

613
All Aspects

Orthopaedic Surgery/Trauma

1851
Surgery of the knee joint

Orthopaedic Surgery/Trauma Surgery

298
Knee surgery and knee injuries

302
All Aspects

532
All Aspects

806
Medical negligence
Repetitive stress disorder
Road and work accidents

825
CDH
Co-inventor of ankle replacement joint
Emergency and accident orthopaedic
  surgery
Feet
Joint replacement surgery
Spine

986
All aspects of orthopaedic trauma
  (fractures, dislocations etc)
Amputations and their rehabilitation
British and international standards on
  orthopaedic implants
Hip and knee replacements
Medical manpower and staffing levels

1137
All Aspects

1248
All Aspects

1361
Alleged Repetitive Strain Injury (RSI)
  defence work
Defence work in cases of
  professional medical negligence
  relating to orthopaedics or trauma
  surgery
Hand surgery
Spinal work
Upper and lower limb surgery

1416
Hand injuries
Injuries to bones and joints
Medical negligence cases
Neck, back and other spinal injuries
Soft tissue injuries
Tenosynovitis and Repetitive Strain
  Injury (RSI)

1607
Joint replacement surgery
Spinal surgery

1617
Surgery of the lower limb

1659
All Aspects

1721
Adult hip and knee surgery
Problems following hip and knee
  replacement

2090
Arthroscopic surgery
Joint replacement
Knee surgery

2097
Neuro-orthopaedic surgery
Paediatric orthopaedic surgery

2101
All Aspects

2258
Hand and upper limb problems
Medical negligence

Orthopaedic Surgery, Trauma Surgery

25
All Aspects

Orthopaedic Trauma

12
All Aspects

17
Assessment of environment
Assessment of functional ability
  (including physical and cognitive
  ability – memory, concentration,
  problem-solving, judgement)
Assessment of need (ie therapy,
  environmental adaptation, specialist
  equipment)
Work assessment

389
Bone and muscle tumours
Joint replacements

482
Paediatric orthopaedics
Paediatric trauma
Skeletal injury

585
Injury compensation
Legal aid cases
Road traffic, industrial and other
  accidents

847
Children's orthopaedics including
  fractures
Dislocated hips, deformity etc
Spinal disorders including back pain

919
Medical negligence litigation
Paediatric orthopaedics
Personal injury litigation

956
Bone and soft tissue tumours
Personal injury
Road traffic accidents

1037
All Aspects

1487
Hip and knee surgery
Joint replacement surgery
Revision joint replacement surgery

1782
Back injuries
Foot and ankle injuries
Knee injuries
Whiplash injuries
Wrist injuries

1806
Children's orthopaedics
Hand surgery

1900
Fracture surgery
Paediatric orthopaedic trauma
Pelvis and hip joint trauma

2043
Foot surgery
Hand surgery
Rheumatoid surgery

2271
Back problems
Sports injuries

2503
Employment issues
Medical negligence
Personal injury

Orthopaedics

48
All Aspects

68
Orthopaedic trauma

174
Back pain
Fractures
Knee injuries
Skeletal injuries
Whiplash injuries

253
Motor vehicle accidents
Personal injuries
Whiplash
Work related injuries, especially of
  the back

409
NOT spine

819
Low back pain
Spine
Trauma

1104
Spine, joint and musculo-skeletal
  conditions

1140
Joint replacement
Sports injuries
Trauma

1274
Hand conditions/injuries

1488
All aspects
Surgery

1490
Medical expert
Orthopaedics
Personal injury
Trauma – all fracture surgery except
  acute spinal trauma

1543
Foot and ankle surgery

1900
Hip surgery
Knee surgery
Paediatric orthopaedic surgery

1918
General
Orthopaedic trauma – including
  fractures

2250
Limb disorders related to
  work/repetitive strain injuries
Limb length inequality
Paediatric orthopaedics (especially
  CDH and TEV)

2289
Trauma orthopaedics

2460
All aspects

Orthopaedics Elective

392
Hip surgery
Knee surgery
Spinal surgery

**Orthopaedics/Musculo-skeletal
  Trauma**

1086
Bone infection (osteo-myelitis)
Hip surgery

1710
Foot injuries
Hand, shoulder, elbow and
  upper-limb injuries
Hip, knee and lower limb injuries
Low back pain and sciatica
Neck and other spinal injuries
Pelvic injuries

Orthopaedics (Non-Surgical)

1785
Non-surgical spinal conditions
Osteopathy
Whiplash

Orthopaedics/Trauma/Personal Injury

1733
Hand and upper limb conditions

Orthopaedics/Traumatology

748
Low back pain
Occupational upper limb disorders
Shoulder pain

1328
Endoscopic arthroscopic knee
  surgery
Hip replacement
Knee surgery/ligament replacement
  and joint replacement

1353
Cervical spine disorders and injuries
Fracture trauma
Lumbar spine disorders and injuries

Osteopathic Malpractice

253
All Aspects

Osteopathy

341
All aspects

1324
Ethics hearings attendance
General advice
Medical negligence
Personal injury treatment – spinal
  and peripheral joints
Professional negligence

1401
Occupational injury
Road traffic accidents
Work-related trauma

2548
All aspects

Other Injuries Leading to Disability

1209
Civil litigation

Otolaryngology

1549
Noise-induced hearing loss
  (particularly in relation to
  motorcycles)

Otolaryngology/Head/Neck Surgery

1642
Laryngology, including laryngeal
  trauma and voice disorders
Otology, including noise-induced
  hearing loss and acoustic tumours
Rhinology, including occupational
  rhinitis

Otorhinolaryngology/Ear/Nose/Throat

778
Ear Nose and Throat (ENT)
Industrial deafness
Occupational nasal/sinus disease
Otology
Rhinology

Otorhinolaryngology/Head/Neck Surgery

955
Audiology
Dysphagia
Head and neck surgery
Voice disorders

Outdoor Pursuits

2211
Instruction in sailing/yachting,
  mountaineering, centre activities
Mountaineering: trekking, hillwalking,
  rock-climbing, navigation,
  campcraft, etc
Sailing instructor for Royal Yachting
  Association training schemes

Package Holiday Operation

168
Association of British Travel Agents
  (ABTA) codes
Disputes
UK and international law

Packaging

892
Causes of damage to
Environmental impact – disposal
Package design and quality
Packaging manufacture
Plastics packaging
Storage and transportation

Packaging for Transport/Distribution

912
Fibreboard and wooden cases
Paper and plastic sacks

Paediatric Adult Neuroradiology

2353
Brain, spine and nervous system
  imaging and interpretation
Head injury and sequelae
Intracranial bleeding
NAI children
Spinal injury
Strokes, brain tumours and multiple
  sclerosis

Paediatric Cardiology

1337
All Aspects

Paediatric Haematology

730
Abnormal bruising (but NOT the
  general aspects of non-accidental
  injury)
Bleeding problems
Management of blood diseases in
  childhood
Transfusions of blood and blood
  products

1003
Acute leukaemia in childhood
General blood problems in childhood
Infection in immuno compromised
  children
Lymphoma in childhood
Paediatric haematology laboratory
  medicine
Paediatric haemophilia and bleeding
  disorders

Paediatric Medicine

1486
All Aspects

Paediatric Nephrology

2347
Ante-natal diagnosis
Congenital abnormalities
Nephrology
Transplantation
Urinary tract infection
Urology

Paediatric Neurology

477
Birth injury and cerebral palsy
Causation of handicap in childhood
Traumatic head injury and spinal
  injury in childhood

1144
All Aspects

Paediatric Nursing

1468
Intravenous therapy in children
Paediatric medical nursing

Paediatric Oncology (Childhood Cancer)

539
All childhood and adolescent cancer
Bone tumours

Paediatric Orthopaedics Fractures

7
Cerebral palsy
Clubfoot and other foot conditions
Congenital dislocation of the hip

Paediatrics

182
Paediatric gastroenterology and
  nutrition

429
Birth asphyxia
Birth trauma
Brain damage in the newborn
Care of the newborn
Causation of handicap in children
Cerebral palsy in children

1354
Child care/child abuse
General paediatrics

1456
Cerebral palsy
Child handicap
Neonatal problems
Neonatal problems arising from birth

1473
All Aspects

1604
Birth asphyxia
Cerebral palsy
Neonatology
Paediatric neurology

1854
Allergy/allergic diseases
General paediatrics
Respiratory disease

2138
Metabolic disease including diabetes
  in childhood
Non-accidental injury and child abuse
Respiratory disorders

2182
Imaging, all aspects
Non-accidental injury, child abuse
  imaging
Trauma

2206
Child abuse
Endocrinology
General Paediatrics
Neonatology

2513
General paediatrics
Neonatal paediatrics

2517
Children and families – assessment
  for medical negligence and
  personal injury

Paediatrics/Child Health

67
Birth trauma
Child abuse and child protection
Child development
Child handicap and disability
Child neurology
Failure to thrive emotionally and
  physically

1415
Child abuse
Neurodevelopmental disorders
Respiratory disorders

Paediatrics/General Clinical

2272
Gastroenterology
Hepatology
Immunisation
Infectious disease
Nutrition and metabolism

Paediatrics/Neonatology

1967
Neonatology (all aspects)
Paediatric infectious disease
Paediatric pulmonary disease

**Paediatrics/Paediatric
  Gastroenterology**

1606
Disorders of the gastrointestinal tract
Problems pertaining to general
  paediatric disorders, excluding
  neonatal problems

Pain

614
Head pain
Spinal pain

693
Post-operative pain
Road traffic accidents (RTA)
Spinal Injury

Pain Management

1729
Back education
Chronic pain disorders
Reflex sympathetic dystrophy
Risk assessment
Work-related disorders

Painting/Polymers

80
Accidents
Cosmetics
On-site investigation
Paints and Polymers
Problem solving
Trading standards

2465
Accidents
Cosmetics
On-site investigations
Paints and Polymers
Problem-solving
Trading standards

Paintings Painters

1072
Gallery/dealer/auction house practice
Methods and materials
Most periods – 17th/18th/19th/20th
  centuries
Schools, artists, living artists

Paints

1394
Analysis
Failure
Formulation

**Paints/Sealants/Adhesives/Printing
  Inks**

421
Investigation of failures-in-service

Palliative/Terminal Care

999
Analgesic pharmacology and use
  generally
Pain control in cancer
The use of drugs such as morphine,
  diamorphine to treat pain

**Paper, Printing, Ink, Finishing,
  Binding etc, Examinations of**

1890
All aspects

Paraplegia/Quadriplegia

1209
Civil litigation

Parental Capacity/Suitability

2352
Adoption
Contact
Local authority care orders
Residence

Parental/Enteral Nutrition

1793
All aspects

Parenting Assessment

1431
Parent-child interactions and
  management
Psychological assessment of parents

**Partially Sighted Children/Young
  People**

512
General purpose assessment for
  educational purposes
Sight loss following medical
  intervention – assessment of
  educational/psychological status
  and needs

**Patent Infringement Cases (most
  cases settled out of court)**

432
All aspects

Paternity Testing

797
All aspects

1770
Deoxribonucleic Acid (DNA) profile
  and fingerprinting
Serological and biochemical typing

Pathological Diagnosis of Cancer

1452
Breast cancer and breast disease
Cervical and breast cancer screening
Cervical cancer and gynaecological
  pathology
Cytological diagnosis (cervical smear
  and breast FNA)
Maligant mesothelioma and
  asbestosis
Medical negligence

**Pathological Interpretation of
  Wounds/Injuries**

1452
Patterns of injuries, assault and
  wounding

Pathological Investigation of Death

1452
Deaths due to natural causes
Deaths following medical treatment
  and surgery
Homicide (murder)
Second post mortems and
  independent witness at first post
  mortems
Suicide
Trauma/motor vehicle, gunshot
  wounds and accidents

Pathology

157
Accidental or unnatural death
Adult death or disease
Death during surgery/anaesthesia
Obstetric death/disease (foetus or
 mother)
Paediatric death or disease (baby or
 child)

276
Bone disease and tumours
Histopathology

519
Death
Malignant melanoma and other skin
 tumours
Skin pathology
Tumour pathology generally

521
Autopsy pathology (but NOT
 specialist forensic work)
Surgical histopathology

1862
Forensic
Haematology
Negligence

Pathology/Diagnostic

931
Cytological misdiagnosis
Cytopathology
Gynaecological and
 non-gynaecological cytology
Histopathology

Pathology/Occupational Medicine

365
Alleged environmentally related
 medical problems
Diving
Drowning and offshore medical
 problems
Occupational related disease and
 injury
Sudden and unnatural death
Trauma

Pedestrian Accidents

942
Compliance with the Code of Good
 Practice for Highway Maintenance
Compliance with the Department of
 Transport's design criteria for public
 highways
Compliance with the Highways Act
 1980
Compliance with the New Roads and
 Street Works Act 1991
Compliance with the Occupiers
 Liability Act 1957

Pension Schemes

142
Benefits
Financing occupational schemes
Investment
Operation

Pensions

187
Actuarial and administrative aspects
 of pension schemes
Division of pension rights on divorce
Pension scheme trusteeship
Quantification of loss as a
 consequence of bad advice or
 maladministration

771
Loss of future income
Matrimonial disputes: pension
 valuation
Pension loss claims
Pension transfers/opt outs
Professional negligence: financial
 services related

779
Disputes over actuarial methodology
Disputes over role of actuary to
 pension scheme
Disputes over surplus

1170
Calculation of current and future
 values
Evaluation of same
Identification of any kind of pension
 arrangement
Investment advice on divorce
 settlements
Spouses lost pension rights

1188
Company sales
Dismissal, redundancy
Divorce
Transfers
Trusteeship
Winding up

1809
Pension aspects of employment
 disputes and personal injury claims
Valuation of pension rights following
 divorce

1885
Allocation of surplus
Compensation for mis-selling of
 policies
Divorce – valuation of pension rights
Mergers and acquisitions
Transfer values – individual and
 group
Wind-up of pension funds

Pensions Advice

189
Evaluation of transfer values offered
 by schemes
Independent trusteeship for pension
 schemes
Insured pension schemes
Investment strategy for pension
 schemes
Occupational pension schemes
Pension scheme design and
 communication
Pensions aspects of mergers and
 take-overs

Pensions/Company Pension Funds/Actuarial Investment

2444
All Aspects

Pensions/Financial Services

1788
Analysis of pension transfers and
 opt-outs
Loss of pension rights following
 personal injury
Negligent pension advice
Pension rights on divorce

Pensions/Life Assurance/Health Insurance

1527
Bad advice
Defective investment schemes
Disputed claims
Negligence of intermediaries
Non-disclosure
Policy terms and conditions

Perinatal/Paediatric Pathology

521
Fetal and neonatal pathology
Sudden infant death

Peripheral Nerve Damage

894
Muscular weakness
Neuralgia
Pain

Peripheral Nerve Injuries/Trauma

586
Neck and back injuries
Nerve entrapment
Nerve problems due to accidents
Obstetric trauma and medicosurgical
 cases (nerve
 problems/operative/peri and post
 operative)
Repetitive strain injuries

Peripheral Vascular Problems

656
Arterial problems
Circulation to the limbs
Venous (vein) problems

Permanent Health Insurance Claims

2372
All aspects

Personal

457
Breach of contract
Divorce
Domestic financial settlements

Personal Accident

1556
Commercial premises
Industrial premises
Machinery

Personal Claims

2477
Matrimonial disputes

Personal Claims for Loss of Earnings/ Dependency

205
Asset valuations in matrimonial
  disputes
Following injury or fatality, including
  medical accident
Loss of pensions entitlement
Valuation of share options

Personal Damages

1299
Compensation for loss of office
Defence and plaintiff reports
Divorce – ancillary relief
Loss of earnings

Personal Disputes

1285
Employment and pension disputes
Family and matrimonial disputes
Fatal accidents
Medical negligence
Personal injury claims

1286
Employment and pension disputes
Family and matrimonial disputes
Fatal accidents
Medical negligence
Personal injury claims

1287
Employment and pension disputes
Family and matrimonial disputes
Fatal accidents
Medical negligence
Personal injury claims

1288
Employment and pension disputes
Family and matrimonial disputes
Fatal accidents
Medical negligence
Personal injury claims

1289
Employment and pension disputes
Family and matrimonial disputes
Fatal accidents
Medical negligence
Personal injury claims

1290
Employment and pension disputes
Family and matrimonial disputes
Fatal accidents
Medical negligence
Personal injury claims

1291
Employment and pension disputes
Family and matrimonial disputes
Fatal accidents
Medical negligence
Personal injury claims

Personal Home Care

2362
Care in the home following accidents
Convalescent care in the home
Financial benefits of domiciliary care
Home care as an alternative to
  residential home care

Personal Injury

see also type of injury eg Burn Injury,
  Chest Medicine and under Medical
  Specialism eg Orthopaedics

21
Building, slipperiness

49
Fairground and playground accidents
Industrial occupational accidents
Machinery accidents
Manual handling accidents,
  cumulative trauma
Road traffic accidents
Tripping and slipping

54
Advice/recommendation on
  adaptation or assistive equipment
Care package costings
Costing of environmental adaptations
  and assistive devices
Defence and plaintiff reports
Functional assessment

96
All aspects

98
Loss of earnings claims
Loss of pension rights claims

106
Assessment of injuries following road
  traffic accidents, especially
  whiplash neck injuries
Implications of splenectomy following
  trauma

133
Defence and plaintiff reports
Loss of earnings claims

135
Industrial accidents
Repetitive Strain Injury (RSI)
Road traffic accidents

143
All accidents (except road traffic)
Chemical accidents
Electrical accidents

156
Claims relating to defective premises

214
Loss of earnings
Loss of pension rights
Medical negligence
Plaintiff and defence reports

230
Psychological effects

234
Construction industry equipment
Lifting equipment including cranes,
  lifts etc
Machinery guarding
Noise
Pressure systems
Process systems eg petrochemicals,
  food etc

241
All Aspects

243
Defence and plaintiff reports
Health and safety

263
Army bullying/assault
Army related injuries
Military inquiries
Mistreatment of subordinates
Negligence allegations
Redress of grievances

264
Attending counsel briefings
Defence and plaintiff reports
Fatal accident
Giving evidence in court
Legal aid

280
Domestic property failures
Neighbour trespass, nuisance and
  damage
Personal injury – defective
  pavements/structures
Personal injury – defective roads
Personal injury – site accidents
  including scaffolding
Personal injury at place of work

309
Cervical whiplash injury
Criminal injuries compensation board
Minor traffic accidents (requiring
  short hospital stay or casualty
  attendance)
Paediatric injuries
Pavement trips
Post-traumatic stress disorder

331
Slipping and tripping, falls, electric
  shock, crushing, systems of work,
  RTAs

355
Alteration for disabled living as part
  of Personal Injury (PI) claims
Reports in personal injury cases
  involving buildings and construction
  sites

387
Resulting from road accidents by the
  self-employed and directors of
  unquoted companies

449
Claims mitigation
Loss of earnings
Quantification of financial losses
  generally

478
Defence and plaintiff reports
Loss of profits/business interruption

485
Defence and plaintiff employment
  reports
Disadvantage on the labour market
Loss of earnings
Residual abilities

491
Care costs and requirements
Continual support needs reports
Court presentation
Current needs reports
Nursing aids recommendations
Patient assessment on discharge
  from hospital
Projected needs reports
Residual disability assessment
Video presentation

501
Major trauma
Whiplash

525
Accidents at work
Leisure accidents

537
Accident investigation
Explosions
Fires
Human error
Impacts
Management of hazardous operations

549
Hazard assessment within the home
Home accident investigation
Slips, trips and falls within and
    outside the home

578
Personal injury
Professional negligence (general
    practice)

601
Defence and plaintiff reports
Loss of Earnings

624
Insurance claim assessment
Loss of profits/earnings

671
Electrical accidents and shock
Engineering
Fires and explosions
Mechanical failure
Toxic chemical

697
Capacity for work or normal life
    activity
Effects of anxiety of exposure to
    infectious diseases at work
Failure to recover from
    injury/suspicions of malingering
Post-traumatic stress disorder
Psychological reactions to
    disfigurement
Repetititve strain injury

723
Resulting from construction materials
Resulting from handling glass
Resulting from use of construction
    plant
Resulting from use of machinery
Resulting from use of tools

745
Defective machinery causing injury
Falling/tripping/slipping accidents
Hazardous substances
Occupational health and hygiene
Working practices/system of work

767
Defence and plaintiff reports
Loss of earnings claims
Loss of profits claims

791
Loss of earnings claims
Loss of profits claims

839
Industrial and non industrial accident
    investigations
Leisure facilities, including pools and
    water slides
Lifting and manual handling accidents
Machinery guarding and safety of
    work equipment
Safety of access and place of work
Safety of systems of work
Slipping accidents

855
All areas of personal injury work
Insurance reports

865
Cosmetic surgery clinics
Industrial burns and accidents
Injury to musicians
Scarring and deformities

866
Paraplegic claims
Specialist reports
evidence in court

867
Asbestos
Chemical inhalation
Electrical, mechanical, electronic
    engineering
Glass
Repetitive Strain Injury (RSI)

868
Asbestos
Chemical inhalation
Electrical, mechanical, electronic
    engineering
Glass
Repetitive Strain Injury (RSI)

870
Cost of employing builder for Do It
    Yourself (DIY) jobs
Defective building works causing
    personal injury

875
Industrial injury

895
Actuarial assessment of loss
Investment advice
Structured settlements

920
Post accident pain/complications
Referral clinic for back/neck pain

929
Fatal accidents
Medical claims
Non-fatal accidents

931
Advice on medical evidence
Child abuse
Defence of plaintiff reports
Mechanisms of injury
Sexual offences

978
'Loss of earnings' and dependency
    claims
Including fatal accident and medical
    negligence

991
Industrial injuries
Injuries arising from criminal assaults
Injuries in public places (paving
    stones, etc)
Injuries on commercial premises
    (supermarkets, etc)
Road traffic accidents

1004
Highway geometry
Highway visibility

1022
Defence reports
Loss of earnings capacity (not
    employees)

1054
Loss of earnings claims

1057
Post-injury evaluation
Rehabilitation
Repeated stress factors
Video Display Unit (VDU) activities

1103
Psychiatric effects

1125
Construction site accidents
Excavation or trench collapse
Highway footpath accidents
Roof, floor and stairway collapse
Tripping accidents

1160
Reports for plaintiffs and defendants

1209
All aspects

1238
Highways
Manhole accidents
Pavement accidents
Road accidents
Road surfacing

1270
Construction site accidents
Defence and plaintiff reports
Manual handling
Occupational disease
Production plant and machinery
Work-related upper limb disorders

1273
Musculoskeletal injury
Shoulder injury

1296
General surgical/medical negligence

1317
Defence and plaintiff reports
Loss of earnings for agricultural
    workers
Loss of earnings for self-employed

1324
Medical reports, defence and plaintiff
Road traffic incidents
Treatment of patients

1332
Loss of earnings

1348
All Aspects

1377
Assessment of additional personal
    expenditure
Assessment of future loss
Assessment of quantum
Assessment of the impact of taxation
Calculation of multipliers
Interpretation of accounts and
    accounting records
Pension rights

1406
General minor injury
Non-catastrophic orthopaedic injuries

1410
Burns and scalds
Falls etc
Fumes and gases (including carbon
    monoxide)
Health and safety
Noise

1426
Accomodation for the disabled
    arising out of Personal Injury (PI)

1428
Consequential loss on share
 purchase agreement – warrantees

1448
Head injury
Post-traumatic stress disorder
The psychological consequences of
 accidents

1459
Accommodation needs
Adaptive equipment
Daily living activities
Leisure activities
Mobility
Personal care

1461
Accidents at work
Accidents in public places
Labelling of chemicals

1462
Defence and plaintiff reports
Fatal accident, 'loss of earnings'
 calculations

1472
Other injuries following accidents
Road traffic accidents injuries
Works accidents/injuries

1474
Medicine

1502
Defence and plaintiff reports
Loss of earnings

1511
All aspects

1530
Loss of earnings and potential
 earnings
Rehabilitation
Reports for plaintiff and defence

1596
Diving and flying injuries
Medical negligence
Occupational deafness (noise
 induced)

1673
Loss of earnings
Plaintiff reports

1680
Anxiety and depression
Chronic pain
Disability
Disfigurement
Post-traumatic stress

1706
Assessing impact of injury on social
 functioning, capacity to study or
 work
Medical negligence
Neuro-psychological impairments
Post-traumatic stress disorder
Road traffic accidents

1719
Employment prospects of personal
 injury litigants

1754
Buildings and home adaptations

1758
Defence and plaintiff reports
Loss of earnings and dependency
 claims

1768
Defence reports
Plaintiffs claims

1793
All aspects

1800
Back pain and injury
Chronic pain
Hand injury and limb claims
Multiple injury and major loss claims
Neck strain
Repetition 'injury' claims

1801
Bone, joint and soft tissue injuries

1803
Building design/personal injuries
Design for accessibility, safety and
 security
Housing/accommodation
Safety and building

1804
Minor injuries suitable for general
 practitioner assessments

1848
Psychological/psychiatric effect of
 Road Traffic Accidents (RTA's)
Road Traffic Accidents (RTA) injuries
Social effects of Road Traffic
 Accidents (RTA's)
Whiplash

1858
All domestic staff, nannies, cooks,
 butlers, handymen etc
Mental and physical injuries,
 schizophrenia, senile dementia,
 body injuries, mental handicap, etc

1881
General accidents with a technical
 involvement
Industrial accidents
Slip and fall accidents

1885
Dependency – assessment of
Fatal accident – pension rights,
 dependency etc
Medical care – evaluation of future
 costs
Pension rights – loss of

1893
All aspects of minor personal injury

1921
Preparation of plans of 'locus in quo'

1940
Fatal accident claims
Loss of dependency
Loss of earnings calculations
Loss of pension calculations
Medical negligence
Plaintiff and defence reports
Structured settlements

1966
Defence and plaintiff reports
Loss of earnings

1998
Buildings and home adaptations

2007
Loss of profits/earnings claims
Plaintiff reports

2077
Compulsive gambling
Post-traumatic stress disorder
Professional negligence/medical and
 nursing
Substance misuse/alcohol and drugs
Suicide

2104
Consumer product defects/injuries
Defence to charges under Health
 and Safety at Work Act
Electric burns
Electric shock
Industrial accidents

2108
Medicine

2132
Reports on site accidents/safe
 method of working etc
Valuing cost of Do It Yourself (DIY)
 repairs that client could do before
 accident

2137
Manual handling operations
Personal protective equipment
Safe guarding of machinery
Safe place of employment
Work equipment
Workplace health, safety and welfare

2153
Death by electrocution
Electric shock
Industrial injury

2163
Dependants' claims
Fatal accident
Loss of earnings

2175
Loss of earnings claims; plaintiff and
 defendant reports

2213
Health and safety on building sites
Methods of work
Pavements and roadways
Slippery floors
Steps/staircases/ramps

2253
Asbestosis
Claims for children
Claims of utmost severity
Criminal injury (CICB work)
Fatal accidents/dependency claims
Medical negligence

2255
Industrial injuries
Road Traffic Accidents (RTA) injuries
 and psychological effects
Whiplash

2350
Incidents involving fire-related death
 and injury

2358
Assessment of post-traumatic stress
 disorder, anxiety, depression
Psychological stress and impairment
 following trauma – children and
 adults
Treatment of psychological
 consequences of trauma including
 hypnosis

2360
Industrial accidents
Road Traffic Accidents (RTA) injuries
 and psychological effects
Whiplash

2361
Industrial injuries
Road Traffic Accidents (RTA) injuries
 and psychological effects
Whiplash

2368
All aspects

2370
Accidents at work
Industrial injury
Road traffic accidents
Sporting injuries
War pensions

2436
Injuries/emergency services
Injuries/fatalities in fire

2495
All Aspects

2509
Construction and industry

2562
Attending counsel briefings
Defence and plaintiff reports
Fatal accident
Giving evidence in court
Legal aid

Personal Injury/Accident Investigation
680
Accidents involving fixed or portable
 plant
Fork lift trucks and lifting equipment
Slips, trips, falls
Work-related upper limb disorders

Personal Injury/Accidents
410
Construction accidents
Industrial accidents
Noise
Road traffic accidents

441
Defence and plaintiff reports
Loss of earnings and dependency
 claims

683
Insurance claims arising out of
 employer liability related accidents
Insurance claims arising out of public
 liability related accidents

1533
Construction site accidents
Pedestrian slip and trip accidents

Personal Injury/Accidents/Medical Negligence
1034
Defence and plaintiff reports

1351
Post-traumatic stress assessment –
 defence and plaintiff reports
Post-traumatic stress treatment
Psychometric assessment of stress
Types of accident – Road Traffic
 Accidents (RTA), industrial, military,
 medical

2174
Loss of earnings claims for both
 plaintiff and defendant

Personal Injury/Case management
1737
Assessment of need with
 recommendation and costs
Care planning and implementation
Counselling
Monitoring and review

1810
Counselling and guidance
Hiring of carers, therapists etc
Purchase and design of housing
Purchase of equipment, transport etc
Reassessments for Public Trust
 Office

2051
Assessment for special equipment

Personal Injury Cases
634
All aspects

921
All aspects

Personal Injury/Children/Adolescents
215
Medical injuries (child psychiatry) or
 trauma
Psychological injuries

Personal Injury Claims
221
Fatal accident and loss of
 dependency
Medical negligence

632
Factory accidents
Industrial diseases – asbestosis,
 Repetitive Strain Injury (RSI),
 asthma, deafness etc
Marine accidents
Public liability claims
Road haulage accidents
Road traffic accident reconstruction

834
Specialist photography

1304
Medico-legal work

1363
Accidents at work
Motor vehicle accidents

Personal Injury Claims Assessment
807
Amputees
Hand injuries
Orthopaedics
Pain
Polimyelitis and long-term neural
 injury

1734
House adaptations
Neurological damage
Specialised equipment

Personal Injury Claims for Plaintiff/Defendant
2433
Hand injuries
Head injuries
Musculo-skeletal/orthopaedic injuries
Surgical aspects of trauma

Personal Injury/Compensation Claims
2125
Assessment of losses
Quantification of loss of
 profits/earnings

Personal Injury Compensation Cost Reports
1736
Analysis and quantification of past,
 present and future care
Assessment of housing needs
Evaluation of specialist equipment
Identification of injured and ongoing
 costs

Personal Injury/Effects of
1800
Effects on couple bonding and family
 units
Personality and psychological
 'drivers' in recovery from trauma
Psychodynamics of claimants in
 adversarial compensation situations
Psychological effects of trauma on
 the personality

Personal Injury/Electrical/Electro-Mechanical Engineering
1741
Lifts and escalators
Machine guarding
Production processes and production
 aids

Personal Injury/Fatal Accidents
367
Calculations of quantum
Loss of earnings calculations
Pension calculations

397
Loss of earnings
Loss of pension
Mitigation
Structured settlements

457
Dependency claims
Loss of earnings
Structured settlements

635
Defence of plaintiff reports
Dependency claims
Loss of earnings

757
Full schedules of special damage
Loss of earning claims
Loss of pension rights
Plaintiff and defendant work
 undertaken (including legal aid)

833
Loss of dependency
Loss of earnings
Pension losses
Plaintiff and defendant work
Schedules of other losses

927
Defence and plaintiff reports
Duxbury calculations
Loss of earnings/dependency claims
Lost pension rights
Special damages claims

1062
Loss of earnings and dependency
   claims

1173
Defence and plaintiff reports
Insurance claims assessment
Loss of earnings and dependency
   claims
Loss of service claims

1218
All branches of industry and
   commerce
Food processing industry
Manual handling and lifting
Plaintiff and defence reports
Slipping, tripping and falling
Structural, scaffolding and general
   construction

1450
Dependency claims
Loss of income

1562
Loss of earnings (for plaintiff)

1740
Loss of earnings and dependency
   claims

2188
Defence and plaintiffs' reports
Dependency claims
Loss of earnings claims

2263
CICB claims
Dependency calculations
Loss of earnings
Loss of pension
Plaintiff and defence reports
Severe injuries – head injuries,
   paraplegics and tetraplegics

2373
Claims

2488
Loss of earnings calculations
   particularly for self-employed
Loss of pension rights calculations
Plaintiff and defence reports

**Personal Injury/Fatal
   Accidents/Insurance Claims**

1924
Confidential video and photographic
   evidence re plaintiff movement
Covert surveillance and enquiries
Defence and plaintiff reports
Detailed proofing of witnesses
Evidence preparation to High Court
   standard
Video/photographic/plan drawing re
   locus

**Personal Injury/Fatal Accidents/
   Matrimonial/Loss of Earnings**

2475
Defence and plaintiff reports
Loss of earnings and dependency
   claims

**Personal Injury/Fatal
   Accidents/Medical Negligence**

29
Dependency claims
Loss of income and pension, profit
   and growth
Other special damages

425
Loss of dependency
Loss of earnings
Loss of pension
Structured settlements

914
'Loss of earnings' and 'dependency'
   claims
Defence and plaintiff reports
Fatal accident

928
Defence and plaintiff reports
Loss of earnings and dependency
   claims
Structured settlements

977
'Dependency' claims
Defendant and plaintiff reports
Loss of earnings
Loss of pension
Structured settlements

1111
Defence and plaintiff reports
Loss of business profits
Loss of earnings and fringe benefits

1284
Defence and plaintiff report
Dependency calculations
Loss of earnings/profit
Loss of pension

1390
Accountants' reports/loss of
   earnings/loss of profits

1839
Calculation of loss of dependency –
   fatal accidents
Calculation of loss of earnings or loss
   of business profits
Calculation of loss of pension rights –
   'Auty' and other methods
Calculation of loss of services

1932
Defence and plaintiff reports
Fatality and dependency claims
Medical negligence – quantum of
   special damages
Quantification of lost earnings

1981
Defendant
Plaintiff
Structured settlements

2129
All Aspects

2134
Future losses
Loss of earnings
Loss of pension benefits
Objective reports for claimant or
   defendant

2330
Defence and plaintiff reports
Loss of earnings/profits

2331
Defence and plaintiff reports
Fatal accident
Loss of earnings and dependency
   claims

2332
Defence and plaintiff reports
Fatal accident – 'loss of earnings'
   and 'dependency' claims

2459
Defendant and plaintiff reports
Loss of earnings
Loss of pension rights

Personal Injury/Fatality Claims

1481
All aspects

Personal Injury/Housing

2473
Accident reports
Breach of repairing obligations
Hazard assessments
Property design/construction reports
Slips, trips and falls within and
   outside the home

**Personal Injury/Housing/Liability
   /Quantum**

2179
Design and construction of housing
   for disabled people
Reports on housing needs of
   disabled people
Reports on liability matters following
   home accident

Personal Injury/Insurance

924
Loss of profits reports
Taxation advice re settlement of
   proceedings

Personal Injury Investigation

210
Airborne pollution measurements
Health and safety law
Injuries at work
Road traffic accidents (surveys and
   reports)

Personal Injury (Leisure Accidents)

525
All aspects

Personal Injury Litigation

232
Psychological assessment of adults
   and children

318
Back injury/back pain
Repetitive Strain Injury (RSI),
   Work-related upper limb disorders

422
Advice on employment and disability
Advice on housing adaptations and
   disability
Advice on specialised equipment –
   wheelchair, bed, special aids
Assessment of disability – effect on
   functional capabilities (personal,
   occupational, social)
Personal injury litigation- individual
   and insurance companies

1020
Care management services
Care requirements – analysis and
  quantification
Equipment and housing needs
Functional assessment

1688
Psychiatric injury

1703
Accidents at work/in the home/leisure
  activities
Accidents in manufacturing
Boilers and pressure systems
Building and civil engineering
Industrial museums
Locomotives

1718
All aspects

2372
Trauma – bone and soft tissue injury

Personal Injury/Locomotor System

2460
All Aspects

Personal Injury/Medical Negligence

360
Defence and plaintiff reports
  including 'loss of earnings' and
  'dependency' claims

728
Defence and plaintiff reports
Fatal accident and long-term disability
Loss of earnings

762
Defence reports
Loss of earnings claims
Plaintiff reports

821
Loss of earnings claims
Plaintiff and defence reports

1228
Assaults
Emergency medical care
Falls
Industrial injuries
Minor injuries
Multiple major injuries
Road traffic accidents

1335
Dependency claims
Loss of earnings
Report drafting

1798
Problems arising from medication or
  prescribing
Problems of medical treatment

1915
Associated compensation claims
Defence and plaintiff reports
Loss of earnings reports

2333
Defence and plaintiff reports
Dependency
Fatal accident
Loss of earnings
Structured settlements

Personal Injury Medical Reports

364
General personal injury reports
Orthopaedic trauma
Soft tissue trauma

Personal Injury/Minor Trauma

2021
Uncomplicated trauma

**Personal Injury Needs
Assessments/Costing**

645
Accident rehabilitation
Care equipment and adaptations
Compensation claim support
Medical negligence cases

**Personal Injury/Occupational Chest
Conditions**

1976
Asbestos-related conditions
Malingering
Medical negligence

Personal Injury Photography

1973
Injury
Scars

Personal Injury/Plaster cast

1877
Application, removal, care and
  aftercare of patients in plaster of
  Paris or synthetic casts

Personal Injury Psychology

842
Medical trauma
Post-trauma anxiety and depression
Post-traumatic stress disorder
Psychological reactions to Road
  Traffic Accident (RTA)

Personal Injury/Quantum

1455
Loss of earnings claims
Loss of pension entitlement
Structured settlements
Use of multipliers

**Personal Injury/Quantum Assessment
of Special Needs**

1208
All other permanent disabilities
  including whiplash, wrongful birth in
  conjunction with the National Foster
  Care Association
Amputee
Brain damage/injury
Cerebral palsy
Paediatric disabilities
Spinal injury including paraplegia and
  tetraplegia

Personal Injury Rehabilitation Reports

2523
Assessment of clients' requirements
  following injury
Costs of care and special equipment
  required
Elderly care and rehabilitation
Housing adaptations, assessment
  and costing

Personal Injury Reports

1251
Occupational assessment reports

2121
All aspects

2365
Employment reports
Loss of earnings calculations
Self-employed earnings

Personal Injury/Trauma

691
Effects of road traffic (and other
  traumatic) accidents
Intellectual/cognitive difficulties
  following mild head injury
Post-traumatic stress (PTSD)

1599
Assessment of general psychological
  effects of accidents
Assessment of post-traumatic shock
  following RTAs, personal injuries,
  medical accidents and trauma
Psychometric assessment of intellect
  and memory following head injuries

Personal Injury Trauma/Criminal Work

1205
All aspects

Personal Injury/Trauma/Orthopaedics

244
Cervical spine injuries
Repetitive stress injury (RSI)

Personal Injury/Upper Limb Disorders

1798
Diffuse painful disorders
Occupational injury
Repetitive Strain Injury (RSI)

**Personal Injury/Work related Injury
Claims**

2216
Computerised modelling and
  visualisation
Defence and plaintiff reports
Industrial accident investigation

Personal Injury, Effects of

1800
All aspects

Personal Litigation

1058
Defamation loss assessment
Loss of earnings
Matrimonial proceedings
Personal injury claims and
  assessment

2162
Divorce and matrimonial disputes
Inland revenue and customs and
  excise investigations
Trust and estate disputes

**Personal, Industrial/Work-Related
Injury**

452
All aspects

Pest Control Contracts/Work

229
Breach of contract
Due diligence and reasonable
  precautions
Negligence

Pests In Buildings/Structures/ Products

229
Determination of damage caused by infestation
Factors conducive to infestation
Identification of infestation
Origin of infestation

Pharmaceutical

953
20 years international arbitration expert in quality dispute
Drugs of abuse, detection, effects, manufacture
Drugs/drink driving
Expert witness in all above areas
Qualified person status (Medicines Act)
Special expertise in pharmaceutical manufacture
Special expertise in quality control

1616
Analytical investigations

1624
Analysis of medicines etc
Medicines and pharmaceutical products

2490
Chemical and biological analysis
Expert opinion and review of documentation
Quality assurance aspects of production and analysis
Regulatory

Pharmaceutical Licensing/Manufacture

1036
Clinical trials
Manufacturer's licences
Product licences
Qualified person services
Quality assurance
Quality systems

Pharmaceutical Medicine

137
Adverse drug reactions
Adverse events

Pharmaceutical Negligence

920
All aspects

Pharmacology

789
Adverse drug relations
Drink driving alcohol cases

1538
Antiepileptic drugs
Clinical pharmacokinetics
General therapeutics

1774
Sedative drugs

2349
Anaesthetics (especially local anaesthetics)
Drug metabolism
Pharmacokinetics

Pharmacology/Clinical Pharmacy

2415
Clinical pharmacokinetics
Clinical trials
Disease effects on drugs
Drug effects on disease
Drug effects, side effects and interactions
General medicine
Prescribing and dispensing errors
Therapeutics and therapeutic misadventure

Pharmacology/Toxicology

764
Adverse reactions to drugs
Errors in prescribing or using medicines
Harm due to medicines (civil and criminal cases)
Murder by poisoning
Poisoning by medicines, alcohol, etc (including drink-driving cases)

Phenolic Resin Application Technology

802
Foundry materials and refractories
Friction materials
High pressure laminates
Virtually all phenolic resin application areas

Photocomparison of the Face (Face Mapping)

1694
Analysis of stature
Face reconstruction from skeletal remains

Photogrammetric Measurement

2474
Critical measurements at scenes of crime
Position of objects
Size of objects
Survey of extent of damage to buildings

Photographic/Video Evidence Examination/Forensic

1600
Accident investigation
Document examination – ESDA
Evidential photography and video recording
Forensic investigation
Scene examination (crime/industrial/insurance)
Video and photographic evidence examination

Photographs of Plaintiff/Locus

1471
Photographs of scene of accident/injury
Preparation of report
Production of detailed plan of locus from ordinance survey master

Photography

800
Macro photography of exhibits
Video of scenes

2165
Record of personal injuries, road traffic accidents, pavement injuries, scenes of alleged crime, scene of arrest etc

2510
Medical negligence – video
Patent infringement documentary evidence
Personal injury – extent of scarring
Planning disputes, documentary evidence
Road traffic accident documentary evidence

Photography/Photogrammetry

1393
Interpretation and precision measurement of photographs
Use of aerial, ground and underwater photography as evidence

Physical Activity/Education

702
All aspects of the national curriculum in schools
Curriculum physical education in schools and colleges
Dance
Extra-curricular activity in schools, colleges and universities
Informal physical activity
Outdoor pursuits/education – management courses

Physical Education in the School Curriculum

1807
Athletics
Dance
Educational visits
Games
Gymnastics
Swimming

Physical Education/Sport

738
Pre-school physical education and activity
Primary school physical education and activity
Secondary school physical education and activity

1339
'Special needs' physical education
All games activities and athletics
Extra-curricular activities
Outdoor education
School gymnastics

2558
Gymnasium accidents
Physical education in schools
Play equipment accidents
Playground accidents
Playing field accidents
Sports centre accidents

Physical Education/Sport/Leisure

1820
Curriculum teaching/coaching
Health and fitness
Outdoor pursuits
Sports facilities

Physical Forensic Science

1060
Fire and explosion investigation
Firearms and ballistics
Paint, glass, fibres, tool marks,
    footwear marks
Vehicle accident investigation

Physics

1025
Fluid flow
Heat exchanger design
Heat transfer
Pressure vessel design

Physics in Medicine

2108
Medicine

Physiology of Handwriting

2424
Empirical research into the effects of
    alcohol, fatigue, stress, drugs,
    shock, environment or implement
    faults, ill-health and/or age

Physiotherapy

719
Long-term physiotherapy needs for
    the spinally injured
Neurological gait (walking)
    assessment
Paraplegia
Quadriplegia
Spinal cord injury
Wheelchair rehabilitation

770
Acute trauma and sports injuries
Back and neck injuries
General physiotherapy problems
Neurological conditions
Orthopaedic problems
Paediatrics
Tetraplegics/paraplegics/spinal
    injuries

Physiotherapy/Hydrotherapy/ Rehabilitation

2483
Amputations
Hydrotherapy provision –
    hydrotherapy pools
Paediatrics – birth injuries, traumatic
    and aesthetic accidents
Physiotherapy negligence re medical
    and surgical treatment
Traumatic head injuries, neurological
    damage and anaesthetic accidents
Traumatic spinal injuries

Physiotherapy/Hydrotherapy/ Rehabilitation/Associated Costs

1150
Hydrotherapy provision-hydrotherapy
    pools
Neurological damage and
    anaesthetic accidents
Paediatric-sporting injuries
Paediatrics-birth injuries, traumatic
    and anaesthetic accidents
Traumatic head injuries
Traumatic spinal injuries

Physiotherapy/Orthopaedic Medicine

2483
Back injuries – neck/whiplash injuries
Handling and lifting issues
Industrial accidents
Orthopaedic injuries, eg fractures,
    ligamentous tears, joint injuries
Physiotherapy negligence re
    electrical treatments/physiotherapy
    techniques
Sporting injuries

Physiotherapy Reports

782
Assess present physical disabilities
Physical disabilities following road
    traffic accidents, orthopaedics,
    medical, surgical and congenital
Physiotherapy costings
Recommendations for future
    physiotherapy needs

Pipelines

1765
Land pipelines
Marine pipelines
Piping systems

Pipework/Mechanical Installations

2336
Construction cost management
Evaluation of disruption costs
Evaluation of loss and expense
Expert report on quantum
Measurement and valuation of
    variations
Prolongation claims

Plan Drawing

2165
Leaseplans, Applications for licensed
    premises
Personal injury cases including road
    traffic accidents, pavement injuries,
    industrial accidents, scenes of
    alleged crime
Pursuits over large distances, scenes
    of arrest

Planning

289
Court hearings
Enforcement appeals
Local plan inquiries
Planning, listed building and
    conservation area appeals

522
Agriculture
Application/appeal documentation
Archaeology
Ecology
Environmental surveys
Landscape

1185
Planning appeals
Planning applications/negotiations
Planning enquiries

1271
Highways
Markets
Safety
Traffic

1362
Appeals
Applications
Conditions
Law
Negotiation with planning authorities
Sections 50 and 51 agreements

1827
Noise-producing developments in
    noise-sensitive areas
Noise-sensitive developments in
    noisy areas
Planning applications, appeals and
    public inquiries

2261
Access planning
Country planning
Town planning
Urban planning

Planning Appeals

2190
Anticipated generated traffic and its
    assignment to roadway network
Appraisal of highway networks
Entry arrangements for
    developments, sight-lines etc
Expert witness evidence for
    highway/traffic aspects of
    developments
Traffic impact assessments

Planning Appeals/Public Inquiries

115
CPO inquiries
Informal hearings
Local plan inquiries
Planning appeals
Structure plan examinations
Written representations

Planning Applications

1701
Environmental impact assessment
    for road traffic
Lorries and freight
Road capacity for access to
    developments
Street markets, golf courses, etc
Traffic generated by new
    developments
Traffic signals and control systems

Planning Consultancy

2541
Environmental assessment
Highways
Listed buildings
Preparation of planning advice
Professional negligence disputes
Public planning inquiries

Planning/Design Of Highway Schemes

2384
Design of civil engineering works
Economic assessment
Environmental assessment of
    highway schemes
Legal procedures for scheme
    implementation
Safety audits and accident
    investigation

Planning/Development

820
Historic buildings consultant

1045
Development appraisals
Planning applications and appeals
Strategic planning
Structure and local plan
  representation

Planning Negotiations/Support

115
Planning application support
Section 106/278/38 agreements
Traffic impact assessment

Planning Noise

3
Environmental noise
Mining and quarrying
Oil and gas exploration
Process industry
Transport noise

Planning Permission Applications

2113
Advice on all planning matters
Preparation and submission of all
  types of planning applications
Preparation of planning appeals,
  written statements and giving
  evidence at public enquiries

Planning/Programming/Construction

104
Analysis of construction delays
Analysis of design delays
Analysis of extension of time
  entitlement
Analysis of procurement delays

Planning/Urban Design

351
Development analysis and appraisal
Pre-application reports
Research/history/dynamics of
  settlement
Townscape analysis

Plant/Machinery

632
Analysis of failure of installed plant
  and machinery
Cost of repairs and replacements
Failure of and damage to
  construction plant and machinery
Fire damage to plant and machinery

1270
Contractors' plant
Fire and flood damage
Mobile cranes
Monitoring of repair costs
On-site investigations

Plant Engineering

261
Building services litigation, including
  heating, ventilation and air
  conditioning
Electrical accidents/fire causation
Machinery disputes

Plant/Machinery Disputes

135
All aspects

Plant/Machinery Valuations/Auctioneering

103
Cars and commercial vehicles
Construction equipment
Machine tools

Plastic/Hand Surgery

2440
Hand surgery
Reconstructive microsurgery

Plastic Materials

1612
Foams
Fracture of plastics products

Plastic/Reconstructive/Aesthetic Surgery

288
Cosmetic (aesthetic) surgery

416
Aesthetic
Burns
Reconstructive

541
Aesthetic surgery
Burns
Hand surgery
Industrial injuries
Microsurgery
Road traffic injuries

612
Aesthetic

617
Burn injuries
Scarring – any site following
  industrial, domestic or road traffic
  accidents
Soft tissue injuries including muscle
  and nerve damage

625
Aesthetic – all aspects of cosmetic
  surgery
Burns
Congenital – cleft lip and palate
Malignancy – skin malignancies,
  head and neck cancer
Trauma – facial and soft tissue
  injuries

709
Burns and scalds
Congenital malformations and drugs
Facial injuries
Hand injuries
NOT environmental pollution
Wounds and scars

898
Cosmetic plastic surgery
Craniofacial surgery
Paediatric plastic surgery

922
Cosmetic and aesthetic surgery

1030
Accident surgery
Hand surgery

1038
Burns
Cosmetic surgery
Hand trauma
Head and neck surgery
Lower limb trauma

1407
Aesthetic/cosmetic surgery
Burns and scalds
Soft tissue trauma/scars

1430
Surgery of the head and neck
  (cancer)

1534
Benign skin tumours (eg moles,
  naevi, cysts etc)
Breast reconstruction
Cleft lip and palate
Malignant skin tumours (eg.
  BCC/rodent ulcer, SCC, melanoma)
Reconstructive head and neck
  surgery
Soft tissue trauma (including
  management scars, grafts, flaps)

1557
Aesthetic surgery
Reconstructive surgery
Surgery of the congenital deformities
  (cleft, lip and palate, hand)
Surgery of the hand

1560
Aesthetic surgery
Burns
Hand surgery (especially trauma)
Head and neck cancer
Post-traumatic reconstruction
Skin malignancy

1610
Burns
Cleft palate
Hand and neurosurgery

1613
Burns
Cosmetic surgery
Scarring

1777
Abdominioplaty, liposuction
Breast augmentation, breast
  reduction, mastopexy
Facelift, blepharoplasty, rhinoplasty
Injury: facial, hand, nerve
Scarring, scar revision
Surgery: cosmetic, aesthetic
Skin grafting and reconstructive
  surgery

1841
Aesthetic (cosmetic) surgery
Burns
Cutaneous laser therapy
Head, neck and skin cancer
Minor hand injuries
Soft tissue trauma

2151
Cosmetic
Hand
Microsurgery
Scar revision
Skin, tendon, nerve, Dupuytren's

2257
Burns
Hand surgery
Microsurgery

2422
Burns
Cosmetic surgery including breast
  reconstruction
General plastic surgery
Head and neck surgery
Microvascular surgery
Skin cancer

Plastic Surgery

2047
Aesthetic surgery
Burns
Military plastic surgery
Plastic surgery in children
Trauma and reconstruction

Plastic Surgery Reconstructive

1000
Aesthetic plastic surgery
Hand surgery

1297
Children's hand surgery
Hand surgery
Major nerve injury (including brachial plexus)
Microvascular surgery

Plastics

892
Environmental impact – disposal
Plastics raw materials – quality
Plastics technology
Process machinery – patents, faults, accidents
Product design and quality – faults, accidents

Plastics/Polymer Technology

2031
Compression moulding
Injection moulding
Materials selection
Transfer moulding and extrusion

Plastics/Rubber Technology

1182
Adhesives, coatings, films
Design, service behaviour
Natural and synthetic materials
Plastics, rubbers, textile fibres
Raw materials, manufacture

Play

702
'One off' installations eg bouncy castles
Holiday camp play areas
Informal play with loose connections to owners
Play areas in public house gardens or annexes
Sports centre play
Vacation play work weeks

Play Equipment/Surfaces

1052
Artificial grass pitches – technical inspections
Playground accidents – inspection and testing
Sports injuries relating to surfaces and equipment

Playground Accidents

1963
Indoor soft play areas
Play accidents generally
School playground accidents

Playground Safety

308
Conformity to British Standard No 5696 Parts 1, 2 & 3
Playground accident reports

525
All Aspects

768
Accidents investigations/falls from equipment
Equipment related accidents

Plumbing

1831
Central heating
Cold water services
Hot water services
Radiators

Plumbing Installations

1869
Design fault diagnosis
Fit for purpose inspections
Health and safety recommendations
Quantum and reports
Statutory regulation audits
Workmanship appraisals

Police

325
Computers, Holmes

Police/Civil Claims Against

2373
Aggravated and exemplary damages
Assault by police officer
Damages for wrongful arrest
Malicious prosecution
Racial abuse
Trial by jury
Unlawful imprisonment

Police Dogs/Training/Operational Use

443
Dead body recovery
Drugs detection
Explosives detection
Normal patrol dog training

Police Major Enquiry Systems

325
Examine for unused material, information and evidence
Investigation of serious and complex crime

Pollution

see Environmental Pollution

2359
Analysis, testing and provider of experts

Pollution Arising from Farming/Related Businesses

1920
Farm building design for pollution control
Farm waste management planning
Investigation of individual pollution cases – liability and quantum

Pollution Assessment/Control

2369
Assessment and control of air pollutants
Assessment of liquid pollution
Assessment of waste handling and disposal
Odour assessment and control

Pollution Control

438
Sewage treatment
Sewerage system discharges
Trade effluent treatment
Treatment process evaluation and optimisation

Polymers/Plastics

423
Catalysts
Manufacturing, plant operation and construction
Purity and specifications
Valuation and markets

1624
Adhesives
Analyses of polymers and plastics
Paints
Rubbers
Water soluble gums and resins

Port/Coastal Engineering

1483
Construction, UK and overseas
Design and management of multidisciplinary projects
Dredging and disposal/reclamation
Risk assessments
River and dam engineering
Sedimentation and hydraulics

Post-Mortem Examinations

237
Bladder biopsies
Prostate biopsies

Post-Trauma Responses

2080
Assessment of post-traumatic stress
Treatment of post-traumatic stress

Post-Traumatic Psychological Disorder/Victimology

23
Adult survival of child abuse (male and female)
Fake memories and allegations of abuse
Post-traumatic stress disorder (PTSD)
Post-traumatic stress disorder (PTSD) after crime
Post-traumatic stress disorder (PTSD) and crime
Treatment of Post-traumatic stress disorder (PTSD)

Post-Traumatic Stress, Assessment of

193
All aspects

Post-Traumatic Stress Disorder

1678
All aspects

1748
Anxiety and panic attacks
Depression
Fitness to maintain relationships
Fitness to work/loss of earnings
Obsessive/compulsive disorder
Phobias

2346
All aspects

2434
Assessment
Rehabilitation

Poultry Husbandry Science/Technology

120
Evaluation of insurance claims
Evaluation of poultry systems
Planning for housing and
    environmental issues
Poultry management which includes
    turkeys, geese, ducks, guinea fowl
Poultry nutrition/breeding
Poultry processing, including
    added-value products

Poultry Nutrition

1857
Animal feeding stuffs
Breeding birds
Laying birds
Meat producing birds
Nutritional deficiencies
Turkeys/waterfowl

Poultry, Especially Commercial Poultry

2251
Diseases and disorders
Game-birds
Husbandry and nutrition
Transport
Welfare

Poultry, Including Feathered Game/Ostriches

2278
Egg production
Poultry insurance
    claims/assessments
Poultry meat production
Poultry transport and slaughter
Poultry unit planning
Poultry welfare

Power/Energy Systems

1665
Economic and technical evaluation of
    power and energy systems
Thermodynamics of power
    generation plant

Power Engineering

185
Control systems
Energy efficiency
Nuclear power
Power and distribution
Power stations

553
Control systems
Energy efficiency
Nuclear power
Power and distribution
Power stations

Power Stations

2222
Boiler operation and maintenance
Pumps and pumping
Stoking practice
Turbine operation and maintenance

2334
CGTS
Contract management
Gas turbines

Practical Consequences of Disability

9
Employment and education
Leisure and recreation
Provision of specialist equipment
Special seating and postural control
Transport, access to the community
Wheelchair assessments

Pre-Press

2242
Colour measurement
Colour separation
Imaging
Proofing
Quality Assurance
Quality Control

Pressure Areas

380
Liability/cost of care ie assessment

Pressure Systems

971
All aspects

Printing

2176
Preparing check quotes (estimates)
Preparing reports
Printing costs
Review of print prices

2242
Colour Reproduction
Quality Assurance
Quality Control
Standards

Printing/Packaging Industries

2520
Colour control
Press room chemicals
Print quality assessment
Printing inks
Varnishes and coatings

Printing/Publishing Technology

1580
Desktop publishing applications
Digital communications and
    networking
Imagesetting and printing plate
    production
Pre-press applications in printing,
    publishing and allied industries
Scanning and digital imaging
Software applications and image
    processing

Printing/Security/General

1397
Counterfeit or suspect document
    examination
Printing quality analysis in civil
    disputes
Security document audit
Security document design and
    counterfeit protection
Security printing

Probability/Statistics

117
Deoxribonucleic Acid (DNA)
    identification evidence
Paternity/relatedness testing
Sample surveys
Scientific evidence
Statistical evidence

Probate Genealogy

1794
Certificate and record searches
Estate distribution and division
    (intestate)
Family tree preparation,
    documentation and verification
Location of missing and unknown
    beneficiaries
Missing beneficiary indemnity
    insurance agency

Probate Research

829
Genealogy

Process Plant/Machinery

2421
Control systems
Electrical generators, motors and
    transformers
Electrical installations
Electrical safety
Power generation and distribution
Power utilisation and control

Process Safety

450
Chemical engineering process plant
    safety
Hazop and Hazan

Product Disputes

1741
Commercial disputes concerning
    machines
Commercial disputes concerning
    volume products
Disputes relating to building services
Disputes relating to scaffolding and
    other access

Product Failure Analysis

2537
Capital equipment
Consumer products
Household goods
Industrial equipment
Manufactured goods
Personal injury

Product Liability

see also under relevant product eg
    Chemical

971
All Aspects

1451
Instructions for use
Product design – consumer
Product design – domestic
Product design – nursery/juvenile
User error prediction

2443
Component failure
State of the art reviews
Testing and standards

Product Liability/Personal Injury Claims Involving Glass

803
Processing problems of glass bottles

Product Safety

1963
Accident statistics – home and public
areas
Consumer products – civil liabilities
Consumer products – risk
assessment
Consumer products – safety
regulations

Production Engineering

525
All Aspects

Professional Indemnity Insurance Related Claims

826
All aspects

Professional Negligence

see also under the profession eg
Architect or the Work eg
Construction, Building

29
Accountancy
Auditing
Taxation advice

133
Accounting negligence
Other professions – consequential
losses

138
Auditing and due diligence work
Failure to detect fraud
Failure to detect money laundering
Negligence claims against
accountants
Preparation of financial statements
Reports on quantum
Tax compliance and planning

146
Building contracts/supervision
Building surveys/home buyers'
reports
Commercial/residential valuations
Landlord/tenant disputes
Party wall matters/boundary disputes

156
Architect negligence requiring
valuation/survey evidence
Solicitor negligence requiring
valuation evidence
Surveyor negligence relating to
survey and valuation work

205
Consideration of circumstances
Quantification of claim
Quantification of error

214
Expert witness work in accounting
negligence claims
Financial effect of negligence, other
professions

221
Accountancy
Auditing
Due diligence reports
High net worth individuals
Privately owned business
Professional partnerships
Taxation

223
Architects

235
Surveyors

260
Professional fees
Professional negligence

285
Tax issues

289
Architects

312
Architects

354
Expert witness work related to
valuations, surveys and building
problems

360
Accounting and tax negligence

391
Expert witness work
Other professions
Planning supervisor
Project management
Quantity/building surveying

397
Accountants
Insolvency practitioners
Quantum in claims against other
professionals
Tax practitioners

405
Pensions adviser's negligence
Quantifying loss as a result of
pensions mis-selling

424
Building disputes

440
Breach of duty of care of accountants
Investigation of potential fraud
Responsibilities of company directors

441
Accounting negligence

449
Accountants' and insolvency
practitioners' negligence
Claims mitigation
Quantification of losses

456
Auditing
Finance
Taxation

457
Accounting negligence
Other professions
Solicitors' negligence

481
Building disputes

499
Court appearances
Expert witness reporting
Investigative studies

511
All Aspects

525
All Aspects

535
Building

551
Building disputes

601
Accounting and taxation negligence

622
Building engineering

634
Architect

635
Accounting negligence
Expert witness work

652
Accountancy

669
Architects

682
Clients representative
Expert witness work
Other disciplines
Project management
Quantity surveying

707
Construction professionals

720
Accountants' negligence
Auditors' negligence
Quantum on professional negligence

728
Accountants' negligence
Auditors' negligence
Other professions

757
Expert witness work in connection
with auditing, accounting or taxation
problems
Plaintiff and defendant work
undertaken

762
Accounting negligence
Computer-related claims

772
Building defects/structural surveys
Valuations

790
Construction professionals

815
Architects

821
Accountants' negligence

833
Accountants' negligence
Medical negligence
Other professional negligence
Solicitors' negligence

927
Accounting/taxation/valuation matters
Director disqualification
Medical negligence

928
Acquisitions, flotations, mergers and disposals
Auditors' negligence
Other professions

929
Auditors' negligence
Other professional negligence

957
Building and construction

977
Accounting/audit negligence
Defendant and plaintiff reports
Tax negligence

978
Accounting negligence
Auditor's negligence
Negligent pensions advice
Negligent tax advice
Other professions
Tax negligence

979
Accountants' negligence
Auditors' negligence
Expert witness

996
Conveyancing
Professional conduct and ethics

1004
Civil engineering
Project management
Structural engineering

1007
Building disputes

1029
Accounting negligence

1039
Expert witness work
Taxation negligence

1054
Accounting negligence claims
Expert witness work

1056
Fraud
Libel
Mal-administration

1058
Accounting matters
Property and construction claims
Taxation matters

1061
Back duty claims
Inland Revenue disputes
Sale and purchase of companies

1062
Application of generally accepted accounting practice
Auditing, taxation and accountancy advice
Quantification of loss arising from claims

1080
Building contract disputes
Copyright infringement
Design and construction failures and rectification
Party wall disputes
Professional appointment and negligence
Professional practice and performance

1085
Architects

1091
Architect's appointment and duty of care
Client's obligations
Design-and-build appointments
Practice management

1105
Maladministration

1125
Building design deficiencies
Collapse of structures
Excavation collapse
Foundation design failures
Structural defects
Subsidence of buildings

1128
Building surveying

1161
Building contract disputes
Building defects – commercial, leisure, residential and medical buildings
Claims for professional fees
Disputes between contractor and subcontractors
Improper contract administration
Infringements of copyright
Party wall infringements
Responsibilities of an architect
disputed subcontractor claims
practica completion certificate improperly withheld

1222
Drug-related negligence
Negligence in medical specialities

1238
Building and civil engineering design and construction

1284
Accounting negligence
Expert witness
Tax advice negligence

1285
Accounting, auditing and IT implementation (liability and quantum)
Other professionals (quantum)

1286
Accounting
Auditing and Information Technology (IT) implementation (liability and quantum)
Other professionals (quantum)

1287
Accounting
Auditing and Information Technology (IT) implementation (liability and quantum)
Other professionals (quantum)

1288
Accounting
Auditing and Information Technology (IT) implementation (liability and quantum)
Other professionals (quantum)

1289
Accounting, auditing and Information Technology (IT) implementation (liability and quantum)
Other professionals (quantum)

1290
Accounting
Auditing and Information Technology (IT) implementation (liability and quantum)
Other professionals (quantum)

1291
Accounting, auditing and Information Technology (IT) implementation (liability and quantum)
Other professionals (quantum)

1332
Accounting negligence
Negligent tax advice

1335
Accountants' negligence
Audit negligence
Expert witness
Report writing and claims analysis
Tax negligence

1377
Accountancy

1404
Engineering surveyors
Land surveyors

1450
Accounting audit and tax negligence
Inland Revenue investigations

1457
Architects

1462
Accounting negligence

1516
Solicitors
Solicitors' alleged negligence

1529
Architects

1533
Building and construction defects

1562
Negligence in audit and similar reports
Negligence in financial advice
Negligence in taxation aspects of trust and estates
Negligence in taxation/compliance and advice

1594
Architects

1636
Application of accounting and auditing standards
Due diligence in business acquisitions
Taxation advice

1650
Civil engineering

1652
Claims involving surveyors
Expert witness work

1681
Consulting engineers
Fee levels
Services provided

1720
Building surveying

1754
Expert witness work, including other
  professions

1766
All aspects

1768
Accounting negligence (liability and
  quantum)
Other professions

1784
Structural surveys

1813
All aspects

1839
Calculation of losses arising
Expert opinion on the standards of
  work undertaken by accountants

1928
Accounting negligence
Assessment of claims

1940
Auditors' negligence
Quantum reports, including other
  professions
Standards of accountancy and
  taxation advice

1955
Building surveying

1956
Architects

1966
Accounting negligence
Expert witness work

1981
Liability and quantum for accountants
Quantum for other professions

2019
Building and construction defects

2029
Architects

2111
Architects

2125
Accountancy

2126
Architects

2129
Accountants
Other profession

2132
Assessment of documentation
Assessment of running of project
Quantity surveyors and architects

2134
Accountancy
Audit
Taxation

2163
Auditors'/accountancy negligence
Lloyd's/insurance markets
Negligence in connection with
  insolvency appointments
Taxation/tax advisers (including
  inland revenue investigations)

2171
Building disputes

2175
Expert witness work

2260
Building disputes

2263
Accountants
Other professions

2325
Building

2330
Accounting negligence
Losses arising

2331
Accounting negligence
Expert witness work
Tax negligence

2332
Accountancy negligence
Expert witness work
Other professions

2333
Accounting profession
Expert witness work
Other professions

2350
Building regulation aspects
Fire-protection aspects
Fire-related negligence claims
Role of architect and contractors

2382
Commercial building
Industrial building
Professional negligence/building
Residential building

2386
Boundary disputes
Building disputes
Residential mortgage
Rights of light
Valuation

2402
Building surveying

2432
Banking practice

2477
Accounting negligence
Expert witness work

2488
Accounting negligence

2541
Architectural
Building supervision duties
Personal injury cases arising from
  building
Property sales misdescription
  matters/property valuations
Structural surveys/house buyers,
  reports/valuation surveys
Town planning consultancy work

2542
Architects

2550
Negligent surveys and valuations
Undiscovered defects in buildings,
  including asbestos

2554
Building surveys (residential and
  commercial)
Construction failures
Mortgage valuations (residential)
RICS/ISVA Home buyers' reports
RICS/ISVA House/flat buyers' reports
Refurbishment and repair

**Professional Negligence/
Accountancy Investigations**

2414
Acquisition investigations and reports
Share valuations

Professional Negligence (Alleged)

1304
Medico-legal work

**Professional Negligence/
Accountants/Auditors**

205
Comparison with prevailing standards
Consideration of circumstances
Quantification of claim
Quantification of error

**Professional Negligence/Building
Defects/Disputes**

1908
Expert reports on poor/defective
  building works
Expert submissions and arbitrations
  on building claims
NHBRC Warranty claims/arbitrations
Negligence claims – surveys
Negligence claims – valuations
Ombudsman referral on building
  insurance claims

Professional Negligence Claims

634
Advising architects on claims for
  non-payment of fees

652
Accountancy and business advice

2125
Accountancy
Audit
Back duty reviews
Forensic accounting
Taxation

Professional Negligence/Fraud

425
Accounting negligence
Evaluation of fraud
Liaison with insurers and authorities
  [police, Crown Prosecution Service
  (CPS)]

914
Accounting negligence
Asset tracing
Expert witness work
Fraud investigations and prevention
  including IT

**Professional Negligence in General
Medical Practice**

106
All aspects

Professional Negligence/Liability Claims

1481
All aspects

Professional Negligence/Medical Negligence

1474
Medicine

Professional Practice

403
Advice on Architects appointment, professional, technical and administrative performance
Copyright infringement
Employer and Contractor obligations and responsibilities

Professional Services

1072
Consultancy, collectors, loss adjusters, underwriters, solicitors
Expert witness work
Valuations – insurance, tax, sale, private treaty

Professionals/Negligence Claims against

138
Reports on quantum

Profits, Loss of

1377
Assessment of future loss
Assessment of loss
Experience of losses arising in tort and contract

Project Completion

969
Clearance defects
Commissioning
Contractual claims
Delays and costs
Incomplete work
System malfunctions

Project Management

857
All aspects

1512
Claims and contract variations
Cost control
Engineering coordination
Estimating
Planning and scheduling
Subcontracts

1609
Audit of performance
Contractual relationships
Effects upon programme
Procurement advice

2122
Contract administration
Procurement selection
Quality, time and value monitoring

Project Management/Construction

104
Analysis of the performance of the client's project manager
Analysis of the performance of the contractor's management

2527
Building
Civil engineering
Mechanical/electrical services

Property

see also Valuation, Surveying

880
Arbitration
Landlord and tenant
Rent review (commercial)
Valuation of commercial property for all purposes

1754
Arbitrations
Compensation
Compulsory purchase
Conveyancing negligence (quantum effects)
Doctors' and dentists' rents
Landlord and tenant disputes
Lease extensions
Matrimonial property valuation
Probate valuation
Rating
Rent reviews
Town planning
Valuation negligence

1850
All aspects

2466
Public houses, hotels, clubs and other licensed premises

Property/Building/Construction

64
Boundary disputes
Building negligence
Surveying negligence
Valuation negligence

Property Commercial

354
Architectural and design work
Building defects
Landlord and tenant problems
Surveys

1099
Contaminated land
Doctors' surgeries
Professional negligence
Valuation disputes

1355
Landlord and tenant negotiations
Lease renewals
Portfolio management
Rent reviews
Valuation

1728
Landlord and tenant disputes
Professional negligence
Valuation disputes

Property Commercial/Industrial

1867
Property consultancy
Valuations
Work experience in more than 35 countries

Property Commercial/Residential

50
Boundary disputes
Building disputes
Landlord and Tenant Act
Professional negligence

Property/Construction

1481
All aspects

Property Development

1842
Commercial
Hospital
Industrial
Leisure
Residential
Retail

Property in the Retail Oil/Motor Trade Industries

131
Development appraisal and viability studies
Easements and covenants
Rent review/lease renewal
Valuation and appraisals

Property Insurance

235
Claim assessment
Rebuilding cost assessments
Risk management
Structural monitoring and damage investigation

Property Litigation

206
Boundary disputes
Disrepair reports – Section II Landlord and Tenant Act 1985
Matrimonial division valuations
Professional negligence (residential valuations, surveys and reports)

1369
Boundary disputes
Dispute
Negligence and divorce
Rent review and lease renewal
Valuation and survey of property/residential/commercial arbitrator or independent expert

Property Management

2431
Commercial properties
Vacant or tenanted

Property Offices

1747
Investment
Landlord and tenant work
Planning
Rating
Rent review/lease renewals
Sales and lettings
Valuation

Property/Residential

1171
Boundary disputes
Development land
House agency including country
  houses and estates
Survey report and valuation
Valuation

Property Residential/Commercial

861
Boundary disputes
Dilapidations
Expert witness reports
Independent expert appointed by
  Royal Institution of Chartered
  Surveyors (RICS)
Rent reviews and lease renewals
Surveys and valuations

Property/Rural

716
Farm and commercial rents
Farm dilapidations
Land drainage works
Rural and urban boundaries
Rural and urban rights of way

Property Surveying/Expert Reports

30
Accident claims
Boundary claims (in-house drawings)
Dilapidation claims
Expert reports and court evidence
Professional negligence claims
Structural surveys and valuations

Property Surveying/Valuation

658
Boundary disputes
Building construction/supervision
Covenants/land tribunal etc
Landlord and tenant disputes
Property management
Rent reviews/lease renewals

Property Valuation

235
Freehold and leasehold
Mortgage valuation
Professional negligence
Residential and commercial

448
Commercial and residential property
  valuations and surveys
Ground rent and investment
  valuations
Lock-up garage and valuations and
  surveys
Matrimonial reports
Professional negligence

530
Arbitration and dispute resolution
Commercial landlord and tenant
Leasehold reform
Restrictive covenants
Valuation of commercial and
  industrial property
Valuation of residential property

572
For insolvency situations
For matrimonial purposes
For probate purposes
Landlord and tenant work, including
  rent reviews and lease renewals
Negligence claims against other
  valuers
Rental valuations for all purposes

1364
Landlord and Tenant
Professional negligence
Property development
Rents
Yields

2550
Boundary and right of way disputes
Business valuations
Partnership disputes
Personal injury
Quantum assessments

Property Valuation/Management

1045
Compensation and rating
Ecclesiastical, charity and education
  property
Landlord and tenant/management
Professional negligence and damage
  assessment
Residential, commercial, industrial
  and land
Retrospective valuations and
  procedures

Property Valuation/Planning

1552
Appeals
Commercial developments and
  residential developments
Planning

Property-Related Matters

1265
Development land
Landlord and tenant disputes
Professional negligence
Rent reviews/lease renewals
Restrictive covenants
Valuation disputes

Providing Support Care to Heavily Dependent Individuals

878
Clients are continuous clients for
  many years
Expert position to cost care for
  individuals over long periods

Psychiatric Aspects of Trauma

2508
All aspects

Psychiatric Assessment

1071
Adults in matrimonial dispute
Child in relation to parents,
  grandparents in disputed custody or
  abuse
Children
Educational needs of
  disturbed/autistic children
Juvenile offenders

Psychiatric Care

1402
Case management
Depression
Occupational stress
Residential care
Suicide and suicidal behaviour

Psychiatric Disorders

2059
Depression/anxiety
Post-traumatic stress disorder
Use and abuse of minor tranquillisers
Violence secondary to mental
  disorder

Psychiatric Nursing

917
Community care
Schizophrenia
Self-harm
Standards of care
Suicide
Violence

Psychiatric Problems in Old Age

2508
All aspects

Psychiatric/Psychological Problems

1405
Aggression
Anxiety
Compulsive gambling
Depression
Post-traumatic stress disorder
Socialisation and intellectual
  assessments

Psychiatric Reports

176
Assessment of psychological trauma
  in damage claims
Expert evidence for pleas in mitigation

Psychiatry

see also under patient eg Child

18
Mental handicap
Neuropsychiatry in childhood and
  adolescence/especially head
  injuries, dyslexia and epilepsy
Reliability of child and adolescent
  witnesses

33
Medical negligence (psychiatric)
Mental Health Act violations
Personal injury – psychological
Post-traumatic stress disorder
Psychological damage due to drugs

56
Co-existence of psychiatric disorder
  and crime
Effects of sexual abuse/rape
Issues related to psychotherapy and
  counselling especially
  psycho-analysis
Parent-child dynamics
Post-traumatic stress disorder

60
Alcohol-drug dependence
Psycho-sexual problems
Stress-related disorders

164
Anorexia nervosa
Post-traumatic stress

177
Personal injury
Post-traumatic stress disorders

181
Crime
Medical negligence
Personal injury

226
Bereavement
Child protection – psychiatric aspects
of factitious or induced illness
(Munchausen syndrome by proxy)
Post-traumatic response to medical
accidents (some aspects)
Post-traumatic stress disorder

286
Affective disorders
Depression
Manic depressive disease

290
Criminal work, including courts martial
Family, child, adolescent, abuse work
Munchauser cases, including 'by
proxy'
Personal injury work
Professional negligence work
Substance abuse work

295
Medical negligence
Mental health legislation
Mental health review tribunals
Mentally disordered offenders
Psychiatric aspects of personal
injuries
Testamentary capacity

366
Child custody
Learning disabilities
Medical negligence
Mental health
Mental health review tribunals
Personal injury

377
Medico-legal work

431
Alcohol dependency
Drug dependency
Litigation
Post-traumatic stress
Substance misuse

433
Alcoholism and drug abuse
Criminal liability and diminished
responsibility
Forensic – difficult and offender
patients
General
Mental Health Act and Mental
Review Tribunal
Personal injury

434
Alcohol-related problems
General adult psychiatry
Occupational stress
Post-traumatic stress

500
Forensic psychiatry
Personal injury

526
Anxiety states
Depression
Personality disorder
Post-traumatic stress disorder
Schizophrenia

607
Cognitive behaviour therapy
Consultation on clinical environments
Dementias
Neuropsychological assessment
Post-traumatic stress disorder
Testamentary capacity

705
Alcohol and drug abuse and addiction
Criminal behaviour
Detention under Mental Health Act
Injury caused by drugs and other
toxic substances
Matrimonial disputes and custody of
children
Post-traumatic stress disorder
Psychiatric sequelae to accidents
and major disasters
Suicide and attempted suicide

714
Chronic pain, eg. low back pain
Cultural psychiatry
Psychophysiology and
psychopharmacology
Psychosomatic conditions, eg.
irritable bowel syndrome, ME
Work-related stresses

724
Criminal
Forensic
Legislative
Medical negligence
Post-trauma

832
Anxiety, depressive disorders
Eating disorders
Electro-convulsive therapy
Post-traumatic stress
Work-related psychiatric disorders

837
Anxiety
Depression
ME
Post-traumatic stress disorder
Repetitive Strain Injury (RSI)
Stress

849
Defences to criminal charges
Discretionary life review panel
reports and evidence
Family law in care proceedings
Mental health review tribunal –
independent reports and evidence
Opinion in mitigation to criminal
offences
Personal injury and medical
negligence

851
General psychiatry
Neuropsychiatry

859
Neurotic and stress-related disorders

888
Alcoholism and other alcohol
problems
Drug misuse and addiction
Gambling addiction
Pathological spending

984
Community and social psychiatry
Depressive states and anxiety
Drug treatment in psychiatry
Eating disorders (anorexia nervosa
etc)
Neuropsychiatry (interface between
psychiatry/neurology)
Stress and post-traumatic stress

990
Anxiety
Depression
Prescribed psychiatric drugs
Tranquilisers

1006
Accident compensation
Post-traumatic stress

1055
All aspects

1245
Post-traumatic stress disorder
Psychological aspects of medical
illness
Psychological effects of alleged
negligence

1302
Forensic psychiatry
Learning disability (mental
retardation)

1448
Criminal work
Drug and alcohol dependency
Examinations related to the Mental
Health Act
Parenting assessment and family
matters
Testamentary capacity

1498
Assessment of parental suitability for
access to children
Family emotional problems,
neurosis/personality difficulties
Forensic problems associated with
accidents, post-traumatic stress
disorder
Forensic problems associated with
mental illness/subnormality
Rehabilitation and treatment for
people with alcohol/drug problems
and dependence
Work in relation to assessing people
in secure hospital settings (Mental
Health Review Tribunal and Mental
Health Act 1983)

1509
Addiction – to benzodiazepine, to
illicit drugs
Cannabis – use and effects
Illicit drugs – use and effects
Panic attacks
Phobic anxiety

1540
Alcoholic dependence
Depression
Drug dependence
Head injuries (psychiatric sequelae)
Post-traumatic stress disorder
Psychoses

1669
Anxiety states
Dementia
Depression
Medical negligence
Post-traumatic stress disorder
Schizophrenia

1724
Alcohol
General psychiatry
Occupational mental health
Post-traumatic stress disorder

1823
General psychiatry
Liaison psychiatry

1906
Cognitive therapy
Maternal mental health
Psychotherapy

1939
Medical negligence (psychiatric
  aspects)
Medico-legal aspects of personal
  injury claims – Mental Health Act
  1983
Nervous shock
Post-traumatic shock disorder (PTSD)
Psychosis (with particular reference
  to schizophrenia)

1960
All aspects

1962
Arson
Child care (assessment of parents
  only)
Criminal behaviour
Medical negligence
Mental health review tribunals
Personal injury

2036
Learning difficulties (mental handicap)
Multiple handicap
Personality disorder

2050
Deafness and mental health
  (mentally disordered offenders)
Forensic psychiatry
Independent opinions, mental health
  review tribunals
Transcultural aspects (mentally
  disordered offenders)

2077
Compulsive gambling
Post-traumatic stress disorder
Professional negligence/medical and
  nursing
Substance misuse/alcohol and drugs
Suicide

2254
Child, adolescent and family
Forensic
Medico-legal

2269
Agoraphobia and panic
Depression
Obsessive-compulsive disorder
Personality disorder
Post-traumatic stress disorder

2417
Forensic psychiatry
Medico-legal issues

2464
Abnormal illness behaviour
Epidemiology
Munchusen's
Psychosomatic medicine/stress
Somatisation

2481
Eating disorders
Head injury/neuro-psychiatry
Liaison psychiatry
Post-trauma eg post-traumatic stress

2533
Psychoanalysis
Psychotherapy

2565
Depression, anxiety etc
Head injury/post concussive states
Post traumatic stress disorder

Psychiatry/Adult

45
Alcohol misuse
Post-traumatic stress disorder
Substance misuse

216
Matrimonial
Mental health review tribunals
Personal injury

241
Alcoholism
Family issues with children over 16
Marital conflict
Post-traumatic stress disorder
Stress-related conditions

283
Assessment and reporting of
  medical/personal (psychiatric) injury
Assessment and reporting on
  criminal matters
Assessment of families (parties) in
  custody/access disputes
Stress management and
  stress-related disorders
Treatment of alcoholism

373
Alcoholism
Depressive illness
Drug misuse and dependence
Post-traumatic stress disorder

375
Benzodiazepine addiction
Medical negligence
Mental Health Act

376
General clinical work

715
Assessment of mental competence
  in relation to retirement, paternity
  and custody
Diagnosis, assessment and
  treatment of psychotic disorders
Effects of mental health due to
  significant specific life events

1176
Anxiety states and depression
Assessment of intellectual ability and
  competence
Personality assessment
Post-traumatic stress disorder
  (assessment and treatment)

1225
Depression
Post-traumatic stress disorder

1283
Medical negligence
Personal injury
Professional negligence

1423
'Shoplifting'
Alcohol-related offences
Depression and post-traumatic
  depression
Pathological grief
Post-traumatic anxiety and phobic
  disorders
Post-traumatic stress disorder
Psychiatric issues in personal injury
  action
Psychological issues regarding the
  Housing Act
Somatoform pain disorder

1525
Diversion from custody to secure
  beds
Post-traumatic stress disorder and
  other sequelae
Reports on non-indictable offenders
Reports on special care psychiatry

1547
Psychopharmacology

1590
Alcohol dependence
Post-traumatic stress disorder

1611
Eating disorders
Mood disorders
Post-traumatic stress disorder
Psychiatry of post-natal period
Sexual disorder

1670
Alcohol problems
Post-traumatic stress disorders

1772
Neuropsychiatry
Post-traumatic stress disorder
Psychiatric efforts of trauma
Psychiatry of old age
Transcultural psychiatry

1843
Anxiety disorders
Post-traumatic stress disorders
Sexual dysfunction

1879
Medical accidents – psychiatric
  aspects
Post-traumatic stress disorder
Professional negligence – psychiatric
  aspects

2082
Forensic
Medical negligence
Post-traumatic stress disorder
Unfit doctors

2083
Medico-legal
Post-traumatic and other stress
  disorders
Psychopharmacology
Psychosomatic disorders
Psychotherapy

2194
Medical negligence
Personal injury

2200
Adjustment disorders
Depression
Post-traumatic stress disorder

2215
Criminal law
Family law – assessment of parents in relation to care proceedings
Independent psychiatric opinion in relation to Mental Health Act
Personal injury

2273
Alcohol related illnesses
Mood disorders, especially depressive illness
Post-traumatic stress disorder (PTSD) – identfication and treatment

2322
Criminal behaviour and psychiatric disorder
Psychiatric disorder and insurance
Psychiatric disorder due to organic disease
Psychiatric sequelae of trauma

2374
Agoraphobia/panic disorder
Anorexia/bulimia nervosa
Body dysmorphic disorder
Depression
Obsessive compulsive disorder
Post-traumatic stress disorder

2407
Civil litigation
Criminal matters
Forensic psychiatry

2499
Anxiety and depression
Assessment of adults in Children Act proceedings
Chronic fatigue syndrome
Medical negligence
Mental health in the work place
Post-traumatic stress disorder
Psychiatric consequences of road accidents and accidents at work

Psychiatry/Civil/Criminal Law

1223
Cases involving drug and alcohol aspects
Effect of dementias, brain injury and mental handicap
Effect of psychosis and neurosis including puerperal psychosis
Epileptic and neurological aspects
Marital and psychosexual problems
Personality disorders
Post-traumatic stress disorder
Pre-menstrual tension
Stress disorders

Psychiatry of Accidents

375
Post-traumatic stress disorder
Psychiatric disorders following injury
Psychiatric sequelae of head injury
Psychiatric sequence of road traffic accidents

Psychiatry/Psychology

750
Alcoholism and drug abuse
Criminal cases
Mental health appeal tribunals
Psychotherapy
Sexual disorders, marital problems, sexual abuse
Stress

Psychiatry/Psychotherapy/ Psychoanalysis

618
Assessment and treatment of neurotic disorders
Assessment and treatment of personality disorders
Assessment and treatment of post-traumatic disorders
Assessment and treatment of psychosomatic disorders

Psychiatry Puerperal

1225
Post-natal depression/psychoses
Post-traumatic stress disorder after childbirth

Psychodiagnostic Assessment for Adults

386
Assessment of psychological aspects in personal injury cases
Fitness to plead/stand trial
Intellectual assessments
Treatment planning and questions of disposition

Psychological

see also Children

Psychological Aspects of Trauma/Adults/Children

2266
Anxiety states
Bereavement reactions
Clinical depression
Medical negligence
Personal injury
Post traumatic stress disorder

Psychological Assessment

395
Pain
Phobic/anxiety/depressive disorders
Post-traumatic stress disorder

1211
Compliance
Emotional disposition
Experience of custody, detention and questioning
Intellectual functioning
Personality
Suggestibility

1405
Alcohol
Depression
IQ
Organicity
Pain pathology
Personality
Psychopathy
Stress

1591
Autism/Asperger syndrome/language
Bilingual children
Child abuse – race, disability and abuse
Deafness and development (fluent in British Sign Language)
Language development and disorder
Language/race issues

1717
Nervous shock following medical accidents
Nervous shock following personal injury
Post-traumatic stress disorder

2210
Criminal injuries compensation
Family proceedings assessments
Mental health/handicap assessments
Personality assessments
Post-traumatic stress disorder
Road traffic accidents

2279
Parenting ability (in residence order conflicts)
Post-traumatic stress syndrome

Psychological Assessment/ Adults/ Families

232
Criminal Injuries Compensation Board
Fitness to plead
Legal aid
Mediation: consultancy on family psychodynamics

Psychological/Assessment of Adults/Children

1679
Cognitive ability and learning capacity
Parenting – emotional, cognitive and development issues
Specific learning difficulties (dyslexia and language)

Psychological Assessment of Adults in Forensic/Compensation Cases

1019
Post-traumatic stress disorder
Psychometric assessment (eg of memory, intellect, personality, mental state)
Suitability for psychological intervention
Witness susceptibility to suggestion

Psychological Assessment of Children

523
Effects of accidents and trauma
Intellectual, educational, emotional development

Psychological Assessment of Children/Families

463
Assessment of family functioning
Child protection and child abuse
Individual assessment of children (emotional and intellectual)
Individual assessment of parents (psychological and intellectual)
Working with social services departments and guardians ad lite

1431
Child dysfunction
Family relations/attachment
Family/child law (Children Act)
Placement of child away from family
Rehabilitation back to family

Psychological Assessment of Children/Young People

119
Advice on computer equipment
Advice on educational placements
Medical negligence
Neuropsychological asessments
  relating to head injury
Post-traumatic stress
Special educational needs
Special schools
Specific learning difficulties

Psychological Assessment of Deaf Clients

1629
Assessment of language
  comprehension
Assessment of understanding
Deaf persons in hospitals, prisons
  and secure institutions
Deviant clinical and criminal minority
  of deaf people
Educational, social and occupational
  background of deaf people

Psychological Assessment/Treatment

2343
Brain injury, epilepsy
Chronic pain
Learning disability
Physical or sensory disability
Psychological trauma
Specific learning difficulties

Psychological/Cognitive/Mental Assessments

678
Emotional and behavioural
  consequences of trauma
Head injury, memory impairments
Mental competence
Personal injury compensation
Psychological damage – quantum
Quantification of cognitive and
  psychological deficits
Road traffic accidents related
  impairments

Psychological Consequences of Road Traffic/Occupational Accidents

150
Chronic invalidism, chronic pain
Concussion
Driving-related anxiety
Hyperventilation
Post-traumatic stress disorder
Whiplash neck injury

Psychological Consequences of Trauma, Assessment of

896
Relationship between mental events
  and physical changes

Psychological Effect of Accidents

2381
Injuries sustained during medical
  treatment

Psychological Effect of Trauma/Injury

1442
Brain damage
Following road traffic accidents
Other psychological effects
Phobias
Post-traumatic stress disorder

1619
Cognitive or intellectual assessment
Family law risk assessments
Post-traumatic stress disorder
  assessments
Psychophysiological assessments of
  fear
Rebuttal of psychological evidence
Suggestability assessments

Psychological Functioning, Assessment of

1442
Dyslexia
Intelligence

Psychological Impairment

2352
Assessments of intelligence and
  suggestibility
Disputed confessions to police
Personal injury
Post-traumatic stress
Testamentary capacity

Psychological Injury

1755
Personal psychological injury arising
  from road accidents

Psychological Medicine/Adult

1641
Adult psychiatry (but NOT criminal
  litigation)
Psychiatric treatment of trauma and
  physical disability

Psychology

see also under patient eg Child
10
Counselling after accidents, illness,
  domestic upheaval, redundancy
Educational assessments
Neurological assessments
Psychological assessment of
  children and adults in personal
  injury disputes

73
Children and families
Custody, access/contact
Personal injury
Psychometric assessment
Recovery from trauma (including
  child abuse)

167
Cognitive assessment
Occupational stress
Personal accident
Traumatic stress [including Post
  Traumatic Stress Disorder (PTSD)]

196
Anxiety, phobias, depression
Health psychology
Pain management and psychological
  rehabilitation
Panic attacks
Post-traumatic stress disorder
Psychological assessment and
  therapy

560
Competency (civil and criminal)
Post-traumatic stress disorder
Psychological assessment
Sanity at time of offence

561
Clinical psychology
Educational psychology
Inspection of children's homes
School inspection
Special educational needs
Working with parents/carers

854
Children
Custody
Educational psychology
People with learning difficulties
Post-traumatic stress
Special educational needs

917
Obsessive compulsive disorder
Phobias, agoraphobia
Post-traumatic stress disorder
Psychological effects of physical
  illness
Schizophrenia

1065
Assessment of psychological
  suffering due to accidents etc
Hypnosis
Post-traumatic stress disorder (adults
  only)
Treatment of adult mental health
  problems

1120
Assessment and treatment of
  criminal behaviour
Clinical and criminal liability
Evaluation of witness statements
Post-traumatic stress disorder
Problems of abnormal behaviour

1241
Abuse/sexual, physical and emotional
Anxiety
Assessment of intellectual ability,
  memory and cognitive state
Assessment of risk
Assessment of verbal, written and
  video evidence
Cognitive analytic and behaviour
  therapy
Depression
Marital and family dynamics
Mental state and diagnosis of
  adolescents and adults
Parenting skills
Post-traumatic stress disorder
Psychological impact of personal
  injury

1244
Educational: special educational
  needs (1993 Education Act);
  dyslexia; negligence; tribunals
  (1993 Education Act); educational
  placement – maintained and
  independent sectors
Family court work
Post-accident assessment –
  insurance claims

1403
Head injury
Memory disorders
Neuropsychological assessment and
  rehabilitation
Neuropsychology
Post-traumatic psychological
  phenomena

1643
Child
Education
Forensic

1663
Adjustment reactions
Brain damage
Post-traumatic stress disorder

1873
Anxiety
Post Traumatic Stress Disorder
  (PTSD)
Recovered memory
Sexual abuse

2010
Advice on treatment
Head injury – neuropsychological
  assessment
Personal injury – assessment of
  effects
Post-traumatic stress
  disorder/post-traumatic anxiety

2063
Neuropsychological assessment
Post-traumatic stress disorder
Psychological assessment and
  treatment of mental health problems

2077
Compulsive gambling
Post-traumatic stress disorder
Professional negligence/medical and
  nursing
Substance misuse/alcohol and drugs
Suicide

2198
Assessment of parents in cases of
  child abuse and neglect
Asssessment of the reliability of
  witness evidence
Evaluation of IQ and learning
  difficulties
Evaluation of all sex offenders and
  their treatability
Evaluation of arsonists, mental state
  etc
Neuropsychological assessment in
  civil compensation and criminal
  cases
Psychological effects of accidents
  and trauma

2275
Anxiety/phobia
Depression
Post-traumatic stress
Psycho-neurological psychometric
  assessment of intellect and memory
Road traffic accidents/injury

2416
Assessment of post-traumatic stress
  disorder
Psychological effects of head injury
Reliability of confessions to the police

2445
Anxiety and depression following
  trauma
Post-traumatic stress disorder
Psychological effects of personal
  injury
Psychometric assessment

2463
Family breakdown
Family interactions – effects on
  children
Parenting competence
Rehabilitation of children to parents

Psychology/Adult

1176
Anxiety states and depression
Assessment of intellectual ability and
  competence
Personality assessment
Post-traumatic stress disorder
  (assessment and treatment)

2143
Neuropsychological assessment
Post-traumatic phobia
Post-traumatic stress disorder

Psychology Assessment

419
Children Act work
Family and matrimonial
Forensic assessment
Personal injury

Psychology/Civil Courts

1294
Educational assessments and
  appeals
Medical accidents
Personal injury
Road traffic accidents
Work-related psychological damage

Psychology/Criminal Courts

1294
Assessment of intent
Coercion and harrassment
Explanation of behaviour
Fitness to plead
Psychological sequelae of criminal
  actions
Trauma assessment

Psychology/Family Courts

1294
'Failure to thrive' issues
Adoption issues
Child abuse – sexual and physical
Custody and access disputes
Parenting skill – assessment
Risk assessment

Psychology/Forensic/Clinical

1964
Family
Mental health – psychological overlay
Personal injury

Psychology Investigative

1210
Analysis of spoken and written
  material
Inferring characteristics from crime
  scene
Linking crimes
Offender profiling
Psychogeography of crime, fraud,
  threat letters, serial killers
Studies of arson, homicide, rape

Psychology Services to Adults

1744
Conference speaker
Post-traumatic stress disorder
Psychological debriefing
Psychological effects of emergency
  services work
Research and literature reviews
War veterans

Psychosexual Medicine

908
Aspects of sexuality in homosexual
  men and woman, paraphiliacs, ie
  fetishists, sadomasochists
Consummation problems in couples
Desire problems, usually as a result
  of injury, tumour or stroke, both
  hypo- and hypersexuality
Hormonal control of transsexuals
  who wish to change sex
Injuries sustained by men/women
  that interfere with sexual functioning
Sexual problems of
  mentally/physically handicapped
  people
Treatment of erectile impotence in
  men, or loss of libido in women
Variant sexuality and its difficulties

Psychotherapist

2476
Child therapy and care
Family mediation
Family therapy

Public Health

2204
Environmental hazards
Water, food

Public Health Engineering

1077
Land drainage and flooding
  assessments
Pollution risk assessments
Private and public sewerage
Small scale sewage treatment
  installations

2408
Compressed air, vacuum
  systems/installations
Fire sprinkler protection, fire survey
  and investigation
Gas, carbon monoxide spillages
Personal injury
Plumbing, drainage, sanitation,
  Closed Circuit Television (CCTV)
  survey
Services for medical buildings,
  modular systems
Water services, pumps

Public Health Entomology/Pest Control

326
Audit of catering, hotel, food premises
Examination of pest control contracts
Litigation under food
hygiene/pesticide legislation
Mosquitoes, cockroaches, bed bugs, flies, etc
Stored product and agricultural insect pests
Tropical entomology and vector control

Public Health Pest Control

292
Incidence/risks of infestation
Methods of control
Pest biology
Pesticides and equipment
UK legislation relating to pest control

Public Houses/Licensed Premises

1942
Brewery and balance sheet valuations
Compulsory purchase and compensation
Open market valuations
Professional negligence and expert witness work
Rent reviews and renewal of leases:
General advice & Expert Witness service, Independent Determination and arbitrator

Public Inquiries/Legal Procedures

1203
Negotiating highway, drainage and planning agreements with local/highway authorities
Presentation of expert highway and transportation evidence

Public Inquiries/Planning Appeals

1667
Development planning
Highway design
Traffic and highway evidence
Traffic planning
Transportation planning

Public Local Inquiries

351
Preparation of reports/evidence
Presentation of evidence
Research

Pulmonary Pathology (Histopathology)

1046
Industrial lung disease
Lung cancer
Mesothelioma

Quality Assurance Systems

723
Evaluation of compliance with ISO 9000

Quality Management/Personal Effectiveness of Solicitors

1351
Personal efficiency and effectiveness programmes
Total quality management programmes

Quantification of Loss of Earnings

1309
Analysis of earnings by occupational area and geographical region.
Career options and levels of earnings in Europe, America, South America and Australia.

Quantity Surveying

see also Civil Engineering

314
Arbitration and litigation
Construction contracts and sub-contracts
Contractual claims
Professional negligence claims (quantity surveyors)
Valuation of construction works

321
Bills of quantities
Cost estimates
Life cycle costings
Repair costs
Valuations

329
Contractual claims
Final accounts
Insurance valuations
Measurement of construction works
Subcontract claims
Valuation of construction works

338
Claim preparation/rebuttal
Contract conditions
Measurement/tender documentation
Offshore and petro-chemical
Quantum
Sub-contracting

361
Civil engineering
Earthworks
Major roadworks

590
Construction: mechanical and electrical
Delay, disruption, extension of time
Measurement and valuation of building work
Professional negligence appointment and fees
Quantification of loss and expense
Refurbishment and new build

592
Contractual claims
Cost expertise in building construction work
Standard forms of building contract

602
Construction contracts
Construction costs
Standard rules of measurement

615
Construction and property related studies and reports
Construction cost consultancy and management
Construction taxation services
Legal support services
Project management

616
Administration of contracts for construction projects
Allegations of negligence in quantity surveying work
Estimating and tendering procedures for construction projects
Evaluation of claims for additional payment
Measurement and costing of construction work
Preparation of feasibility studies and budgets for construction
Preparation of tender documents and final accounts
Valuation of changes/variations etc in construction projects

822
Construction cost consultancy
Contract and sub-contract relationships
Estimating the costs of construction
Life cycle costing
Management and administration of builders

857
Advice on building contracts
Building disputes
Employer's agent
Insurance valuations

874
Costing
Quantum reports
Scott schedules – preparation and pricing

973
Adjudication
Contractors' loss and expense claims
Costs of building reinstatement
Professional negligence – procurement and certification

1016
Construction disputes/claims
Cost estimates and planning
Development appraisals
Development disputes
Procurement advice
Professional negligence

1090
Cost control
Delay and disruption
Estimating and tendering
Loss and expense
Valuation of variations

1124
Arbitration
Building defects
Extension of time claims
Loss and expense claims
Structural surveys
Valuations of building costs

1146
Compliance with building contracts
Compliance with terms of
  professional appointment
Disruption to programmed works and
  loss and expense entitlement
Quantum of contractor's entitlements
Remedial works

1155
Measurement and analysis of
  disputed quantities and valuation
Review and analysis of the content of
  bills of quantities, schedules and
  contract documents

1180
Building
Civil engineering

1321
Commercial developments
Final accounts
Interior finishes

1517
Cost control
Delay and disruption
Estimating and tendering
Loss and expense
Valuation of variables

1524
Construction costs and costs of
  changes
Delay and disruption claims in
  building contracts
Insurance related matters
Valuation of defective works costs

1609
Ascertainment of loss and expense
Estimation of remedial costs
Evaluation of claims
Professional negligence
Quantum meruit: work/fees
Valuation of building works

1614
Contractual claims (causation and
  liability)
Professional duties and obligations
  (negligence)

1723
Construction contracts
Construction costs

1821
All specialist trades
Building and civil engineering
Claims for loss and expense
Extensions of time and delay
  causation
Final accounts
Specialised experience on
  landscaping

1840
Building and civil engineering works
  valuations
Contract delays and extensions of
  time
Contractual claims and disputes
Professional fees and professional
  liability
Professional negligence
Quantum

1875
Acceleration
Delays and disruptions
Extensions of time
Loss and expense
Quantity surveying
Valuations/final accounts

1955
Ascertainment of claims for loss
  and/or expense, extensions of time,
  disruption etc
Estimating and cost planning
Measurement and valuation of
  construction works
Procurement and contractual
  arrangements and administration
Professional negligence
Remedial works

2122
Construction claims
Construction contracts (JCT etc)
Construction costs/estimates
Dispute resolution

2228
Assessment of claims for delays and
  loss and expense
Construction contracts and their
  application
Construction procedures – pre and
  post contract
Measurement and valuation of
  quantum
Valuation of work in progress for
  financial institutions

2320
Delay and disruption claims
Extension of time
Loss and expense claims
Quantum issues
Valuation of variations

2338
Cost planning
Professional indemnity cases
Professional practice and procedures
Quantum

2411
Building and civil engineering works
  – mechanical and electrical services
  contracts – refurbishment and
  maintenance works
Contractual disputes including
  preparation of claims and expert
  opinion on contract matters
Preparation of expert reports and
  evidence
Quantum evaluation

2493
Adjudication
Commercial management of
  contract, prevention of claims
Preparation of expert reports, giving
  expert evidence
Preparation/resolution of claims
Resolution of disputes in
  construction/engineering/energy/insu
  rance

**Quantity Surveying/Building Cost
Disputes**

1184
Advising of costs, contracts and
  obtaining tenders – building
Reports of disputes, acting as expert
  witness
Schedules of condition and
  dilapidation
Tender documents, negotiating and
  reporting in tenders
Valuation of work in progress,
  assessing variations, accounts and
  claims
Valuations for fire insurance and loss
  assessment

**Quantity Surveying/Building/
Engineering**

573
Defective construction and remedial
  works
Insurance and fire damage valuation
Project funding and taxation
Project planning and management
Specialised construction:
  military/airforcre installations
Specialised construction:
  petrochemical plant
Specialised construction: pipelines
Workmanship and materials quality
  standards

**Quantity Surveying/Chartered
Quantity Surveyor**

222
Building defects assessment and
  analysis
Construction costs
Contractual claims assessment and
  appraisal
Contractual claims preparation
Design and construction of petrol
  filling stations
Professional negligence

**Quantity Surveying/Construction
Consultancy**

1628
Building – new and refurbishment
Civil engineering
Electrical engineering
Mechanical engineering
Process engineering

**Quantity Surveying/Cost
Consultancy/Planning**

511
All Aspects

**Quantity Surveying/Project
Management**

1986
Analysis of land and property
  speculation
Building contract disputes
Professional negligence
Quantity surveying matters from
  feasibility to final account

Quantity Surveying Services

870
Professional fees
Professional negligence

Quantity Surveyor/Project Manager

2239
Building and civil engineering works
Contract administration and dispute
  resolution
Marine works
Mechanical and electric service
  contracts
Preparation of expert reports and
  evidence
Project management and
  co-ordination
Quantum evaluation
Refurbishment, restoration and
  maintenance

Quantum

see also Loss of Profit,
Compensation, Employment,
Income Loss, Loss of Earnings

543
Employability/rehabilitation service

599
Building and construction works
Mechanical and electrical
engineering services
Professional negligence

720
Breach of warranty
Calculations of damages
Foreign exchange
Loss of earnings
Loss of profits
Share valuations

1309
Analysis of earnings by occupational
area and geographical region.
Career options and levels of earnings
in Europe, America, South America
and Australia.

1460
Cost of disability, help and assistance

1838
Construction quantity surveying

2547
Construction

Quantum Calculations

1266
Cost of care in medical negligence
claims
Loss of earnings, including pensions
Self-employed persons

Quantum/Construction

1667
Civil engineering and building
contracts
Claims arising from design problems
Claims for unforeseen conditions
Costs of delay and disruption
Professional indemnity claims

1834
Boundary disputes
Professional negligence – quantity
surveying
Programming/planning – construction
projects
Quantum – building projects
Quantum – civil engineering projects
Quantum – mechanical and electrical
services

2527
Building
Civil engineering
Mechanical/electrical services

Quantum/Construction Claims

270
Claims evaluation – loss and
expense and/or damages
Claims preparation – loss and
expense and/or damages
Insurance claims – preparation or
evaluation
Latent defects – claims and
evaluation
Valuation of work in progress
Variation account – preparation or
evaluation

Quantum/Construction Contracts

1855
Evaluation of accounts for measured
work
Evaluation of loss/expense and
damages claims
Planning analysis of claims for
extensions of time

Quantum Evaluation of Construction Work

1344
Assessing costs of disruption and
delay
Building construction
Civil engineering construction
Consequential costs of variations
Fair and reasonable quantum meruit
evaluation

Quantum in Commercial Litigation, Assessment of

414
Breach of contract, Breach of
warranty
Business valuations
Fraud investigations
Loss of profits/business interruptions
Matrimonial and partnership disputes
Personal injury and fatal accident –
loss of earnings
Professional negligence

Quantum/Liability/Construction Industry

92
Alternative Dispute Resolutions
(ADR)

Quantum of Damages in International/Domestic Civil Litigation/Arbitration

1398
Banking and finance disputes
Breach of contract
Business interruption
Construction
Insurance
Intellectual property
Pension disputes
Professional negligence
Warranty claims

Quantum of Loss, Assessment of

440
Advice on structured settlements
Breach of contract
Consequential loss in construction
disputes
General commercial litigation
Loss resulting from professional
negligence
Personal injury/medical
negligence/fatal accident

Quantum Reports For Specific Damages

1810
Care
Education and training
Equipment and housing adaptations
Nursing
Therapy
Transport and hollidays

Questioned Computer Evidence

2354
Computer evidence – Computer
Misuse Act
Computer evidence – civil
Computer evidence – crime

Questioned Document Examination

1570
Forgery detection
Handwriting identification
Typescript comparisons

Questioned 'Handwriting'

805
Cheque and fraud related cases
Comparison of disputed handwriting

2061
Anonymous letters
Questioned printing
Wills, contracts, agreements

Radar

2256
Doppler speed detection
Hand-held equipment

Radiological Safety

835
Assessment of statutory compliance
Industrial/environmental radiological
hazard assessment
Nationally accredited laboratory
facilities
On-site radiation monitoring
Radiological risk evaluation

Radiology

16
CT scanning
Contrast media
Diagnostic x-ray
procedures/investigations
General radiology
Interventional radiology
Radiology of trauma

2182
Antenatal ultrasound diagnosis
Gynaecology imaging/scans
Obstetrics imaging
Paediatric imaging

Radiology/Diagnostic

925
Cardiovascular radiology
Contrast medium pharmacology and
clinical usage
General radiology
Neuroradiology
Respiratory radiology
Skeletal radiology

2556
Accident and orthopaedic cases
Chest
Gastro-intestinal
Genito-urinary work
Isotopes
Myelography
Ultra-sound

Radiology/Imaging of Brain/Spine

345
Computed tomography
Diagnostic and interventional
angiography
Magnetic resonance imaging
Myelography
Plain radiography

Radiotherapy

1982
Accident
Damage and overdose/underdose

Railway Mechanical/Electrical Engineering

1948
Mishap investigations
Train performance
Vehicle design
Vehicle maintenance
Warranty claims

Refined Product Characterisation

1464
Additive analysis
Fuel analysis
Impurity analysis
Lubricating oil analysis
Racing fuel compliance

Refrigeration

787
Components
Equipment
Food production, storage and
transportation
Refrigerants
Systems
Testing performance

1118
Insurance claims
Refrigerated transport
Technical reports

Refurbishment/Repairs

1852
Alterations to existing buildings
Domestic alterations
Restoration of listed buildings

Regulatory

382
Competition-related enquiries
Monopolies and Mergers
Commission (MMC)/Office of Fair
Trading (OFT) enquiries
Price cap/rate of return regulation

1277
Health and social services
Inspection
Quality systems
Registration

1637
Conspiracy to defraud
Department of Trade and Industry
(DTI) investments
Tax fraud/negligence

Regulatory Authority Matters

1981
Inland Revenue and Customs and
Excise inquiries
Investigations under the Companies
Act and the Financial Services Act
Serious Fraud Office (SFO) inquiries

Regulatory Disputes

979
Compliance arrangements
Financial services
IMRO and SFA rules

Regulatory (Financial Services Act)

1732
Compliance
Fraud investigation

Regulatory Investigations

1285
Investigations and accounting
assistance for regulatory authorities
and those under investigation

1286
Investigations and accounting
assistance for regulatory authorities
and those under investigation

1287
Investigations and accounting
assistance for regulatory authorities
and those under investigation

1288
Investigations and accounting
assistance for regulatory authorities
and those under investigation

1289
Investigations and accounting
assistance for regulatory authorities
and those under investigation

1290
Investigations and accounting
assistance for regulatory authorities
and those under investigation

1291
Investigations and accounting
assistance for regulatory authorities
and those under investigation

Rehabilitation

909
(including social and home
background)
Neurological or arthritic disability
assessment

Rehabilitation After Traumatic Brain Injury

732
Assessment of disability and
dependency
Clinical evaluation of outcome
Quantifying dependency

Rehabilitation Cost Consultancy/Occupational Therapy

1760
Care and equipment
Medical negligence
Orthopaedics
Road traffic accidents

Rehabilitation Costs

2284
Assessment of future needs for
people who suffer traumatic injury
Assessments undertaken by spinally
injured person
Detailing accommodation, aids and
adaptions, care, mobility and leisure
costs
For solicitors or insurers
Injuries covered: brain injuries, spinal
injuries, cerebral palsy, limb loss

Rehabilitation Medicine (Neurological/Rheumatological Conditions)

1674
Acute brain injury from stroke,
trauma, anoxia
Gait analysis (mainly for cerebral
palsy)
Mobility assessment (especially
disabled car drivers)

Rehabilitation/Rheumatology

1246
Adult cerebral palsy
Chronic back pain
Chronic disability, especially
neurological disability
Head injuries
Orthopaedic rehabilitation
Rheumatological problems

Reinforced Plastics

2031
Adhesives and rubbers
Composites
GRP
Osmosis
Thermosets

Reinsurance

75
Casualty
Property
broking/underwriting/wordings/accoun
ts

367
Calculation of quantum arising from a
dispute

428
Litigation support

Reinsurance/Insurance Law

218
Dispute resolution in UK and USA
London market
USA market

Reinsurance Investigations

2418
Inspections of records
Reinsurance collections
Reinsurance contract interpretations

Reinsurance/Non Marine

2011
Claims inspections and claims
management
Lloyds and London market practice
Loss reserving
Reinsurance to close

Renal (Kidney) Disease

2515
Dialysis
Renal failure
Transplantation

Renal Medicine

528
Acute renal failure, complications and
treatment, including dialysis
Chronic renal failure, complications
and treatment
Glomerulonephritis, pyelonephritis
Haemodialysis and peritoneal dialysis
Hypertension, renal damage
secondary to drugs
Multiple myeloma and the kidney
Polyarteritis nodosa, Wegener's
Renal biopsy, techniques and
complications
Renal involvement in SLE

1033
Dialysis and transplantation
Drug and environmental toxicity

Renal/Transplant Medicine

846
Chronic and acute renal failure
Dialysis
General Kidney Diseases
Nephritis
Renal transplantation
Withholding or withdrawal of dialysis
support

Rent Reviews/Lease Renewals

2166
Arbitrations and awards
Commercial and industrial properties
Independent expert determinations

Rental Valuation

1696
Lease renewals – Landlord and
Tenant Act 1954
Rent reviews – arbitration

Repairing Leases

511
All Aspects

Repetitive Strain Injury (RSI)/Work-Related Upper Limb Disorders

1474
Medicine

Reports on Liability/Negligence

100
Back injuries to nurses and carers
Lack of care in hospitals and
institutions
Lack of care in mental hospitals

Research/Development

1750
Concrete
Materials

Residential Property

354
Architectural and design work
Building defects
Surveys
Tenancy matters including repairs
and rents
Valuations

Resins

1394
Formulation
Use in paints and coatings

Respiratory Disease

188
Asthma and occupational asthma
Industrial lung disease
Lung infections, including tuberculosis
Pneumothorax
Pulmonary embolism

2017
Lung cancer
Medical negligence

Respiratory Disease/Occupational

2017
Asbestosis
Inhalation accidents
Mesothelioma
Occupational asthma
Pneumoconiosis

Respiratory Medicine

402
Alcohol breath tests
Asbestos-related lung disease
Asthma
General respiratory medicine
Respiratory infection
Sleep apnoea

900
Asthma
Lung cancer
Occupational lung disease

2117
Respiratory failure
Sleep medicine, including sleep
apnoeas
Spinal cord injuries

2312
Asthma, with specific expertise in
steroid litigation

2519
Alcohol breath tests
Chronic respiratory ailments eg
asthma, chronic bronchitis
Industrial lung disease including
occupational asthma, asbestos
related lung disease, inhalation
accidents eg chlorine gassings,
smoke inhalation
Lung cancer

Respiratory Medicine/Adult

2183
Asbestos-related lung disease
Asthma (general and occupational)
Asthma death
Chest diseases generally
Cystic fibrosis
Industrial lung disease

Restoration of Erased Numbers

242
Stolen vehicles – erased engine and
chassis numbers

Retail Planning/Impact Assessment

2388
Retail impact analysis
Retail planning policy
Vitality and viability assessments

Rheumatology

893
Medical orthopaedics
Orthopaedic neurology
Persistent pain syndromes
Psychosomatic disorders
Rehabilitation
Trauma

909
Arthritis
Soft tissue rheumatic pains (including
work-related)
Spinal pain

1668
Arthritis
Medical negligence
Over-use injury
Post-injury musculo-skeletal disease
Repetitive Strain Injury (RSI)

2511
Accidents to involve bone muscle
joint, fracture, injury
Acute and chronic locomotor
disorders
Inflammatory polyarthropathies
Sprain injuries, Repetitive Strain
Injuries (RSI) and occupational
injuries
Various road traffic and industrial
accidents
Whiplash and back injuries

Rheumatology/Rehabilitation

444
Community rehabilitation
Complex disability
General rheumatology
Head injury
Soft tissue disease and injury
(including back and neck pain)
Soft tissue disease and injury
[Repetitive Strain Injury (RSI)] etc
Sports medicine

Riding/Training Horses

2237
Equine-related competition
Training students for equine-related
examinations

Rights of Way

1644
Investigation, reports, guidance and
litigation support
Private – nuisance arising from
interference, closure on obstruction
Public – Re-establishment, ancient
highways
Public – definitive map upgrading,
closure of obstruction

Risk Assessment

971
All Aspects

Risk Consultancy/Inspection Services

1938
Banks
Construction projects
Factories
Hotels
Jewellers
Natural perils, including earthquake
Warehouses

Risk Management

1057
Application to industrial and health
care activities
Claims management
Training

2181
Acute units
Community units
Operating theatres

River Basins Management/their Engineering Geology

2119
Engineering geology in glaciated
areas (slope stabilities etc)
Flooding and drainage disputes
(Lands Tribunal claims etc)
Public inquiries into floodplain
developments etc
Water aspects of planning
applications
Water resources problems,
boreholes, low flows, etc

River Engineering

122
Flood protection
Land drainage
River engineering

1665
Bank erosion
Bed scour
Dredging
Flood damage, including structural
failure

Road Defects/Resulting Accidents

1961
Inadequate signing and safety
measures
Public utility plant – manholes,
hydrants, tobies, etc
Surface-dressing failures (flying
chippings)
Surface-water drainage standards,
French drains, etc
Trip spots on footways, potholes etc
on carriageways

Road/Footway Design/Maintenance

1961
Carpark design and maintenance
Proper design of camber, crossfall,
drainage, etc
Safety inspections
Signing at roadworks
Types of surfacing – asphalt,
bituminous, macadam, slabs,
paviour

Road Haulage/Goods in Transit

1454
Carriage by sea
Containerised cargo
Road haulage

Road/Rail Traffic Accidents

1665
Interpretive study of damage of
impact
Mechanics of moving vehicles under
and out of control

Road Traffic

see also Road Transport, Motor
Vehicle, Vehicle, Automobile

834
Damaged vehicle assessment

Road Traffic Accident Injuries

2293
Back
Soft tissue
Whiplash

Road Traffic Accident Injuries/Causes/Preventions

1108
Effect of crash helmets on injuries
Effect of cycle helmets on injuries
Effect of seat belts on injuries
Pedestrian injuries

Road Traffic Accident Investigation

217
Advanced driving
Driving instruction
Full Road Traffic Accidents (RTA)
investigation
Independent dossier analysis
Motor vehicle examination
Road Traffic Accidents (RTA) scale
plans and photographs
Scenes and evidence video filmed etc
Statements, interviews, fraud and
injury investigations

246
Cause of and responsibility for road
accidents

305
Causing death by dangerous and
careless driving
Collision involving emergency
vehicles – police, fire and
ambulance
Commercial vehicle wheel
detachment
Motorway accidents, multiple
vehicle/casualty
Pedestrian accidents
Speed allegations, speed from skid
marks, critical speed on corners

566
All Aspects

798
Analysis of accident data
Analysis of accident sites
Surveys, plans, photographs and
video

838
Accident investigation and
associated matters
Accident reconstruction
Scene examination
Stolen/suspect vehicle examination
Tachograph analysis
Vehicle examination
Verification of police accident reports
and reconstructions

934
Photography
Plans
Speed measurement
Tachograph analysis
Video

1097
Calculation of vehicle speed from
tyre skid marks and scuff
Pedestrian/vehicle collisons
Scene measurement and plan
drawing
Time and distance studies

1198
Agricultural accidents (vehicles)
Plant and machinery
Vehicle examination

1350
Accident scene examination
Expert opinion
Interpretation of written evidence
Scale plan and photographs
Vehicle examination – basic

1701
Accident reconstruction and
investigation
Claims for damages in road traffic
accidents
Motorcycle accidents
Negligence by highway authorities
Pedestrian accidents
Road safety audits stages 1 and 2

1761
Compliance with legal requirements
Mathematical reconstructions
Photographs
Plan drawing
Vehicle examinations

1881
Acccident reconstruction and analysis
Computer simulation of driver
sightline dynamics
Vehicle defect investigation and
analysis

2079
Collision mechanics
Highway engineering
Human factors
Injury causation
Seat belts
Vehicle examination

2185
Calculations associated with vehicle
speeds etc
Interviewing and obtaining
statements of witnesses
Photographs and site plans
Review and analysis of documentary
evidence

2447
Accident investigation
Heavy Goods Vehicles (HGV) load
 safety
NOT damage claim assessor
NOT insurance loss adjuster
Tachograph analysis
Vehicle examination
Witness interview

**Road Traffic Accident
Investigation/Reconstruction**

46
Interviewing parties and witnesses
Photography
Reconstruction and interpretation of
 findings, analysis
Scale plan drawing
Vehicle examinations, testing and
 inspection
Voluntary and Criminal Justice Act
 (CJA) statement taking

1531
Skidding

1651
Locus reports
Scale plans and photographs
Tachograph analysis

1687
Plan drawing
Road traffic criminal work
Statement taking
Tachograph chart analysis
 (non-microscopic)

**Road Traffic Accident
Investigation/Road Vehicle Safety**

1958
Expert witness for court purposes
Goods vehicle underrun guards
Investigation of road accidents for
 criminal or civil cases
Large goods vehicle safety generally
Road vehicle braking including
 anti-lock brakes
Road vehicle handling, stability and
 overturning

Road Traffic Accident Reports

1921
Preparation of plans of 'locus in quo'

**Road Traffic Accident/Road Safety
Investigation**

1359
Photography
Sketch plans of accident sites
Technical report writing
Vehicle handling effect of road
 surface on stability
Vehicle impact/severity into
 pedestrians, vehicles, barriers,
 bridge parapets, crash cushions,
 fixed objects in general
Vehicle speed from braking,
 skidding, vehicle damage

Road Traffic Accidents

40
Two-vehicle collisions, full frontal,
 off-set or rear
Vehicle and cyclist collisions

110
Analysis of the accident

130
Full reconstruction
Photography, still and video
Scale plans

149
Chest injury following Road Traffic
 Accidents (RTA)
Mesothelioma
Testing failed alcohol breath test

346
Plans and reports

374
Heavy Goods Vehicles (HGV)
Motorcycle
Pedestrian
Vehicle inspections [Heavy Goods
 Vehicles (HGV) and Passenger
 Carrying Vehicles (PCV)]
Vehicle valuations

629
Accident analysis
Presentation of evidence
Reconstruction reports

942
Compliance with BS 5489
Compliance with the Department of
 Transport's design criteria for public
 highways
Compliance with the Health and
 Safety at Work etc Act 1974
Compliance with the Highway Code
Compliance with the New Roads and
 Street Works Act 1991
Compliance with the Traffic Signs
 Manuals
Compliance with the relevant Road
 Traffic Acts

971
All Aspects

2190
Expert reports
Expert witness at court
Highway and traffic aspects
Investigation
Performance review of traffic signals
 and roadway lighting
Review of road conditions

2220
Brake performance/malfunctions
Highway design/engineering
Highway maintenance
Road accident analysis and
 reconstruction
Tyre characteristics/faults
Vehicle handling

2335
Complete investigations and reports
Expert witness
Operators' licensing authority public
 enquiries and disciplinary hearings

2443
Motorcars
Motorcycles
Personal injury and damage

2496
Estimation of vehicle speeds
Jack-knifing of articulated vehicles
Roll-over of lorries

Road Traffic Act Alcohol Matters

793
Alcoholic strength of drinks etc
Back calculations
Body samples
Current instrumentation
Failure to provide
Interfering substances

**Road Traffic/Industrial Accident
Investigation**

26
Report writing
Scale plans, photographs and videos
Tachograph analysis
Vehicle and component examination

Road Traffic Law/Enforcement Policy

38
Drivers' hours and tachographs
Goods and passenger vehicle
 legislation
Government enforcement
 policy/application

Road Transport

 see also Road Traffic, Motor Vehicle,
  Vehicle, Automobile

2294
Classic and vintage vehicles
Road traffic accident reconstruction
Tachographs
Transport/garage management and
 finance etc
Vehicle engineering – workshops –
 repair standards
Vehicle overloading – insecure loads
 – operation etc

Road Transport/Distribution

2335
Accident investigations
Expert witness – civil and criminal
 cases
Litigation spadework
Operators' licensing offence reports
Reporting for counsel
Tachograph analysis (forensic)

**Road Transport/Operation/
Engineering**

1771
Commercial vehicle accident
 investigation
Commercial vehicle maintenance
 and repairs
Personal injury investigations
 involving commercial vehicles
Vehicle and component failure
 investigation
Vehicle condition and valuation
 assessment
Vehicle loading and load security

Road Vehicle Engineering/Operation

1197
Accident reconstruction
Goods vehicle operation
Large fleet operations
Motor trade operations
Vehicle design and engineering
Vehicle maintenance

Roadway Lighting

2190
Appraisals
Assessment of need
Design

Roof Construction

1965
Asbestos cement and replacement
materials
Built-up felt
Long strip
Mastic Asphalt
Panel
Profiled steel

Roofing

1603
Asphalt
Cladding
Membranes
Sheeting
Slate
Tiles

Ruminant Nutrition

1167
All aspects of ruminant nutrition
Loss from incorrect feed supply –
negligence

Rural Land Management

2235
Agricultural economics
Land use reporter
Landlord and tenant practice
Valuations – agricultural (freehold
and rental)
Valuations – residential (freehold and
rental)

Safety

see also Health/Safety, Industrial
Accidents, Machinery

Safety Engineering

234
Safe systems of work
Safety at construction site
Safety audit
Safety in lifting

798
Design and assessment of highway
layouts
Road safety
Safety audit of highway projects
Signing and signalling of roads,
junctions and accesses
Traffic accident prevention
Traffic management and traffic
calming

Safety/Health

2261
Building safety
CDM regulations implementation
Construction safety
Loss control and risk assessment
Personal injury investigation
Slips and falls
Stadium safety

**Safety/Health in Construction/
Mining/Quarrying/Landfill**

2270
Advising solicitors on accident claims

Safety/Health/Personal Injury

1993
Asbestos-related disease claims
Defence and plaintiff work
Investigation of accidents at work

Safety of Agricultural Machinery

2028
Accident investigation of agricultural
and other machines on and off
roads
Safety of vehicles operating on slopes

**Sampling/Examination/Chemical/
Physical/Instrumental Analysis**

2135
Air, soil, water, quality, foodstuffs,
pharmaceutical, polymers
Compliance with regulations,
legislation and specification,
commercial disputes
Forensic analysis – criminal and civil,
expert witness
Health and safety
Identification of contaminants, taint,
sabotage investigation
Inorganic materials
Sampling, insurance, loss adjusters
investigations, cargoes shipping

Scaffolding/Access/Support

640
Contractual
Giving evidence in court
Health and safety
Personal injury
Professional negligence
Security

Scalp/Hair Advice/Treatment

1370
Allergy reactions on skin (scalp)
Chemical/physical reactions of scalps
Damage to scalp/hair from chemical
products

Scalp/Hair Disorders

2112
Clinical and diagnostic care of scalp
and hair
Defence and plaintiff reports
Hairdressing negligence and
personal injury
Insurance litigation : defence reports
Professional negligence – expert
witness work

Scarring

415
Following injuries of all types,
including burns

Scars

212
Burns
Cosmetic plastic surgery
Plastic surgery

**Scene Analysis (from Photographic
or Video Images)**

1421
Height computations
Perspective geometry

**Scene Examinations/Photography/
General Investigations**

2560
Crime scene examinations
Fingerprints – evidence consultant
Forensic matters – evidence
consultants
Investigations – tracing witnesses
etc, statements, general
Photography – scene, injuries,
accident scenes
Plan drawer – plans in relation to
scenes and accident scenes
Process – service

Scene of Crime Investigation

2454
Blood stain distribution
Processing of evidential materials

Science/Engineering

2265
Automobile accidents
Chemical risk
Component failure
Construction defects/failures
Fire investigation
Mechanical equipment failure

Scientific Advice

1
Drink driving
Interpretation of scientific documents

793
All aspects

Scientific Examination of Documents

62
Erasures and altered documents
Foreign script
Handwriting comparison
Photocopy fraud
Printing examination
Typescript identification

Scientific Instrumentation

982
Aero, industrial, meteorological,
medical

Seat Belts/Restraint Systems

1913
Air bags
Child restraints
Injury mechanisms
Seat belt effectiveness
Seat belt failures and defects
Seat belt usage

Securities

207
Compliance reviews
Dealing practices
Exchange and SFA regulations
Investment advice
Negligence
Operations procedures

Securities Trading Procedures/ Controls

845
Derivatives, options, futures, interest and currency swaps
Equities
Fixed interest and convertible bonds
Foreign exchange

Security

5
Audits of systems and procedures
Codes of practice and standards
Computer misuse investigations
Forensic studies
Regulatory compliance, national and international
Software product authentication

2454
Tagging
Traps and markers

Security Instrumentation

982
Commercial – remote signalling
Domestic – remote signalling and wire free

Security/People/Property/Information

2055
Counter industrial espionage
Criminal and civil investigations
Fraud investigations including maritime matters
NACOSS – approved expert in intruder alarm systems

Security Printing Expert

706
Advice on protection of documents against counterfeiting
Examination of suspect documents for authenticity
Identification of the means of counterfeiting

Security Procedures/Documentation

972
Documentation systems and BS5750
Knowledge of NACOSS policy, certification and inspection
Knowledge of legal process
Knowledge of relevant British Standards
Knowledge of third party support services (central station and BT)
Risk assessment and surveys

Security Products

1541
Locks
Safes
Security system components
Strongrooms

Security Recommendations

1541
Plans
Project management
Risk assessment
Screening
Specifications
Tenders

Security/Risk Management Consultants

1191
Building and property security
Corporate and information security
Counter-terrorist audits and explosive effects analysis
Electronic countermeasures and debugging services
Emergency procedures and disaster recovery planning
Fraud prevention and investigation
Information Technology (IT) and computer security
Risk assessments
Security equipment and alarm systems
Security guarding and special event security

Security/Safety Lighting

1853
Car parks
Exterior maintenance standards
Interior maintenance standards

Security Systems/Procedures

972
Access control, Closed Circuit Television (CCTV), perimeter protection, integrated systems
Communications and signalling
Electronic and physical security
Guarding and contingency plans
Product evaluation, suitability, liability
Survey of risk assessment

Security Systems/Services

1541
Access systems
Closed circuit television systems
Integrated security systems
Intruder alarms
Manned guarding
Perimeter alarms

Sequestration/Court Appointment as Receiver

1957
Family disputes

Serious Fraud

1428
Companies Act offences
Serious crime with financial motive
Theft Act offences

Services

1628
Adjudication
Arbitration
Court expert
Litigation
Mediation
Planning applications and enquiries

Settlements/Negotiations

1002
Calderbank offers
Fixed fees/contingency fees
Security for costs schedules

Sewage Disposal

980
Pollution control
Septic tanks and cesspools
Sewage treatment
Sewers and drains
Waste water

Sex Offenders

1405
Assessments
Exhibitionists
Paedophiles
Therapy work (individual cognitive therapy and group)

Sexual Abuse

1620
Assessment of families where sexual abuse has taken place
Assessment of sexual offenders/alleged offenders (adolescent)
Assessment of sexual offenders/alleged offenders (adult)
Training of professional bodies in the assessment of sexual abusers
Treatment of family members
Treatment of sexual offenders (adolescent)
Treatment of sexual offenders (adult)

Sexual Abuse/Assault Assessment

2352
Adult's alleged 'recovered' memories of childhood abuse
Adults' recollections of childhood sexual abuse
Children's testimony of sexual abuse
Schedule 1 sex offenders

Sexual Assault/Adult

697
Rape trauma

Sexual Behaviour

941
Gender identity
Homosexuality
Pornography
Recovered memories
Sexual abuse
Transsexualism

Share/Business Valuations

1481
All aspects

Share Valuation

133
Company share valuations
Valuation of unincorporated business

1638
Business valuation
Commercial
Matrimonial dispute
Partnership valuation
Taxation

Shareholder Disputes/ Reorganisations

1284
Corporate reconstructions
Minority oppression actions
Share, business and goodwill
valuation

Ship

see Naval, Marine, Cargo

Ship/Engine Surveys

766
Charter party disputes
Condition surveys
Hull damage
Safety surveys
Structural surveys
Vetting surveys

Ship/Leisure Craft Surveys

628
Damage claim investigations
Hull and equipment surveys for
British and foreign owners
Insurance and valuation reports
Marina and yacht centre accidents

Ship Surveying

1894
Draught surveys and stability/loading
analysis
Fishing vessel application of statutory
requirements
Fishing vessel general condition and
evaluation surveys
Hull and machinery damage surveys
Towage approval surveys

Shipbroking/Ship Management

1598
Chartering
Forensic shipbroking
Fraud
Laytime calculating
Ship operations
Voyage estimating and quantum

Shipping/Fishing Industry

1636
Alleged scuttling claims – financial
motive
Charter party disputes
Forecasting
Joint venture disputes
Recreating trading accounts past and
present

Shops/Offices/Railway Premises/Schools

159
Dermatitis
Manual handling
Slipping

Ski

1276
Ski slopes

Ski Accidents

901
Artificial ski slopes design and
management
Professional practice in ski instruction
Ski bindings adjustment and testing
Ski collisions
Ski equipment
Ski lift operation and safety

Ski Equipment/Lifts

741
Ski binding settings and adjustments
Ski binding testing and verification
Ski equipment product liability/issues
Ski equipment related injuries
Ski lift design, maintenance,
construction and rescue from lifts

Ski Instruction/Mountain Safety

741
Mountain safety and leadership;
conduct of skiers
Professional negligence of ski
instructors
Ski guiding and guides' conduct
Ski instructional practice on artificial
ski slopes
Ski teaching on snow
Training and assessment of
instructors and coaches

Ski Law International

1539
All matters

Ski Slopes/Snowmaking

741
Design and construction of artificial
ski slopes
Design and construction of
refrigerated ski centres
Lifespan and use of artificial skiing
surfaces
Snowmaking
Supply and adjustment of ski
eqiupment on ski slopes

Skiing

460
Collisions and FIS rules
Off-piste skiing
Piste skiing
Ski touring/mountaineering

818
Artificial ski slope safety, design and
maintenance
Instructing, teaching, coaching,
guiding, leading
Mountain safety (including weather,
altitude and avalanche hazards)
Safe practice for school parties
Ski area safety
Ski equipment selection, adjustment
and safety
Skiing accidents and injuries

2142
Artificial ski slopes – design and
construction
Ski coaching – snow and artificial
surfaces
Ski instruction – snow and artificial
surfaces
Ski school management
Skiing safety

Skiing/Ski Filming/Video Reports

1708
Accidents on snow and ice
Mountain resorts
Ski guiding
Ski rules – European (FIS) and
American
Snow and weather conditions
Winter holidays – all aspects

Skin Organ/Diseases/Tumours

739
Cancer of the skin – in particular
melanoma
Cosmetic dermatological surgery
Dermatological surgery including hair
transplants
Hair disorders
Industrial skin disorders

Sleep

2498
Falling asleep while driving
Loss of sleep and accidents generally
Nightshift working
Soporific clinical drugs

Slipping/Tripping/Falling Accidents

148
Accident investigation: floors, steps
and stairways (but NOT ladders or
scaffolding)
Cleaning and polishing: effect on
floor safety
Dance floors: required floor friction
Effect on pedestrian saftey, eg
multi-function floors
Flooring materials: suitability and
condition of floor

971
All Aspects

Social Care

1277
Care of the elderly
Child care
Community care
Management
Mental health
Professional practice

Social Work

951
Child care issues
Family relationships

1414
Child care issues
Complaints proceedings
Family and domestic proceedings
Juvenile justice issues
Local authority social services
practice

2321
Child care issues
Family problems

Soft Furnishings

1936
Blinds
Curtain tracks
Curtains
Loose covers

Soft Tissue Injuries

1263
Lacerations
Ligament injuries
Nerve injuries
Strain injuries
Tendon injuries
Tenosynovitis

Software Applications

1532
Accounting software
Payroll software
Retail and point of sale software
Sales order processing software
Stock control software
Wholesale and distribution software

Software Engineering/Modelling

740
C/C ++
Hardware description language
Image processing
Mathematical modelling and
simulation
Microprocessor assembler design
Multi-media
Personal Compputer (PC) systems –
Windows applications

Software/Programs

5
Authentication plans and procedures
Copyright investigations
Fitness for purpose
Intellectual property matters
Patents
Standards compliance

Soil/Land Management Advice

841
Analysis
Erosion, structure and stability
Land drainage
Pollution and contamination
Problem investigation
Surveys and land utilisation

Soil Mechanics/Foundation Engineering

2531
Foundation failures including piles
Natural subsidence
Settlement of structures
Shrinkable soils and tree roots
Slope stability and landslips
Subsidence over abandoned
mineworkings

Solicitors

1351
Personal efficiency and effectiveness
programmes

1516
Breach of professional practice rules

1769
All aspects

Solicitors, Training of

1280
Seeking rights of audience in higher
courts

Solvents

2359
Anaslysis, testing and provider of
experts

Special Needs Education

220
Attention deficit disorder
Educational appeals/tribunals
Expert witness work
Specific learning difficulties (dyslexia)

Special Needs Reports

1208
Aids and equipment
Conversions/adaptations
Cost of care
Extra household expenditure
Holidays
Special housing
Vehicle requirements

1209
Care requirements (personal,
domestic, therapy etc)
Holiday needs
Living costs for disabled pesons
Specialised equipment requirements
of physically disabled
Specialised housing
Specialised transport eg vehicle
conversion/adaptions

Specialised/Lightweight Structures

1505
Fibre reinforced polymers (FRP,
GRP, composites)
Lightweight surface transportation
structures
Specialised building structures
Specialised marine structures
(vessels, boats, craft, etc)
Stress analysis

Specialisms

1628
Causation and quantum
Claims
Insurance
Professional negligence
Programming and planning
Valuations

Specialist Accounting Reports

233
Accounting reports in fraud cases
Accounting systems and records
All accounts and audit functions
Audited accounts
Loss of earnings and dependency
claims

Specialist in the Practice of the Law

1769
Comparative labour law
Litigation expert
Multi-party actions
Structure of law firms

Specialist Interviewing/ Suspects/Witnesses

1211
Cognitive (memory enhancement)
interviewing
Testimony derivation for reliability
assessment

Specialist Photography

1973
Any form of photographic evidence
Defence or plaintiff
To assist negotiation or litigation

Specialist Testing

1965
Concrete testing – ultrasonics, cover,
carbonation, chloride content
Load tests
Pull – off and bond strength
Temperature monitoring
Vibration monitoring

Spectrography

2359
Analysis, testing and provider of
experts

Speech/Language Delays or Disorders in Children/Adolescents

1882
Disorders of written language
(dyslexia)
Specific language disorder
Use of technological aids to
communication in cases of severe
speaking or writing difficulty

Speech/Language Therapy

163
Cerebral palsy: assessment, therapy
Deafness: assessment, habilitation,
signing, cochlear implants
Learning difficulties: assessment,
therapy
Profound and multiple learning
difficulties: assessment,therapy
Specific language impairment:
assessment, therapy

1343
Dyslexia in children and adolescents
Educational problems due to speech
and language difficulties
Head injury in children and
adolescents
Stammering and learning difficulties

2504
Augmentative communication
Communication aids
Computers

2535
Neurological damage (eg cerebral
palsy)
Paediatrics

Spinal Disorders

25
All Aspects

Spinal Injury

894
Nerve root damage
Pain syndromes
Spinal cord injury
Whiplash injury

2170
Back problems
Spinal cord injuries

Spinal Injury/Paralysis

380
Disability
Home assessment and cost of care
Nursing medical negligence liability

Spinal Surgery

25
all Aspects

Spine

614
Arachnoiditis
Cervical spine (whiplash)
Lumbar spine
Spinal degeneration
Spinal injury
Thoracic spine

Spine/Injuries to

1263
Car injuries (impact injuries)
Lifting injuries
Low back injuries
Whiplash injuries

Sport

702
All sports and minor games
Contact sports –
　rugby/gaelic/american football
Golf, snow ski-ing, volleyball
Gymnastics, hockey, tennis, games
　from overseas cultures
Martial arts, self defence, arrest
　training
Swimming, basketball, soccer

Sport/Leisure/Recreation Safety

2034
Crisis management
Management
Risk assessment
Safety audit
Training

Sport/Physical Education

864
Content of lessons and/or training
　programmes
Defective equipment and premises
Negligence claims against teachers,
　employers and others
Teachers'/instructors'
　qualifications/experience

Sport/Recreation

768
Accident investigations/synthetic
　sports surfacing
Accidents investigations/equipment
　related – high jump etc.
Gymnasium matting problems
Inflatable structures (bouncy castles)

Sports/Recreational Accidents

971
Adventure playgrounds, gymnasiums
　and swimming pools
Stairs and ramps

Stablelads/Workriders/Studmen

see also Equestrian

761
Problems in their work, especially
　injuries sustained at work

Stairs/Ramps

971
All Aspects

Standards/Codes of Practice

2526
British and International
Temporary works

Statistics

1008
Engineering and process industries
Environmental pollution
Medical, epidemiological
Seismic and environmental risk
Uncertainty in forensic evidence

Statutory Nuisance

1064
Condensation dampness
Hazardous building materials or
　design
Insect infestations
Rodent and avian infestations

Statutory Tribunals/Committees

448
Land tribunal reports
Leasehold valuation tribunal reports
Rent assessment committee reports
Valuation and community charge
　tribunal reports

Statutory Undertakers' Costs

511
All Aspects

Steam Systems/Boilers

971
All Aspects

Steroid Endocrinology

1231
Steroid analysis, pharmacology,
　physiology

Storage Systems/Racking

971
All Aspects

Stress

375
Expatriate stress
Stress in overseas employees
Work-relates stress

1599
Assessment of pccupational stress
　and its effects
Psychological effects of harassment
　etc
Psychological effects of industrial
　accidents

Stress Conditions

2464
Chronic fatigue syndrome
ME/post viral fatigue
Stress-related conditions

Stress Management

1351
Stress audit
Stress management programmes:
　individual and group

Structural

47
Airports
Leisure
Listed buildings
Nuclear/seismic
Structural steel
Theme parks, rides, equipment

Structural/Building

1261
Defective design/construction
Durability
Foundation settlement
Industrial floors
Structural movement
Tree damage

Structural/Civil Engineering

499
Building collapses
Building defects
Foundation problems

662
Geotechnical: subsidence,
　underpinning, retaining walls,
　foundations
Structural materials: steelwork,
　timber, stonework, masonry
Structural: failures, defects in
　concrete, fire damage, blast
　damage, demolition
Structures: industrial, commercial,
　domestic, agricultural, institutional

681
Contractual matters
Historic and traditional building
　methods
Subsidence related matters

1633
Commercial buildings
Design/construction
Industrial buildings
Investigation of soils and construction
　(existing buildings)
Residential buildings

Structural Defects in Traditional Building Construction

577
Contaminated land
Defective workmanship
Foundations/subsidence
Timber frame – historic and new

Structural Design

516
Domestic buildings
Industrial buildings

1852
Calculations and drawings
Commercial buildings
Residential schemes

Structural Engineering

109
Reinforced concrete
Retaining structures
Structural steelwork

321
Contract administration
Defective construction
Defective design and detailing
Soil movements
Timber frame
Water penetration

493
Concrete structures
Plastering, rendering and screeding
  defects
Refurbishment of listed buildings
Retaining walls
Structural failure investigation
Structural repair

749
Building defects
Structo/mechanical engineering
Structural design of bulk handling
  plant
Structural design of mechanical
  handling equipment
Structural design of mobile access
  equipment
Structural design of mobile storage
  equipment

792
Commercial
Fire damage
Industrial
Masonry
Offshore structures
Public buildings
Reinforced concrete
Residential
Restoration
Structural steelwork
Timber
Underpinning

811
Brickwork
Concrete
Foundations
Steelwork
Structural adequacy
Structural surveys
Subsidence
Timber

812
Structural surveys
Subsidence matters

1067
Explosion hazards (risk assessment
  and enhancement)
Glass fibre reinforced cement
Historic building structures
Reinforced concrete, steel,
  aluminium and timber structures

1338
Bridges
Chimney masts
Commercial properties
Historic buildings
Private properties

1482
Accidents associated with building
  maintenance
Defective building construction
Defects of structural materials
  including concrete and steel
  reinforcement
Foundation failures, subsidence and
  heave
Structural failures

1735
Bridges
Buildings
Construction failures
Design errors – negligence
Engineering failures

1765
Applied mechanics
Blast
Explosions
Ice
Offshore structures
Pipelines

1781
Concrete
Deterioration of structures
Non-traditional housing
Prefabricated reinforced concrete
  (PRC) housing
Repairs for Housing Defects Act 1984

2214
Investigation of structural defects etc
  in buildings
Preparing remedial work proposals
  for problems identified

2305
Building settlement
Crane failure
Floor slab performance
Forensic investigations
Reinforced concrete
Structural failure
Structural monitoring
Structural steelwork
Wall performance

2366
Building failures
Design faults
Foundation movements
Personal accidents

2389
Contractual disputes
Foundation failures
Structural failures

2500
Building construction
Masonry
Reinforced concrete
Structural engineering aspects of
  personal injury accidents
Structural steelwork
Structural timber

2501
Composite materials and resin
  adhesives
External cladding and envelopes (the
  glazing systems)
Flat slabs
Foundations and superstructures
Precast concrete
Waterproof basements, roofing and
  deck finishes

2532
Construction contracts
Dock damage
Structural defects

Structural Engineering/Surveying

661
Subsidence, settlement, heave,
  structural surveying
accident investigation, fall, trip, slip
failures, defects, repairs, dilapidations
personal injuries, safety, health and
  safety
professional negligence, fees
reinforced concrete, steelwork,
  masonry

Structural Failures/Accidents

412
Falsework and formwork
Rostrums
Scaffolding
Seating and standing showstands
Studio and outside stages, sets and
  towers

Structural/Forensic Engineering

2261
Building
Foundations
Historic structures
Hospitals
Refurbishment

Structural/Geotechnical Engineering

369
Building contracts disputes
Building subsidence and heave
Professional negligence (structural
  and geotechnical engineering)

Structural Investigations

1666
High rise buildings
Historic buildings
Large panel system buildings
Subsidence

Structural/Mechanical Engineering/Failure Assessment

1665
Crash dynamics
Dynamic and static stress analysis
  and assessment of failure
  mechanisms
Fatigue and brittle fracture of metals
Investigation into failures, collapses
  and accidents to bridges, buildings,
  industrial plant, machines, vehicles
  and vessels
Plastic failure of thin-walled structures

Structural Mechanics

2359
Analysis, testing and provider of
  experts

Structural Reports

516
Defects in buildings
Mining subsidence
Subsidence of foundations

Structures

357
Corrosion
Fatigue and fracture
Metallurgy
Structural failure

Summarising Medical Notes

1292
Detailed summaries of medical notes
  to assist experts
Preparing letters of instruction
Writing medical notes, paraphrased
  into plain English

Sunglasses

2031
Eye protection
Impact testing
UVA/UVB analysis

Surgery

89
General surgery
Hernia
Personal injury; neck injury
Professional and medical negligence

165
Abdominal surgery
NOT vascular surgery
Parathyroid gland surgery
Thyroid gland surgery

275
Arterial surgery
Gastro-intestinal surgery
General abdominal surgery
Laparoscopic cholecystectomy
Surgery of the veins

418
Vascular surgery (including all
  arteries and veins)

557
Abdominal surgery
Colo-rectal surgery
Hernia
Major trauma
Transplantation
Vasectomy

609
Endocrine surgery
Gastroenterology

656
Hernia problems

685
Vascular surgery

686
Hernia

918
Colorectal surgery

1010
Abdominal surgery
Breast
Herniae
Thyroid and parathyroid

1109
Hepatobiliary and pancreatic surgery

1122
Endocrine surgery
Medical negligence (general surgery
  only)
Personal injury

1205
Adult cardiac surgery
Adult oesophageal surgery
Adult pulmonary surgery
Trauma to chest

1521
Vascular (arterial and venous)
  surgery

1573
Occupational related vascular injury
Vascular injury
Vascular surgery
Vascular thrombosis
Vibration White Finger (VWF)

1574
Hepatobiliary and pancreatic surgery
Laparoscopic surgery
Transplantation

1777
Keloid scars
Removal of skin lesions and
  blemishes
Scar hypertrophy
Skin cancer
Skin, dermatological
Surgical scarring, including painful
  scars

1870
Elective general surgery
Emergency general surgery
Hernia surgery
Laparoscopic general surgery
Medical negligence and court work

2005
Endocrine surgery

2076
Deep vein thrombosis
Surgical oncology/cancer
Vascular surgery
Venous/varicose vein surgery

2085
Organ transplantation

2091
Day surgery
Minimally – invasive surgery
Vascular surgery

2116
Abdominal surgery
Colo rectal surgery
Gastroenterology
Hepatobiliary surgery

2120
Breast
General
Trauma
Vascular

2180
Breast care
Coloproctology
General surgery
Hernia repairs

2450
Biliary, colonic, appendix
Breast disease and surgery
Inguinal and other hernias
NOT laparoscopic surgery
Non-gynaecological, clinical cytology
Some abdominal surgical operations
Sporting groin strains
Thyroid disease and surgery

2482
Cancer

Surgery/Coloproctology

1306
Bowel perforation
Colorectal cancer: radiotherapy,
  chemotherapy
Functional bowel disease
Incontinence
Infections
Stomas

Surgery/Gastrointestinal

1899
Adult practice
Colorectal
Faecal incontinence
Minimal invasion

Surgery of Face/Mouth/Jaws

1523
Facial deformity
Facial trauma
Facial/head/neck oncology
Salivary gland disease
Surgical dentistry

Surgery to Face/Jaw/Jaw Joints/ Mouth/ Teeth

571
Cosmetic jaw surgery
Dental injuries and implants
Facial injuries, soft and bony
Mouth and face soft tissue injuries
Salivary glands
Temporomandibulum joints

Surgery/Trauma/Orthopaedic

489
Cruciate ligament reconstruction
Micro-discectomy
Total joint replacement arthroplasty

1568
All aspects

2006
Arthroscopy
Joint replacement problems
Knee injuries
Paediatric problems
Sports injuries

Surveillance

644
Bugging and de-bugging
Covert operatives
Observations
Vehicle (including motorcycle) and
  foot surveillance
Video and photographic evidence
  supplied

Surveillance Motor Cyclist

1528
Foot surveillance
Motor cycle surveillance
Motor vehicle surveillance
Static observation surveillance

Surveying

see also Property, Valuation

39
Arbitration services
Construction disputes
Fraud investigations
Negligence claims
Valuations

146
Building design/contract
  administration
Building refurbishment
Building surveys/home buyers'
  reports
Landlord and tenant/dilapidations
Maintenance/repair works
Party wall matters
Planning/building regulation matters

183
Building construction disputes –
  property value, scotts schedules
Dilapidations – schedules –
  preparation and pricing
Housing acts, environmental notices
  – correct, appropriate
Party wall matters – London building
  acts and elsewhere
Rent acts – rent officer consultations,
  panel appeals

417
Commercial valuations
Compulsory purchase and
  compensation
Landlord and tenant
Planning
Rating

486
Building defect diagnosis
Building work (design, specification,
  supervision of alteration, extension,
  repair)
Dilapidations
Home buyers' reports
Party wall
Structural surveys (commercial and
  residential)

812
Boundary matters
Condition surveys
Dimensional surveys
Inspections
Insurance work
Specifications and schedules

937
Arbitrator and independent expert
  specialising in Shop Property
  throughout the UK
Department stores and chain stores
Rent review and lease renewals on
  shop premises
Shopping centres
Supermarkets and superstores

1268
Boundary disputes
Building work and disputes
Expert witness
Valuation disputes

1381
Dilapidations – Scott schedules
Party wall and boundary disputes
Professional negligence – building
  works/surveys
Schedules of condition
Structural surveys

1796
Boundary disputes
Dilapidation
Plans for personal injury claims
Rent review and lease renewal
Surveyors' negligence – valuations
Valuation disputes

1836
Building disputes
Compulsory purchase
Valuation of property

1849
Boundary disputes
Land surveying
Planning disputes (precise
  3-dimensional surveys)

1923
Inspections and advice
Insurance claims
Party wall disputes
Structural surveys – residential and
  commercial
Supporting evidence in plan or map
  form
Traffic accidents

2283
Boundary disputes
Defective building work
Professional negligence claims
Survey reports
Valuation

2555
Building and civil engineering
  disputes
Construction programmes and
  procurement
Contract duration/extension of time
Defective workmanship
Electrical and mechanical services
Environmental and engineering
  projects
Professional practice and procedure

Surveying by Land/Air/Hydrographic Techniques

890
Boundary disputes
Measurement of settlement
  (monitoring of structural movement)
Subdivision and demarcation of land
  parcels
Surveying accuracy (quality of
  surveying information)
Volumetric disputes (ie fly-tipping)

Surveying/Construction

568
Building disputes
Building surveying
Contract
Design/supervision
Dilapidations
Surveyors negligence

Surveying/General Practice

1484
Compensation
Compulsary purchase
Residential valuations
Structural surveys/house or flat
  buyers' reports

Surveying/Housing/Building

1757
Boundary disputes
Building
Dilapidations
Housing law
Structural surveys
Window installations

Surveying/Land/Engineering/Building

1404
Buildings – measurement of size,
  position, verticality
Construction – staking out and
  surveying
Disputes – boundary, land,
  construction surveying or staking out
Specification – land, engineering,
  building surveying
Volumes – land, soil, materials

Surveying/Valuation

703
Boundary disputes
Commercial and domestic valuation
Domestic building disputes
Domestic construction
Double glazing
Surveying negligence claims

1201
Boundary disputes
Building disputes/defective buildings
Dilapidations
Negligence claims
Valuation

1518
Building surveys and home buyers
  reports
Negligence/personal injury (plaintiff
  and defendant)
Valuations for mortgage, tax,
  matrimonial, etc

1653
Bank and building society mortgage
  valuation
Building disputes generally
Home buyers' survey and valuation
Structural surveys and valuations

1865
Boundary disputes
Building defects reports
Landlord and tenant disputes
Professional negligence claims
Valuations

2375
Boundary/building/landlord and
  tenant dispute reports
Professional negligence – defence
  and plaintiff reports
Site plans and photographs for
  personal injury/accidents/Road
  Traffic Accidents (RTA)

Surveying/Valuation/Development

647
Boundary disputes
Development of land matter
Personal injury
Professional negligence
Valuation (commercial and
  residential)

Surveying/Valuation/Residential

2449
All aspects of surveying and valuing
  of residential property
Boundary disputes
Professional negligence
Schedules of dilapidations
  (residential and commercial)

Surveyor/General Professional Work

2202
Compulsory purchase
Rating
Structural advice
Valuations

Surveyors

114
Building disputes
Building maintenance, repair,
  renovation, refurbishment
Dilapidations and leasehold repair
  liabilities
Domestic and commercial property
Party walls
Professional negligence
Roof defects and maintenance
Structural surveys
Subsidence, foundation settlement,
  heave, fire, flood and other insured
  perils

235
Professional negligence

362
Alteration, extension and conversion
  of buildings
Building defect investigation/analysis
Negligence claims against surveyors
Residential pre-purchase (structural)
  surveys (excluding valuations)
Schedules of dilapidations/condition

379
Professional negligence

690
Negligence

1186
Building contract and procedure
  advice
Building defect analysis
Design, supervision and contract
  administration of building works
Structural movement in buildings
  analysis
Structural surveys of residential and
  commercial buildings

1775
Professional negligences

1796
Building disputes
Surveyors' neglligence – structural
  surveys

Surveyors' Professional Negligence

2
Building (structural) surveys
Building design

400
Client relationships
Landlord and tenant – some aspects
Valuation for mortgage purposes
Valuation of commercial property
  investments
Valuation of redevelopment sites
Valuation of vacant commercial
  properties for occupation

1446
Building society valuations
Faulty valuations
General matters
Structural surveys

1815
Surveyor's practice and procedure
Surveys of buildings

1917
Building or structural surveys of
  residential property
RICS/ISVA flat buyers report and
  valuations
RICS/ISVA home buyers survey and
  valuations
RICS/ISVA house buyers report and
  valuations

Survival in Water at Sea

717
Cold shock and drowning
Escape from ditched helicopter
Survival suit limitations
Underwater breathing apparatus

Swimming Pool Safety

2034
Lifeguarding
Management
Spinal injury
Training
Waterslides
Written procedures

Swimming Pools

811
Earth retaining works
Foul and surface drainage
Swimming pools

814
Construction
Contractual disputes
Design
Operation and maintenance
Related personal injury claims
Water treatment

Synthetic Resins

2448
Coatings – resin based
Corrosion protection
Floors – resin based
Glass reinforced plastics
Paint failure

Systems Design/Development

307
Assessing business/user
  requirements
Evaluation
Implementation and training
Setting business and project
  objectives
System development
System, detailed design and review

Tachograph

797
Chart analysis
Route tracing

2154
Accident evaluation
Criminal investigations
Operation and interpretation of
  recordings

Tachograph Chart Analysis

242
Accident evaluations
Driver's hours analysis
Falsification of chart investigations
Theft/fraud investigations

1172
European Community (EC) hours
  and tachograph regulations
Falsification of charts and/or records
Microscopic analysis of tachograph
  charts
Road traffic accidents
Route plotting for thefts, route/load
  disputes, drug smuggling

1435
Chart falsification investigation
Driver's hours analysis
Road traffic accident analysis
Theft/fraud investigation

Tamperings/Alterations/Erasures etc, Investigation of

1890
All Aspects

Tax Fraud

1536
Common Agricultural Policy (CAP)
  fraud
Customs and Excise duty frauds
VAT fraud (criminal and civil)

Tax Investigations

285
Customs and Excise: all agencies
DSS
Inland Revenue: all other agencies
Inland Revenue: special compliance
  office

506
Basic rate tax/composite rate tax
  investigations
Mortgage interest relief at source
  (MIRAS) analysis
Pay As You Earn (PAYE)
  investigations
Special Inland Revenue investigations

507
Basic rate tax/composite rate tax
  investigations
Mortgage interest relief at source
  (MIRAS) analysis
Pay As You Earn (PAYE)
  investigations
Special Inland Revenue investigations

Tax Litigation

1898
Capital taxes
Corporation tax
Fiscal share valuations

Tax Matters/Investigations

472
All Aspects

Taxation

169
Capital gains tax
Corporation tax
Duties of tax agents
Income tax
Inland Revenue
  investigations/fraudulent and
  negligent conduct
Partnership taxation

294
Capital gains tax
Corporation tax
Income tax
Inheritance tax

1039
Capital gains
Corporate
Investigations
NOT inheritance tax or Value Added
  Tax (VAT)
Personal

1284
Business and personal taxation
Professional negligence

1335
Critical analysis of advice
Negligence claims
Reports on structure and
  effectiveness

2095
Capital gains tax
Corporation tax
Income tax
Inheritance tax
Value added tax

2546
Business valuation
Professional negligence liability and
  quantum
Share valuation
Taxation planning

Taxation of Law Costs

1002
Advice
Negotiated settlements
Objections
Preparation and attendance
Responses

Technical Advice on Crop/Livestock Production

1920
Agronomy of most agricultural and
  horticultural crops
Husbandry and management of most
  types of grazing and intensive
  livestock
Irrigation requirements and systems

Technical Standards

5
Determination of accedence
Implementation
Preparation

74
Determination of accedence
Implementation
Preparation

Technology Cost Reports

1208
Communication equipment
Computer equipment
Paediatrics
Wheelchairs/special seating

Technology Transfer

2302
Capacity building
Institutional strengthening
Working in developing countries
  (mainly with United Nations)

Telecommunications

173
Charging disputes
Contractual disputes
Outstanding and strategic studies
Product comparisons
Service comparisons
Supplier comparisons

465
Malicious calls
Payphone fraud
Radio
Radio telephones
Systems, networks
Voice, telex, data, digital

796
Data communications and fax
  machines
Fraud and misuse
Mobile telephones
Radio systems
Telephone systems

Telecommunications/Broadcasting/Media

399
Advanced voice telephony services
Digital television
New venture business development
  and public prospectus
Telecommunications and
  broadcasting and satellite contracts
  (private and inter-governmental)
Telecommunications and
  broadcasting regulation
Value added data services

Telemetry

1148
Control centres
Outstations
Point-to-point communications
Scanning networks

Telephone Advice

1292
Immediate advice on personal
  injury/medical negligence

Temporary Works

2526
Access scaffolding
Construction methods
Falsework
Formwork for concrete
Precast concrete unit handling
Safety requirements
Structural rehabilitation

Testamentary Capacity

1103
All Aspects

2508
All aspects

Testimony (Spoken/Written), Analysis/Assessment of

1211
Investigator testimony (police officers
  and other professionals)
Suspect testimony (especially
  confessions)
Witness testimony

Textile/Garment Technology

219
Factory operations
Functional textiles
Performance of textiles
Protective clothing
Safety harnesses
Textile testing and specification

Textile Machinery

219
Guards
Operations
Patent infringement
Performance to specification
Processes

Textile Technology

718
Dyeing
Fabrics
Fibres
Garments
Industrial, engineering, medical and
  surgical textiles
Narrow fabric/tapes, labels, etc
Yarns

949
Cotton production and utilisation
Flax and linen
Quality
Textile dyeing and finishing

Textile Testing

850
Chemical, fibre composition, oil
  content
Colour fastness, fading resistance
Flammability and retardancy
Physical performance, strength,
  durability, shrinkage

Textiles

2031
Carpets, floor coverings and
  upholstery
Construction and performance testing
Garments/apparel
Workwear/protective clothing
Woven, knitted and non-woven
  fabrics
Yarns, fibres

2240
Apparel
Carpets
Fabrics
Fitness-for-purpose
Inspections
Upholstery

2359
Analysis, testing and provider of
　experts

Thai Language

85
Cross-cultural issues
Education
Interpretation
Labour relations

Therapy Reports on Children/Adults

633
Care reports
Occupational therapy reports
Rehabilitation cost reports
Speech and language therapy reports

Thoracic/Respiratory Disease

2150
Medicine

Timber Consultancy

2478
Dampness
Fungal decay
Insect attack
Preservation
Selection, preparation and use of
　timber
Timber drying

Timber Technology

2267
Fungal decay and woodworm
Preservatives
Species identification
Surface finishes
Visual stress grading
Wood-based sheet materials

Timber Utilisation

2267
Architectural detailing
Condition surveys
Construction – timber frame, floors,
　roofs
Engineering appraisals
Failure – buildings, tools, equipment
Joinery – design, manufacture and
　installation

**Topographical Surveys/Mineral
Planning**

129
Accident surveys/surface and
　underground
Digital computer applications to same
Dimensional surveys of precise
　structures
Mine surveys and quarry surveys
Planning inquiries
Property boundary measurement

Town/Country Planning

11
Development plan representations
Enforcement notices
Planning appeals

383
Acting on behalf of third party
　objectors
Certificate of Lawful Development
　Applications
Giving expert planning evidence at
　planning inquiries
Planning and enforcement appeals
Planning applications
Site analysis and development
　appraisal

469
Environmental Assessment
Tourism and recreation

869
Planning appeals
Private bills
Statutory plan inquiries
Transport and Works Act

957
Applications, appeals, enquiries
Economic studies
Enforcement
Green belt issues
Mixed use and town centre
　development
Retail planning including impact
　assessment

1004
Foul drainage
Highway engineering
Land use transportation studies
Surface water drainage
Traffic engineering

1837
Development plan representations
　and development plan
Inquiry evidence
Planning application, enforcement
　and lawful development appeals
Planning applications and Lawful
　Development Certificate applications
Preparing and submitting
　representations
　(applications/Development Plans
　for third parties)
Site analysis and development
　appraisals

2387
Business
Commercial
Development Plan policy
Environmental assessment
Housing
Industrial
Retail development
Waste planning

Town/Country Planning/Development

175
Applications/appeals/public inquiries
　(all types)
Enforcement
Green belt issues
Mixed use and town centre
　development
Residential planning (including
　housing land availability)
Retail planning (including impact
　assessment)

Town Planning

510
Development control, including
　permitted development
Enforcement
Local plans
Marinas, boatyards and shore sites
Planning in Hampshire
Presentation and interpretation of
　plans

584
Commercial –
　offices/industrial/warehousing
Housing
Listed buildings and conservation
　areas
Retail
Strategic land use planning
Urban regeneration schemes

844
Certificates of lawful use
Enforcement of planning control
Major commercial mixed use
　development
Public inquiries
Residential
Retail
Urban regeneration

1095
Design

2029
Conservation
Listed buildings
Planning appeals
Public inquiries

2177
Advising protest groups
Individual projects – housing,
　industrial, highways and leisure
Town centre redevelopment

Town Planning Consultancy

1980
Development plan inquiries
Economic studies
Planning appeals
Planning applications
Planning inquiries

**Town Planning/Development
Consultancy**

1078
Development plans
Environmental assessment
Planning applications; preparation,
　negotiation
Public inquiry work
Retail planning
Roadside services

Town Planning/Environmental Law

250
Enforcement appeals
Local plan representations
Planning appeals
Planning applications
Site development appraisals

Town Planning Services

694
Appeals
Architects' appraisals/opinions
Objections to applications

Toxicology

579
Hazard/risk evaluation
Health effects of toxic substances

665
Carbon monoxide
Firefighters and smoke inhalation
Health effects of damp and moulds in
  housing
Irritant gases and vapours
Occular effects of irritants
Smoking

1196
Cancer/carcinogenicity
Chemical toxicity/poisoning
Immunotoxicity
Industrial chemical toxicity
Laboratory investigations and
  analysis
Occupational exposure
Personal injury
Pollution, chemical or radiation

Toys

2031
EN71 – Safety testing
HD271 – Electrical safety
Pencils and Graphics

Trace Evidence

800
Footwear impressions
General debris
Glass fragments
Paint flakes
Soil
Toolmarks

Tracing Individuals

1449
Missing persons
Probate

Trading Performance/Potential, Assessment of

2453
Assessment of viability of business
  location
Calculation of damages due to lost
  profits

Traditional Building Construction

959
Building construction failure related
  to personal injury
Investigations into faulty workmanship
Investigations into workmanship with
  NHBC guarantee
Professional services provided by
  architect
Services provided by contractor or
  sub-contractors

Traffic Accident Consultancy

1978
Accident site surveys, plans and
  photographs
Expert evidence at court
Expert opinion on traffic accidents
Mathematical analysis and
  reconstruction

Traffic Accident Evidence

1667
Traffic accident studies
Traffic and highway design standards
Traffic signs and signalling adequacy

Traffic Accident Investigation

19
Driving/vehicle-related incidents
Scene
  survey/plans/photography/video
Speed detection devices
Stolen vehicle examination
Tachograph analysis/interpretation

834
Full Road Traffic Accident (RTA)
  investigation and reconstruction,
  and reports
Locus reports and detailed plans

883
Accident reconstruction
Braking
Heavy Goods Vehicles (HGVs)
Motorcycles
Roads
Training

1435
Accident reconstructions
Component failure investigations
Crash helmets
Seat belts
Wheels/tyre investigations

1954
Photographs of scenes, damage
Reconstruction of accidents from
  witness evidence
Scale plans
Witness statements in civil, industrial
  and traffic accidents

2154
Causation and evaluation
Comprehensive investigation of car
  and commercial vehicle accidents
Plaintiff and defence reports
Scene recording and interpretation

2305
Accident reconstruction
Braking
Heavy Goods Vehicles (HGV)
Motorcycles
Roads
Training

Traffic Accident Investigation (Civil/Criminal Work)

2106
Accident reconstruction
Scale plan drawing
Tachograph analysis

Traffic Accident Reconstruction

1996
Cause analysis
Computer animation
Computer simulation
Criminal and civil cases
Forensic vehicle examination
Site surveys, scale CAD plans and
  photographs

Traffic Control

2388
Motorway control
Traffic monitoring and surveillance
Traffic signal systems
Transport control systems

Traffic Engineering

826
Generation and capacity studies
Traffic calming measures
Urban traffic management

2316
Evidence at public enquiries

Traffic Engineering/Accident Analysis

947
Highway aspects of road traffic
  accidents
Traffic aspects of small developments
Traffic signals
Traffic signs

Traffic Engineering/Accident Investigation

1575
Highway and junction design
Parking
Road safety
Traffic accident investigations
Traffic generation and impact studies
Traffic-related town planning matters

Traffic Engineering/Transportation Planning

1701
Access facilities at railway stations
Taxi ranking and licensing
Traffic and economic assessment of
  trunk roads and motorways
Traffic calming, pedestrians and
  cycles
Traffic forecasting
Traffic modelling and impact
  including London

Traffic Impact Assessment

2384
Design of parking and circulation
  systems
Environmental impact assessment
Planning for access by public
  transport and pedestrians

Traffic Signals

2190
Appraisals
Assessment of needs
Design

Traffic/Transport Analysis/Highway Planning

2388
Development proposals
Environmental impact analysis
Highway planning, design and
  appraisal
Public inquiry expert witness
Traffic impact analysis

Traffic/Transportation

1475
Damage only accidents
Design of transporation facilities
Higways Acts
New Roads and Street Works Act
Personal injury accidents
Town and Country Planning Acts

Training

211
Mounted police
Show jumpers

1388
Presentation needs and skills
Safety and ergonomics training
Training course design
Training needs analysis

1530
Consultancy

Training Opportunities/Placements by Vocational Area/Disabled People

1309
Evaluation
Local provision

Transfer Pricing

1638
International taxation

Transfusion Medicine

1083
Donor selection and care
Transfusion transmitted infection

Translation

2037
Arabic/English translation and interpretation
Expert evidence in court/affidavits

Translation/Interpreting

1983
Banking/insurance
Business including shipping
Legal documents
Medical
Technical including patent
Translation from the Scandinavian languages

Transport

525
All Aspects

Transport Accidents

971
Rail, air, sea, bus/coach, and road haulage

Transport Equipment

1424
Aviation ground handling equipment
City transit systems, people-movers and LRT
Environmental engineering
Heavy-load transporters
Marine Roll on/Roll off (RORO) and container-handling equipment
Pharmaceutical and industrial blenders and robots
Tractor, trailer and storage systems

Transport/Heavy Goods Vehicles/Passenger Carrying Vehicles/Trailers

975
Hours of work and tachograph analysis
Mechanical condition reports
Operator's licence
Servicing/maintenance, construction and use regulations
Vehicle testing regulations

Transport Infrastructure

2305
Contracts
Feasibility studies
International
Roads

Transport Law

2423
Industrial insurance claims
Light Goods Vehicles (LGV) and Passenger Carrying Vehicles (PCV) law
Operators' licensing
Public inquiries

Transport Noise/Vibration

2053
Aircraft noise impact
Mitigation of transportation noise
Railway noise and vibration impact
Road traffic noise prediction

Transport Planning

47
Cycling
Environmental
Hazards
Highways
Modelling
Planning/Public Inquiry

2305
Enforcement appeals
Highway appraisal
Public inquiries
Section 78 appeals
Traffic impact assessment
Transport modelling
Transport policy

2388
Development impact assessments
Highway provision and design
Traffic forecasting
Traffic impact
Traffic modelling
Transport feasibility and economic assessment studies
Transport inputs to planning inquiries and appeals
Transport policy in structure and local plans

Transport Safety

1189
Occupant injuries
Public transport
Road accidents
Transport systems
Vehicle layout and controls

Trauma

48
All Aspects

392
Knee injuries
Severe multiple trauma
Spinal injuries
Sports injuries

409
Fractures and dislocations
Multiple injuries
NOT Repetitive Strain Injury (RSI)
Soft tissue injuries

416
Burns
Hand injury
Lower limb reconstruction
Scarring
Soft tissue injury – skin

1507
Accidents – road traffic/other
Child Sexual Abuse
Trauma due to medical negligence

Trauma Medico-Legal

1866
Hand injury
Skin loss and burn injuries
Soft tissue injuries

Trauma/Musculo-Skeletal System/Orthopaedics

1018
Bone and joint infections
Deformities in children
Foot conditions
Hip and bone replacement
Low back pain problems

Trauma/Orthopaedic Surgery

830
Back pain
Children's orthopaedics

1023
Hand surgery
Not head injury

1152
General orthopaedic surgery
Hip and knee replacement
Limb fractures and general trauma excluding head injuries
Revision hip and knee replacement

1789
Paediatric orthopaedics
Surgery of neuromuscular disorders

1905
Fractures and joint injuries
Joint replacement
Paediatric orthopaedics and fractures
Sports injuries
Surgery of the lumbar spine

2205
NOT head and spinal cord injuries

2286
General adult orthopaedic conditions
Paediatric orthopaedics including congenital abnormalities and child abuse
Trauma – fractures and soft tissue injuries

Trauma/Orthopaedics

194
Backache
Knee disorders except knee
  replacement
Road accidents and whiplash injuries
Work-related upper limb disorders

932
Arthroscopy of the knee
Back pain and sciatica
Fracture management
Hand injuries
Injuries at work
Whiplash

1545
Injuries to the upper limb
Peripheral nerve injuries
Tendon injuries
Wrist injuries

1822
Including work-related disorders

1994
Backache
Fractures and soft-tissue injuries
Infection in orthopaedics
Surgery of arthritis

2020
Fractures
Injuries: joint, neck
Medical negligence (NOT back pain)
  [NOT Repetitive Strain Injury (RSI)]

Trauma/Personal Injury

1328
Industrial injury
Road traffic accidents

Trauma Surgery

1910
Paediatric trauma
Sports injuries

Travel Agency Operation

168
Association of British Travel Agents
  (ABTA) codes
Disputes
Equipment and practices
UK and international law

Treatment Processes for Sewage/Industrial Effluent

1139
Activated sludge
Biofiltration
Dissolved air flotation
Odour control

Tree Consultancy

2478
Planning appeals
Tree preservation orders
Tree safety
Trees in relation to buildings

Trees

202
Accidents and insurance claims
  involving trees
Tree preservation orders
Tree root damage to buildings

1074
Amenity valuation of trees
Effects of tree roots on buildings etc
Effects on the tree of damage to tree
  roots
Tree management

1135
Hazard analysis of trees
Tree design schemes
Tree inspection
Tree law –
  conservation/TPOS/boundaries etc
Tree surveys
Tree valuation

1278
Tree accidents
Tree damage
Treeroots/buildings

1303
Contraventions of statute and
  planning law
Industrial injuries
Insurance claims – building
  subsidence
Third-party injuries or damage

1725
Electric utility vegetation management
Health and safety at work
Local plans and supplementary
  planning guidance
Planning and development – appeals
Public inquiries
Special projects, study and
  commissions
Training and continuing professioanl
  development
Tree preservation orders
Trees and building failure
Trees and pollution control
Vegetation and environmental law

Trees/Personal Injury

2280
Accidents caused by trees
Accidents to tree-work operatives
Condition and safety of trees

Trees/Planning

2280
Conservation areas
Planning applications and appeals
Tree preservation orders

Trees/Property

2280
Damage to pavements etc
Overhanging branches – pruning and
  management
Root trespass and nuisance
Roots and subsidence/heave

Trichology (Hair/Scalp)

2022
Biochemistry with reference to hair
  and scalp
Cosmetic issues related to hair and
  scalp
Forensic – hair related aspect
Hair loss, metabolism, growth
Hormones – hair growth, loss and
  effects
Surgery related to hair and scalp

Trust Funds, Appointment of

189
Actuarial apportionment of trust funds
Valuation of life interests and
  reversions

Tunnelling

2388
Building damage from tunnelling
Hardground tunnelling
New Austrian tunnelling method
  (NATM)
Softground tunnelling

Turnkey Projects

2177
Construction of major projects
Design and management

Twins/Triplets/Higher Order Births

313
Adoption of twins
Bereaved adult twins
Bereavement in multiple pregnancy
Development and behaviour of twins
  children
Education of twins
Psychosocial effects of multiple births
  on the family

Typewriting/Faxes/Photocopies/ Computer-Generated Material, Examination of

1890
All Aspects

Typewriting/Printing

1922
Authentication of printed counterfeits
  (including currency)
Comparison of typing
Examination of printing plates
Identification of typewriter
Photocopies
Ribbon reading

Tyre Consultancy

1702
Examination of tyres for compliance
  with legal requirements
Forensic and accident tyre
  examination and forensic reports
Quality consultancy – BSEN1SO9000
Tyre and retread production
  consultancy
Tyre research and development

Unfair Competitive Activity

514
'Grey market' trading
Parallel trading
Product counterfeiting
Product diversion

Unfit Housing

2213
Disrepair
Fitness for human habitation
Houses in multiple occupation
Landlord and tenant
Means of escape
Nuisance

United Kingdom Health/Social Security

1489
Personal and industrial injuries
Social security and medical appeal
 tribunals

Unquoted Share Valuations

2244
Valuations for purchase of own
 shares by companies
Valuations for purchases and sales
 of shares
Valuations for tax purposes
Valuations in disputes and for
 petitions under s 459, Companies
 Act 1985
Valuations in professional negligence
 claims
Valuations under articles of
 association and shareholder
 agreements

Upper Respiratory Tract/Disease/Injuries

2124
Injuries to nose and throat and ears
Medical negligence cases/people
 claiming after unsatisfactory
 treatment
Mucous membrane
 diseases/disorders following
 industrial exposure
Noise-induced deafness

Urban Design

1233
All aspects of design and construction
Development control

Urban Real Estate Valuation/Advice

2060
Building repair and maintenance
Landlord and tenant matters
Lease and service charge details and
 impact
Rent review disputes

Urban Regeneration

2081
Financial management
Market and economics
Public and private partnership
 structures
Tourism and leisure development

Urodynamics

380
Assessment/cost of care/liability
Traumatic and post-operative
 incontinence

Urological

1790
Consultant urological surgeon

Urological Surgery

1634
Bladder surgery
Kidney surgery
Prostate surgery

Urology

155
Damage to ureter or bladder
Fistulae
Urinary incontinence

940
Parathyroid surgery

1076
Gynaecological injuries
Infertility
Urological cancer

1778
Female urology
Paediatric urology
Reconstructive urology
Urological complications of
 gynaecology and obstetrics
Urological trauma

2086
Impotence (andrology)
Urological cancers

2159
Genital surgery
Gynaecology
Vasectomy

2553
Reconstructive urology
Urinary incontinence

Valuables

1072
Consultancy, collectors, loss
 adjusters, underwriters, solicitors
Expert witness work
Valuations – insurance, tax. sale,
 private treaty

Valuation

146
Capital gains tax valuations
Leasehold Reform Act valuations
Mortgage valuations (commercial
 and residential)
Probate valuations

440
Valuations of businesses/assets in
 matrimonial disputes
Valuations of shares in companies
Vaulations of partnerships

486
Asset and mortgage (commercial
 and residential)
Independent expert
Rent reviews

509
Arbitrator
Valuer of residential property

584
Captial valuations
Funding/development agreements
Industrial/warehousing
Leasing agreements
Leisure, retail, hotels
Offices/commercial
Private hospitals/nursing homes
Rental valuations
Residential

914
Business valuation
Loss of profits/business interruption
Other assessments of quantum

1059
Compulsory purchase/law and
 valuation
Negligence claims
Planning compensation/law and
 valuation
Statutory valuation
Valuation and land compensation
 claims
Valuation jurisprudence

1171
Agency-industrial, retail and office
Compulsorypurchase and
 compensation
Development land consultancy
Landlord and tenant-rent review etc
Valuation

1238
Delay analysis
Final account
Loss and expense
Quantum evaluation

1308
Commercial property
Compulsory purchase and
 compensation
Mortgage valuations
Rating
Residential (central London)
Residential investments and
 development schemes

1595
Industrial property
Investment property
Office property

1636
Business valuations
Divorce/separation
Partnership disputes
Security for costs
Share valuation disputes

1692
Doctors' surgery

1754
Arbitrations
Compensation
Compulsory purchase
Conveyancing negligence (quantum
 effects)
Doctor's and dentists' rents
Landlord and tenant disputes
Lease extensions

1951
Valuation of commercial property
Valuation of residential property

2201
Development finance
Landlord and tenant disputes
Mortgage valuations
Rent reviews

2202
Business property (hotels, nursing
  homes)
Commercial property
Development valuation and
  appraisals
Leisure property
Rental valuations and valuations for
  lending purposes
Residential property

2234
Country houses, cottages
Farms and estates

2431
Commercial and residential properties
Current or retrospective
Vacant or tenanted

Valuation/Acquisition/Management of Predominantly Arable Farms/ Estates

620
Agricultural rental valuations
Contract farm management
  agreements
Farms – valuation and aquisition
Mineral (sand and gravel) valuation,
  acquisition and disposal

Valuation/Agricultural/Commercial

1264
Agricultural matters/tenant/landlord
Agricultural quotas
Boundary disputes
Land compensation acts
Property valuations/litigation
Residential, small buildings disputes

Valuation/Appraisal of Businesses

2453
Hotels
Nursing and residential care homes
Public houses, nightclubs,
  restaurants, caravan sites and
  leisure establishments
Retail businesses
Valuation having regard to trading
  potential

Valuation/Compulsory Purchase

289
Commercial and residential
  valuations
Compulsory purchase and
  compensation
Rent reviews and lease renewals

Valuation Disputes

2131
Commercial, land and residential
Landlord and tenant
Negligence

Valuation for Tax Purposes

58
Capital Gains Tax (CPG)/Inheritance
  Tax (IHT) and probate values
March 1982 rebasing valuations
Negotiating with shares valuation
  division
Share option valuations

Valuation/Investment Appraisal

76
Companies
Corporate finance
Fiscal valuations
Intangible assets
Royalty rates/licensing

Valuation/Landlord/Tenant

1381
Arbitration
Commercial valuations
Lease renewals
Professional negligence
Property management disputes
Residential valuations

Valuation of Antiques/Fine Art/ Chattels/Forensic

2168
Inheritance tax assessment
  valuations
Matrimonial dispute valuations

Valuation of Collectors' Motor Vehicles

30
Insurance claims
Valuation of vintage and classic cars,
  etc

Valuation of Commercial/Industrial Property

754
Asset value disputes and arbitrations
Disputes on property assets – capital
  market transactions
Disputes on value
Section 18 Landlord and Tenant Act
  1927 disputes
Value negligent actions

Valuation of Commercial Property

704
Breach of lease covenants,
  easements etc
Golf courses and leisure properties
Office and industrial properties and
  development sites
Rent reviews, arbitrations and lease
  renewals
Restaurants

957
Appraisals easements and covenants
Asset value
Disputes
Landlord and tenant
Negligence
Rent review

1275
Developments
Industrial and warehouses
International
Negligence
Offices
Shops and shopping centres

1445
Diminution of value following
  negligent construction
Diminution value resulting from
  negligent surveys
Negligent valuations

2429
Industrial and warehousing
Specialised properties valued by
  depreciated replacement cost

Valuation of Commercial/Residential Property

1365
General practice professional
  problems

1692
Boundary disputes
Landlord and Tenant Act applications
  to Court
Mortgage valuation disputes
Professional negligence

Valuation of Land/Buildings

869
Capital valuation, especially
  valuations for loan purposes
  (negligence)
Compulsory purchase
Landlord and tenant (especially rent
  review)
Leasehold enfranchisement
Rating appeals (valuation tribunals)
Restrictive covenants

Valuation of Lost Pension Rights

405
Arising from divorce
Loss of office
Personal injury

Valuation of Property

267
Agricultural properties
Development land and sites
Dispute resolution
Estates
Gravel extraction and landfill
Management of leased estates
Planning appeals
Residential properties

2166
Commercial and industrial properties
Compulsory purchase and
  compensation
Divorce and matrimonial proceedings
Leasehold reform acts
Rating and conducting valuation
  tribunal hearings
Taxations for capital gains and
  inheritance

2232
Compulsory purchase compensation
Dilapidations
Landlord and tenant
Lease renewal
Rent review and lease renewal
Rent review arbitration

Valuation of Shares/Companies

58
Intellectual property valuations
Marital splits
Overseas companies
Shareholder disputes
Shares with unusual rights
Tax and commercial valuations

Valuation of Unquoted Company Shares for Commercial/Tax Purposes

1783
Commercial litigation
Fiscal litigation
Matrimonial
Professional negligence

Valuation of Wills/Trusts

405
'Trust busts'
Valuing life interests and reversions

Valuation Research/Forensic

2453
All Aspects

Valuation/Structural Surveys/Building Defects

2391
Building defects
Structural surveys
Valuation

Valuation/Survey of Commercial/ Residential Property

1510
Commercial property: expert reports, lease renewals
Professional negligence: expert witness work; valuation and surveyors, estate agency negligence
Residential property: expert reports for all purposes, marital disputes

2052
Boundary disputes
Contractors' claims
Dilapidations
Landlord and tenant matters
Valuation and survey

Valuation/Survey of Residential/ Commercial Property

35
Boundary disputes
Building disputes
Dilapidations
Historic buildings
Landlord and tenant
Structural survey

785
Commercial property lease renewals
Dilapidations of commercial property
Landlord and tenant disputes
Residential mortgage valuations
Structural surveys
Surveyor's professional indemnity claims
Surveyors' negligence

Valuation/Survey of Residential Property

2295
Boundary and other property disputes
Building surveys
Dilapidation claims
Open market/retrospective valuations
Valuations for insurance purposes

Valuation/Town Planning/Rating

708
Arbitrations
Rent reviews, lease renewals
Water disposal, scrap yards, waste transfer stations

Valuations in Central London Residential

2075
Development appraisals
Leasehold enfranchisement
Mortgage valuations
Party walls
Professional negligence
Structural surveys

Valuations Residential

1917
Capital gains tax
Matrimonial
Probate
Valuer negligence

Valuations Residential/Commercial

1365
General practice surveys
Rating valuations
Rental valuations

Value Added Tax

978
Value Added Tax (VAT) fraud
Value Added Tax (VAT) investigations

Valuers of Intangible Assets

515
Brand Names Goodwill eg hotels, nursing homes, restaurants and schools
Client and service contracts
Information Technology
Research and development
Trade secrets and proprietary technology

Valuers of Intellectual Property

515
Copyright/especially computer software
Design rights and Registered Designs
Moral Rights and Service Marks
Patents
Royalties/royalty rates
Trade Marks and Trade Names

Valuers of Unquoted Share/Private Companies/Unincorporated Businesses

515
Fair value eg required by the Articles of Association
Litigation and dispute resolution eg, dissident shareholder actions, negligence claims, matrimonial proceedings and asessment of damages
MBO's or buy-ins; employee share schemes
Pre-flotation planning
Sales of companies or shareholdings
Tax valuation [eg Inheritance Tax (IHT) and apital Gains Tax (CGT)]

Vascular/General Surgery

1695
Complex venous disorders
Leg ulcers
Varicose veins, recurrent varicose veins

Vascular Surgery

686
Arterial diseases
Diseases of the microcirculation
Reconstructive arterial surgery
Surgery of carotid artery
Venous diseases

1234
Arterial, excluding cardiac
Lymphatic
Venous

Vegetable/Petroleum Oils

1616
Analytical investigations

Vehicle

see also Motor Vehicle, Road Transport, Road Traffic, Automobile

939
Commercial vehicle bodywork constructions and mounting
Compresed gases systems and sylinder storage
Metal fabrication, welded or bolted
Off-road vehicles and light construction plant, hydraulics
Road tanakers for liquids, powders, cryogenic and compressed gases

2062
Design, development and testing – all classes
Heavy haulage and abnormal loads
Military and off-roaad vehicles
Scammell and leyland vehicles
Special-purpose wheeled vehicles
Vehicle recovery – all kinds

Vehicle/Automobile

683
Forensic examination of automobiles
Forensic examination of tyres and wheels
Insurance accident, fire and theft investigations
Mechanical failures, reasons and causes
Road traffic accidents, investigations and reconstruction

Vehicle/Automobile Assessors

2161
Automobile damage assessment
Automobile valuations

Vehicle/Automobile Consulting Engineering

2161
Automobile defective repair evaluations
Automobile mechanical failure evaluations
Automobile roadworthiness examinations

Vehicle/Automobile Engineering

672
Forensic examination for 'clocking' of speedometer odometer
Photomicrography
Road accident investigation
Vehicle damage assessment
Vehicle examinations

Vehicle/Automotive Engineer

1832
Accident locus reports and survey
Automotive component failure
Consulting automotive engineer
Motor trade disputes
Motor vehicle damage or defect reports
Motor vehicle valuation
Traffic accident investigation

Vehicle/Automotive Engineering

971
All aspects

Vehicle/Automotive/Related Matters

368
'Locus' scale drawings (and photographs)
Civil and industrial accidents
Condition reports (merchantable quality)
Road traffic accidents/reconstruction
Valuations/paintwork/tyres

Vehicle Secondary Safety Design

1913
Injury mechanisms and causation
Product liablility
Safety design
Safety legislation

Vehicle Theft

242
Erased engine and chassis numbers

1435
Erased engine and chassis numbers

Vehicle Valuation

1096
Accident/theft vehicle valuation
Valuation cherished numbers
Valuation of assets for sale due to liquidation (light and heavy commercials)

Ventilation

1831
Air conditioning
Cooling
Extract ventilation
Fans

2359
Analysis, testing and provider of experts

Ventilation/Air Conditioning

1991
Ductwork distribution and extract systems
Fans, filtration, air-handling units
Sound attenuators

Veterinary

2072
Aquaculture/fish farming
Deoxribonucleic Acid (DNA) profiling
Exotic animals and birds/zoo species
Ornamental fish

2359
Analysis, testing and provider of experts

2490
Animal health and welfare
Expert opinion and review of documentation
Negligence
Nutrition
Toxicology

Veterinary Medicine

483
Animal behaviour
Chemical pathology
Food contamination
Metabolic nutrition deficiency diseases – all species of animals
Pollution in environment in relation to animal matters
Professional negligence cases
Salmonella
Veterinary forensic medicine
Veterinary pharmacology

2419
Bovine lameness
Bovine medicine
Bovine nutrition
Bovine reproduction

Veterinary Medicine/Surgery/Equine

558
Cardiology
Lameness
Pre-purchase examination of horses
Stud work

Veterinary Pathology

776
Domestic, farm, laboratory and zoo animals
Good laboratory practice quality assurance
Histology
Histopathology
Post mortem pathology

Vibration

3
Environmental vibration
Vibration White Finger (VWF) investigations

1569
Industrial
Occupational

1716
Building
Construction and demolition
Environmental
Industrial
Transportation

Vibration Injuries

952
Back injuries caused by vibration
Hand-arm vibration syndrome
Vibration-induced White Finger (VWF)

Vibration Measurement/Control

266
Assessment and control of vibration in building services
Assessment and control of vibration in industry

Vibration/Noise

2189
Effect of vibration on man

Video-Filming

1810
'Day in the Life Of' films
Dying depositions
Films of examinations/assessments and therapy
School and college filming

Visual Handicap/Rehabilitation/Management Services

1345
Daily living, mobility, need for care, recreation and employment of blind and partially sighted
Monocular vision
Multiple handicap
Visually handicapped children

Visual Problems

586
All aspects

Visually Impaired Young People/Adults

2209
Assessment of functional vision
Daily living skills training
Educational programmes
Employment of visually impaired people
Rehabilitation, training and education
Training for work
Use of technical equipment

Voice/Speech Analysis/Tape Recordings/Documents

1219
Acoustic analysis of gun shots
Linguistic analysis of documents
Sound propagation
Tape authentication
Tape enhancement
Transcription
Voice identification
Voice identity parades

Wall Cladding Systems

421
Investigation of failures

Waste Disposal

1196
Clinical waste disposal and risk assessment
Hazardous and toxic waste disposal
Military waste disposal and risk assessment
Waste pollution

Waste Disposal Plant/Desalination Plant

1069
Education and training
Total quality management

Waste/Landfills/Environmental Geotechnics

698
Contaminated land
Design of waste facilities, landfills, tips and lagoons
Groundwater/hydrogeology/monitoring

Landfill liners – geomembranes
Public inquiries

Waste Management

1499
Design of landfills
Geosynthetics
Quality assurance

2025
Design of landfills
Geosynthetics
Quality assurance

2141
Marine discharges
Pollution control
Sewage treatment
Sewerage

2388
Assessment and remediation of landfill pollution
Groundwater protection
Landfill investigation, planning and design
Strategic planning and need assessment
Waste management planning and licensing

Water

47
Coastal engineering
Dock works
Drainage
Effluent treatment
Processes
Sewerage treatment

Water Engineering

545
Drainage and flooding
Sewage treatment
Sewerage
Water distribution
Water supply and resources

826
Drainage – storm and foul water sewerage
Flood protection, land drainage and river engineering
Hydrology and water resource engineering
Pumping stations
Waste water treatment
Water treatment and distribution

2261
Drainage

2388
Flooding arising from leaking pipes
Leakage from pipes
Pipelines and pipes
Pumping stations
Water supply
Water treatment

Water/Environment

2388
Dams, construction and inspection
Environmental assessment
River flooding
Water demand and its management
Water resources
Water supply, treatment and distribution

Water/Environmental Health

817
'Sick buildings'
Agricultural pollution
Drainage design
Flood damage
Sewage and waste treatment
Water pollution
Water supplies and treatment

Water/Infrastructure Planning

383
Negotiations with National Rivers Authority and water companies
Planning liaison and development control research with National Rivers Authority

1837
Negotiations with National Rivers Authority and water companies
Planning liaison and development control research with National Rivers Authority

Water Supply

980
Dams
Pumps
Reservoirs
Water mains
Water treatment

2388
Cracking of water structures
Pipeline design and construction
Treatment plant design and construction
Water retaining structures/design and construction

Water Supply/Sewerage

525
All Aspects

Water Supply/Water Pollution Control

122
Industrial wastewaters
River pollution control
Sewerage and sewerage treatment
Sludge treatment
Water quality
Water supply

Water/Waste Engineering

185
Waste water/effluent treatment
Water cooling installations
Water treatment

553
Waste water/effluent treatment
Water cooling installations
Water treatment

2334
Contract management
System process verification

Water/Wastewater

450
Drinking water treatment and distribution
Incineration
Industrial water treatment
Ion exchange
Sludge treatment and disposal
Wastewater treatment, biological and physio-chemical
Water/wastewater treatment plant design and operation

Water Well Design/Construction

271
Contamination/quality deterioration
Drilling techniques
Loss of yield assessment
Pump selection and operation
Well design
Well field operation

Welded Products

1087
Design
Fabrication procedures
Failure analysis
Fatigue cracking and brittle fracture
Inspection
Material specifications

Welded Structures

2540
Aluminium welding and fabricating
Boat-building in metal
Failure analysis of welded structures

Welding Engineering

348
Bridges and buildings
Mechanical handling
Metallurgy
Pressure vessels
Process plants
Quality assurance

Whiplash

1209
Civil litigation

Wills/Trusts/Probate/Estate/Inheritance Tax Planning

1506
English law of succession for foreign jurisdictions
Professional negligence, especially defective will drafting and inheritance tax planning

Wind Engineering/Wind Turbines

2388
Buildings, towers and wind turbines
Dynamic response
Fatigue
Structural and mechanical strength
Wind loading